TENTH BRIEF EDITION

Music
An Appreciation

Roger Kamien
Zubin Mehta Chair in Musicology, Emeritus
The Hebrew University of Jerusalem

with Anita Kamien

McGraw Hill

MUSIC: AN APPRECIATION (BRIEF), TENTH EDITION

Published by McGraw Hill LLC, 1325 Avenue of the Americas, New York, NY 10121. Copyright © 2022 by McGraw Hill LLC. All rights reserved. Printed in the United States of America. Previous editions © 2018, 2015, and 2011. No part of this publication may be reproduced or distributed in any form or by any means, or stored in a database or retrieval system, without the prior written consent of McGraw Hill LLC, including, but not limited to, in any network or other electronic storage or transmission, or broadcast for distance learning.

Some ancillaries, including electronic and print components, may not be available to customers outside the United States.

This book is printed on acid-free paper.

1 2 3 4 5 6 7 8 9 LWI 26 25 24 23 22 21

ISBN 978-1-260-71935-2 (bound edition)
MHID 1-260-71935-9 (bound edition)
ISBN 978-1-264-02971-6 (loose-leaf edition)
MHID 1-264-02971-3 (loose-leaf edition)

Portfolio Manager: *Sarah Remington*
Product Developer: *Betty Chen*
Marketing Manager: *Meredity Leo Digiano*
Content Project Manager: *Rick Hecker*
Buyer: *Susan K. Culbertson*
Designer: *David W. Hash*
Content Licensing Specialist: *Brianna Kirschbaum*
Cover Image: *©Joshua Kamien*
Compositor: *MPS Limited*

All credits appearing on page or at the end of the book are considered to be an extension of the copyright page.

Library of Congress Cataloging-in-Publication Data

Names: Kamien, Roger, author. | Kamien, Anita, author.
  Title: Music : an appreciation / Roger Kamien with Anita Kamien.
  Description: Tenth brief edition. | New York : McGraw Hill, 2021. |
  Identifiers: LCCN 2020033228 | ISBN 9781260719352 (hardcover)
  Subjects: LCSH: Music appreciation.
  Classification: LCC MT90 .K342 2021 | DDC 781.1/7—dc23 LC record available at
  https://lccn.loc.gov/2020033228

The Internet addresses listed in the text were accurate at the time of publication. The inclusion of a website does not indicate an endorsement by the authors or McGraw Hill LLC, and McGraw Hill LLC does not guarantee the accuracy of the information presented at these sites.

mheducation.com/highered

About the Author

Joshua Kamien

ROGER KAMIEN was born in Paris and raised in the United States. He received his BA in music from Columbia College in New York, and his MA and PhD in musicology from Princeton University. He studied piano with his mother—composer-conductor Anna Kamien—and with Nadia Reisenberg and Claudio Arrau. He returned to Paris as a Fulbright scholar for research on eighteenth-century music.

Professor Kamien taught music history, theory, and literature for two years at Hunter College and then for twenty years at Queens College of the City University of New York, where he was coordinator of the music appreciation courses. During this time he was active as a pianist, appearing both in the United States and in Europe. In 1983, he was appointed to the Zubin Mehta Chair of Musicology at the Hebrew University of Jerusalem.

In addition to *Music: An Appreciation,* Dr. Kamien was the editor of *The Norton Scores,* one of the coauthors of *A New Approach to Keyboard Harmony,* and a contributor to *The Cambridge Companion to Beethoven.* He has written articles and reviews for journals including *Music Forum, Beethoven Forum, Musical Quarterly, Journal of Music, The Music Theory Spectrum, Journal of Musicology,* and *Journal of the American Musicological Society.* Roger Kamien has been honored as a "musician, theorist and teacher" by the volume *Bach to Brahms: Essays on Musical Design and Structure,* edited by David Beach and Josef Goldenberg (University of Rochester Press: 2015).

Professor Kamien has appeared as a piano soloist in thirty-two countries on five continents. He frequently performs together with his wife, the conductor-pianist Anita Kamien, who has contributed immeasurably to *Music: An Appreciation.* The Kamiens have three children and eight grandchildren.

Contents

PART III   The Baroque Period   99

PART VII Nonwestern Music 421

Preface

Music: An Appreciation welcomes nonmajors to the art of listening to great music. Roger Kamien continues to focus on coverage of the elements of music, fostering each student's unique path to listening and understanding. The brief 10th edition of *Music: An Appreciation* equips students with the language, tools, and listening skills required to sustain a lifelong enthusiasm for music.

Building a Solid Foundation: Resources on the Elements of Music

Typically the first material that a Music Appreciation student encounters in the semester is about the elements of music. Often it is a student's first exposure to musical vocabulary and concepts. The new edition features four learning tools that supplement and expand on Roger Kamien's narrative on the elements.

Elements of Music Interactives
More than 100 interactives, accessed through the eBooks, give students hands-on experience with the elements of music in an approachable digital format. These interactives cover topics such as pitch, tone, and rhythm.

Fundamentals of Music Video Tutorials
Each of the 15 video tutorials, found in the eBooks and Media Bank, covers a broad topic of music fundamentals. These videos reinforce what students read in *Music: An Appreciation*.

Spotify Playlists
Recognizing the elements in an unfamiliar piece of music is a learned skill. Spotify playlists, accessed through the eBooks, help students develop that skill by providing an avenue into the musical elements through music they are already familiar with.

Targeted Guidance in Listening Outlines and Vocal Listening Guides
Roger Kamien includes specific pointers about the elements that students will encounter in each piece accompanied by a Listening Outline or Vocal Music Guide. These points are located at the beginning of each guide and are intended as brief, approachable refreshers that are relevant specifically to each piece.

More Music to Appreciate: Expanded Repertoire

New recordings have been added to the new edition. All selections can be accessed in Connect, or students can purchase an access card that allows them to download MP3 files of selections.

McGraw–Hill Connect®: An Environment for Active Listening and Learning

Interactive Music Listening Guides
Interactive guides for audio selections in *Music: An Appreciation* are included in the eBook and can be assigned for listening completion. The guided listening experience point out meaningful elements, themes, and instrumentation. They include brief contextual information and key terms for each piece.

Writing Assignments
Available within McGraw-Hill Connect®, the Writing Assignment tool delivers a learning experience to help students improve their written communication skills and

conceptual understanding. As an instructor you can assign, monitor, grade, and provide feedback on writing more efficiently and effectively.

Remote Proctoring & Browser–Locking Capabilities

New remote proctoring and browser-locking capabilities, hosted by Proctorio within Connect, provide control of the assessment environment by enabling security options and verifying the identity of the student.

Seamlessly integrated within Connect, these services allow instructors to control students' assessment experience by restricting browser activity, recording students' activity, and verifying students are doing their own work.

Instant and detailed reporting gives instructors an at-a-glance view of potential academic integrity concerns, thereby avoiding personal bias and supporting evidence-based claims.

New and Updated Content

The tenth Brief Edition expands the range of composers, performers and music genres discussed. New composers and performers include Barbara Strozzi, Elisabeth Jacquet de la Guerre, Fanny Mendelsohn Hensel, Lili Boulanger, Maurice Ravel, Sergei Prokofiev, Lin-Manuel Miranda, Bob Dylan, Prince, Beyoncé, Taylor Swift, and Kendrick Lamar. New music genres discussed include the secular cantata, piano trio, hip-hop musical, and rap music. **Part I: Elements** has new musical examples throughout and revised discussions of rhythm and melody.

In **Part III: The Baroque Period,** discussion of baroque vocal music has been revised, along with reorganization of chapters to break the discussion of the cantata between secular and sacred contexts. This part now includes a section on the baroque cantata and considers the lives of Barbara Strozzi and Elisabeth Jacquet de la Guerre and movements from their secular cantatas.

New to **Part V: The Romantic Period** are discussions of Fanny Mendelsohn Hensel and the second movement from her String Quartet in E-Flat major. Also added is a discussion of the third movement of Clara Wieck Schumann's Piano Trio in G Minor.

Part VI: The Twentieth Century and Beyond now includes a discussion of Ravel's *Boléro,* one of the most widely-performed orchestral works. Also new to this part is a discussion of Lili Boulanger's *Psalm 24* for Chorus and Orchestra, a chapter on primitivism, and a discussion of the first movement of Prokofiev's *Classical Symphony* as an example of neoclassicism. The chapter **Music for Stage and Screen** now includes a discussion of the hip-hop musical *Hamilton* and its hit song *My Shot* as well as John William's music for the *Desert Chase* scene from the film *Raiders of the Lost Ark,* starring Harrison Ford. **Popular Music Genres**, a new chapter, covers rock, country, rap, hip hop, and other genres and styles of American music from 1945 to the present. Examples presented in the narrative include Bob Dylan's *Blowin' in the Wind,* The Beatles' *Lucy in the Sky with Diamonds,* Prince's *Purple Rain,* Beyoncé's *Irreplaceable,* Taylor Swift's *Shake It Off,* and Kendrick Lamar's *GOD.*

New musical selections and recordings include the following:

- Lili Boulanger, *Psaume 24* (*Psalm 24*)
- Elisabeth Jacquet de la Guerre, *La Têmpete* (*The Storm*), from *Le sommeil d'Ulisse* (*The Sleep of Ulysses*)
- Fanny Mendelssohn Hensel, String Quartet in E Flat Major, second movement
- Sergei Prokofiev, *Classical* Symphony in D Major, Op. 25, first movement
- Clara Wieck Schumann, Trio for Violin, Cello, and Piano in G Minor, Op. 17
- Barbara Strozzi, *Che si può fare* (*What can you do?*)

Teaching resources such as the Instructor's Manual and lecture PowerPoints have been updated and can be accessed through McGraw-Hill Connect®.

Acknowledgments

My deep thanks go to John d'Armand (University of Alaska) for class-testing the section on Music in America; Catherine Coppola (Hunter College, CUNY) for suggestions concerning *Don Giovanni* and Part I: Elements; Hubert Howe (Queens College, CUNY) for updating the discussions of electronic music and instruments; James Hurd (El Camino College) for assistance in choosing repertoire; Daniel Kamien for suggestions concerning string instruments; Roger Vetter (Grinnell College), Edwin Seroussi, and Amazia Bar-Yosef (The Hebrew University of Jerusalem) for information concerning nonwestern music.

A number of other instructors were instrumental in the development of this edition. Thank you to those reviewers whose input and ideas were invaluable in the process:

Olga Amelkina, Collin College
Carol Ayres, Iowa Lakes Community College
Vincent Biggam, Forsyth Tech Community College
Michael Boyle, Oklahoma City Community College
Andrew Briggs, Houston Community College Central
Dorothy Bryant, Ohio University
Kristin Clark Randles, Central Piedmont Community College
Julie Clemens, Illinois Central College
David T. Curtin, Lock Haven University
David Cyzak, Bradley University
William Darwin, Jr., Western Iowa Tech Community College
Andy David, University of North Georgia
Ellen Denham, Texas AM University Corpus Christi
James Easteppe, Central Piedmont Community College
William Fitzhugh, Volunteer State Community College
Brett Fuelberth, Iowa Lakes Community College
Ingrid Gordon, LaGuardia Community College
Kurt Gorman, University of Tennessee at Martin
Mari Hahn, University of Alaska Anchorage
John Harrell, Gadsden State Community College
Michael Heffley, Baker College
Karen R. Hickok, Southern Union Community College
Peggy Hinkle, Pellissippi State Community College
Lisa Hughes, West Georgia Technical College
Robyn James, Pellissippi State Community College
Donald Mack, Piedmont Technical College
Blake McGee, University of Wyomoing
Patrick McGuffey, Volunteer State Community College
Myrna Meeroff, Broward College

Julia Miller, Tri-County Technical College
Heather Murray, Rowan College at Burlington County
Scott Pool, Texas A&M University Corpus Christi
Holly Powe, Calhoun Community College
James Lee Reifinger Jr., Southern Illinois University Carbondale
Michael Ritter, Austin Peay State University
Jocelyn Sanders, University of Tennessee at Chattanooga
Anthony Scelba, Kean University
Kathleen Scheide, Rowan College at Burlington County
James Siddons, Liberty University
Sayaka Tanikawa, Hunter College
Jamie Taylor, East Mississippi Community College
Nikolasa Tejero, The University of Tennessee at Chattanooga
Jason Terry, Bradley University
Lia Uribe, University of Arkansas
Cristina Verdesoto, Broward College
Roxanne H. Watson, Central Piedmont Community College
John Wilborn, West Georgia Technical College
Bill Witwer, Collin College

I would like to thank those who gave valuable input about *Music: An Appreciation* during the preparation of this new edition:

Lynne Brandt
Cathy Callis
Thomas Dempsey
Ellen Denham
Donna Doyle
Joel Denson
James Easteppe
Giordana Fiori
Will Fulton
Benjamin Graves
Karen Henson
Peggy Hinkle
Anthony Jones
Susanna Loewy
Myrna Meeroff
Alisha Nypaver
Jason Sagebiel

I would also like to thank Aviva Stanislawski for her suggestions concerning Part I: Elements, Joshua Kamien for his photographs of musicians with their instruments, Stephen Horenstein for his help with the discussion of bebop, Ephraim Schafli for his suggestions concerning Music for Stage and Screen and Popular Music Genres, Kwasi Ampene for his translation of the *Ompeh* text, and Michael Staron for suggestions on the Listening Outlines.

A very special thank you goes to Steven Kreinberg at Temple University for helping create the Part Summary features.

My wife, conductor-pianist Anita Kamien, has contributed to every aspect of this book. She clarified ideas, helped choose representative pieces, and worked tirelessly to improve the Listening Outlines and Vocal Music Guides. Her advice and encouragement were essential to the completion of *Music: An Appreciation,* Tenth Edition.

Roger Kamien

Instructors: Student Success Starts with You

Tools to enhance your unique voice

Want to build your own course? No problem. Prefer to use our turnkey, prebuilt course? Easy. Want to make changes throughout the semester? Sure. And you'll save time with Connect's auto-grading too.

65%
Less Time Grading

Laptop: McGraw Hill; Woman/dog: George Doyle/Getty Images

Study made personal

Incorporate adaptive study resources like SmartBook® 2.0 into your course and help your students be better prepared in less time. Learn more about the powerful personalized learning experience available in SmartBook 2.0 at **www.mheducation.com/highered/connect/smartbook**

Affordable solutions, added value

Make technology work for you with LMS integration for single sign-on access, mobile access to the digital textbook, and reports to quickly show you how each of your students is doing. And with our Inclusive Access program you can provide all these tools at a discount to your students. Ask your McGraw Hill representative for more information.

Padlock: Jobalou/Getty Images

Solutions for your challenges

A product isn't a solution. Real solutions are affordable, reliable, and come with training and ongoing support when you need it and how you want it. Visit **www.supportateverystep.com** for videos and resources both you and your students can use throughout the semester.

Checkmark: Jobalou/Getty Images

SUPPORT AT every step

Students: Get Learning that Fits You

Effective tools for efficient studying

Connect is designed to make you more productive with simple, flexible, intuitive tools that maximize your study time and meet your individual learning needs. Get learning that works for you with Connect.

Study anytime, anywhere

Download the free ReadAnywhere app and access your online eBook or SmartBook 2.0 assignments when it's convenient, even if you're offline. And since the app automatically syncs with your eBook and SmartBook 2.0 assignments in Connect, all of your work is available every time you open it. Find out more at **www.mheducation.com/readanywhere**

"I really liked this app—it made it easy to study when you don't have your text-book in front of you."

- Jordan Cunningham, Eastern Washington University

Calendar: owattaphotos/Getty Images

Everything you need in one place

Your Connect course has everything you need—whether reading on your digital eBook or completing assignments for class, Connect makes it easy to get your work done.

Learning for everyone

McGraw Hill works directly with Accessibility Services Departments and faculty to meet the learning needs of all students. Please contact your Accessibility Services Office and ask them to email accessibility@mheducation.com, or visit **www.mheducation.com/about/accessibility** for more information.

Top: Jenner Images/Getty Images, Left: Hero Images/Getty Images, Right: Hero Images/Getty Images

All musical elements come together when people play or sing.

PART I

Rhythm and harmony find their way into the inward places of the soul…

—Plato

Elements

LEARNING OBJECTIVES

- Describe the properties of sound and explain how music is part of the world of sound.

- Identify basic voice ranges for men and women and the categories of instruments in western music.

- Explain how rhythm is basic to life and how it forms the lifeblood of music.

- Recognize how music notation indicates pitch and rhythm.

- Discuss some elements of melody.

- Explain basic principles of chords and harmony.

- Compare and contrast major and minor scales.

- Identify and describe the three kinds of musical texture.

- Explain the techniques that create musical form.

- Discuss the different meanings of the term "musical style."

Music plays a vital role in human society. It provides entertainment and emotional release, and it accompanies activities ranging from dances to religious ceremonies. Music is heard everywhere: in auditoriums, homes, elevators, sports arenas, places of worship, and on the street.

Live performances provide special excitement. In a live performance, artists put themselves on the line; training and magnetism must overcome technical difficulties to involve the listener's emotions. What is performed, how it sounds, how the artist feels about it that evening—all this exists for a fleeting moment and can never be repeated. An audience responds to the excitement of such a moment, and feelings are exchanged between stage and hall.

Recorded performance was a sensational innovation of the twentieth century. Today, the Internet gives access to a practically unlimited variety of recorded sounds and images. Portable audio and media players permit us to hear and watch what we want, wherever we want.

Our response to a musical performance or an artist is subjective and rooted in deep feeling. Even professional critics may differ strongly in their evaluations of a performance. There is no one "truth" about what we hear and feel. Does the performer project a concept, an overall idea, or an emotion? Can you figure out why? It's up to us as listeners to evaluate performances of music. Alert and repeated listening will enhance our ability to compare performances so that we can fully enjoy them.

People listen to music in many ways. Music can be a barely perceived background or a totally absorbing experience. Part I of this book, "Elements," introduces concepts that can contribute to your enjoyment of a wide range of musical styles. For example, awareness of tone color—the quality that distinguishes one instrument from another—can heighten your pleasure when a melody passes from a clarinet to a trumpet. Perceptive, aware listening makes any musical experience more intense and satisfying.

Informal music making is a source of pleasure for players and listeners.
RimDream/Shutterstock

Whether in a public park or a concert hall, live performances have a special electricity.
Media Union/Shutterstock

Bruce Springsteen: The exchange between singer and audience contains something magical, direct, and spellbinding.
Jamie Squire/Getty Images

The use of computers and electronics has revolutionized the way we create, play, and listen to music.
Eugenio Marongiu/Shutterstock

Music making transcends boundaries of many kinds. Pictured here are musicians playing in a gamelan, an ensemble found in Indonesia.
ASK Images/Alamy Stock Photo

1 Sound: Pitch, Dynamics, and Tone Color

Sounds bombard our ears every day—the squeaks and honks of traffic, a child's laugh, the bark of a dog, the patter of rain. Through them we learn what's going on; we need them to communicate. By listening to speech, cries, and laughter, we learn what others think and how they feel. But silence, an absence of sound, also communicates. When we hear no sound in the street, we assume no cars are passing. When someone doesn't answer a question or breaks off in the middle of a sentence, we quickly notice, and we draw conclusions from the silence.

Sounds may be perceived as pleasant or unpleasant. Fortunately, we can direct our attention to specific sounds, shutting out those that don't interest us. At a party, for instance, we can choose to ignore the people near us and focus instead on a conversation across the room. Actually, we shut out most sounds, paying attention only to those of interest. The composer John Cage (1912–1992) may have meant to show this with his "composition" entitled *4'33"*, in which a musician sits at a piano for 4 minutes and 33 seconds—and does nothing. The silence forces the people in the audience to direct their attention to whatever noises, or sounds, they themselves are making. In a sense, the audience "composes" this piece. To get the effect, listen to the sounds that fill the silence around you right now.

What are these sounds that we hear? What is "sound"? What causes it, and how do we hear it?

Sound begins with the vibration of an object, such as a table that is pounded or a string that is plucked. The vibrations are transmitted to our ears by a *medium,* which is usually air. As a result of the vibrations, our eardrums start vibrating too, and *impulses,* or signals, are transmitted to the brain. There the impulses are selected, organized, and interpreted.

Music is part of this world of sound, an art based on the organization of sounds in time. We distinguish music from other sounds by recognizing the four main properties of musical sounds: *pitch, dynamics* (loudness or softness), *tone color,* and *duration.* We'll look now at the first three of these properties of musical sound. Duration—the length of time a musical sound lasts—is discussed in Chapter 3, "Rhythm."

Pitch: Highness or Lowness of Sound

Pitch is the relative highness or lowness we hear in a sound. Sing or listen to the song *Happy Birthday to You.* Notice that the highest tone comes on the third *birth-*day, just before the name of the person celebrating his or her birthday.

The pitch of a sound is determined by the frequency of its vibrations—that is, their speed, which is measured in cycles per second. The faster the vibrations, the higher the pitch; the slower the vibrations, the lower the pitch. All other things being equal, smaller objects vibrate faster and have higher pitches; thus, plucking a short string produces a higher pitch than plucking a long string.

In music, a sound that has a definite pitch is called a **tone.** It has a specific frequency, such as 440 cycles per second. The vibrations of a tone are regular and reach the ear at equal time intervals. On the other hand, noiselike sounds (squeaking brakes or clashing cymbals) have an indefinite pitch because they are produced by irregular vibrations.

Two tones will sound different when they have different pitches. The "distance" between any two tones is called an **interval.** When tones are separated by the interval called an **octave,** they sound very much alike. Sing or listen to the opening of the song *Over the Rainbow:* "Somewhere over the rainbow." Notice that the tone on *-where* sounds like the tone on *Some-,* even though it is higher. An octave lies between them. The vibration frequency of the tone on *Some-* is exactly half that of the tone on *-where.* If the *Some-* tone was 440 cycles per second, the *-where* tone—an octave higher—would be 880 cycles per second. A tone an octave lower than the *Some-* tone would be half of 440, or 220 cycles per second. When sounded at the same time, two tones an octave apart blend so well that they almost seem to merge into one tone.

The interval of an octave is important in music. It is the interval between the first and last tones of the familiar scale. Sing or listen to this scale.

Octave: See Arlen's *Over the Rainbow,* opening (page 39).

```
                                          do
                                      ti
                                  la
                              sol
                          fa
                      mi
                  re
              do
```

Notice that the octave is filled by seven different pitches before arriving at the high *do,* which "duplicates" the low *do.* This group of seven tones was the basis of music in western civilization for centuries. The seven tones are produced by the white keys of the piano keyboard, as shown in the illustration at the bottom.

As time passed, five pitches were added to the original seven. These five are produced by the black keys of the keyboard. All twelve tones, like the original seven, are "duplicated" in higher and lower octaves. (In nonwestern music, the octave may be divided into a different number of tones.)

The distance between the lowest and highest tones that a voice or instrument can produce is called its **pitch range,** or simply its **range.** The range of the average untrained voice is about 1½ octaves; a piano's range is over 7 octaves.

Organization of pitch is a composer's first resource. In Chapters 5 and 6, where melody and harmony are explored, we look at how pitch is organized. For now, we'll simply observe that composers can create a special mood by using very low or very high pitches. For example, low pitches can intensify the sadness of a funeral march; high pitches can make a dance sound lighter. And a steady rise in pitch often increases musical tension.

Though most music we know is based on definite pitches, indefinite pitches—such as those made by a bass drum or by cymbals—are important as well. Some percussion instruments, such as gongs, cowbells, and woodblocks, come in different sizes and therefore produce higher or lower indefinite pitches. Contrasts between higher and lower indefinite pitches play a vital role in contemporary western music and in musical cultures around the world.

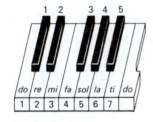

Seven different tones are produced by the white keys of the piano.

Dynamics

Degrees of loudness or softness in music are called *dynamics*—our second property of sound. Loudness is related to the amplitude of the vibration that produces the sound. The harder a guitar string is plucked (the farther it moves from the fingerboard), the louder its sound. When instruments are played more loudly or more softly, or when there is a change in how many instruments are heard, a dynamic change results; such a change may be made either suddenly or gradually. A gradual increase in loudness often creates excitement, particularly when the pitch rises too. On the other hand, a gradual decrease in loudness can convey a sense of calm.

A performer can emphasize a tone by playing it more loudly than the tones around it. We call an emphasis of this kind an *accent.* Skillful, subtle changes of dynamics add spirit and mood to performances. Sometimes these changes are written in the music; often, though, they are not written but are inspired by the performer's feelings about the music.

When notating music, composers have traditionally used Italian words and their abbreviations to indicate dynamics. The most common terms are

Term	Abbreviation	Meaning
pianissimo	*pp*	*very soft*
piano	*p*	*soft*
mezzo piano	*mp*	*moderately soft*
mezzo forte	*mf*	*moderately loud*
forte	*f*	*loud*
fortissimo	*ff*	*very loud*

For extremes of softness and loudness, composers use *ppp* or *pppp* and *fff* or *ffff*.

The following notations indicate gradual changes in dynamics:

Symbol	Term	Meaning
	decrescendo (decresc.) *or diminuendo* (dim.)	gradually softer
	crescendo (cresc.)	gradually louder

Like many elements of music, a dynamic indication is not absolutely precise. A tone has a dynamic level—is soft or loud—in relation to other tones around it. The loudest sound of a single violin is tiny compared with the loudest sound of an entire orchestra, and even tinier compared with an amplified rock group. But it can be considered fortissimo (very loud) within its own context.

Tone Color

We can tell a trumpet from a flute even when each of them is playing the same tone at the same dynamic level. The quality that distinguishes them—our third property of musical sound—is called *tone color,* or *timbre* (pronounced *tam'-ber*). Tone color is described by words such as *bright, dark, brilliant, mellow,* and *rich.*

Changes in tone color create variety and contrast: for example, the same melody will have different expressive effects when it is played by one instrument and then another, or a new tone color may be used to highlight a new melody. Tone colors also build a sense of continuity; it is easier to recognize the return of a melody when the same instruments play it each time. Specific instruments can reinforce a melody's emotional impact—in fact, composers often create a melody with a particular instrument's tone color in mind.

A practically unlimited variety of tone colors is available to composers: instruments (see Chapter 2) can be combined in various ways, and modern electronic techniques allow composers to invent entirely new tone colors.

Listening Outlines, Vocal Music Guides, and the Properties of Sound

Reading about pitch, dynamics, and tone color without hearing music is too abstract. To understand and recognize the properties of sound, we must *listen for them*. In this book, Listening Outlines (for instrumental music) and Vocal Music Guides (for music with vocal texts) will help focus your attention on musical events as they unfold. These outlines and guides must be read *as you listen to the music;* otherwise, their value to you is limited.

In a Listening Outline, each item describes some musical sound. It may point out dynamics, instruments, pitch level, or mood. (Remember, though, that indications of mood in music are subjective. What one person calls "triumphant," for instance, someone else may call "determined.") In a Vocal Music Guide, the vocal text appears with brief marginal notes that indicate the relationship between words and music and help the listener follow the thought, story, or drama.

The outlines and guides are preceded by descriptions of the music's main features. Within the guide or outline, timings appear in the margin. In addition, the outlines include instrumentation, notes about our recordings (where important), and the duration of selections in our recordings.

Before you listen to a piece of music, you will find it helpful to glance over the entire Listening Outline or Vocal Music Guide. Then, while hearing one passage, look ahead to learn what's next. For example, in the Listening Outline for the second scene of Igor Stravinsky's ballet *The Firebird,* the first item (1a) is "Slow melody in French horn, soft (*p*), quivering string accompaniment." While listening to the music described by item *a,* glance at item 1*b*: "Violins, soft, melody an octave higher. Flutes join."

Sometimes, not all the instruments playing are listed; instead, only those that are prominent at a given moment are shown. For example, item 2*a* in the Listening Outline for *The Firebird* reads "Brasses, very loud (*ff*), melody in quick detached notes, timpani." Although other instruments can be heard, this description focuses attention on the instruments that play the melody.

Music selection in the text with an outline or guide can be streamed in Connect or downloaded after purchasing the mp3 card.

The Firebird, Scene 2 (1910), by Igor Stravinsky

In the second—and final—scene of the ballet *The Firebird,* Igor Stravinsky (1882–1971) repeats one melody over and over, creating variety and contrast through changes of dynamics, tone color, and rhythm. During this scene, the hero triumphs and becomes engaged to a beautiful princess.

The second scene begins softly but becomes increasingly grand as the music gradually grows louder (crescendo), more instruments play, and the melody is repeated at higher pitches. After this slow buildup to a climax, there's a sudden quiet as all the instruments but the strings stop playing. A quick crescendo then leads to a brilliant concluding section.

Listening Outline

Piccolo, 3 flutes, 3 oboes, English horn, 3 clarinets, bass clarinet, 3 bassoons, contrabassoon, 4 French horns, 6 trumpets, tuba, timpani, triangle, cymbals, bass drum, 3 harps, 1st violins, 2d violins, violas, cellos, double basses (Duration 3:06)

Listen for gradual crescendo (*dynamics*) and the repetition of the main melody in increasingly higher octaves (*pitch*) during 1.a-e.

0:00	**1. a.** Slow melody in French horn, soft (*p*), quivering string accompaniment.
0:29	**b.** Violins, soft, melody an octave higher. Flutes join.
0:43	**c.** Grows louder (crescendo) as more instruments enter.
1:03	**d.** Violins and flutes, loud (*f*), melody at even higher octave, crescendo to
1:17	**e.** Full orchestra, melody very loud (*ff*), timpani (kettledrums).
1:34	**f.** Suddenly very soft (*pp*), strings, quick crescendo to
1:41	**2. a.** Brasses, very loud (*ff*), melody in quick detached notes, timpani.
2:04	**b.** Melody in slower, accented notes, brasses, *ff*, timpani, music gradually slows.
2:35	**c.** High held tone, *ff*, brass chords, extremely loud (*fff*), lead to sudden *pp* and crescendo to extremely loud close.

C-Jam Blues (1942), by Duke Ellington and His Famous Orchestra

A succession of different tone colors contributes to the variety within *C-Jam Blues* (1942), as performed by Duke Ellington and His Famous Orchestra. A repeated-note melody is played first by the piano and then by saxophones. Then we hear solos by the violin, cornet (brass instrument of the trumpet family), tenor saxophone, trombone, and clarinet. These solos are improvised by the players. ***Improvisation*** is the term used for music created at the same time as it is performed. Each instrument is first heard alone and then heard with accompaniment. The cornet and trombones are played with mutes, devices inserted into the instrument to alter its sound. *C-Jam Blues* ends climactically when the full band is heard for the first time.

Listening Outline

Piano (Duke Ellington), violin (Ray Nance), 2 trumpets (Wallace Jones, Ray Nance), cornet (Rex Stewart), 2 trombones (Joe "Tricky Sam" Nanton, Lawrence Brown), valve trombone (Juan Tizol), clarinet (Barney Bigard), 2 alto saxophones (Johnny Hodges, Otto Hardwick), 2 tenor saxophones (Barney Bigard, Ben Webster), baritone saxophone (Harry Carney), guitar (Fred Guy), bass (Junior Raglin), percussion (Sonny Greer) (Duration 2:38)

Listen for different *tone colors* of the piano, saxophone, violin, muted cornet, muted trombone, and clarinet (during 1-7), and the contrast between instruments playing with and without accompaniment.

0:00	**1.** Piano, repeated-note melody, accompanied by bass, guitar, drums.
0:17	**2.** Saxophones, repeated-note melody, accompanied by rhythm section (piano, bass, guitar, percussion).
0:33	**3.** Violin alone, then accompanied by rhythm section.
0:54	**4.** Muted cornet alone, then accompanied by rhythm section.
1:15	**5.** Tenor saxophone alone, then accompanied by rhythm section.
1:37	**6.** Muted trombone alone, then accompanied by rhythm section.
1:59	**7.** Clarinet alone, then accompanied by band.
2:20	**8.** Full band.

2 Performing Media: Voices and Instruments

Voices

Soprano: See Puccini's *La Bohème*, Mimi's aria (Vocal Music Guide, Part V, ch. 19).

Mezzo-soprano: See Bizet's *Carmen*, Carmen's Habanera (Vocal Music Guide, Part V, ch. 17).

Tenor: See Puccini's *La Bohème*, Rodolfo's aria (Vocal Music Guide, Part V, ch. 19).

Baritone: See Bizet's *Carmen*, Toreador song (Vocal Music Guide, Part V, ch. 17).

Bass: See Mozart's *Don Giovanni*, Leporello's solo (Vocal Music Guide, 00:15 to 01:41, Part IV, ch. 11).

Chorus: See Handel's *Messiah, Hallelujah* Chorus (Vocal Music Guide, Part III, ch. 18) and *Ompeh* (Listening, Outline, Part VII, ch. 2).

Throughout history, singing has been the most widespread and familiar way of making music. Singers seem always to have had a magnetic appeal, and the exchange between singer and audience contains a bit of magic, something direct and spellbinding. The singer becomes an instrument with a unique ability to fuse words and musical tones.

For many reasons, it is difficult to sing well. In singing we use wider ranges of pitch and volume than in speaking, and we hold vowel sounds longer. Singing demands a greater supply and control of breath. Air from the lungs is controlled by the lower abdominal muscles and the diaphragm. The air makes the vocal cords vibrate, and the singer's lungs, throat, mouth, and nose come into play to produce the desired sound. The pitch of the tone varies with the tension of the vocal cords; the tighter they are, the higher the pitch.

The range of a singer's voice depends both on training and on physical makeup. Professional singers can command 2 octaves or even more, whereas an untrained voice is usually limited to about 1½ octaves. Men's vocal cords are longer and thicker than women's, and this difference produces a lower range of pitches. The classification of voice ranges for women and men follows, arranged from highest to lowest. (The four basic ranges are soprano, alto, tenor, and bass.)

Women	Men
soprano	*tenor*
mezzo-soprano	*baritone*
alto (or contralto)	*bass*

Methods and styles of singing vary widely from culture to culture and even within a culture: for instance, in the west, classical, popular, jazz, folk, and rock music are all sung differently.

Until the late 1600s, most music of western culture was vocal. Since then, instrumental music has rivaled vocal music in importance; but composers have continued to

write vocal works—both solo and choral—with and without instrumental accompaniment (which can range from a single guitar or piano to an entire orchestra).

Musical Instruments

An *instrument* may be defined as any mechanism—other than the voice—that produces musical sounds. Western musicians usually classify instruments in six broad categories: *string* (such as guitar and violin); *woodwind* (flute, clarinet); *brass* (trumpet, trombone); *percussion* (bass drum, cymbals); *keyboard* (organ, piano); and *electronic* (synthesizer).

An instrument is often made in different sizes that produce different ranges. For instance, the saxophone family includes sopranino, soprano, alto, tenor, baritone, and bass saxophones. An instrument's tone color may vary with the *register* (part of the total range) in which it is played. A clarinet sounds dark and rich in its low register, but its high register is brilliant and piercing. Most instruments have a wider range of pitches than the voice does. A trained singer's range is about 2 octaves, but many instruments command 3 or 4 octaves, and some have 6 or 7. Also, instruments usually produce tones more rapidly than the voice. When writing music for a specific instrument, composers have to consider its range of pitches and dynamics and how fast it can produce tones.

People around the world use musical instruments that vary greatly in construction and tone color, and instruments have had many functions—at different times and in different cultures. They may provide entertainment; they may accompany song, dance, ritual, and drama; they have sometimes been considered sacred or thought to have magical powers; they have been used for communication; and they have even been status symbols.

Instruments' popularity rises and falls with changing musical tastes and requirements. Today only a fraction of all known instruments are used. Interest in music of earlier times has led to the revival of instruments such as the harpsichord, an ancestor of the piano, and the recorder, a relative of the flute. Modern replicas of instruments used before 1800 are being built and played. Today, musicians are flexible and far-ranging in their choice of instruments. Rock composers have used nonwestern instruments, such as the Indian sitar (a plucked string instrument). Some jazz musicians have turned to classical instruments, such as the flute, and classical composers have used instruments associated with jazz, such as the vibraphone.

A symphony orchestra.

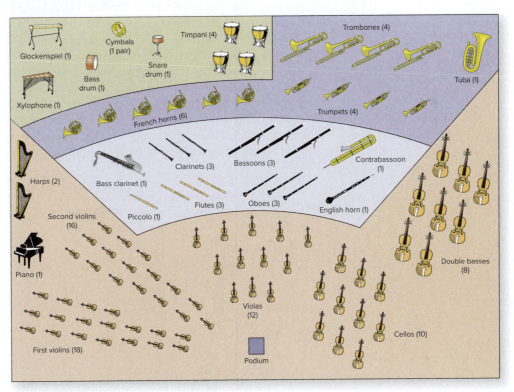

Typical seating plan for a large orchestra (about 100 instrumentalists),
showing the distribution of instruments.

Compositions may be written for solo instruments, for small groups, and for orchestras with more than 100 musicians. Modern symphony orchestras contain string, woodwind, brass, and percussion instruments. (The previous page shows a photograph of a symphony orchestra and a typical seating plan for a large orchestra.) Keyboard instruments also find their way into the modern orchestra as needed. Bands consist mainly of brass, woodwind, and percussion instruments.

Orchestras and bands—as well as choruses—are usually led by a **conductor,** who coordinates the performers and shapes the interpretation of a musical composition. Many conductors hold a thin stick called a **baton** in one hand to beat time and indicate pulse and tempo. With the other hand they control the balance among the instruments—or voices—so that the most important musical ideas will be brought out. In an orchestra, the principal first violinist, the **concertmaster,** plays solo violin passages and coordinates the bowing of string instruments.

Instruments commonly used for western music are described in this chapter, by categories. Nonwestern instruments are discussed in Part VII.

String Instruments

The **violin, viola, cello** (*violoncello*), and **double bass** (sometimes called simply a *bass*) form the symphony orchestra's string section. They vary in tone color as well as in size and range: the violin is the smallest and has the highest range; the double bass is the largest and has the lowest range. For symphonic music the strings are usually played with a **bow,** a slightly curved stick strung tightly with horsehair (see the illustration below.) Symphonic strings also may be plucked with the finger.

Of all the instrumental groups, the strings have the greatest versatility and expressive range. They produce many tone colors and have wide ranges of pitch and dynamics. String players can produce tones that are brilliant and rapid or slow and throbbing; they can control tone as subtly as a singer. Orchestral works tend to rely more on the strings than on any other group. Even with their differing tone colors, the four string instruments blend beautifully. Here it will be helpful to consider the construction and tone production of the string instruments; the violin can represent the entire family.

The hollow wooden body of the violin supports four strings usually made of metal or synthetic material. (Even today, some players prefer traditional gut strings made of tightly wound intestine.) The strings stretch, under tension, from a *tailpiece* on one end over a wooden *bridge* to the other end, where they are fastened around wooden *pegs*. The bridge holds the strings away from the *fingerboard* so that they can vibrate freely; the bridge also transmits the strings' vibrations to the *body,* which amplifies and colors the tone. Each string is tuned to a different pitch by tightening or loosening the pegs. (The greater the tension, the higher the pitch.)

Violin and bow.

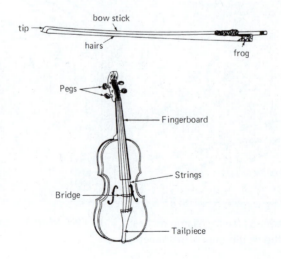

The violin is often used as a solo instrument. In the orchestra, the violins are divided into first and second violins, with the first violins frequently playing the main melody. The violinist shown here is Joshua Bell.

Paul Morigi/Getty Images

The body of the viola is about two inches longer than that of the violin, and thus the viola's range is somewhat lower. Its tone color is darker, thicker, and a little less brilliant than the violin's. The violist here is Tabea Zimmermann.

Brill/ullstein bild via Getty Images

Although eighteenth-century composers generally used the cello in its bass and baritone registers, later composers exploited its upper registers as well. The cellist shown here is Yo-Yo Ma.

Alex Wong/Getty Images

The double bass (or bass) has a very heavy tone and is less agile than other instruments. It is generally played with a bow in symphonic music, but in jazz and popular music it is commonly played by plucking the strings.

Jan Šmydke

The harp—with forty-seven strings stretched on a triangular frame—has a wide range of 6 octaves. The harpist plucks with the fingers of both hands.
Joshua Kamien

The guitar has six strings, which are plucked with the fingers or strummed with a plectrum, or pick. The frets on the fingerboard mark the places where the strings must be pressed with the fingers of the other hand.
Olena Yakobchuk/Shutterstock

The musician makes a string vibrate by drawing the bow across it with the right hand. The speed and pressure of the bow stroke control the dynamics and tone color of the sound produced. Pitch is controlled by the musician's left hand. By pressing a string against the fingerboard, the player varies the length of its vibrating portion and so changes its pitch. This is called *stopping* a string (because the vibrations are stopped at a certain point along the string's length). Thus, a range of pitches can be drawn from each of the four strings.

Basically the viola, cello, and double bass are made in the same manner and produce sound by similar means. How the string instruments are played—what string performance techniques are used—determines which of many musical effects they will produce. The most frequently used techniques are listed here.

Pizzicato (plucked string): The musician plucks the string, usually with a finger of the right hand. In jazz, the double bass is played mainly as a plucked instrument, rather than being bowed.

Double stop (two notes at once): By drawing the bow across two strings, a string player can sound two notes at once. And by rotating the bow rapidly across three strings (*triple stop*) or four strings (*quadruple stop*), three or four notes can be sounded almost—but not quite—together.

Vibrato: The string player can produce a throbbing, expressive tone by rocking the left hand while pressing the string down. This causes small pitch fluctuations that make the tone warmer.

Mute: The musician can veil or muffle the tone by fitting a clamp (mute) onto the bridge.

Tremolo: The musician rapidly repeats tones by quick up-and-down strokes of the bow. This can create a sense of tension, when loud; or a shimmering sound, when soft.

Harmonics: Very high-pitched tones, like a whistle's, are produced when the musician lightly touches certain points on a string.

Though the violin, viola, cello, and double bass are similar, they, like members of any family, have their differences. The photographs in this section show why each adds something distinctive to the orchestra's total sound.

Some string instruments are not played with a bow but are plucked instead, with the fingers or with a *plectrum* (plural, *plectra*). The most important of these are the **harp** and the **guitar.** The harp is the only plucked string instrument that has gained wide acceptance in the symphony orchestra.

Woodwind Instruments

The woodwind instruments are so named because they produce vibrations of air within a tube that traditionally was made of wood. During the twentieth century, however, piccolos and flutes came to be made of metal. All the woodwinds have little holes along their length that are opened and closed by the fingers or by pads controlled by a key mechanism. By opening and closing these holes, the woodwind player changes the length of the vibrating air column and so varies the pitch.

The main woodwind instruments of the symphony orchestra are as follows, arranged in four families, in approximate order of range from highest (piccolo) to lowest (contrabassoon). (Only the two most frequently used instruments of each family are listed.)

Flute Family	Clarinet Family	Oboe Family	Bassoon Family
piccolo			
flute	*clarinet*		
		oboe	
		English horn	
	bass clarinet		*bassoon*
			contrabassoon

A woodwind instrument (unlike a string instrument) can produce only one note at a time. In symphonic music, woodwinds are frequently given melodic solos.

Woodwind instruments are great individualists and are much less alike in tone color than the various strings. The woodwinds' unique tone colors result largely from the different ways in which vibrations are produced. Flute and piccolo players blow across the edge of a mouth hole (players of the *recorder,* a relative of the flute, blow through a "whistle" mouthpiece); but the rest of the woodwind instruments rely on a vibrating reed. A *reed* is a very thin piece of cane, about 2½ inches long, that is set into vibration by a stream of air.

In *single-reed woodwinds* the reed is fastened over a hole in the mouthpiece and vibrates when the player blows into the instrument. The clarinet and bass clarinet are single-reed woodwinds. The *saxophone,* too, an instrument used mainly in bands, has a single reed. In *double-reed woodwinds* two narrow pieces of cane are held between the musician's lips. The oboe, English horn, bassoon, and contrabassoon are double-reed woodwinds.

Tone colors differ greatly not only between single-reed and double reed woodwinds, but also among the various registers of each woodwind instrument. In general, low registers tend to be breathy and thick, and top registers are more penetrating.

The piccolo—whose name is short for *flauto piccolo,* or small flute—is half the size of the flute and plays an octave higher. The piccolo's high register is shrill and whistlelike.

Joshua Kamien

The flute has a high range and is extremely agile, capable of producing a rapid succession of tones. Its tone is full and velvety in the low register and bright and sparkling at the top. Shown here is the flutist James Galway.

Richard E. Aaron/Redferns/Getty Images

The oboe has a nasal, intense, expressive tone. Because the oboe's pitch is difficult to adjust, the entire orchestra is tuned to its A.

Joshua Kamien

The English horn is neither English nor a horn, but simply a low, or alto, oboe. The English horn player is Dmitry Malkin.

Joshua Kamien

The recorder, like the flute and piccolo, has no reed. The recorder's tone resembles a flute's but is softer and gentler. It is commonly found in five sizes: sopranino, soprano, alto, tenor, and bass.
Joshua Kamien

The clarinet can produce tones very rapidly and has a wide range of dynamics and tone color. Pictured here is Sabine Meyer.
Jazz Archiv Hamburg/ullstein bild via Getty Images

The tone of the bassoon is deeply nasal. The bassoonist is Richard Paley.
Joshua Kamien

The contrabassoon can produce the lowest pitch in the orchestra.
Joshua Kamien

The bass clarinet is larger than the clarinet and has a much lower range.
imageBROKER/Alamy Stock Photo

The saxophone has a single-reed piece like a clarinet, but its tube is made of brass. Its tone is rich, husky, and speechlike. Shown here is the jazz saxophonist Sonny Rollins.
Tim Mosenfelder/Corbis via Getty Images

Brass Instruments

From high register to low, the main instruments of the symphony orchestra's brass section are the **trumpet, French horn** (sometimes called simply a *horn*), **trombone,** and **tuba.** Trumpets and trombones are often used in jazz and rock groups. Other instruments, such as the **cornet, baritone horn,** and **euphonium** are used mainly in concert and marching bands.

The vibrations of brass instruments come from the musician's lips as he or she blows into a cup- or funnel-shaped *mouthpiece.* The vibrations are amplified and colored in a tube that is coiled (to make it easy to carry and play). The tube is flared at the end to form a *bell.* The pitch of brass instruments is regulated both by varying lip tension and by using *slides* and *valves* to change the length of the tube through which the air vibrates. The trombone uses a slide, a U-shaped tube that fits into two parallel straight tubes. By pulling the slide in or pushing it out, the player changes the length of tubing and makes it possible to play different pitches. The trumpet, French horn, and tuba use three or four valves to divert air through various lengths of tubing. When valves came into use around 1850, these instruments could produce many more tones and became much more flexible. Brass players can alter the tone color of their instruments by inserting a **mute** into the bell. Mutes for brass instruments come in different shapes and are made of wood, plastic, or metal. They are most common in jazz, where they create a variety of effects, including a buzzing sound, a mellowing of the tone, and the comical "wah-wah."

Brass instruments are very powerful, so they are often used at climaxes and for bold, heroic statements. Since the late nineteenth century, they are frequently given rapid solo passages as well. Today, brass instruments are very popular, owing to ensembles such as the Canadian Brass and soloists like the trumpeter Wynton Marsalis.

The trumpet sounds brilliant, brassy, and penetrating. The trumpeter shown here is Wynton Marsalis.
Erika Goldring/Getty Images

The French horn has a tone that is less brassy, more mellow, and more rounded than the trumpet's.
Lawrence Migdale/Science Source

The trombone has a tone that combines the brilliance of a trumpet with the mellowness of a French horn.
Joshua Kamien

The thick, heavy tone of the tuba is used to add weight to the lowest register of an orchestra or band.
Carl Court/Getty Images

Percussion Instruments

Most percussion instruments of the orchestra are struck by hand, with sticks, or with hammers. Some are shaken or rubbed. Percussion instruments are subdivided into instruments of definite and indefinite pitch, depending on whether they produce a tone or a noiselike sound.

Definite Pitch	Indefinite Pitch
timpani (kettledrums)	*snare drum (side drum)*
glockenspiel	*bass drum*
xylophone	*tambourine*
celesta	*triangle*
chimes	*cymbals*
	gong (tam-tam)

The vibrations of percussion instruments are set up by stretched membranes, like the calfskin of the kettledrum, or by plates or bars made of metal, wood, or other sonorous materials. Extremely loud sounds may be drawn from percussion instruments like the bass drum or cymbals. In a symphony orchestra, one percussionist may play several different instruments.

Percussion instruments have long been used to emphasize rhythm and to heighten climaxes. But until the twentieth century, they played a far less important role in western music than strings, woodwinds, or brasses. Since 1900, composers have been more willing to exploit the special colors of the percussion group and have occasionally written entire pieces to show it off, such as *Ionisation* (1931) by Edgard Varèse. Jazz and rock musicians, of course, have made good use of percussion instruments. Yet, for all these recent explorations, western musicians barely approach the incredibly varied use of percussion found in Africa and Asia, where subtle changes of rhythm, tone color, and dynamics are used with great imagination.

Percussion

The timpani (kettledrums) are the only orchestral drums of definite pitch. A calfskin head is stretched over a hemispherical copper shell. Varying the tension of the head using adjustable screws around the head or a pedal changes the pitch of the timpani. One percussionist generally plays two to four timpani, each tuned to a different pitch.
Vital Sharepchankau/Alamy

The xylophone consists of a set of wooden bars that are struck with two hard hammers to produce a dry, wooden tone.
Harold Smith/Alamy

The metal bars of the glockenspiel (orchestral bells) are struck with two hammers to produce a tone that is bright and silvery.
Joshua Kamien

The bass drum—the largest of the orchestral drums—is almost three feet in diameter.
Joshua Kamien

Chimes are a set of metal tubes hung from a frame. They are struck with a hammer and sound like church bells.
Rolf Haid/dpa/picture-alliance/Newscom

The celesta looks like a small upright piano, but its sounding mechanism is like a glockenspiel's. Metal bars are struck by hammers that are controlled by a keyboard. The celesta's tone is tinkling and graceful.
Lebrecht Music & Arts/Alamy

The triangle is struck with a metal beater and makes a tinkling, bell-like sound.
Ted Thai/The LIFE Images Collection/Getty Images

The dry rattling sound of the snare drum (or side drum) is produced by the vibration of snares—strings that are tightly stretched against the bottom head. The snare drum is often used in marches.
Joshua Kamien

When struck by a beater, the gong (or tam-tam) produces long-lasting sounds that can seem solemn, mysterious, or frightening.
Joshua Kamien

The tambourine is often used to create a Spanish or Italian effect. The player shakes it or strikes it with the knuckles.
Giambra/iStock/Getty Images

Cymbals are round brass plates. They usually are struck together with a sliding motion, and their sound penetrates like a sharp crash.
Comstock Images/SuperStock

Keyboard Instruments

The piano, harpsichord, organ, and accordion are the best-known keyboard instruments. Although they are quite different from each other in the way they produce sound, each has a keyboard that permits the performer to play several tones at the same time easily and rapidly.

The *piano* was invented around 1700 and mechanically perfected by the 1850s. It produces sound through vibrating strings held under tension by an iron frame: striking a key causes a felt-covered hammer to hit a string (the harder the pianist strikes the key, the louder the sound); releasing the key causes a felt damper to come down on the string and end the tone. Pianos have two or three pedals: the *damper pedal* lets the pianist sustain a tone after releasing the key; the *una corda pedal* (*soft pedal*) veils the sound; the *sostenuto pedal* (which not all pianos have) sustains some tones but not others.

The piano is exceptionally versatile. A pianist can play many notes at once, including both a melody and its accompaniment. Its eighty-eight keys span more than 7 octaves. The dynamic range is broad, from a faint whisper to a powerful fortissimo. Today it is among the most popular instruments and is used for solos, for accompaniments, and in combination with one other instrument or many other instruments.

The *harpsichord* was important from about 1500 to 1775 (when it was gradually replaced by the piano) and was revived in the twentieth century for performance of early music and some new works. It has strings that are plucked by a set of *plectra* (little wedges of plastic, leather, or quill). These are controlled by one or two keyboards.

Keyboard

The piano is exceptionally versatile and its eighty-eight keys span more than seven octaves. Shown here is the pianist Murray Perahia.

Amy T. Zielinski/Getty Images

The harpsichord has plucked strings controlled by one or two keyboards.
Matthew Chattle/Alamy

The **pipe organ** was most prominent from 1600 to 1750 (when it was known as the "King of instruments") but is still in wide use today, particularly in religious services. It has a wide range of pitch, dynamics, and tone color. There are many sets of pipes controlled from several keyboards, including a pedal keyboard played by the organist's feet. The keys control valves from which air is blown across or through openings in the pipes. Various sets of pipes are brought into play by pulling knobs called *stops*. Each set of pipes has a particular tone color that the organist uses alone or with others. Dynamic change is produced by adding to or reducing the number of pipes being played, by moving from one keyboard to another, or by opening and closing shutters around some of the pipes.

A pipe organ has many sets of pipes controlled from several keyboards and pedals. The organist varies the sound by selecting different combinations of the pipes.
Lawrence Migdale/Science Source

The accordion is used most often in folk and popular music.
Wilfried Krecichwost/Getty Images

Invented during the early nineteenth century, the **accordion** is used most often in folk or popular music. An accordion has strips of brass or steel that are controlled by a keyboard with piano keys, played by the right hand; and a keyboard with buttons, played by the left hand. The metal strips are caused to vibrate by pressure from a bellows.

Electronic Instruments

Electronic instruments produce or amplify sound through electronic means; they were invented as early as 1904 but have had a significant impact on music only since 1950. Today, electronic and computer technologies are developing rapidly, changing continually, and increasingly blending together. Electronic instruments for performing and composing music include amplified instruments, such as the electric piano, organ, and guitar; tape studios; synthesizers; computers; and various "hybrid" technologies.

The **tape studio** was the main tool of composers of electronic music during the 1950s. (In Part VI we study Edgard Varèse's *Poème électronique,* which was created in a tape studio.) The raw material in tape studios consisted of recorded sounds that might be electronic or from "real life"—flutes, birdcalls, percussion, church bells, people singing, and so forth. The composer manipulated these in various ways: by speeding them up or slowing them down, altering their pitch and duration, giving them echoes, filtering them to change tone color, mixing them, and editing the tape (as by cutting and splicing) to play them in any desired order. Rhythm could be fully controlled because the duration of a sound depended only on the length of a tape segment. However, tape splicing and rerecording were difficult, inaccurate, and time-consuming processes, and many composers of the 1960s turned to synthesizers, which appeared around 1955.

Synthesizers are systems of electronic components that generate, modify, and control sound. They can generate a huge variety of musical sounds and noises, and the composer has complete control over pitch, tone color, loudness, and duration. Most synthesizers can be "played" by means of a keyboard—an addition to the mechanisms of the tape studio.

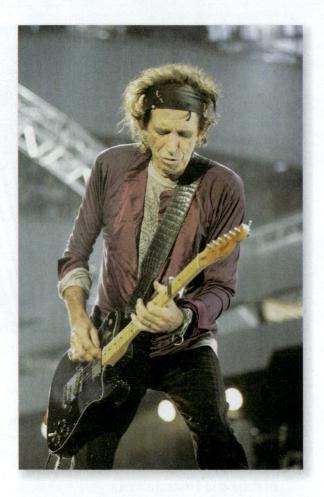

The **electric guitar** uses a built-in pickup to convert the vibration of its strings into electrical impulses for amplification. Keith Richards is the guitarist shown here.
Getty Images Entertainment/ Getty Images

Synthesizers vary in size and capacity. The mid-1950s saw the invention of the RCA Mark II synthesizer, an enormous (and unique) vacuum-tube synthesizer occupying an entire wall of the Columbia-Princeton Electronic Music Center in New York City. During the 1960s and 1970s, smaller, less expensive transistorized synthesizers such as the Moog and Buchla were developed; these were installed in electronic music studios at universities and advertising agencies, played in live rock concerts and concerts of electronic music, and used to create film and television scores. They permit manipulation of the sounds, such as adding reverberation. Highly sophisticated synthesizers using computer capabilities have been developed. Though synthesizers are still in use, most of what they do has been replaced by personal computers, which are now extremely powerful.

A significant development in synthesizing technology is known as *musical instrument digital interface (MIDI)*: this is a standard adopted by manufacturers for interfacing synthesizer equipment. MIDI has allowed the device actually played to be separated from tone generation; thus there are now keyboards that look, feel, and play like a piano; wind controllers played like a woodwind instrument; and string controllers played like a violin or cello. Also, control signals can be fed to and from a MIDI instrument into and out of a personal computer, and users can store and edit music and convert to and from musical notation.

Now ***computers*** are used to generate music notation, to control synthesizing mechanisms, and to store samples of audio signals.

Sampling is a technology that enables composers to hear what their music sounds like on the instruments for which their pieces are written. Sampling involves taking

Today's electronic music studios create a wide range of sounds.
yanyong/Getty Images

brief digital recordings of acoustic instruments and placing them under the control of a keyboard or computer. Today, sampling is integrated into notation software so composers can enter music notation and hear what their piece will sound like when performed by live musicians.

Drum machines are electronic instruments that create percussive sounds and allow musicians to program rhythms. They are primarily used in popular music.

Several programs known as digital audio workstations (DAWs) enable composers to record audio onto separate tracks and mix and synchronize the results into compositions. After the audio is recorded (or synthesized), all properties of sound—such as pitch, duration, dynamics, and tone color—can be manipulated in many ways. This is how electronic music composers now generally assemble their pieces.

Composers also write for acoustic instruments whose sound is fed live into a laptop computer and processed or mixed with synthesized sounds in real time. In Part VI we'll study Kaija Saariaho's opera *L'amour de loin* (Love from Afar), in which such "live electronics" is used.

To increase the variety of sound and the composer's control over it, today's electronic music studios often contain and integrate a wide variety of equipment, including synthesizers, computers, and devices for mixing and filtering sound.

All this equipment enables the composer to exploit the entire spectrum of sound as never before. But the quality of the music produced still depends on the imagination and organizing power of the human mind.

The Young Person's Guide to the Orchestra, Op.* 34 (1946), by Benjamin Britten

Benjamin Britten (1913–1976), an English composer, wrote the attractive *Young Person's Guide to the Orchestra* in 1946 as an introduction to the instruments of the orchestra. He used a theme by Henry Purcell, a great English composer of the seventeenth century. (A *theme* is a melody used as the basis for a musical composition.) The majestic theme is presented first by the full orchestra, and then by each section of the orchestra in turn: woodwinds, brasses, strings, and percussion. Thirteen *variations,*

---

* The abbreviation *op.* stands for *opus,* Latin for *work.* An opus number is a way of identifying a piece or set of pieces. Usually, within a composer's output, the higher a composition's opus number, the later it was written.

or varied repetitions of the theme, are then heard. Each highlights a different instrument. The variations differ in dynamics, speed, and tone color, as well as mood. They follow each other without pause and last from about 30 seconds to 1 minute each. (Variation 13, however, which features many percussion instruments, lasts almost 2 minutes.) Woodwind, string, and brass instruments are generally presented from highest to lowest in range.

Variation 13 is followed immediately by a concluding section beginning with a lively new tune played by an unaccompanied piccolo. Then other instruments enter, each playing the same tune. After woodwind, string, brass, and percussion instruments have had their turn, the brasses bring back the main theme and provide an exciting ending.

Listening Outline

BRITTEN, *The Young Person's Guide to the Orchestra*

Piccolo, 2 flutes, 2 oboes, 2 clarinets, 2 bassoons, 4 horns, 2 trumpets, 3 trombones, tuba, timpani, bass drum, snare drum, cymbals, tambourine, triangle, Chinese block, xylophone, castanets, gong, whip, harp, 1st violins, 2d violins, violas, cellos, double basses
(Duration 17:23)

Listen for the characteristic *tone colors* of the woodwind, brass, string, and percussion sections (Theme b-e) and individual instruments from these sections (Variations 1-13).

Theme

0:00	**a.** Full orchestra
0:41	**b.** Woodwind section
1:11	**c.** Brass section
1:42	**d.** String section
2:07	**e.** Percussion section
2:26	**f.** Full orchestra

Woodwinds

3:00	**Variation 1:** Flutes and piccolo
3:30	**Variation 2:** Oboes
4:33	**Variation 3:** Clarinets
5:16	**Variation 4:** Bassoons

Strings

6:13	**Variation 5:** Violins
6:58	**Variation 6:** Violas
7:46	**Variation 7:** Cellos
8:43	**Variation 8:** Double basses
9:41	**Variation 9:** Harp

Brasses

10:31	**Variation 10:** French horns
11:14	**Variation 11:** Trumpets
11:48	**Variation 12:** Trombones and tuba

Percussion

12:48	**Variation 13:**
	a. Timpani (kettledrums); bass drum and cymbals
13:20	**b.** Tambourine and triangle; snare drum (side drum) and Chinese block (a hollow wooden block that is struck with a drumstick)
13:38	**c.** Xylophone
13:49	**d.** Castanets and gong
14:03	**e.** Whip (two hinged pieces of wood that are slapped against each other)
14:08	**f.** Entire percussion section; xylophone and triangle

Concluding Section

14:44	**a.** Unaccompanied piccolo, lively new tune, tune played in turn by flutes, oboes, clarinets, and bassoons, crescendo.
15:22	**b.** Lively tune played in turn by 1st violins, ***p***; 2d violins, violas, cellos, double basses, woodwinds accompany, crescendo; quick decrescendo introduces
15:51	**c.** Harp, lively tune, crescendo in strings and woodwinds.
16:03	**d.** Lively tune played in turn by French horns, ***ff***, trumpets, trombones and tuba, orchestra accompanies.
16:21	**e.** Percussion, ***f***, accompanied by orchestra, ***p***, crescendo to
16:31	**f.** Main theme in brasses, ***ff***, together with lively tune in high woodwinds and strings. Full orchestra, percussion, long-held closing chord, ***fff***.

3 Rhythm

Rhythm is basic to life. We see it in the cycle of night and day, the four seasons, the rise and fall of tides. More personally, we feel rhythm as we breathe. We find it in our heartbeats and our walking.

The essence of rhythm is a recurring pattern of tension and release, of expectation and fulfillment. This rhythmic alternation seems to pervade the flow of time. Time, as we live it, has fantastic diversity; each hour has sixty minutes, but how different one hour may seem from another!

Rhythm forms the lifeblood of music too; it is the flow of music through time. In music, ***rhythm*** refers to the ordered durations of sounds and silences. Rhythm has several interrelated aspects, which we'll consider in turn: beat, meter, accent and syncopation, and tempo.

Dancing is closely linked to the rhythms of music. Shown here is Carlos Acosta in *Diana & Acteon* by Agrippina Vaganova, December 2015, London Coliseum.

Lidia Crisafulli/Photoshot/Newscom

Beat

When you clap your hands or tap your foot to music, you are responding to its beat. **Beat** is a regular, recurrent pulsation that divides music into equal units of time. Beats can be represented by marks on a time line:

Beats can be shown as a succession of marks on a time line.

In music, beats occur as often as every ¼ second or as seldom as every 1½ seconds. Sometimes the beat is powerful and easy to feel, as in marches or rock music; but sometimes it may be barely noticeable, suggesting feelings like floating or aimlessness.

The pulse of music is communicated in different ways. Sometimes the beat is explicitly pounded out—by a bass drum in a marching band, for instance. At other times the beat is sensed rather than actually heard.

Sing or listen to the beginning of *Happy Birthday to You:*

Each of the vertical lines below the words represents a beat. Did you notice that you automatically held *you* for 2 beats? You *sensed* the beat because you were aware of it and expected it to continue.

Beats form the background against which the composer places tones of varying lengths. Beats are the basic units of time by which all tones are measured. A tone may last a fraction of a beat, an entire beat, or more than a beat.

At the beginning of *Happy Birthday,* each of the two syllables in the word *hap-py* lasts ½ beat; each of the three syllables in the words *birth-day to* lasts one beat. It was already noted that *you* is held for two beats. Thus, at the beginning of the song, we have tones ranging in length from ½ beat to two beats.

When we talk about the combination of different durations of tones in *Happy Birthday,* we are considering its rhythm. The rhythm of a melody is an essential feature of its character. Indeed, we might recognize *Happy Birthday* merely by clapping out its rhythm without actually singing the tones. The *beat* of *Happy Birthday* is an even, regular pulsation. But its *rhythm* flows freely, sometimes matching the beat, sometimes not.

Meter

Sing or listen to the beginning of *London Bridge Is Falling Down*:

Lon-don	bridge is	fall-ing	down,	fall-ing	down,	fall-ing	down
beat	beat	**beat**	beat	**beat**	beat	**beat**	beat

When we hear this song, some beats feel stronger or more stressed than others. The stress comes on the first of every 2 beats. Therefore we count the beats of *London Bridge* as **1**–2, **1**–2.

In music we often find a repeated pattern of a strong beat plus one or more weaker beats. The organization of beats into regular groups is called **meter.** A group containing a fixed number of beats is called a **measure** or **bar.** There are several types of meter, which are based on the number of beats in a measure. *London Bridge*, which has two beats to the measure, is in **duple meter.**

Lon-	don	bridge	is	fall-	ing	down,		fall-	ing	down,		fall-	ing	down	
1		2		|1		2		|1		2		|1		2	|

The vertical lines mark the beginning or end of the measure. The first, or stressed, beat of the measure is known as the **downbeat.**

Another basic metrical pattern is **quadruple meter,** which has 4 beats to the measure. As usual, the downbeat is strongest; but there is another stress on the third beat, which is stronger than the second and fourth beats and weaker than the first: **1**–2–*3*–4, **1**–2–*3*–4.

Twin-	kle,	twin-	kle	lit-	tle	star,	How I	won-	der	what you	are!	
1		2		*3*		4	|**1**	2		*3*	4	|

Jazz and rock are usually in quadruple meter. Both duple and quadruple meter reflect the left-right, left-right pattern of walking or marching.

A pattern of 3 beats to the measure is known as **triple meter.** We count **1**–2–3, **1**–2–3, and so on.

Hap-	py	birth-	day	to	you,		hap-	py	birth-	day	to	you,	
	|1	2	3	|1	2	3		|1	2	3	|1	2

In this example of triple meter, the first word is on the **upbeat,** an unaccented pulse preceding the downbeat.

Sextuple meter contains 6 rather quick beats to the measure. The downbeat is strongest, and the fourth beat also receives a stress: **1**–2–3–*4*–5–6.

Row,			row,			row		your	boat			
1	2	3	*4*	5	6	|1	2	3	*4*	5	6	|

Gent-		ly	down		the	stream.						
1	2	3	*4*	5	6	|1	2	3	*4*	5	6	|

Mer-	ri-	ly,	mer-	ri-	ly,	mer-	ri-	ly,	mer-	ri-	ly,	
1	2	*3*	*4*	5	6	|1	2	3	*4*	5	6	|

life		is	but		a	dream.						
1	2	3	*4*	5	6	|1	2	3	*4*	5	6	|

Note that the measure is subdivided into two groups of 3 beats each: **1**–2–3\|*4*–5–6. Thus, sextuple meter is a combination of duple and triple meter.

Accent and Syncopation

An important aspect of rhythm is the way individual notes are stressed—how they get special emphasis. A note is emphasized most obviously by being played louder than the notes around it, that is, by receiving a dynamic *accent.* A note is sometimes especially accented when it is held longer or is higher in pitch than those notes near it.

When an accented note comes where we normally would *not* expect one, the effect is known as **syncopation.** There is a syncopation when an "offbeat" note is accented—that is, when the stress comes *between* two beats.

In the song *I Got Rhythm,* by the American composer George Gershwin (1898–1937), a syncopation occurs when the accented tone on *I* comes on the "offbeat," between beats 1 and 2.

A syncopation also occurs when a weak beat is accented, as in 1–**2**–3–4 or 1–2–3–**4**. Such contradictions of the meter surprise the listener and create rhythmic excitement. Syncopation is a characteristic feature of jazz.

Tempo

Tempo—the speed of the beat—is the basic pace of the music. A fast tempo is associated with a feeling of energy, drive, and excitement. A slow tempo often contributes to a solemn, lyrical, or calm mood.

A *tempo indication* is usually given at the beginning of a piece. As with dynamics, the terms that show tempo (at the left) are in Italian.

largo	very slow, broad
grave	very slow, solemn
adagio	slow
andante	moderately slow, a walking pace
moderato	moderate
allegretto	moderately fast
allegro	fast
vivace	lively
presto	very fast
prestissimo	as fast as possible

Qualifying words are sometimes added to tempo indications to make them more specific. The two most commonly used are *molto* (*much*) and *non troppo* (*not too much*). We thus get phrases like *allegro molto* (*very fast*) and *allegro non troppo* (*not too fast*). The same tempo is not always used throughout a piece. A gradual quickening of tempo may be indicated by writing **accelerando** (*becoming faster*), and a gradual slowing down of tempo by **ritardando** (*becoming slower*).

All these terms (again like dynamics) are relative and approximate; different performers interpret them differently, and there is no "right" tempo for a piece. This is true even though, since about 1816, composers have been able to indicate their preferred tempos by means of a **metronome,** an apparatus that produces ticking sounds or flashes of light at any desired musical speed. The metronome setting indicates the exact number of beats per minute.

I Got Rhythm (1930), by George Gershwin

Pervasive syncopations give a jazzy feeling to the song *I Got Rhythm,* which was written by George Gershwin (1898–1937) for the musical comedy *Girl Crazy.* The song is in duple meter, with two quick beats to the measure. In our recording, it is performed by a soprano, with orchestral accompaniment.

As discussed earlier, the accented tone on *I* is syncopated because it comes *between* the first and second beats of the measure. The next emphasized tone *rhy-(thm)* falls *on* the first beat and therefore is *not* syncopated. This opening rhythmic pattern is repeated

Syncopation: See Dvorak's *New World* Symphony, I, exposition, 1.a (Listening Outline, Part V, ch. 15).

Largo: See Vivaldi's *Spring* Concerto, II (Part III, ch. 13).

Adagio: See Dvorak's *New World* Symphony, I (Listening Outline, Part V, ch. 15).

Andante: See Haydn's *Surprise* Symphony, II (Listening Outline, Part IV, ch. 4).

Allegretto: See Bartok's Concerto for Orchestra, II (Listening Outline, Part VI, ch. 14).

Allegro: See Vivaldi's *Spring* Concerto, I (Listening Outline, Part III, ch. 13).

Presto: See Beethoven's Fifth Symphony, IV (coda, Part IV, ch. 12).

Prestissimo: See Beethoven's String Quartet in C Minor, IV (Listening Outline, 7, Part IV, ch. 6).

Accelerando: See Schoenberg's *A Survivor from Warsaw* (Vocal Music Guide, 04:08, Part VI, ch. 12).

Ritardando: See Puccini's *La Boheme* (Vocal Music Guide, 03:40, Part V, ch. 19).

for *I got music* and for later parts of the melody. The recurrence of the rhythmic pattern on different pitches helps give *I Got Rhythm* its wonderful sense of unity and drive.

4 Music Notation

We use written words to express our thoughts and communicate with others when we can't be with them. In music, ideas are also written down, or *notated,* so that performers can play pieces unknown to them.

Notation is a system of writing music so that specific pitches and rhythms can be communicated. It is explained here—very briefly—primarily to help you recognize rising and falling melodic lines and long and short notes so that you can follow the music examples in this book.

Notating Pitch

With music notation, we can indicate exact pitches by the upward or downward placement of symbols—called *notes*—on a *staff.* A **note** is an oval. (Its duration is indicated by whether it is black or white or has a *stem* and *flags,* as will be explained later, under "Notating Rhythm.") A **staff** (plural, *staves*) is a set of five horizontal lines. Notes are positioned either on the lines of the staff or between them, in the spaces; the higher a note is placed on the staff, the higher its pitch:

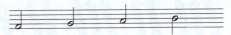

If a pitch falls above or below the range indicated by the staff, short, horizontal **ledger lines** are used:

Seven of the twelve pitches (tones) that fill the octave in western music are named after the first seven letters of the alphabet: A, B, C, D, E, F, G. This sequence is repeated over and over to represent the "same" tones in higher and lower octaves, and it corresponds to the white keys of the piano. The other five tones of the octave correspond to the black keys of the piano and are indicated by one of the same seven letters plus a **sharp sign** (♯) or a **flat sign** (♭) (see the illustration below). Thus, the pitch between C and D may be called C sharp (♯; higher than C) or D flat (D♭; lower than D). A **natural sign** (♮) is used to cancel a previous sharp or flat sign.

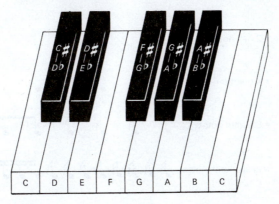

The twelve pitches of the octave and their positions on the piano keyboard.

A **clef** is placed at the beginning of the staff to show the pitch of each line and space. The two most common clefs are the **treble clef**, used for relatively high ranges (such as those played by a pianist's right hand), and the **bass clef**, used for relatively low ranges (played by the pianist's left hand):

Treble Clef   Bass Clef

Keyboard music calls for a wide range of pitches to be played by both hands; for such music, the **grand staff**—a combination of the treble and bass staves—is used. The following illustration shows how the notes on the grand staff are related to the piano keyboard. Note that the C nearest to the middle of the keyboard is called **middle C.**

Notes on the grand staff and their positions on the piano keyboard.

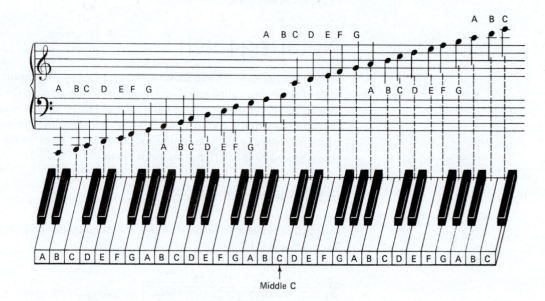

Middle C

Notating Rhythm

Music notation does not indicate the exact duration of tones; instead, it shows how long one tone lasts in relation to others in the same piece. A single note on the staff lasts longer or shorter depending on how it looks—on whether it is white or black and has a **stem** or **flags.** Following is a chart that shows the relationships of the duration symbols:

1 whole note

= 2 half notes:

= 4 quarter notes:

= 8 eighth notes:

= 16 sixteenth notes:

One whole note lasts as long as 2 half notes or 4 quarter notes, and so on. As shown, the flags of several eighth notes or sixteenth notes in succession are usually joined by a horizontal **beam.**

To lengthen the duration of a tone (and add rhythmic variety), we can make it a *dotted note;* adding a dot (.) to the right of a note increases its duration by half. Thus, 1 quarter note ordinarily equals 2 eighth notes, but 1 dotted quarter note equals 3 eighth notes:

Frequently, a dotted note is followed by one that is much shorter; this long-short pattern, called **dotted rhythm,** strongly emphasizes the beat (and is therefore often used in marches).

A *tie* (⌢) is another way to lengthen the duration of a note. When two notes in a row are the same pitch and are connected by a tie, the first note is lengthened by the duration of the second. In the following example, the note on *dell* lasts as long as 1 dotted quarter note plus 1 quarter note; the two tied notes become one continuous sound:

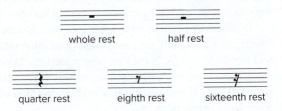

The farm - er in the dell, ___ The farm - er in the dell, ___

We also can add rhythmic variety by shortening the duration of a note. One method is the **triplet,** three notes of equal duration notated as a group within a curved line and the number 3. Such a group lasts only as long as if it were two notes of equal value:

Notating Silence (Rests)

Duration of silence is notated by using a symbol called a **rest.** Rests are pauses; their durations correspond to those of notes:

whole rest	half rest

quarter rest	eighth rest	sixteenth rest

Notating Meter

A *time signature* (or *meter signature*) shows the meter of a piece. It appears at the beginning of the staff at the start of a piece (and again later if the meter changes) and consists of two numbers, one on top of the other. The upper number tells how many beats fall in a measure; the lower number tells what kind of note gets the beat (2 = half note, for instance, and 4 = quarter note). Thus the time signature $\frac{2}{4}$ shows that there are 2 beats to the measure (duple meter) and a quarter note gets 1 beat. Duple meter may also be shown as $\frac{2}{2}$ (or by its symbol, ¢); quadruple meter is usually $\frac{4}{4}$ (or **C**). The most common triple meter is $\frac{3}{4}$.

5 Melody

For many of us, music means melody. A ***melody*** is a series of single tones that add up to a recognizable whole. A melody begins, moves, and ends; it has direction, shape, and continuity. The up-and-down movement of its pitches conveys tension and release, expectation and arrival. This is the melodic *curve*, or *line*. As you get deeper into the music explored in this book, you'll find a wealth of melodies: vocal and instrumental, long and short, simple and complex. This section will help you sort them out by introducing some terms and basic melodic principles.

A melody moves by small intervals called ***steps*** or by larger ones called ***leaps.*** A step is the interval between two adjacent tones in the familiar *do-re-mi-fa-sol-la-ti-do* scale (from *do* to *re* or *re* to *mi*, and so on). Any interval larger than a step is a leap (*do* to *mi*, for example). Besides moving up or down by step or leap, a melody may simply repeat the same tone.

At the opening of *Happy Birthday to You*, for example, the two syllables, *Hap-py*, are sung to the same notes. To emphasize the word *Birth-day*, the melody moves up a step to *Birth-* and back down a step to *-day*. A small upward leap connects *-day* and *to*, followed by a downward step between *to* and *you*.

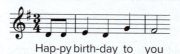

Hap-py birth-day to you

A melody's range is the distance between its lowest and highest tones. Range may be wide or narrow. Melodies written for instruments tend to have a wider range than those for voices, and they often contain wide leaps and rapid notes that would be difficult to sing. Often the highest note of a melody will be the ***climax***, or emotional focal point.

The rhythmic patterns of a melody contribute to its distinctive character. A well-known melody can be almost unrecognizable if it is not sung in proper rhythm. How the tones of a melody are performed can vary its effect too. Sometimes they are sung or played in a smooth or connected style called ***legato.*** Or they may be performed in a short, detached manner called ***staccato.***

Many melodies are made up of shorter units called phrases. A ***phrase*** is a musical segment that can be sung on one breath and ends at a point of full or partial rest. A resting place at the end of a phrase—a point of arrival—is called a ***cadence.***

In discussing music, letters are customarily used to represent sections of a piece: lowercase letters (a, b, etc.) for phrases and other relatively short segments or sections, and capital letters (A, B etc.) for longer sections. If two sections, such as phrases, differ significantly, we use different letters: a, b. If one exactly repeats another, the letter is repeated: a a. If one section is a varied repetition of a previous section, the repeated letter has a prime mark: a a'.

As you get deeper into the music explored in this book, you will find a wealth of melodies, vocal and instrumental, long and short, simple and complex. To help sort them out, let's see how some basic principles apply to two familiar tunes. These are short melodies, easy to sing and easy to remember.

Sing or listen to the song *Happy Birthday to You.*

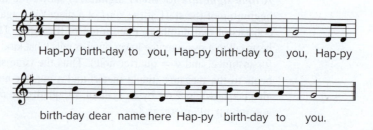

Hap-py birth-day to you, Hap-py birth-day to you, Hap-py

birth-day dear name here Hap-py birth-day to you.

What makes *Happy Birthday* one of the best-known melodies worldwide, with its text translated into more than two hundred languages? One reason is the good feeling when we sing the word *Hap-py*, four times, each time on a repeated tone. Another is the way the melody gradually builds up to an emotional focal point on the third *Happy Birthday dear ...* through increasingly large upward leaps.

The first *Happy Birthday* includes a small upward leap (between *-day* and *to* [*you*]) and the second *Happy Birthday* brings a slightly larger leap on the same words. The third time we sing *Happy Birthday*, there is a wide leap up an octave to the climax of the song on the highest note of the melody (on *Birth-*). This climax highlights the melodic descent to the name of the person celebrating his or her birthday. The final *Happy Birthday to You* ends the song on a complete cadence, which creates a sense of satisfaction and conclusion.

Next sing or listen to the tune *London Bridge Is Falling Down*:

The melody consists of two balanced phrases of equal length. The first phrase (a) ends with a questioning upward motion on the third "falling down." This is an incomplete cadence, one that sets up expectations for a continuation. The second phrase (a′) begins exactly like the first, but continues to a different, conclusive ending, a complete cadence on the words "my fair lady." As we'll see, melodic repetition, both exact and varied, contributes to a sense of continuity and plays an important role in the music of all cultures.

After considering two simple tunes, we'll now study the beloved popular song, *Over the Rainbow,* which is composed of two contrasting melodies.

Over the Rainbow (1938), by Harold Arlen

The classic ballad *Over the Rainbow*, with music by Harold Arlen and words by E. Y. Harburg, was voted the best movie song of all time by the American Film Institute and the National Endowment for the Arts. This song was written for the movie *The Wizard of Oz* (1939), starring the seventeen-year-old Judy Garland as the Kansas farm girl Dorothy Gale.

In this song, Dorothy—an orphan—is unhappy and yearns to escape from Kansas to a land where dreams "really do come true."

Like many popular songs, *Over the Rainbow* is made up of a main melody (A) and a contrasting one (B), called a *bridge*. It has the popular song form A A B A, with changes in lyrics after the first A.

The main melody is made up of two related phrases: the first ends inconclusively on *way up* **high** (an incomplete cadence); the second ends conclusively on the rhyming syllable of *once in a lulla-**by*** (a complete cadence).

The yearning quality of the main melody comes from its slow upward leaps combined with a quicker pattern of notes. Evoking Dorothy's dream to fly over the rainbow to a better place, the main melody begins with a wide upward leap of an octave, from the low tone on *Some* to the high tone on *-where*. Smaller upward leaps, on **way up** high and **There's a** land reinforce the melody's feeling of longing.

Sequence: See Beethoven's Symphony No. 5, I, exposition 1.a, (Listening Outline, Part IV, ch. 12).

After the opening leap on *Some-where*, the words *over the rainbow* are sung more quickly to a mostly stepwise melodic pattern. This pattern provides a beautiful conclusion to the melody when it returns on *land that I heard of* and is repeated at a lower pitch on *once in a lullaby*. Such a repetition of a melodic pattern on a higher or lower pitch is called a *sequence.*

Contrasting melody B is speechlike as Dorothy muses dreamily about life in her fantasy land. This melody (B) moves in a narrower range than melody A, uses quicker rhythms, and repeats two-note patterns (*Some-day, I'll wish* etc.). It consists of two phrases (b b′) that begin with the same tones, but have different endings. Phrase b ends with long repeated notes on *far be- hind me*. The second phrase (b′) rises to a climax on its next-to-last tone on *where you'll find me*, on the highest note of the song. Phrase b′ has an inconclusive ending that leads us to anticipate the return of the main melody.

Together, melodies A and B are masterfully composed and create a satisfying feeling of balance in this enchanting song. In our recording, *Over the Rainbow* is sung by the legendary performer Frank Sinatra accompanied by an orchestra.

The following outline will help the listener perceive the AABA form of *Over the Rainbow*:

0:00	A	Somewhere over the rainbow way…
0:22	A	Somewhere over the rainbow skies…
0:41	B	Some day I'll wish…
1:03	A	Somewhere over the rainbow bluebirds…

Melody and Words

In most songs, the melody—along with the accompaniment—expresses the meaning and emotion of the words. Song texts deal with topics ranging from the pleasures and pains of love and the beauties of nature to the realm of the supernatural and the approach of death. A melody can evoke the overall mood of a text and call forth the feelings and images of individual words and lines. Changes of mood in the text often give rise to changes of tempo, rhythm, melody, and accompaniment in the music.

Song lyrics usually are poetry, rather than prose. Composers prefer poetry because of its rhymes, rhythmic quality, and emotional intensity.

Vocal music often contains *word painting,* the musical representation of specific poetic images. For example, the words *descending from heaven* might be set to a descending melodic line, and the word *running* might be heard as a series of rapid notes. We have already seen in the song *Over the Rainbow* that the opening upward octave leap expresses the words of the title, and the word *up* appears on a high note.

In most kinds of vocal music, melodies are composed to preexisting texts. However, lyricists or composers have also written words especially to fit existing melodies; this is true of most popular songs of the twentieth century. For example, Harold Arlen first wrote the melody of *Over the Rainbow* and then E. Y. Harburg fit his lyrics to the melody. Sometimes a composer and a lyricist collaborate on the lyrics of a song, and occasionally a composer will write both words and music.

6 Harmony

When folksingers accompany themselves on a guitar, they add support, depth, and richness to the melody. We call this *harmonizing.* Most music in western culture is a blend of melody and harmony (much nonwestern music, on the other hand, emphasizes melody and rhythm rather than harmony).

Harmony refers to the way chords are constructed and how they follow each other. A *chord* is a combination of three or more tones sounded at once. Essentially, a chord is a group of simultaneous tones, and a melody is a series of individual tones heard one after another. As a melody unfolds, it provides clues for harmonizing, but it does not always dictate a specific series, or *progression,* of chords. The same melody may be harmonized in several musically convincing ways. Chord progressions enrich a melody by adding emphasis, surprise, suspense, or finality.

Ed Sheeran blends melody and harmony by accompanying himself on the guitar.
Richard Isaac/Shutterstock

New chords and progressions continually enter the language of music, but the basic chordal vocabulary has remained fairly constant. We'll look now at a few principles of harmony.

Consonance and Dissonance

Some chords have been considered stable and restful, others unstable and tense. A tone combination that is stable is called a *consonance.* Consonances are points of arrival, rest, and resolution. A tone combination that is unstable is called a *dissonance.* Its tension demands an onward motion to a stable chord. Dissonant chords are "active"; traditionally they have been considered harsh and have expressed pain, grief, and conflict. A dissonance has its *resolution* when it moves to a consonance. When this resolution is delayed or accomplished in unexpected ways, a feeling of drama, suspense, or surprise is created. In this way a composer plays with the listener's sense of expectation.

Consonance and dissonance can exist in varying degrees. Some consonant chords are more stable than others, and some dissonant chords are more tense than others. Dissonant chords have been used with increasing freedom over the centuries, so that often a chord considered intolerably harsh in one period has later come to seem rather mild.

The Triad

A great variety of chords have been used in music. Some chords consist of three tones; others have four, five, or even more. The simplest, most basic chord is the **triad** (pronounced *try'-ad*), which consists of three tones. To indicate that a triad's three tones are played at one time, it is notated as follows:

A triad is made up of alternate tones of the scale, such as the first tone (*do*), the third (*mi*), and the fifth (*sol*). The bottom tone is called the *root*; the others are a third and a fifth above the root. (From *do* to *mi* in the scale is the interval of a third; from *do* to *sol* is the interval of a fifth.)

A triad built on the first, or tonic, note of the scale (*do*) is called the **tonic chord** (*do- mi-sol*); it is the main chord of a piece, the most stable and conclusive. Traditionally, the tonic chord would usually begin a composition and almost always end it.

The **subdominant chord** is the triad based on the fourth note—*fa*—of the scale (*fa-la-do*). It often leads to the **dominant chord,** built on the fifth note—*sol*—of the scale (*sol-ti-re*). The dominant chord is next in importance to the tonic chord and is strongly pulled to it. This attraction has great importance in music. A dominant chord sets up tension that is resolved by the tonic chord. The progression from dominant to tonic gives a strong sense of conclusion, and that's why it is used so often at the end of a phrase, a melody, or an entire piece. A progression such as the one from dominant chord to tonic chord is called a cadence. The word **cadence** means both the resting point at the end of a melodic phrase (as was noted in Chapter 5) and a chord progression that gives a sense of conclusion. Here is a typical closing cadence composed of four chords: tonic-subdominant-dominant-tonic.

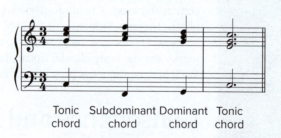

Tonic   Subdominant Dominant   Tonic
chord   chord   chord   chord

Broken Chords (Arpeggios)

When the individual tones of a chord are sounded one after another, it is called a **broken chord,** or an **arpeggio.** *The Star-Spangled Banner* begins with such a broken chord:

Arpeggio: See Mozart's Symphony No. 40, IV, opening (Part IV, ch. 11).

In this example, the notes of the tonic chord are heard in succession rather than together. Throughout this book, the importance of harmony will become more and more apparent. It helps give music variety and movement; and its effects are endless, varying with the style of a particular era and the desires of individual composers.

Prelude in E Minor for Piano, Op. 28, No. 4 (1839), by Frédéric Chopin

Chopin's harmony makes a vital contribution to the brooding quality of this miniature lasting around 2 minutes. Without the pulsating chords of its accompaniment, the melody might seem aimless and monotonous. It hardly moves, alternating obsessively between a long note and a shorter one right above it. But the returning long note seems to change in color, because each time there is a different dissonant chord below it. The dissonant chords underscore the melancholy of this prelude, which is meant to be played *espressivo* (*expressively*).

In the middle of the prelude, a return of the opening melody leads to a brief but passionate climax with a crescendo, faster rhythm, and an acceleration of tempo (accelerando). The agitation rapidly subsides as we again hear returning long notes in the melody. Toward the end of the piece, a mildly dissonant chord is followed by a brief pause. This silence is filled with expectancy, as we wait for the dissonance to resolve. Finally the tension is released in the three solemn chords of the closing cadence.

Listening Outline

CHOPIN, Prelude in E Minor for Piano

Largo, Duple meter (²⁄₂), E minor
Piano
(Duration 2:16)

Listen for the pulsating dissonant *harmonies* that add tension to a *melody* that obsessively alternates between two notes.

0:00   **1.** Sad melody with obsessively returning long notes, accompanied by pulsating dissonant chords, *p*,

accompaniment stops, melody rises to

1:00   **2. a.** Return of sad melody; tempo acceleration and crescendo to *f* climax, decrescendo.
1:25   **b.** Obsessive long notes in melody, *p*, soft dissonant chord, brief pause.
1:56   **c.** Final cadence of three low chords.

Performance Perspectives

Roger Kamien, Pianist, Playing Chopin's Prelude in E Minor

A performer conveys to the listener the sound and emotional message of music. Like an actor playing a role, a performer breathes life into symbols on a page. Both actors and musicians move their audiences through changes of pace and emphasis.

Because indications of tempo, dynamics, legato, and staccato are not absolutely precise, much is left to the interpretation of the performer. A composition marked allegro (fast), for example, might be played more rapidly by one performer than another. Fine singers or instrumentalists put a personal stamp on the music they perform, so the same piece can sound quite different when interpreted by different artists.

To illustrate the role of the performer, I would like to share with you some of the decisions involved in my performance of Chopin's Prelude in E Minor, Op. 28, No. 4, included in the recording set (see the discussion and Listening Outline on page 43). For me, the Prelude in E Minor is an emotional journey from the profound grief of the beginning, through a climactic outburst of despair, to a final acceptance

Joshua Kamien

of death. My tempo is very slow (largo), as Chopin indicates, but not excessively so. To emphasize the changes in color of the long notes in the melody, which return obsessively, I play each one at a slightly different dynamic level. In the pulsating accompanying chords, I stress the dissonant tones, either by subtly lengthening them, or by playing them a little louder than the consonant tones. To intensify the climax that grows out of the return of the opening melody, I momentarily quicken the tempo, as Chopin indicates. Toward the end of the prelude, I give extra time to the pause following the questioning dissonant chord, thus heightening expectancy before the final low cadence.

You may find it interesting to compare my recorded performance of Chopin's Prelude in E Minor with performances by two other pianists. How do the three performances differ in expression, tempo, dynamic range, and relationship between melody and accompaniment? All three pianists have played the same notes, and yet they have made three different statements. That is what molding an interpretation means.

7 Key

Practically all familiar melodies are built around a central tone toward which the other tones gravitate and on which the melody usually ends. To feel the gravitational pull, sing or listen to *Row, Row, Row Your Boat*, pausing for a few seconds between *a* and *dream*.

Row, row, row your boat, Gent - ly down the stream,

Mer - ri - ly, mer - ri - ly, mer - ri - ly, mer - ri - ly, Life is but a dream.

You probably felt uneasy until you supplied the last tone. This central tone is the **keynote,** or **tonic.** A keynote can be any one of the twelve tones in an octave. When a piece is in the key of C, for example, C is the keynote, or tonic.

Key involves not only a central tone but also a central scale and chord. (*Chord* was defined in Chapter 6.) The basic chord of a piece in C is a tonic triad with C as its root, or bottom tone. A *scale* is made up of the basic pitches of a piece of music arranged in order from low to high or from high to low. A piece in the key of C has a basic scale, *do-re-mi-fa-sol-la-ti-do,* with C as its *do,* or tonic. *Key,* then, refers to the presence of a central note, scale, and chord within a piece, with all the other tones heard in relationship to them. Another term for key is ***tonality.***

After 1900, some composers abandoned tonality, but even today, much of the music we hear is tonal.

The Major Scale

The basic scales of western music from the late 1600s to 1900 were the *major* and *minor,* and they continue to be widely used today.

The ***major scale***—the familiar *do-re-mi-fa-sol-la-ti-do*—has two kinds of intervals in a specific pattern: *half steps* and *whole steps.* The ***half step*** is the smallest interval traditionally used in western music. The ***whole step*** is twice as large as the half step. Here is the pattern of whole and half steps making up the major scale:

Pattern of whole and half steps making up the major scale.

whole step	whole step	half step	whole step	whole step	whole step	half step
do	re	mi	fa	sol	la	ti do

The illustration that follows shows a major scale with C as the beginning tone. The C major scale uses only the white keys of the piano. There are half steps between the tones E and F, and between B and C; these pairs of tones are not separated by black keys.

We can construct similar major scales by starting on any one of the twelve tones that fill an octave; thus there are twelve possible major scales. The other major scales use one or more black keys of the piano, but the pattern sounds the same.

Major scale beginning on C.

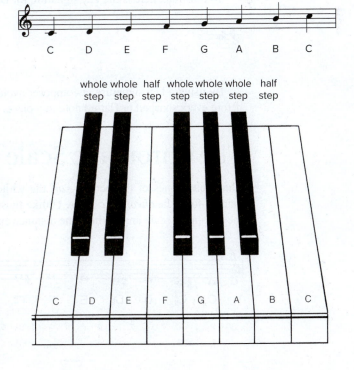

The Minor Scale

Along with the major scale, the minor scale is fundamental to western music. Sing or listen to the opening of *Greensleeves,* a tune based on a minor scale.

A - las my love you   do me wrong To cast me off dis- cour-teous- ly, And

I have lov- ed   you so long De - light-ing in   your com - pan- y.

The *minor scale*—like the major—consists of seven different tones and an eighth tone that duplicates the first an octave higher; but it differs from the major scale in its pattern of intervals, or whole and half steps. Because (again, like the major) it can begin on any of the twelve tones in an octave, there are twelve possible minor scales.

The crucial difference is that in the minor scale there is only a half step between the second and third tones. This small difference greatly changes the sound of a scale and the mood of music using that scale. Music based on minor scales tends to sound serious or melancholy. Also, the tonic triad built from a minor scale is a minor chord, which sounds darker than a major chord.

Major and Minor Keys

When a piece of music is based on a major scale, we say it is in a *major key;* when it is based on a minor scale, it is said to be in a *minor key.* For instance, a piece based on a major scale with D as its keynote is in the key of D major. Similarly, if a composition is based on a minor scale with the keynote F, the composition is in the key of F minor. Each major or minor scale has a specific number of sharps or flats ranging from none to seven. To indicate the key of a piece of music, the composer uses a *key signature,* consisting of sharp or flat signs immediately following the clef sign at the beginning of the staff.

To illustrate, here is the key signature for D major, which contains two sharps:

By using a key signature, a composer avoids having to write a sharp or a flat sign before every sharped or flatted note in a piece.

The Chromatic Scale

The twelve tones of the octave—*all* the white and black keys in one octave on the piano—form the *chromatic scale.* Unlike those of the major or minor scales, tones of the chromatic scale are all the same distance apart, one half step:

The word *chromatic* comes from the Greek word *chroma* (color). The traditional function of the chromatic scale is to color or embellish the tones of the major and minor scales. The chromatic scale does not define a key. Its tones contribute a sense of motion and tension. Composers throughout history have used the chromatic scale to evoke strong feelings of grief, loss, and sorrow. Since 1900 it has become independent of major and minor scales and has been used as the basis for entire compositions.

Modulation: Change of Key

Most short melodies remain in a single key from beginning to end. However, in longer pieces of music, variety and contrast are created by using more than one key. Shifting from one key to another within the same piece is called *modulation.*

A modulation is like a temporary shift in the center of gravity—it brings a new central tone, chord, and scale. Though modulations are sometimes subtle and difficult to spot, they produce subconscious effects that increase our enjoyment of the music.

Tonic Key

No matter how often a piece changes key, there is usually one main key, called the *tonic* or *home key.* The tonic key is the central key around which the whole piece is organized. Traditionally, a piece would usually begin in the home key and practically always end in it. A composition in the key of C major, for example, would begin in the home key, modulate to several other keys—say, G major and A minor—and finally conclude in the home key of C major. The other keys are subordinate to the tonic.

Modulating away from the tonic key is like visiting: we may enjoy ourselves during the visit, but after a while we're glad to go home. In music, modulations set up tensions that are resolved by returning to the home key. For centuries, the idea of a central key was a basic principle of music. But after 1900, some composers wrote music that ignored the traditional system and replaced it with new ways of creating tension and resolution. The results of this revolutionary step are explored in Part VI, "The Twentieth Century and Beyond."

8 Musical Texture

At a particular moment within a piece, we may hear one unaccompanied melody, several simultaneous melodies, or a melody with supporting chords. To describe these various possibilities, we use the term *musical texture;* it refers to how many different layers of sound are heard at once, to what kind of layers they are (melody or harmony), and to how they are related to each other. Texture is described as transparent, dense, thin, thick, heavy, or light; and variations in texture create contrast and drama. We'll look now at the three basic musical textures—*monophonic, polyphonic,* and *homophonic.*

Monophonic Texture

Monophony: See *Vidimus stellam* (Vocal Music Guide, Part II, ch. 1).

The texture of a single melodic line without accompaniment is *monophonic,* meaning literally *having one sound.* If you sing alone, you make monophonic music. Performance of a single melodic line at the same pitch by more than one instrument or voice is playing or singing in *unison* and results in a fuller, richer-sounding monophonic texture.

Polyphonic Texture

Polyphony: See Bach's Organ Fugue in G Minor (Listening Outline, Part III, ch. 4).

Simultaneous performance of two or more melodic lines of relatively equal interest produces the texture called **polyphonic,** meaning *having many sounds.* In polyphony several melodic lines compete for attention. Polyphony adds a dimension that has been compared to perspective in painting: each line enriches the others.

The technique of combining several melodic lines into a meaningful whole is called **counterpoint.** (The term *contrapuntal texture* is sometimes used in place of *polyphonic texture.*) To fully enjoy polyphony, you may have to hear a piece of music a few times. It's often helpful to listen first for the top line, then for the bottom line, and then for the middle lines.

Imitation: See Bach's Organ Fugue in G Minor (Listening Outline, 1.a-b, Part III, ch. 4).

Polyphonic music often contains **imitation,** which occurs when a melodic idea is presented by one voice or instrument and is then restated immediately by another. A *round*—a song in which several people sing the same melody but each starts at a different time—uses imitation. *Row, Row, Row Your Boat* is a familiar example:

Here the imitation is "strict"; each voice sings exactly the same melody. But in polyphonic texture, imitation is often freer, with the imitating line starting like the first one but going off on its own.

Homophonic Texture

Homophony: See Arlen's *Over the Rainbow* (Part I, ch. 5).

When we hear one main melody accompanied by chords, the texture is **homophonic.** Attention is focused on the melody, which is supported and colored by sounds of subordinate interest. *Row, Row, Row Your Boat,* when harmonized by chords, is an example of homophonic texture:

Accompaniments in homophonic music vary widely in character and importance, from subdued background chords to surging sounds that almost hide the main melody. When a subordinate line asserts its individuality and competes for the listener's attention, the texture is probably best described as being between homophonic and polyphonic.

Changes of Texture

Textures: See Handel's *Hallelujah* chorus (Vocal Music Guide, 00:23-01:25), (Part III, ch. 18).

A composer can create variety and contrast by changing textures within a composition. He or she might begin with a melody and a simple accompaniment and later weave the melody into a polyphonic web, or create drama by contrasting a single voice with massive chords sung by a chorus. *Farandole* by Georges Bizet (1838–1875), from *L'Arlésienne* Suite No. 2, is a good example of textural variety.

Farandole from *L'Arlésienne* Suite No. 2 (1879), by Georges Bizet*

The *Farandole* comes from music by Georges Bizet for the play *L'Arlésienne* (*The Woman of Arles*), set in southern France. Two contrasting themes are heard in this exciting orchestral piece. The first, in minor, is a march theme adapted from a southern French folksong. The lively second theme, in major, has the character of the *farandole,* a southern French dance.

Many changes of texture contribute to the *Farandole*'s exciting mood. The piece contains two kinds of homophonic texture: in one, the accompaniment and melody have the same rhythm; in the other, the rhythm of the accompaniment differs from that of the melody. The *Farandole* opens with the march theme and its accompaniment in the same rhythm. But when the lively dance theme is first presented, its accompanying chords do not duplicate the rhythm of the melody; instead, they simply mark the beat.

The *Farandole* also includes two kinds of polyphony: with and without imitation. Soon after the opening, the march theme is presented by the violins and then is imitated

---

* *L'Arlésienne* Suites No. 1 and No. 2 are sets of pieces from the theater music composed by Bizet. Suite No. 2 was arranged by Bizet's friend Ernest Guiraud in 1879, after the composer's death.

by the violas. At the end of the piece, polyphony results when the march and dance themes—previously heard in alternation—are presented simultaneously. In this concluding section, both themes are in major.

The *Farandole* also contains monophonic texture, which sets off the homophony and polyphony. Monophony is heard when the march theme is played by the strings in unison.

Listening Outline

BIZET, *Farandole* from *L'Arlésienne* Suite No. 2

Allegro deciso (forceful allegro), march tempo, quadruple meter ($\frac{4}{4}$), D minor

Piccolo, 2 flutes, 2 oboes, 2 clarinets, 2 bassoons, 4 French horns, 2 trumpets, 2 cornets, 3 trombones, timpani, tambourine, bass drum, cymbals, 1st violins, 2d violins, violas, cellos, double basses

(Duration 3:08)

Listen for the contrast between the *homophonic* texture of the opening for full orchestra and the *polyphonic* texture when the main melody played by violins is imitated by violas (in 1.a-b). Also notice the *polyphonic* texture when two different melodies are set against each other (in 4).

0:00   **1. a.** Full orchestra, ***ff***, march theme; homophonic (accompaniment in same rhythm as melody), minor.

0:16   **b.** Violins imitated by violas, march theme; polyphonic, minor.

0:33   **2. a.** High woodwinds, ***ppp***, dance theme; faster tempo, homophonic (accompanying chords on beat), major; decorative rushes in violins, long crescendo to ***ff*** as dance theme is repeated.

1:17   **b.** Full orchestra, ***fff***, dance theme.

1:28   **3. a.** Strings only, ***ff***, march theme in faster tempo; monophonic, minor.

1:39   **b.** High woodwinds, ***ppp***, dance theme; homophonic.

1:45   **c.** Strings only, ***ff***, continue march theme; monophonic, then homophonic as lower strings accompany melody.

1:56   **d.** High woodwinds, ***ppp***, dance theme; homophonic. Crescendo to

2:19   **4.** Full orchestra, ***fff***, dance and march themes combined; polyphonic, major. Homophonic ending.

9 Musical Form

The word *form* is associated with shape, structure, organization, and coherence. Form calls to mind the human body or a balanced arrangement of figures in a painting. ***Form*** in music is the organization of musical elements in time. In a musical composition, pitch, tone color, dynamics, rhythm, melody, and texture interact to produce a sense of shape and structure. All parts of the composition are interrelated. Our memory lets us perceive the overall form by recalling the various parts and how they relate to each other. The form becomes clearer as we develop awareness and recall these parts through repeated listening. As listeners, we can respond more fully to the emotional power and meaning of a musical composition when we appreciate its form.

Techniques That Create Musical Form

Repetition, contrast, and variation are essential techniques in short tunes as well as in compositions lasting much longer. ***Repetition*** creates a sense of unity; ***contrast*** provides variety; and ***variation,*** in keeping some elements of a musical thought while changing others, gives a work unity and variety at the same time.

Repetition

Musical repetition appeals to the pleasure we get in recognizing and remembering something. In music the repetition of melodies or extended sections is a technique widely used for binding a composition together.

The passage of time influences our reaction to repetition: when a musical idea returns, the effect is not duplication but balance and symmetry.

Contrast

Forward motion, conflict, and change of mood all come from contrast. Opposition—of loud and soft, strings and woodwinds, fast and slow, major and minor—propels and develops musical ideas. Sometimes such contrast is complete, but at other times the opposites have common elements that give a sense of continuity.

Variation

In the variation of a musical idea, some of its features will be retained while others are changed. For example, the melody might be restated with a different accompaniment. Or the pitches of a melody might stay the same while its rhythmic pattern is changed. A whole composition can be created from a series of variations on a single musical idea.

Types of Musical Form

Composers have traditionally organized musical ideas by using certain forms or patterns, and listeners can respond more fully when they recognize these patterns. It's important to note, however, that two compositions having the same form may be different in every other respect. We'll look now at two basic types of musical form. (Remember from Chapter 5 that lowercase letters represent phrases or short sections, and capital letters represent longer sections.)

Three-Part (Ternary) Form: A B A

Three-Part Form (ABA):
See Bartók, *Game of Pairs,*
(Part VI, ch. 14).

During the past few centuries ***three-part form*** (**A B A**) has probably been used most frequently. This form can be represented as *statement* (A), *contrast* or *departure*

(B), *return* (A). When the return of A is varied, the form is outlined A B A′. The contrast between A and B can be of any kind; A and B can be of equal or unequal length; and the way A returns after B differs from piece to piece. A may come back unexpectedly, or it may be clearly signaled (if B comes to a definite end with a cadence and a pause), or a transition may smoothly link the two.

The sections of an A B A composition can be subdivided, for example, as follows:

	A			B			A
	a b a			c d c			a b a

In some pieces, a listener might mistake subsection b within the first A for the arrival of B; but as the music progresses, the greater contrast one hears with B will make it clear that b is a subsection. (For example, in Tchaikovsky's *Dance of the Reed Pipes*, studied next, the English horn melody in item 1c in the Listening Outline introduces a brief contrast within the A section, whereas the trumpet melody in item 2a brings a greater contrast and initiates the B section.)

Dance of the Reed Pipes from *Nutcracker* Suite (1892), by Peter Ilyich Tchaikovsky

The *Nutcracker* Suite is a set of dances from the fairytale ballet *The Nutcracker* by Peter Ilyich Tchaikovsky (1840–1893). *Dance of the Reed Pipes* is a particularly clear example of A B A′ form. Section A features three flutes playing a staccato melody that conveys a light, airy feeling and is repeated several times. The B section contrasts in tone color, melody, and key—it features a trumpet melody accompanied by brasses and cymbals. This melody moves by step within a narrow range, in contrast to the opening flute melody, which has a wide range and many leaps as well as steps. The F sharp minor key of the middle section contrasts with the D major key of the opening section. The concluding A′ section, in D major, is a shortened version of the opening A section.

Listening Outline

TCHAIKOVSKY, *Dance of the Reed Pipes* from *Nutcracker* Suite

Three-part (ternary) form: A B A′

Moderato assai (very moderate), duple meter ($\frac{2}{4}$), D major

3 flutes, 2 oboes, English horn, 2 clarinets, bass clarinet, 2 bassoons, 4 French horns, 2 trumpets, 3 trombones, tuba, timpani, cymbals, 1st violins, 2d violins, violas, cellos, double basses

(Duration 2:05)

Listen for the *three-part form* (A B A′) and the differences between sections A and B in *tone color, melody,* and the use of *major* and *minor keys.*

A

0:00	**1. a.**	Low pizzicato strings, ***p***, introduce
0:03	**b.**	3 flutes, staccato melody in major, pizzicato strings accompany. Melody repeated.

0:29   **c.** English horn melody, legato, flutes accompany, staccato.

0:41   **d.** 3 flutes, staccato melody, pizzicato strings accompany. Melody repeated. Cadence.

1:06   **2. a.** Trumpet melody in minor, brasses and cymbals accompany.

1:19   **b.** Strings repeat trumpet melody. Flutes lead back to

1:37   **3.** 3 flutes, staccato melody in major, strings accompany. Melody repeated. Cadence.

Two-Part (Binary) Form: A B

Two-Part Form (AB): See Bach, *Air* from Suite No. 3, (Part III, ch. 15).

A composition made up of two sections is in ***two-part form*** (**A B**). Two-part form, frequently called ***binary form,*** gives a sense of *statement* (A) and *counterstatement* (B). Usually, compositions in two-part form repeat both parts: A A B B. Like the sections in three-part form, parts A and B in two-part form are often divided into subsections.

The two sections of a composition in binary form are often similar in rhythm, melody, and texture. However, the conclusion of each section is usually signaled by a cadence, held tones, or a brief pause. Part A begins in the tonic (home) key and ends either in the tonic or in a new key. Part B ends in the home key and brings a feeling of completion.

Bourrée from Suite in E Minor for Lute (probably around 1710), by Johann Sebastian Bach

This lighthearted bourrée—a type of dance-inspired piece in duple meter—comes from the Suite in E minor for lute, by Johann Sebastian Bach (1685–1750). The *lute* is a plucked string instrument popular during the sixteenth and seventeenth centuries. In our recording, Julian Bream performs this bourrée—a favorite of classical guitarists—on an acoustic guitar.

Lasting about 1½ minutes, this bourrée is in two-part (binary) form and is outlined A A B B because each section is repeated. Throughout the bourrée, a lilting three-note rhythm, short-short-long, pervades the dancelike melody, which is supported by a steadily moving bass line. Within each section, rhythmic motion is almost continuous except for long, held tones that close parts A and B. These longer notes help define the conclusion of each section.

Part A, about 15 seconds in duration, is made up of two brief balancing phrases (a a′). The melody of these phrases gradually descends, almost entirely by step. The first phrase (a), in minor, closes with a quick downward scale pattern in the melody. The second phrase (a′) begins exactly like the first but proceeds to a different ending on a held major chord. In our recording, the guitarist chooses to repeat part A more loudly. (There are no indications of dynamics in Bach's score of the bourrée.)

Part B, about 30 seconds in length, is twice as long as A. The melody of B is more playful because it moves by leap as well as by step. It contains four brief phrases, each ending with a held note in the melody. The fourth phrase of B differs from the previous phrases because it quickly descends, repeating a three-note melodic pattern at increasingly lower pitches. (This is a downward *sequence*.) Part B ends in minor with a low, held octave. In our recording, the guitarist plays part B at a fairly soft dynamic level and concludes the repetition of B with a slight slowing of tempo to heighten the feeling of finality.

Listening Outline

BACH, *Bourrée* from Suite in E Minor for Lute

Two-part (binary) form: A A B B
Duple meter ($\frac{2}{2}$), E minor
Acoustic guitar
(Duration 1:32)

Listen for the *two-part form* (A A B B) and how a short-short-long *rhythm* pervades the entire piece. Also notice the downward sequence in the *melody* near the end of part B.

A

0:00   **1.** Dancelike melody (a) in minor, short-short-long rhythm, moves downward mostly by step. Melody repeats (a′), descends to long, low, major chord. Soft dynamic level.

A   0:14   Part A repeated more loudly.

B

0:26   **2.** Three soft phrases with skips and steps, short-short-long rhythm continues; each brief phrase ends with long note in melody.

Fourth phrase quickly descends in sequential repetition of short-short-long pattern; minor key, long low octave ends B.

B   0:57   Part B repeated.

Listening for Form

The musical patterns covered in this section fall into clearly defined units. However, music is continuous in its flow and sometimes can't be subdivided quite so easily. Some music seems to fit none of the frequently used patterns. But such music is not formless—it has a unique form that can be discovered through repeated hearings.

Again, it's important to lean on memory when you listen to music. Spotting musical ideas when they occur is fine, but it's only the beginning. The goal is to put the related ideas together by recognizing and remembering them and by finding the relationships between them. Through alert, repeated listening, their overall shape will be made clear, and your response to music will be more satisfying.

10 Musical Style

We use the word *style* in reference to everything from clothing to cooking, automobiles to paintings. In music, **style** refers to a characteristic way of using melody, rhythm, tone color, dynamics, harmony, texture, and form. The particular way these elements are combined can result in a total sound that's distinctive or unique. We speak of the musical style of an individual composer, a group of composers, a country, or a particular period in history. Compositions created in the same geographical area or around the same time are often similar in style, but individuals using the same musical vocabulary can create a personal manner of expression.

Musical styles change from one era in history to the next. These changes are continuous, and so any boundary line between one stylistic period and the next can be only an approximation. Though sudden turning points do occur in the history of music, even the most revolutionary new styles are usually foreshadowed in earlier compositions; and few changes of style sweep away the past entirely.

The history of western art music can be divided into the following stylistic periods:

Middle Ages (450–1450)
Renaissance (1450–1600)
Baroque (1600–1750)
Classical (1750–1820)
Romantic (1820–1900)
Twentieth century to 1945
1945 to the present

The chapters that follow describe the general features of each period and show how that period differs from the preceding one. An awareness of the characteristics of a style helps you to know what to listen for in a composition and helps you to recognize innovative or unique features.

Music is not created in a vacuum. To fully understand the style of a composition, one has to be aware of its function in society. Is a piece meant to provide entertainment in an aristocrat's castle, a concert hall, or a middle-class home? Is it designed to accompany singing, dancing, religious rites, or drama? Musical style is shaped by political, economic, social, and intellectual developments as well. And often, similar features of style can be found in different arts of the same period.

Music is probably as old as the human race itself. There is pictorial evidence of musical activity in Egypt as early as 3000 BCE. We know that music played an important role in the cultures of ancient Israel, Greece, and Rome. But hardly any notated music has survived from these ancient civilizations.

The first stylistic period to be considered in this book is the European Middle Ages, from which notated music has come down to us. Through the power of notation, music created more than 1,000 years ago can come alive today.

Elements: Summary

IMPORTANT TERMS

Sound, p. 6
Pitch, p. 6
Tone, p. 7
Interval, p. 7
Octave, p. 7
Pitch range (range), p. 7
Dynamics, p. 8
  pianissimo
  piano
  mezzo piano
  mezzo forte
  forte
  fortissimo
  decrescendo (diminuendo)
  crescendo
Accent, p. 8
Tone color (timbre), p. 8
Improvisation, p. 10
Voices, p. 11
  Women
    soprano
    mezzo-soprano
    alto (contralto)
  Men
    tenor
    baritone
    bass
Musical instruments
  string, p. 12
  woodwind, p. 12
  brass, p. 12
  percussion, p. 12
  keyboard, p. 12
  electronic, p. 12
  register, p. 12
  conductor, p. 14
  baton, p. 14
  concertmaster, p. 14
String instruments
  violin, p. 14
  viola, p. 14
  cello, p. 14
  double bass, p. 14
  bow, p. 14
  pizzicato, p. 16
  stop (double, triple, quadruple), p. 16
  vibrato, p. 16
  mute, p. 17
  tremolo, p. 17
  harmonics, p. 17
  plectrum, p. 17
  harp, p. 17

  guitar, p. 17
Woodwind instruments
  piccolo, p. 17
  flute, p. 17
  clarinet, p. 17
  bass clarinet, p. 17
  oboe, p. 17
  English horn, p. 17
  bassoon, p. 17
  contrabassoon, p. 17
  recorder, p. 17
  reed, p. 17
  single-reed woodwinds, p. 17
  saxophone, p. 17
  double-reed woodwinds, p. 17
Brass instruments
  trumpet, p. 20
  French horn, p. 20
  trombone, p. 20
  tuba, p. 20
  cornet, p. 20
  baritone horn, p. 20
  euphonium, p. 20
  mute, p. 20
Percussion instruments
  Definite pitch
    timpani (kettledrums), p. 22
    glockenspiel, p. 22
    xylophone, p. 22
    celesta, p. 22
    chimes, p. 22
  Indefinite pitch
    snare drum (side drum), p. 22
    bass drum, p. 22
    tambourine, p. 22
    triangle, p. 22
    cymbals, p. 22
    gong (tam-tam), p. 22
Keyboard instruments
  piano, p. 25
  harpsichord, p. 25
  pipe organ, p. 26
  accordion, p. 27
Electronic instruments
  tape studio, p. 27
  synthesizer, p. 27
  computer, p. 28
  electric guitar, p. 28
Theme, p. 29
Variation, p. 29
Rhythm, p. 31
Beat, p. 31
Meter, p. 33

  duple meter
  triple meter
  quadruple meter
  quintuple meter
  sextuple meter
  septuple meter
Measure (bar), p. 33
Downbeat, p. 33
Upbeat, p. 33
Accent, p. 34
Syncopation, p. 34
Tempo, p. 34
Tempo indication, p. 34
  largo
  grave
  adagio
  andante
  moderato
  allegretto
  allegro
  vivace
  presto
  prestissimo
Accelerando, p. 34
Ritardando, p. 34
Metronome, p. 34
Notation, p. 35
Note, p. 35
Staff, p. 35
Ledger lines, p. 35
Sharp sign, p. 35
Flat sign, p. 35
Natural sign, p. 35
Clef (treble and bass), p. 36
Grand staff, p. 36
Middle C, p. 36
Stem (flag), p. 36
Beam, p. 37
Dotted note, p. 37
Dotted rhythm, p. 37
Tie, p. 37
Triplet, p. 37
Rest, p. 37
Time signature (meter signature), p. 37
Melody, p. 38
Step, p. 38
Leap, p. 38
Climax, p. 38
Legato, p. 38
Staccato, p. 38
Phrase, p. 38
Cadence, p. 38

Sequence, p. 40
Word painting, p. 41
Harmony, p. 41
Chord, p. 41
Progression, p. 41
Consonance, p. 41
Dissonance, p. 41
Resolution, p. 41
Triad, p. 42
Tonic chord, p. 42
Subdominant chord, p. 42
Dominant chord, p. 42
Broken chord (arpeggio), p. 42
Keynote (tonic), p. 44
Key (tonality), p. 45
Scale, p. 45
Major scale, p. 45
Half step, p. 45
Whole step, p. 45
Minor scale, p. 46
Major key, p. 46
Minor key, p. 46
Key signature, p. 46
Chromatic scale, p. 46
Modulation, p. 47
Tonic key (home key), p. 47
Musical texture, p. 47
Monophonic texture, p. 47
Unison, p. 47
Polyphonic texture, p. 48
Counterpoint, p. 48
Imitation, p. 48
Homophonic texture, p. 48
Form, p. 51
Repetition, p. 51
Contrast, p. 51
Variation, p. 51
Three-part (ternary) form (A B A), p. 51
Two-part (Binary) form (A B), p. 53
Style, p. 55

FEATURED COMPOSERS

Igor Stravinsky (1882–1971)
Duke Ellington (1899–1974)
Benjamin Britten (1913–1976)
George Gershwin (1898–1937)
Harold Arlen (1905–1986)
Frédéric Chopin (1810–1849)
Georges Bizet (1838–1875)
Peter Ilyich Tchaikovsky (1840–1893)
Johann Sebastian Bach (1685–1750)

Design Elements: (Listening Icon): McGraw Hill Education; (Baroque violin): McGraw Hill Education

■ Most medieval music was vocal, though musicians also performed on a wide variety of instruments. A page from the *Manesse Codex,* early 1300s.

The Middle Ages and Renaissance

*The man that hath no music in himself,
Nor is not mov'd with concord of sweet
sounds, Is fit for treasons, strategems and
spoils.*

—William Shakespeare

LEARNING OBJECTIVES

- Explain the roles of musicians in medieval society.

- Discuss the texture, melody, rhythm, mood, and texts of Gregorian chant.

- Describe different types of secular music in the Middle Ages.

- Trace the development of polyphonic music in the Middle Ages.

- Identify the musical innovations in music of the fourteenth century.

- Explain the shift in musical patronage during the Renaissance.

- Compare and contrast polyphonic vocal music of the Middle Ages and the Renaissance.

- Describe two types of sacred vocal music during the Renaissance.

- Compare and contrast two types of secular vocal music during the Renaissance.

- Discuss the development of Renaissance instrumental music.

Middle Ages 450–1450

450-1000	1000-1300	1300-1450

Historical and Cultural Events

455 Sack of Rome by Vandals

590–604 Reign of Pope Gregory I (the Great)

800 Charlemagne crowned Holy Roman Emperor

1066 Norman Conquest

1096–1099 First Crusade

1215 Magna Carta signed

1337–1453 Hundred Years' War

1347–1352 Black death

1431 Joan of Arc executed by the English

Arts and Letters

c. 700 *Beowolf*

c. 800 *Book of Kells*

1163 Beginning of Notre Dame Cathedral in Paris

1273 Thomas Aquinas, *Summa Theologica*

1321 Dante, *The Divine Comedy*

1351 Boccaccio, *Decameron*

1387–1400 Chaucer, *The Canterbury Tales*

Ayhan Altun/Getty Images

Music

c. 900 Earliest notated Gregorian chant manuscripts

c. 1100–1300 Troubadours and trouvères

c. 1150 Hildegard of Bingen, *O successores*

begun c. 1170 School of Notre Dame

c. 1360 Guillaume de Machaut *Notre Dame* Mass

David Lees/Getty Images

The History Collection/Alamy

Renaissance 1450–1600

1450–1500	1500–1600

Historical and Cultural Events

1453 Fall of Constantinople

1456 Gutenberg Bible

1492 Columbus reaches America

1517 Martin Luther's ninety-five theses, start of the Reformation

1545–1563 Council of Trent

1558–1603 Elizabeth I, queen of England

1588 Spanish Armada defeated

Arts and Letters

c. 1482 Botticelli, *La Primavera*

c. 1503 Leonardo da Vinci, *Mona Lisa*

1504 Michelangelo, *David*

1505 Raphael, *School of Athens*

c. 1570 Titian, *Venus and the Lute Player*

1596 Shakespeare, *Romeo and Juliet*

muratart/Shutterstock

Music

c. 1475 Josquin Desprez, *Ave Maria . . . Virgo Serena*

DEA PICTURE LIBRARY/ Getty Images

1563 Giovanni Pierluigi da Palestrina, *Pope Marcellus Mass*

c. 1600 John Dowland, *Flow My Tears*

1601 Thomas Weelkes, *As Vesta Was Descending*

The Middle Ages
(450–1450)

Athousand years of European history are spanned by the phrase *Middle Ages*. Beginning around 450 with the disintegration of the Roman empire, the early Middle Ages were a time of migrations, upheavals, and wars. But the later Middle Ages (until about 1450) were a period of cultural growth: Romanesque churches and monasteries (1000–1150) and Gothic cathedrals (1150–1450) were constructed, towns grew, and universities were founded. The later Middle Ages also witnessed the Crusades, a series of wars undertaken by European Christians—primarily between 1096 and 1291—to recover the holy city of Jerusalem from the Muslims.

During the Middle Ages a very sharp division existed among three main social classes: nobility, peasantry, and clergy. Nobles were sheltered within fortified castles surrounded by moats. During wars, noblemen engaged in combat as knights in armor, while noblewomen managed estates, ran households, and looked after the

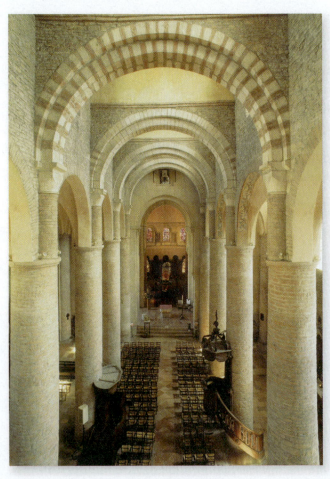 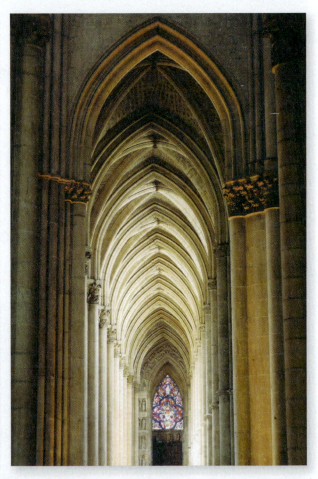

Architecture changed during the Middle Ages from the Romanesque style, seen in the eleventh-century nave at left, to the Gothic style of the thirteenth-century Cathedral of Reims, at right.

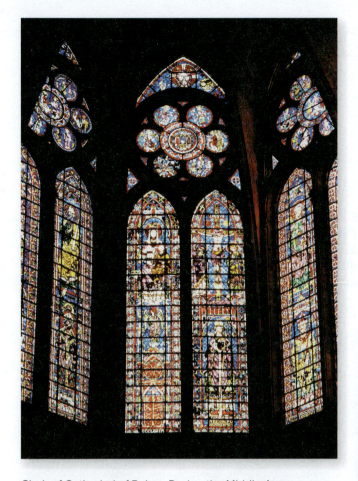

Choir of Cathedral of Reims. During the Middle Ages, religious teachings were imparted, and beliefs were strengthened, by biblical scenes depicted in stained-glass windows.

DeAgostini/Getty Images

During the Middle Ages, artists were more concerned with religious symbolism than with lifelike representation. *Virgin and Child Enthroned, and Prophets* (*Santa Trinita Maestà*), ca. 1290–1300, by Cimabue.

Alfredo Dagli Orti/Shutterstock

sick. In peacetime, the nobles amused themselves with hunting, feasting, and tournaments. Peasants—the vast majority of the population—lived miserably in one-room huts. Many were serfs, bound to the soil and subject to feudal overlords. All segments of society felt the powerful influence of the Roman Catholic Church. In this age of faith, hell was very real, and heresy was the gravest crime. Monks in monasteries held a virtual monopoly on learning; most people—including the nobility—were illiterate.

In the fourteenth century, an age of disintegration, Europe suffered through the Hundred Years' War (1337–1453) and the black death—or bubonic plague (around 1350)—which killed one-fourth of its population. By this time, both the feudal system and the authority of the church had been weakened. From 1378 to 1417, two rival popes claimed authority; and at one time there were three. Even devout Christians were confused. Literature of the time, such as Chaucer's *Canterbury Tales* (1387–1400) and Boccaccio's *Decameron* (after 1348), stressed graphic realism and earthly sensuality rather than virtue and heavenly rewards.

The Renaissance (1450–1600)

The fifteenth and sixteenth centuries in Europe have come to be known as the ***Renaissance***. People then spoke of a "rebirth," or *renaissance*, of human creativity. It was a period of exploration and adventure—consider the voyages of Christopher Columbus (1492), Vasco da Gama (1498), and Ferdinand Magellan (1519–1522). The Renaissance was an age of curiosity and individualism, too, as can be seen in the remarkable life of Leonardo da Vinci (1452–1519), who was a painter, sculptor, architect, engineer, and scientist—and a fine musician as well.

During the Renaissance, the Virgin Mary was depicted as a beautiful, idealized young woman. Renaissance painters emphasized balance and used perspective to create an illusion of depth. *The Virgin and Child with Saint Anne* (ca. 1503), by Leonardo da Vinci.
Corbis Historical/Fine Art/Getty Images

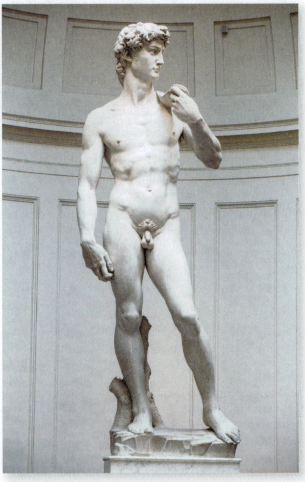

Renaissance sculptors and painters once again depicted the nude human body, which had been an object of shame and concealment during the Middle Ages. *David* (1504) by Michelangelo.
muratart/Shutterstock

Classical mythology was an important source of inspiration for Renaissance art. *La Primavera* (*Spring;* c. 1482) by Sandro Botticelli depicts Venus (center), the Three Graces and Mercury (left), and Flora, Spring, and Zephyrus (right).

Alfredo Dagli Orti/Shutterstock

During the Renaissance, the dominant intellectual movement, which was called **humanism,** focused on human life and its accomplishments. Humanists were not concerned with an afterlife in heaven or hell. Though devout Christians, they were captivated by the cultures of ancient Greece and Rome. They became intoxicated with the beauty of ancient languages—Greek and Latin—and with the literature of antiquity. Humanism strongly influenced art throughout the Renaissance. Painters and sculptors were attracted to subjects drawn from classical literature and mythology. Once again they depicted the nude human body, which had been a favorite theme of antiquity but an object of shame and concealment during the Middle Ages. Medieval artists had been concerned more with religious symbolism than with lifelike representation.

They had conceived of a picture as a flat, impenetrable surface on which persons or objects were shown. Renaissance painters, such as Raphael (1483–1520) and Leonardo da Vinci, were more interested in realism and used linear perspective, a geometrical system for creating an illusion of space and depth. During the Renaissance, painters no longer treated the Virgin Mary as a childlike, unearthly creature; they showed her as a beautiful young woman.

The Catholic church was far less powerful during the Renaissance than it had been during the Middle Ages, for the unity of Christendom was exploded by the Protestant Reformation led by Martin Luther (1483–1546). No longer did the church monopolize learning. Aristocrats and the upper-middle-class now considered education a status symbol, and they hired scholars to teach their children. The invention of printing with movable type (around 1450) accelerated the spread of learning. Before 1450, books were rare and extremely expensive because they were copied entirely by hand. But by 1500, 15 million to 20 million copies of 40,000 editions had been printed in Europe.

Renaissance artists were strongly influenced by the cultures of ancient Greece and Rome. *The School of Athens* (1505) by Raphael, showing the Greek philosophers Aristotle and Plato (center). Plato is painted in the likeness of Leonardo da Vinci. Universal History Archive/Getty Images

1 Music in the Middle Ages (450–1450)

Just as the cathedral dominated the medieval landscape and mind, so was it the center of musical life. Most of the important musicians were priests and worked for the church. An important occupation in thousands of monasteries was liturgical singing. Boys received music education in schools associated with churches and cathedrals. Women were not allowed to sing in church but did make music in convents. Nuns learned to sing, and some—like Hildegard of Bingen (1098–1179), abbess of Rupertsberg—wrote music for their choirs. With this preeminence of the church, it is not surprising that for centuries only sacred music was notated.

Most medieval music was vocal, though musicians also performed on a wide variety of instruments. Church officials required monks to sing with proper pronunciation, concentration, and tone quality. For example, Saint Bernard, the twelfth-century mystic and head of the abbey at Clairvaux in France, ordered his monks to sing vigorously, "pronouncing the words of the Holy Spirit with becoming manliness and resonance and affection; and correctly, that while you chant you ponder on nothing but what you chant."

The church frowned on instruments because of their earlier role in pagan rites. After about 1000, however, organs and bells became increasingly common in cathedrals and monastic churches. For three centuries or so, organs were played mainly on feast days and other special occasions. Sometimes the clergy complained about noisy organs that distracted worshippers. "Whence hath the church so many Organs," complained St. Aethelred, a twelfth-century abbot. "To what purpose, I pray you, is that terrible blowing of bellows, expressing rather the cracks of thunder than the sweetness of a Voyce." Aethelred criticized people who watched the organ as if "in a theater not a place of worship."

Today, we know relatively little about how medieval music sounded. Few medieval instruments have survived; and music manuscripts of the time do not indicate tempo, dynamics, or names of instruments. In some kinds of medieval music, the notation indicates pitch, but not rhythm. Singers and instrumentalists often appear together in pictures and in literary descriptions, but it is not certain whether polyphonic music was performed with voices alone or with voices and instruments.

Gregorian Chant

For over 1,000 years, the official music of the Roman Catholic Church was *Gregorian chant,* which consists of melody set to sacred Latin texts and sung without accompaniment. (The chant is monophonic in texture.) The melodies of Gregorian chant were meant to enhance specific parts of religious services. They set the atmosphere for prayers and ritual actions. For centuries, composers have based original compositions on chant melodies. (Since the Second Vatican Council of 1962–1965, however, most Roman Catholic services have been celebrated in the native language of each country, and so today Gregorian chant is no longer common.)

Gregorian chant conveys a calm, otherworldly quality; it represents the voice of the church, rather than that of any single individual. Its rhythm is flexible, without meter, and has little sense of beat. The exact rhythm of chant melodies is uncertain because precise time values were not notated. But its free-flowing rhythm gives Gregorian chant a floating, almost improvisational character. The melodies tend to move by step within a narrow range of pitches. Depending on the nature and importance of the text, they are simple or elaborate; some are little more than recitations on a single tone; others contain complex melodic curves.

Gregorian chant is named after Pope Gregory I (the Great), who reorganized the Catholic liturgy during his reign from 590 to 604. Although medieval legend credits Pope Gregory with the creation of Gregorian chant, we know that it evolved over many centuries. Some of its practices, such as the singing of psalms, came from the Jewish synagogues of the first centuries after Christ. Most of the several thousand melodies known today were created between 600 and 1300 CE.

At first Gregorian melodies were passed along by oral tradition, but as the number of chants grew to the thousands, they were notated to ensure musical uniformity throughout the western church. (The illustration on page 69 shows an example of medieval chant notation.) The earliest surviving chant manuscripts date from about the ninth century. The composers of Gregorian chant—like the sculptors who decorated early medieval churches—remain almost completely unknown.

Medieval monks and nuns spent several hours of each day singing Gregorian chant in two types of services: the office and the mass. Each type included both sung and spoken texts in Latin. The office consisted of eight services, the first before sunrise and the last at sunset. The *mass,* the highlight of the liturgical day, was a ritual reenactment of the Last Supper. Some texts of the mass remained the same from day to day throughout most of the church year, whereas other texts were meant only for particular feasts, such as Christmas, Epiphany, or Easter.

The Church Modes

The "otherworldly" sound of Gregorian chant results partly from the unfamiliar scales used. These scales are called **church modes** (or sometimes simply *modes*). Like major and minor scales, church modes consist of seven different tones and an eighth tone that duplicates the first an octave higher. However, their patterns of whole and half steps are different. The church modes were the basic scales of western music during the Middle Ages and Renaissance and were used in secular as well as sacred music. Much western folk music follows the patterns of the church modes. For example, the sea chantey *What Shall We Do with the Drunken Sailor?* is in a mode called *Dorian.*

Alleluia: Vidimus stellam (We Have Seen His Star)

An elaborate and jubilant Gregorian chant is the Alleluia from the Mass for Epiphany. The word *alleluia* is a Latinized form of the Hebrew *hallelujah* (*praise ye the Lord*). In this chant (shown on page 70 in modern notation), many notes are sung to single syllables of text. The long series of tones on *ia* is a wordless expression of joy and religious ecstasy. The monophonic texture of the chant is varied by an alternation between a soloist and a choir singing in unison. The chant is in A B A form; the opening *alleluia* melody is repeated after a middle section that is set to a biblical verse.

Vocal Music Guide

Alleluia: *Vidimus stellam* (*We Have Seen His Star*)

(Duration 2:11)

Listen for the *monophonic texture* of the Gregorian chant, and the difference in tone color between a solo voice and a choir singing in *unison*.

0:00

A

| Solo, opening melody, many tones on *ia* | *Alleluia.* | Hallelujah. |
| Choir repeats melody | *Alleluia.* | Hallelujah. |

0:39

B

| Solo, second melody | *Vidimus stellam ejus in Oriente et venimus cum muneribus adorare Dominum.* | We have seen his star in the east and are come with gifts to worship the Lord. |

1:48

A

| Choir, opening melody | *Alleluia.* | Hallelujah. |

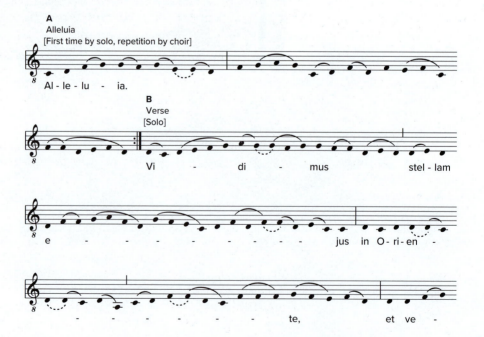

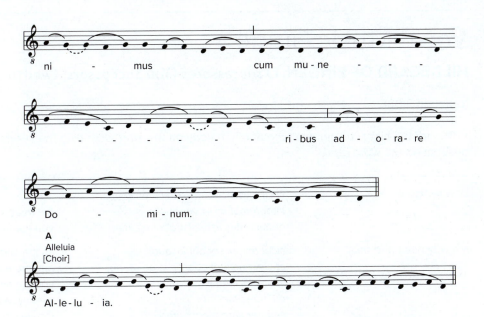

ni - mus cum mu - ne - - -

- - - - - ri - bus ad - o - ra - re

Do - mi - num.

A
Alleluia
[Choir]

Al - le - lu - ia.

O successores (*You Successors*), by Hildegard of Bingen

A late, highly expressive example of Gregorian chant is *O successores* (*You Successors*) by the nun Hildegard of Bingen (1098–1179), abbess of Rupertsberg in Germany. Hildegard was one of the most creative and many-sided personalities of the Middle Ages. A visionary and mystic, she was active in religious and diplomatic affairs. She also wrote poetry and music; treatises on theology, science, and medicine; and a musical drama, *Ordo virtutum* (Play of the Virtues), which is the earliest known morality play. She was the first woman composer from whom a large number of works—monophonic sacred songs—have survived.

The chant *O successores* was composed to be sung by the nuns in Hildegard's convent. It is in praise of the holy confessors who are successors of Christ. (Christ is referred to as *lion* and *lamb* in the text.) Hildegard explained that the words came to her in a vision: "Then I saw the lucent sky, in which I heard different kinds of music…. I heard the praises of the joyous citizens of heaven, steadfastly persevering in the ways of truth."

The chant is notated in the manuscript as a single melodic line, without accompaniment. However, in our recording the performers have added a drone accompaniment. A **drone** consists of one or more long, sustained tones accompanying a melody. In *O successores*, two simultaneous sustained notes at the interval of a fifth are played on a fiddle, a medieval bowed string instrument. It may well be that such an accompaniment accords with medieval performance practice.

The melody is sung by a women's choir and is made up of several phrases. This chant usually has one to four notes to each syllable; only at the end are many notes sung on the final syllable. The melody creates a sense of progression and growth as it moves gradually through a wide pitch range (an octave and a sixth). At first, the melody seems calm as it proceeds primarily by step within a low register. However, beginning with the word *sicut* there are several ascents to high notes and wide upward leaps of a fifth (on the words *et, vos, qui*, and *semper*). The climactic tone (on the important word *officio, service*) is reserved for the concluding phrase, which gently descends by step (on the word *agni, lamb*) to the original low register. *O successores* seems more speech-like than *Alleluia: Vidimus stellam*, where many tones are sung to single syllables of text. Hildegard's chant has a larger pitch range, more wide leaps, and a greater feeling of motion toward a climax near the end.

Vocal Music Guide

HILDEGARD OF BINGEN, O successores (You Successors; twelfth century)

(Duration 2:08)

Listen for the climactic highest *tone* of the *melody* on the word *officio*, in the service, and the long melodic descent on the word *agni*.

Low register	O successores fortissimi leonis inter templum et altare— dominantes in ministratione eius—	You successors of the mightiest lion between the temple and the altar— you the masters in his household—
Melody rises and falls	sicut angeli sonant in laudibus, et sicut adsunt populis in adiutorio, vos estis inter illos, qui haec faciunt, semper curam habentes	as the angels sound forth praises and are here to help the nations, you are among those who accomplish this, forever showing your care
Climax on *officio,* long descent on *agni*	in officio agni.	in the service of the lamb.

Hildegard of Bingen, 1098–1179, Abbess of Rupertsberg in Germany, was one of the most creative and many-sided personalities of the Middle Ages.

The History Collection/Alamy

Secular Music in the Middle Ages

Despite the predominance of Gregorian chant throughout the Middle Ages, there was also much music outside the church. The pleasures of secular music and dance were vividly evoked by the thirteenth-century theologian Henri de Malines, as he reminisced about his life as a young student in Paris. "This servant of God gladly heard music performed upon reed instruments, pipes, and every kind of musical instrument." Henri "knew how to play a fiddle, bringing together in harmonious fashion, a melodious touching of the strings and drawing of the bow. He was familiar with and willingly sang all kinds of monophonic songs in various languages." Henri created poems and melodies and was a "merry and amorous leader … of dances in wooded places, arranging parties and games, and interspersing the sport of dancing with others."

Troubadour and Trouvère Song

A large and highly important body of secular songs was created by poet-composers who were called *troubadours* and *trouvères*, active in courts of the nobility and in towns during the twelfth and thirteenth centuries. Troubadours lived in southern France and wrote poems in the Provençal language; trouvères flourished in northern France and wrote in Old French. The terms *troubadour* and *trouvère* come from words meaning "to invent" or "to find." Most troubadour and trouvère songs were about courtly or idealized love for an unattainable noble lady. Other songs deal with the Crusades, political satire, and dance.

Troubadours and trouvères came from diverse social backgrounds: some were nobles, such as William IX, Duke of Aquitaine (1071–1126), the first known troubadour, and Prince Jaufre Rudel (mid-twelfth century), a troubadour who died during the second Crusade around 1147. (Jaufre Rudel is the subject of Kaija Saariaho's opera, *L'amour de loin* (Love from afar), studied in Part VI, "The Twentieth and Beyond.") Others came from modest backgrounds, such as the troubadour Bernart de Ventadorn (c. 1140–1200), son of a baker, and the trouvère Guillaume le Vinier (c. 1190–1245), whose parents were middle-class.

The written music notation of troubadour and trouvère songs indicates the pitches of the melodies, but not the rhythm. We do not know whether these melodies were performed with a clear beat and meter, or in the free rhythm of Gregorian chant. Troubadour and trouvère songs are notated as single melodic lines; their texture is monophonic. However, instrumentalists probably accompanied the singers. These songs were performed either by their composers or by wandering minstrels (see p. 74).

There were women troubadours, called *trobairitz,* and trouvères, who addressed their songs to men. The example we are about to study is a song by Beatriz, Countess of Dia.

A Chantar (I must sing), by Beatriz, Countess of Dia (Late Twelfth Century)

Beatriz, Countess of Dia—a *trobairitz* from the town of Dia in southern France—wrote love songs that have survived. One of these, *A Chantar,* is the only song by a female troubadour with its melody preserved in music notation. Only about a tenth of the 2,500 existing troubadour songs have survived with their melodies.

Beatriz di Dia, the Countess of Dia, was the best-known female troubadour of the Middle Ages.
MS cod. fr. 12473 located at Bibliothèque Nationale
The History Collection/Alamy

Vocal Music Guide

BEATRIZ, *A Chantar* (*I must sing*); late twelfth century

Voice, vielle

(Duration 5:21)

Listen for the difference between phrases with open and closed endings and for the climax in phrase d.

	0:00		
Vielle Introduction			
	0:25		
Open ending.	a	*A chanter m'er de so q'ieu no volria,*	I must sing of what I'd rather not,
	0:39		
Closed ending.	b	*tant me rancor de lui cui amia*	I am so angry about him whose friend I am,
	0:51		
Open ending.	a	*car eu l'am mais que nuilla ren que sia;*	For I love him more than anything;
	1:04		
Closed ending.	b	*vas lui nom val merces ni cortesia;*	Mercy and courtliness don't help me
	1:17		
Open ending.	c	*ni ma beltatz ni mos pretz ni mos sens,*	With him, nor does my beauty, or my rank, or my mind,
	1:26		
Climax on *sui*.	d	*c'atressi.m sui enganada e trahia*	For I am every bit as betrayed and wronged
	1:38		
Closed ending.	b	*Com degr' esser s'ieu fos desavinens.*	As I'd deserve if I were unattractive.

A Chantar is about Beatriz's love for a man who has betrayed her, even though she is beautiful, intelligent, and of high rank. The haunting, highly ornamental melody of *A Chantar* moves mostly by step, within the pitch range of an octave, and has one to three tones on each syllable of the text. This melody is repeated for each of the poem's seven-line stanzas. The spacious melodic line is composed of four phrases, a, b, c, and d, arranged in the pattern ab ab cdb. Phrase a ends with an open feeling, whereas phrase b ends more conclusively.

Phrase d rises to the climax of the melody, conveying emotional tension.

The melody of *A Chantar* is preserved only in *Le Manuscrit du Roi* (The King's Manuscript), collected by Charles of Anjou, brother of Louis IX, king of France from 1226 to 1270.

In our recording, the singer is introduced and then accompanied by a *vielle*, a medieval bowed string instrument somewhat larger than a modern violin. The vocal soloist sings in a free rhythm, without any clear beat. In phrase d, the singer embellishes the melody to emphasize the words *wronged* and *betrayed*.

Minstrels

During the Middle Ages, wandering *minstrels* (or *jongleurs*—*juggler* comes from this French word) entertained in castles, taverns, and town squares. They performed music, acrobatics, told stories, and danced, hoping to get food or a few coins in return. Minstrels had no civil rights and were on the lowest social level, with prostitutes and slaves; only a lucky few found steady work in the service of the nobility. But they were an important source of information in a time when there were no newspapers. They usually sang songs composed by troubadours and played instrumental dances on harps, fiddles (ancestors of the violin), and lutes (plucked string instruments).

Estampie (Thirteenth Century)

The *estampie*, a medieval dance, is one of the earliest surviving forms of instrumental music. In the manuscript for this **estampie,** a single melodic line is notated and, as usual, no instrument is specified. In our recording, the melody is played on a *rebec* (a bowed string instrument) and a *pipe* (a tubular wind instrument). Because medieval minstrels probably improvised modest accompaniments to dance tunes, the performers have added a drone—two simultaneous, repeated notes at the interval of a fifth, played on a *psaltery* (a plucked or struck string instrument). The estampie is in triple meter and has a strong, fast beat.

Dances in the Middle Ages were often accompanied by instrumental music.
Art Reserve/Alamy

The Development of Polyphony: Organum

For centuries, western music was basically monophonic, having a single melodic line. But sometime between 700 and 900, the first steps were taken in a revolution that eventually transformed western music. Monks in monastery choirs began to add a second melodic line to Gregorian chant. In the beginning, this second line was improvised, not written down; it duplicated the chant melody at a different pitch. The two lines were in parallel motion, note against note, at the interval of a fourth or a fifth. (The interval from *do* to *fa* is a fourth; from *do* to *sol* is a fifth.)

Sit glo - ri - a Do - mi - ni in se - cu - la

Medieval music that consists of Gregorian chant and one or more additional melodic lines is called **organum**. Between 900 and 1200, organum became truly polyphonic, and the melody added to the chant became more independent. Instead of moving strictly parallel to the chant, it developed a melodic curve of its own. Sometimes this line was in contrary motion to the chant, moving up as the chant moved down. The second line became even more independent around 1100, when the chant and the added melody were no longer restricted to a note-against-note style. Now the two lines could differ rhythmically as well as melodically. The chant, on the bottom, was generally sung in very long notes while the added melody, on top, moved in shorter notes.

Medieval listeners must have been startled to hear religious music in which the added melody was more attractive than the chant. In fact, at times the chant tones were so slow and dronelike that the original melody was hardly recognizable. Nonetheless, the chant represented the authority of the church. And respect for the church was so great that for centuries most polyphonic music was created by placing new melodic lines against known chants.

School of Notre Dame: Measured Rhythm

After 1150, Paris—the intellectual and artistic capital of Europe—became the center of polyphonic music. The University of Paris attracted leading scholars, and the Cathedral of Notre Dame (begun in 1163) was the supreme monument of Gothic architecture. Two successive choirmasters of Notre Dame, Leonin and Perotin, are among the first notable composers known by name. They and their followers are referred to as the *school of Notre Dame*.

From about 1170 to 1200, the Notre Dame composers developed rhythmic innovations. Earlier polyphonic music was probably performed in the free, unmeasured rhythms of Gregorian chant. But the music of Leonin and Perotin used *measured rhythm*, with definite time values and clearly defined meter. For the first time in music history, notation indicated precise rhythms as well as pitches. At first the new notation was limited to only certain rhythmic patterns, and the beat had to be subdivided

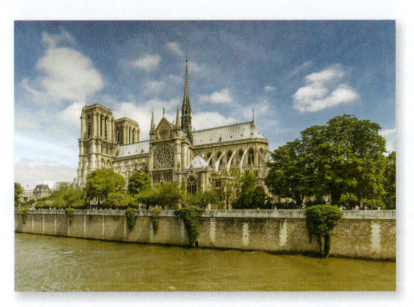

The Cathedral of Notre Dame in Paris.
Ayhan Altun/Getty Images

into threes, the symbol of the Trinity. Despite these limitations, much fine polyphonic music was composed during the late twelfth century and in the thirteenth century.

Modern listeners sometimes find medieval polyphony hollow and thin, probably because it has relatively few triads, which in later periods became the basic consonant chords. The triad contains two intervals of a third; medieval music theorists considered this interval a dissonance. (An interval of a third separates *do* and *mi*, and *mi* and *sol*.) But as the Middle Ages advanced, triads and thirds were used more often, and polyphonic music gradually became fuller   and richer by our standards.

Fourteenth-Century Music: The "New Art" in France

As we have seen in the opening to Part II (page 63), the fourteenth century was an age of disintegration that witnessed the Hundred Years' War, the catastrophic plague known as the black death, and a weakening of the feudal system and the Catholic church. Literary works of the fourteenth century stressed sensuality more than virtue.

Given this atmosphere, it's not surprising that secular music became more important than sacred music in the fourteenth century. Composers wrote polyphonic music that was *not* based on Gregorian chant, including drinking songs and pieces in which birdcalls, dogs' barks, and hunters' shouts were imitated.

By the early fourteenth century, a new system of music notation had evolved, and a composer could specify almost any rhythmic pattern. Now beats could be subdivided into two as well as three. Syncopation—rarely used earlier—became an important rhythmic practice. Changes in musical style in the fourteenth century were so profound that music theorists referred to Italian and French music as the **new art** (**ars nova** in Latin).

As contrasting examples of fourteenth-century music, we'll study a love song and a mass by Guillaume de Machaut, the leading French composer of the time.

Guillaume de Machaut

Guillaume de Machaut (about 1300–1377), who was famous as both a musician and a poet, was born in the French province of Champagne. He studied theology and spent much of his life in the service of various royal families. Around 1323, he became secretary and chaplain to John, king of Bohemia, whom he accompanied on trips and military campaigns throughout Europe. In his later years he lived mainly in Reims, where he served as a church official.

Machaut traveled to many courts and presented beautifully decorated copies of his music and poetry to noble patrons. These copies make Machaut one of the first important composers whose works have survived. The decline of the church in the fourteenth century is reflected in Machaut's output, which consists mainly of courtly love songs for one to four performers. We'll consider, first, one of his love songs, and then the *Notre Dame* Mass, the best-known composition of the fourteenth century.

Puis qu'en oubli sui de vous (Since I am forgotten by you; c. 1363)

When he was about sixty, Machaut fell in love with Peronne, a beautiful young noblewoman. For several years they exchanged poems and letters, but the difference in age eventually proved too great and their relationship ended in mutual disappointment. Machaut immortalized their love in his greatest narrative poem, *Le Livre Dou Voir Dit* (*The Book of the True Poem*, 1363–1365). Along with the narrative, the *Voir Dit* contains lyric poems and letters by Machaut and Peronne as well as nine musical compositions, including the song *Puis qu'en oubli sui de vous* (*Since I am forgotten by you*).

This melancholy work expresses Machaut's "farewell to joy," because he has been forgotten by his beloved. The song consists of a vocal melody and two accompanying parts in an exceptionally low pitch range. These lower parts have no texts in the medieval manuscript, so it is not certain whether they are meant to be sung or to be played by instruments. In our recording, they are performed by two solo voices.

Puis qu'en oubli sui de vous is a **rondeau,** one of the main poetic and musical forms in fourteenth- and fifteenth-century France. The poem has eight lines, each ending with either the syllable *mis* or the syllable *mant* (see the French text in the Vocal Music Guide). Lines 1–2 constitute the poetic refrain, which returns as lines 7–8; line 1 appears again as line 4.

The music consists of two phrases, a and b. (These phrases are indicated to the left of the French text in the Vocal Music Guide.) Phrase a is used for lines ending with *mis*. It begins with long notes, pauses in the middle, and ends with an incomplete cadence.

Phrase b is set to lines ending with *mant*. It begins with short notes, flows continuously, and ends with a complete cadence.

The endings of both phrases contain syncopation, a rhythmic feature of fourteenth-century music. *Puis qu'en oubli* is a heartfelt message of courtly love.

Vocal Music Guide

MACHAUT, *Puis qu'en oubli (Since I am forgotten by you; c. 1363)*

(Duration 1:47)

Listen for the *incomplete cadence* ending melodic phrase a and the *complete cadence* ending melodic phrase b.

a	*Puis qu'en oubli sui de vous dous amis*	Since I am forgotten by you, sweet friend,
b	*Vie amoureuse et joie a dieu commant*	I say farewell to joy and a life of love.
a	*Mar vi le jour que m'amour en vous mis*	Ill-fated was the day I placed my love in you,
a	*Puis qu'en oubli sui de vous dous amis*	Since I am forgotten by you, sweet friend.
a	*Mais ce tenray que je vous ay promis*	But what I have promised you I will maintain,
b	*C'est que jamais n'aray nul autre amant*	Which is that I shall never have any other lover.
a	*Puis qu'en oubli sui de vous dous amis*	Since I am forgotten by you, sweet friend.
b	*Via amoureuse et joie a dieu commant*	I say farewell to joy and a life of love.

Notre Dame Mass (Mid-Fourteenth Century)

Machaut's *Notre Dame* Mass, one of the finest compositions known from the Middle Ages, is also of great historical importance: it is the first polyphonic treatment of the mass ordinary by a known composer.

The **mass ordinary** consists of texts that remain the same from day to day throughout the church year. The five sung prayers of the ordinary are the Kyrie, Gloria, Credo, Sanctus, and Agnus Dei. Since the fourteenth century, these five texts have often been set to polyphonic music and have inspired some of the greatest choral works. (In the service, the Kyrie and Gloria were sung in succession, whereas the Credo, Sanctus, and Agnus Dei were separated by liturgical activity and by other texts sung as Gregorian chant.) In each age, composers have responded to the mass in their own particular style. This centuries-old tradition of the mass gives invaluable insight into the long span of music and its changing styles.

The *Notre Dame* Mass is written for four voice parts. How Machaut wanted his mass to be performed in unknown, but it is likely that four solo voices were employed. In our recording, the four voice parts are sung by a small group of male singers. The *Notre Dame* Mass was probably composed in the early 1360s for performance at the cathedral of Reims. We'll examine the Agnus Dei of the mass as an example of fourteenth-century polyphony.

Agnus Dei

Machaut's music for the Agnus Dei—a prayer for mercy and peace—is solemn and elaborate. It is in triple meter. Complex rhythmic patterns contribute to its intensity. The two upper parts are rhythmically active and contain syncopation, a characteristic of fourteenth-century music. The two lower parts move in longer notes and play a supporting role.

The Agnus Dei is based on a Gregorian chant, which Machaut furnished with new rhythmic patterns and placed in the tenor, one of the two lower parts. Because the chant, or cantus firmus, is rhythmically altered within a polyphonic web, it is more a musical framework than a tune to be recognized. The harmonies of the Agnus Dei include stark dissonances, hollow-sounding chords, and full triads.

Like the chant melody on which it is based, the Agnus Dei is in three sections. It may be outlined as follows:

Agnus Dei (I)	Agnus Dei (II)	Agnus Dei (III)
A	B	A

The same text appears in each section, except for a change from *miserere nobis* (*have mercy on us*) to *dona nobis pacem* (*grant us peace*) in the concluding Agnus Dei (III). A and B are similar in mood, rhythm, and texture and end with the same hollow-sounding chord. The division into three sections is thought to symbolize the Trinity. In Machaut's time, music was meant to appeal to the mind as much as to the ear.

Vocal Music Guide

MACHAUT, Agnus Dei from *Notre Dame* Mass; mid-fourteenth century

(Duration 3:27)

Listen for syncopations in the melody and for the ABA form.

A	0:00	*Agnus Dei, qui tollis peccata mundi: miserere nobis.*	Lamb of God, who taketh away the sins of the world, have mercy on us.
B	1:01	*Agnus Dei, qui tollis peccata mundi: miserere nobis.*	Lamb of God, who taketh away the sins of the world, have mercy on us.
A	2:15	*Agnus Dei, qui tollis peccata mundi: dona nobis pacem.*	Lamb of God, who taketh away the sins of the world, grant us peace.

2 Music in the Renaissance (1450–1600)

The Renaissance in music occurred between 1450 and 1600. (Some historians place the beginning of the Renaissance as early as 1400.) As in the other arts, the horizons of music were greatly expanded. The invention of printing with movable type (c. 1450) widened the circulation of music. The first book of polyphonic music printed completely from movable type appeared in Venice in 1501.

In keeping with the Renaissance ideal of the "universal man," every educated person was expected to be trained in music. "I am not pleased with the courtier if he be not also a musician," Castiglione wrote in *The Book of the Courtier* (1528). Shakespeare's stage directions call for music more than 300 times, and his plays are full of beautiful tributes to music:

> The man that hath no music in himself,
> Nor is not mov'd with concord of sweet sounds,
> Is fit for treasons, stratagems and spoils.
> *(The Merchant of Venice)*

As in the past, musicians worked in churches, courts, and towns. Church choirs grew in size. (The papal choir in Rome increased from ten singers in 1442 to twenty-four in 1483.) Although polyphonic church music in the Middle Ages was usually sung by several soloists, during the Renaissance it was performed by an entire (male) choir. The church remained an important patron of music, but musical activity gradually shifted to the courts. Kings, princes, and dukes competed for the finest composers. A single court might have ten to sixty musicians, including singers as well as instrumentalists. Women functioned as virtuoso singers at several Italian courts during the late Renaissance. A court music director would compose secular pieces to entertain the nobility and sacred works for the court chapel. The nobility often brought their musicians along when traveling from one castle to another.

Renaissance town musicians played for civic processions, weddings, and religious services. In general, musicians enjoyed higher status and pay than ever before. Composers were no longer content to remain unknown; like other artists, they sought credit for their work.

Many leading Renaissance composers came from the Low Countries (Flanders), an area that now includes parts of the Netherlands, Belgium, and northern France. These Flemish composers were regarded highly and held important positions throughout Europe, but especially in Italy, which became the leading music center in the sixteenth century. Other countries with a vibrant musical life in the Renaissance were Germany, England, and Spain.

Characteristics of Renaissance Music

Words and Music In the Renaissance, as in the Middle Ages, vocal music was more important than instrumental music. The humanistic interest in language influenced vocal music, creating a close relationship between words and music. Renaissance composers wrote music to enhance the meaning and emotion of the text. "When one of the words expresses weeping, pain, heartbreak, sighs, tears and other similar things, let the harmony be full of sadness," wrote Zarlino, a music theorist of the sixteenth century. By contrast, medieval composers had been relatively uninterested in expressing the emotions of a text.

Renaissance composers often used **word painting,** a musical depiction of specific words. For example, the word *high* might be set to a high note, and the word *arch* might be heard with a series of notes that form the curved shape of an arch. Yet despite this emphasis on capturing the emotion and imagery of a text, Renaissance music may seem calm and restrained to us. While there *is* a wide range of emotion in Renaissance music, it is usually expressed in a moderate, balanced way, with *no* extreme contrasts of dynamics, tone color, or rhythm.

Texture The texture of Renaissance music is chiefly polyphonic. A typical choral piece has four, five, or six voice parts of nearly equal melodic interest. Imitation among the voices is common: each presents the same melodic idea in turn, as in a round. Homophonic texture, with successions of chords, is also used, especially in light music, like dances. The texture may vary within a piece to provide contrast and bring out aspects of the text as it develops.

Renaissance music sounds fuller than medieval music. The bass register was used for the first time, expanding the pitch range to more than four octaves. With this new emphasis on the bass line came richer harmony. Renaissance music sounds mild and relaxed because stable, consonant chords are favored; triads occur often, while dissonances are played down.

Renaissance choral music did not need instrumental accompaniment. For this reason, the period is sometimes called the "golden age" of unaccompanied—*a cappella*—choral music. Even so, on special occasions instruments were combined with voices. Instruments might duplicate the vocal lines to reinforce the sound, or they might take the part of a missing singer. But parts written exclusively for instruments are rarely found in Renaissance choral music.

Rhythm and Melody In Renaissance music, rhythm is more a gentle flow than a sharply defined beat. This is because each melodic line has great rhythmic independence: when one singer is at the beginning of his or her melodic phrase, the others may already be in the middle of theirs. This technique makes singing Renaissance music both a pleasure and a challenge, for each singer must maintain an individual rhythm. But pitch patterns in Renaissance melodies are easy to sing. The melody usually moves along a scale with few large leaps.

Sacred Music in the Renaissance

The two main forms of sacred Renaissance music are the motet and the mass. They are alike in style, but a mass is a longer composition. The Renaissance **motet** is a polyphonic choral work set to a sacred Latin text other than the ordinary of the mass. The Renaissance **mass** is a polyphonic choral composition made up of five sections: Kyrie, Gloria, Credo, Sanctus, and Agnus Dei.

Josquin Desprez and the Renaissance Motet

Josquin Desprez (c. 1450–1521), a contemporary of Leonardo da Vinci and Christopher Columbus, was a master of Renaissance music. Like many Flemish composers, he had an international career. Josquin was born in the province of Hainaut—today part of Belgium—and spent much of his life in Italy, serving in dukes' private chapels and in the papal choir at Rome. In his later years, he worked for Louis XII of France and held several church posts in his native land.

Josquin's compositions, which include masses, motets, and secular vocal pieces, strongly influenced other composers and were praised enthusiastically by music lovers. Martin Luther, for example, remarked: "God has His Gospel preached also through the medium of music; this may be seen from the compositions of Josquin, all of whose works are cheerful, gentle, mild, and lovely; they flow and move along and are neither forced nor coerced and bound by rigid and stringent rules, but, on the contrary, are like the song of the finch."

Ave Maria … virgo serena (Hail, Mary … serene virgin; c. 1475)

Josquin's four-voice motet *Ave Maria … virgo serena* is an outstanding Renaissance choral work. This Latin prayer to the Virgin is set to delicate and serene music. The opening uses polyphonic imitation, a technique typical of the period.

The short melodic phrase on *Ave Maria* is presented by the soprano voice and then imitated in turn by the alto, tenor, and bass. The next two words, *gratia plena* (*full of grace*), have a different melody, which also is passed from voice to voice. Notice that each voice enters while the preceding one is in the middle of its melody. This overlapping creates a feeling of continuous flow. Josquin adapted the melody for the opening phrases from a Gregorian chant, but the rest of the motet was not based on a chant melody.

Josquin skillfully varies the texture of this motet; two, three, or four voices are heard at one time. In addition to the imitation among individual voices, there is imitation between pairs of voices: duets between the high voices are imitated by the two lower parts. Sometimes the texture almost becomes homophonic, as at the words *Ave, vera virginitas*. Here, also, is a change from duple to triple meter, and the tempo momentarily becomes more animated. But soon the music returns to duple meter and a more peaceful mood. *Ave Maria* ends with slow chords that express Josquin's personal plea to the Virgin: *O Mother of God, remember me. Amen.*

Vocal Music Guide

JOSQUIN, *Ave Maria ... virgo serena (Hail, Mary ... serene virgin; c. 1475)*

(Duration 4:47)

Listen for the *polyphonic imitation* among four voice parts and for the change from *duple to triple meter* at *Ave, vera virginitas*.

0:00	Each soprano phrase imitated in turn by alto, tenor, and bass. Duple meter.	*Ave Maria gratia plena dominus tecum, virgo serena.*	Hail Mary, full of grace, the Lord is with thee, serene Virgin.
0:49	High duet imitated by three lower voices.	*Ave, cuius conceptio,*	Hail, whose conception,
	All four voices. Increased rhythmic animation reflects "new joy."	*solemni plena gaudio, coelestia terrestria nova replet laetitia.*	full of great jubilation, fills Heaven and Earth with new joy.
1:32	High duet imitated by low duet. Soprano phrase imitated by alto, tenor, and bass.	*Ave, cuius nativitas nostra fuit solemnitas, ut lucifer lux oriens verum solem praeveniens.*	Hail, whose birth brought us joy, as Lucifer, the morning star, went before the true sun.
2:17	High duet imitated by low duet. High duet. Low duet.	*Ave, pia humilitas, sine viro fecunditas, cuius annuntiatio nostra fuit salvatio.*	Hail, pious humility, fruitful without a man, whose Annunciation brought us salvation.
2:50	Triple meter.	*Ave, vera virginitas, immaculata castitas, cuius purificatio nostra fuit purgatio.*	Hail, true virginity, immaculate chastity, whose purification brought our cleansing.
3:16	Duple meter, high duets imitated by lower voices.	*Ave praeclara omnibus angelicis virtutibus, cuius assumptio nostra glorificatio.*	Hail, glorious one in all angelic virtues, whose Assumption was our glorification.
	Brief pause.		
	Sustained chords.	*O mater Dei, memento mei. Amen.*	O Mother of God, remember me. Amen.

Palestrina and the Renaissance Mass

During the sixteenth century, Italian composers attained the excellence of such earlier Flemish musicians as Josquin Desprez. Among the most important Italian Renaissance composers was Giovanni Pierluigi da Palestrina (c. 1525–1594), who devoted himself to music for the Catholic church. His career was thus centered in Rome, where he held important church positions, including that of music director for St. Peter's.

Palestrina's music includes 104 masses and some 450 other sacred works; it is best understood against the background of the Counter-Reformation. During the early 1500s, the Catholic church was challenged and questioned by the Protestants and, as a result, sought to correct abuses and malpractices within its structure, as well as to counter the move toward Protestantism. This need to strengthen the church led to the founding of the Jesuit order (1540) and the convening of the Council of Trent (1545–1563), which considered questions of dogma and organization.

During its deliberations, the council discussed church music, which many felt had lost its purity. Years before, the scholar Desiderius Erasmus (c. 1466–1536) had complained: "We have introduced an artificial and theatrical music into the church, a bawling and agitation of various voices, such as I believe had never been heard in the theaters of the Greeks and Romans.... Amorous and lascivious melodies are heard such as elsewhere accompany only the dances of courtesans and clowns." At the council sessions, church music was attacked because it used secular tunes, noisy instruments, and theatrical singing. Some complained that complex polyphony made it impossible to understand the sacred texts; they wanted only monophonic music—Gregorian chant—for the mass. The council finally decreed that church music should be composed not "to give empty pleasure to the ear," but to inspire religious contemplation.

The restraint and serenity of Palestrina's works reflect this emphasis on a more spiritual music. For centuries, church authorities have regarded his masses as models of church music because of their calmness and otherworldly quality. Even today, the technical perfection of his style is a model for students of counterpoint.

Pope Marcellus Mass (1562–1563)

Palestrina's *Pope Marcellus* Mass, his most famous mass, was long thought to have convinced the Council of Trent that polyphonic masses should be kept in Catholic worship. Although we now know that this work did *not* play that role, it does reflect the council's desire for a clear projection of the sacred text. It is dedicated to Pope Marcellus II, who reigned briefly in 1555 while Palestrina was a singer in the papal choir.

The *Pope Marcellus* Mass is written for an a cappella choir of six voice parts: soprano, alto, two tenors, and two basses. We'll focus on the first section of the mass, the Kyrie.

Kyrie

The Kyrie has a rich polyphonic texture. Its six voice parts constantly imitate each other, yet blend beautifully. This music sounds fuller than Josquin's *Ave Maria*, in part because six voices are used rather than four. The elegantly curved melodies summon the spirit of Gregorian chant. They flow smoothly and can be sung easily. Upward leaps are balanced at once by downward steps, as in the opening melody:

A miniature showing a mass at the court of Philip the Good in Burgundy.

DEA PICTURE LIBRARY/Getty Images

The Kyrie of the *Pope Marcellus* Mass is written in three different sections:

1. *Kyrie eleison.*   Lord, have mercy.
2. *Christe eleison.*   Christ, have mercy.
3. *Kyrie eleison.*   Lord, have mercy.

This text is short, and words are repeated with different melodic lines to express calm supplication. The rhythm flows continuously to the end of each section, when all voices come together on sustained chords. Each of the three sections begins in a thin texture with only some of the voices sounding; but as the other voices enter, the music becomes increasingly full and rich. In our recording, the third section sounds climactic because it is performed in a somewhat faster tempo and at a louder dynamic level than the first two sections.

Vocal Music Guide

PALESTRINA, Kyrie from *Pope Marcellus* Mass; 1562–1563

(Duration 4:49)

Listen for *polyphonic imitation* among six voice parts, and the sustained *chord* defining the end of each section.

0:00	Tenor quickly imitated in turn by three other voice parts; remaining two voice parts join. Voices imitate each other and repeat words. Sustained chord, pause end section.	1. *Kyrie eleison.*	Lord, have mercy.
1:35	Three voice parts begin at same time; other three voice parts join in turn. Voices imitate each other. Sustained chord, pause.	2. *Christe eleison.*	Christ, have mercy.
3:29	Soprano phrase quickly imitated in turn by three lower voice parts; two other voice parts join. Voices imitate each other.	3. *Kyrie eleison.*	Lord, have mercy.
4:35	Sustained chord ends *Kyrie.*		

Secular Music in the Renaissance

Vocal Music

During the Renaissance, secular vocal music became increasingly popular. Throughout Europe, music was set to poems in various languages, including Italian, French, Spanish, German, Dutch, and English.

The development of music printing helped spread secular music, and thousands of song collections became available. Music was an important leisure activity; every educated person was expected to play an instrument and read notation. The Elizabethan composer Thomas Morley describes the embarrassment of being unable to participate in after-dinner music making: "But supper being ended, and Musicke bookes (according to the custome) being brought to the tables, the mistresse of the house presented me with a part, earnestly requesting me to sing. But when, after many excuses, I protested unfainedly that I could not: every one began to wonder. Yea, some whispered to others, demanding how I was brought up."

Renaissance secular music was written for groups of solo voices and for solo voice with the accompaniment of one or more instruments. Word painting—musical illustration of a text—was common. Composers delighted in imitating natural sounds such as birdcalls and street cries. In a famous piece entitled *La Guerre* (*The War*), the Frenchman Clément Janequin (c. 1485–1560) vividly imitated battle noises, drumbeats, and fanfares. Secular music contained more rapid shifts of mood than sacred music. As Morley advised one composer, "You must in your music be wavering like the wind, sometimes wanton, sometimes drooping, sometimes grave and staid; ... and the more variety you show the better shall you please."

An important kind of secular vocal music during the Renaissance was the **madrigal,** a piece for several solo voices set to a short poem, usually about love. A madrigal, like a motet, combines homophonic and polyphonic textures. But the madrigal uses word painting and unusual harmonies more often.

The Renaissance madrigal originated in Italy around 1520, during a creative explosion in Italian poetry. Madrigals were published by the thousands in sixteenth-century Italy, where they were sung by cultivated aristocrats and members of the upper middle class. Among the many madrigal composers were Maddalena Casulana (c. 1544–c. 1590s), who favored dramatic dialogues in her music and was the first female composer to have her works printed (starting in 1566); Luca Marenzio (1553–1599), noted for his use of word painting; and Carlo Gesualdo, Prince of Venosa (c. 1560–1613), whose highly chromatic harmonies expressed extremes of emotion. He is infamous for killing his wife and her lover after finding them together in bed.

In 1588—the year of the defeat of the Spanish Armada—a volume of translated Italian madrigals was published in London. This inspired a spurt of madrigal writing by English composers, and for about thirty years there was a steady flow of English madrigals and other secular vocal music. The time of Queen Elizabeth I (1533–1603) and William Shakespeare (1564–1616) was as much a golden age in English music as it was in English literature. The impetus for both arts arose in Italy. But the English madrigal became lighter and more humorous than its Italian model, and its melody and harmony were simpler.

As Vesta Was Descending (1601), by Thomas Weelkes

Among the finest English madrigalists was Thomas Weelkes (c. 1575–1623), an organist and church composer. Weelkes's *As Vesta Was Descending* comes from *The Triumphes of Oriana* (1601), an anthology of English madrigals written to honor Queen Elizabeth, who was often called Oriana. The text of this six-voice madrigal pictures Vesta (the Roman goddess of the hearth) coming down a hill with her attendants,

"Diana's darlings." (Diana was the Roman goddess of chastity, hunting, and the moon.) At the same time, the "maiden queen," Oriana (Elizabeth), is climbing the hill with her shepherd gallants. Vesta's attendants desert her and race down the hill to join Oriana.

As Vesta Was Descending has the light mood typical of English madrigals. Word painting is plentiful. For example, the word *descending* is sung to downward scales, and *ascending* to upward ones.

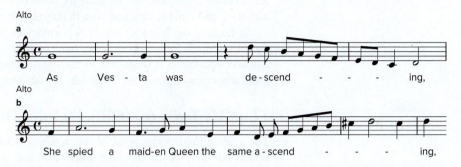

When Vesta's attendants run down the hill, "first *two* by *two*, then *three* by *three together*, leaving their goddess all *alone*," we hear first *two* voices, then *three* voices, then *six* voices, and finally a *solo* voice. In the extended concluding section, "*Long* live fair Oriana," a joyous phrase is imitated among the voices. And in the bass this phrase is sung in long notes, with the longest note on the word *long*.

Vocal Music Guide

WEELKES, *As Vesta Was Descending*; 1601

(Duration 3:11)

Listen for the *word painting* in this madrigal. The word *descending* is sung to downward scales, and *ascending* to upward scales.

Descending scales.	As Vesta was from Latmos hill *descending*,
Ascending scales.	she spied a maiden queen the same *ascending*,
Rapid descending figures.	attended on by all the shepherds swain,
	to whom Diana's darlings came *running down* amain.
Two voices,	First *two* by *two*,
Three voices; all voices.	then *three* by *three* together,
Solo voice.	leaving their goddess *all alone*, hasted thither,
	and mingling with the shepherds of her train
	with mirthful tunes her presence entertain.
	Then sang the shepherds and nymphs of Diana,
Brief joyful phrase imitated among voices; long notes in bass.	*Long* live fair Oriana!

The Renaissance Lute Song

A simpler type of secular music than the madrigal is the song for solo voice and lute. The **lute,** which derives from the Arab instrument known as the 'ūd (literally, *the wood*), is a plucked string instrument with a body shaped like half a pear. The lute's versatility—like that of the guitar today—made it the most popular instrument in the Renaissance home. It could be used for solos or for accompaniments; to play chords, melodies, and rapid scales; and even in polyphonic music.

In England the lute song was widely cultivated from the late 1590s to the 1620s. In contrast to much Renaissance music, **lute songs** are mostly homophonic in texture. The lute accompaniment is secondary to the vocal melody. During the Renaissance, singers could accompany themselves, or have the lute accompaniment played by another musician.

Flow My Tears (c. 1600), by John Dowland (1563–1626)

The leading English composer of lute songs was John Dowland, a virtuoso performer on the lute famous throughout Europe. His lute song *Flow My Tears* was extraordinarily popular in Shakespeare's time, and in our own day it has been recorded by many singers, including the rock star Sting.

Flow My Tears expresses the intense melancholy of someone whose happiness has been abruptly shattered. Such emotionally charged words as *tears, despair, woes, sighs, groans, fear*, and *grief* dominate the song's text, a poem that may have been written by Dowland himself. The expression of melancholy was a prominent feature of English literature and music in the time of Elizabeth I and Shakespeare. Dowland, especially, seems to have cultivated a melancholy public image, and he composed many pieces with sad titles such as *Semper Dowland semper dolens* (*Always Dowland, always sorrow*).

Flow My Tears consists of three brief musical sections (A, B, C) that are each immediately repeated: AA (stanzas 1 and 2), BB (stanzas 3 and 4), CC (stanza 5 repeated to the same melody). Dowland's music heightens the mood of grief through its slow tempo, minor key, and descending four-note melodic pattern that represents falling tears. This descending pattern appears throughout the song with variations of pitch and rhythm.

The opening four-note descent, in minor, on *Flow my tears*, is immediately repeated—with greater emotional intensity—on higher, slower notes to the words *fall from your springs.*

Part B begins with a contrasting major-key version of the four-note descent on the words *Never may my.*

Dowland creates variety by opening part C with a stepwise ascent, turning the four-note pattern upside down on the words *Hark you shadows.*

During the Renaissance, music was an important leisure activity; every educated person was expected to play an instrument and read music notation. *A Concert* (c. 1485–1495), by the Italian painter Lorenzo Costa, shows a man playing a lute accompanying himself and two other singers.

Fine Art Images/Heritage Images/Getty Images

In much of the song, the lute accompaniment is subordinate to the voice. However, in part B, the lute momentarily gains prominence as it imitates the voice's gasping upward skips on *and tears, and sighs*, heightening the agitated mood.

As Sting has observed, even though *Flow My Tears* is "a song about hopelessness, it is strangely uplifting."

Vocal Music Guide

DOWLAND, *Flow My Tears*; 1600

(Duration 3:59)

Listen for the *minor key* that expresses the melancholy of the text. Notice the descending four-note pattern, representing falling tears, that is varied in *pitch* and *rhythm* throughout the song.

0:00	A	Minor key.	Flow my tears, fall from your springs, Exiled for ever: Let me mourn where night's black bird her sad infamy sings, there let me live forlorn.
0:38	A	Minor.	Down vain lights, shine you no more, No nights are dark enough for those That in despair their lost fortunes deplore, light doth but shame disclose.
1:18	B	Major. Minor. Lute imitates voice.	Never may my woes be relieved, since pity is fled, and tears, and sighs, and groans my weary days, of all joys have deprived.
1:55	B	Major. Minor. Lute imitates voice.	From the highest spire of contentment, my fortune is thrown; and fear, and grief, and pain for my deserts, are my hopes since hope is gone.
2:31	C	Minor.	Hark you shadows that in darkness dwell, learn to condemn light, Happy, happy they that in hell feel not the world's despite.
3:13	C	Minor.	Hark you shadows that in darkness dwell, learn to condemn light, Happy, happy they that in hell feel not the world's despite.

Instrumental Music

Though still subordinate to vocal music, instrumental music did become more important during the Renaissance. Traditionally, instrumentalists accompanied voices or played music intended for singing. Even in the early 1500s instrumental music was largely adapted from vocal music. Instrumental groups performed polyphonic vocal pieces, which were often published with the indication *to be sung or played*. Soloists used the harpsichord, organ, or lute to play simple arrangements of vocal works.

During the sixteenth century, however, instrumental music became increasingly emancipated from vocal models. More music was written specifically for instruments. Renaissance composers began to exploit the particular capacities of the lute or organ for instrumental solos. They also developed purely instrumental forms, such as theme and variations.

Much of this instrumental music was intended for dancing, a popular Renaissance entertainment. Every cultivated person was expected to be skilled in dance, which was taught by professional dancing masters. Court dances were often performed in pairs. A favorite pair was the stately *pavane*, or *passamezzo*, in duple meter, and the lively *galliard*, in triple meter. Dance music was performed by instrumental groups or by soloists such as harpsichordists and lutenists. A wealth of dance music published during the sixteenth century has come down to us.

A wide variety of instruments were used during the Renaissance. Hans Burgkmair's woodcut of the emperor Maximilian with his musicians (1505–1516) shows (left) an organ and a cornett; (center) a harp; (on floor) a drum, a kettledrum, a trumsheit (string instrument), and a sackbut; (on table) a viola da gamba, an oblong keyboard instrument, a flute, recorders, a cornett, and a krummhorn.
Lebrecht Music & Arts/Alamy

Much instrumental music of the Renaissance was intended for dancing. *Wedding Dance in the Open Air* (1566) by Pieter Bruegel the Elder.

Renaissance musicians distinguished between loud, outdoor instruments like the trumpet and the *shawm* (a double-reed ancestor of the oboe), and soft, indoor instruments like the lute and the *recorder* (an early flute). The many instruments used in the Renaissance produced softer, less brilliant sounds than we hear from instruments today; most came in families of from three to eight instruments, ranging from soprano to bass. Among the most important Renaissance instruments were recorders, shawms, *cornetts* (wooden instruments with cup-shaped mouthpieces), *sackbuts* (early trombones), lutes, *viols* (bowed string instruments), organs, *regals* (small organs with reed pipes), and harpsichords. Often several members of the same instrumental family were played together, but Renaissance composers did not specify the instruments they wanted. A single work might be performed by recorders, viols, or several different instruments, depending on what was available. Today's standardized orchestra did not exist. Large courts might employ thirty instrumentalists of all types. On state occasions such as a royal wedding, guests might be entertained by woodwinds, plucked and bowed strings, and keyboard instruments all playing together.

Passamezzo and Galliard, by Pierre Francisque Caroubel, from *Terpsichore* (1612), arranged by Michael Praetorius

This passamezzo and galliard illustrate the Renaissance practice of pairing contrasting court dances in duple and triple meter. These dances come from *Terpsichore*, a collection of over 300 dance tunes arranged for instrumental ensemble by Michael Praetorius (1571–1621), a German composer and theorist. (Terpsichore was the Greek muse, or goddess, of the dance.) A few dances in the collection, including the passamezzo and galliard studied here, were composed by the French violinist Pierre Francisque Caroubel (1576–1611). Both dance types originated in Italy and were popular during the sixteenth century and the early seventeenth century.

The passamezzo is a stately dance in duple meter and the galliard is a quick dance in triple meter. The dance-pair studied here is written for five unspecified instrumental parts. In our recording the two dances are performed by a Renaissance string ensemble including violins, violas, and bass violins (ancestors of the cello), lutes, and harpsichord. Both the passamezzo and galliard are made up of three brief sections (a, b, c). The two dances can be outlined as follows:

Passamezzo: aa bb cc abc
Galliard: aa bb cc

The music of the galliard is a variation of the preceding passamezzo, but sounds very different because its tempo is faster and its meter is triple rather than duple.

Passamezzo, section a

In each dance, section b brings greater rhythmic animation. Section b of the passamezzo introduces quicker note values (eighth notes).

Section b of the galliard brings delightful rhythmic irregularity because $\frac{6}{4}$ meter alternates with the prevailing $\frac{3}{2}$ meter. That is, six fast pulses divide alternatively into *two* groups of three pulses (**1**-2-3 **4**-5-6) and *three* groups of two pulses (**1**-2 **3**-4 **5**-6).

A similar alternation can be heard in *America*, from Leonard Bernstein's *West Side Story*, studied in Part VI, "The Twentieth Century and Beyond," in Chapter 24, "Music for Stage and Screen."

The Middle Ages and Renaissance: Summary

Music in Society—Middle Ages

- Musicians worked for churches, courts, and towns.
- Churches and cathedrals were the center of musical life and education during the Middle Ages.
- Vocal music was more important than instrumental music.
- Women were not permitted to sing in church, but they could make music in convents, where they also could receive musical training.
- Secular music and dance flourished.
- Troubadour and trouvère songs were highly influential in medieval society.
- Minstrels performed in castles, taverns, and town squares.

Important Style Features—Middle Ages

Mood and Emotional Expression
- Gregorian chant conveys a calm, otherworldly, spiritual quality.
- Medieval composers were relatively uninterested in expressing the emotions of a text.

Rhythm
- Gregorian chant rhythm is flexible, without meter, and has little sense of beat; as a result, the music has a floating quality.
- Notre Dame composers developed the first instances of western notation that indicated specific pitches as well as measured rhythms with definite time values.
- Dances have a regular, clearly defined beat.
- In ars nova, the beat could be subdivided into two as well as three, and syncopation became an important rhythmic practice.

Tone Color
- Occasionally, vocal or instrumental music will be accompanied by a drone.

Melody and Harmony
- For centuries, medieval composers based original compositions on chant melodies.
- Chant melodies of the Middle Ages often move by step within a narrow range.
- Medieval music theorists considered the interval of a third a dissonance; thus, the music occasionally can sound hollow to us.
- Music is based on church modes rather than major and minor scales.

Texture
- For hundreds of years, western music was basically monophonic.
- Sometime between 700 and 900 CE, a second line of music was added to Gregorian chant, creating organum.
- Starting around 1200, composers wrote polyphonic music in three- and four-voice parts.

Performance Practice

- We know very little about how medieval music sounded and how it was performed.
- Music manuscripts do not indicate tempo, dynamics, or names of instruments.
- Much music was passed down for generations through oral tradition and memorization because music notation was either nonexistent or rudimentary.

Music in Society—Renaissance

- Musical patronage gradually shifted from the church to the courts.
- Music was an important leisure activity, and every educated person was expected to be trained in music.
- As in the Middle Ages, vocal music was more important than instrumental music; however, instrumental music increased in importance.
- The invention of printing during the Renaissance widened the circulation of music.
- Secular music and dance continued to flourish.

Important Style Features—Renaissance

Mood and Emotional Expression

- Renaissance composers wrote vocal music to enhance the meaning and emotion of a text.
- Renaissance madrigals express a wide range of emotions and imagery through word painting.
- Secular music contains more rapid shifts of mood than does sacred music.

Rhythm

- Rhythm is more of a gentle flow than a sharply defined beat, particularly in a cappella choral music. Each line of music has great rhythmic independence.
- Secular music, both vocal and instrumental, usually has a more clearly defined beat.

Tone Color

- In Renaissance music, instruments may or may not accompany vocal music by doubling one or more of the parts.

Melody and Harmony

- Compared with music of the Middle Ages, Renaissance music sounds mild and relaxed because stable, consonant triads occur frequently and are favored over dissonances.
- Melodies usually move stepwise along a scale, with few large leaps.
- The bass register was used for the first time, resulting in a fuller sound and richer harmonies.
- In Renaissance vocal music especially, each melodic line has great independence; phrases often overlap to create a seamless flow of sound among the parts.

Texture

- The main texture of Renaissance vocal music is polyphonic, with a typical choral piece having four to six different parts of nearly equal melodic interest.
- Imitation among voices is common, particularly in a cappella choral music.
- Homophonic texture is also used, especially in light music, such as dances.
- Secular music written for solo voices and for solo voice with accompaniment of one or more instruments was popular.

Performance Practice

- Sacred choral music was sung by an a cappella male choir; women were excluded from participating in liturgical services, although nuns could perform music in convents.
- In courts, the number of musicians could be from ten to as many as sixty, and women functioned as virtuoso singers in several Italian courts during the late Renaissance.
- Renaissance music does not indicate tempos and dynamics or the specific instruments or number of performers on a part.

Design Elements: (Listening Icon): McGraw Hill Education; (Baroque violin): McGraw Hill Education

FEATURED COMPOSERS

Hildegard of Bingen (1098–1179)

Beatriz, Countess of Dia (late twelfth century)

Guillaume de Machaut (1300–1377)

Josquin Desprez (c. 1450–1521)

Giovanni Pierluigi da Palestrina (about 1525–1594)

Thomas Weelkes (1575–1623)

John Dowland (1563–1626)

Pierre Francisque Caroubel (1576–1611)

■ During the baroque period, music making was a favorite activity in middle-class homes and palaces of the aristocracy. *The Music Lesson* (1662-65), by the Dutch painter Johannes Vermeer (1632-75), shows a young woman playing a virginal—a small harpsichord-like instrument—and a young man standing next to her. Inscribed on the virginal are the words "Music is the accompaniment of joy, a remedy for sorrow." On the floor is a viola da gamba, a fretted, bowed string instrument popular from the 16th through much of the 18th century.

PART III

The Baroque Period

The figured bass is the most perfect foundation of music, being played with both hands in such a manner that the left hand plays the notes written down while the right adds consonances and dissonances, in order to make a well-sounding harmony to the Glory of God and the permissible delectation of the spirit.

—Johann Sebastian Bach

LEARNING OBJECTIVES

- Identify key features of the late baroque style in music.

- Explain how composers were an integral part of baroque society.

- Discuss baroque concerto grosso and ritornello form.

- Describe the main elements of a fugue.

- List the special characteristics of opera, and opera of the baroque period.

- Enumerate the features of a baroque suite.

- Discuss the chorale and church cantata during the baroque era.

- Compare and contrast baroque opera and baroque oratorio.

Baroque Period 1600–1750

1600–1680	1680–1750

Historical and Cultural Events

1607 Jamestown founded

1610 Galileo confirms that the earth revolves around the sun

1611 King James Bible

1618–1648 Thirty Years' War

1643–1715 Louis XIV reigns in France

1687 Newton, *Principia Mathematica*

1692 Witchcraft trials in Salem, Massachusetts

1715–1774 Louis XV reigns in France

1740–1786 Frederick the Great reigns in Prussia

Arts and Letters

1600 Shakespeare, *Hamlet*

1605 Cervantes, *Don Quixote*

1613 Gentileschi, *Judith Slaying Holofernes*

1614–16 Rubens, *Daniel in the Lions' Den*

1623 Bernini, *David Slaying Goliath*

1656 Velasquez, *Las Meninas*

1659 Rembrandt, *Self-Portrait*

1667 Milton, *Paradise Lost*

1689 Locke, *Essay Concerning Human Understanding*

1717 Watteau, *The Embarkation for Cythera*

1719 Defoe, *Robinson Crusoe*

1726 Swift, *Gulliver's Travels*

National Gallery of Art, Washington, D.C.
Ailsa Mellon Bruce Fund

Music

1607 Monteverdi, *Orfeo*

1642 Monteverdi, *The Coronation of Poppea*

1664 Strozzi, *Che si può fare* (*What can be done?*)

1689 Purcell, *Dido and Aeneas*

1689 Corelli, Trio Sonata in A Minor, Op. 3, No. 10

c. 1709 Bach, Organ Fugue in G Minor (*Little Fugue*)

c. 1715 Jacquet de la Guerre, *Le Sommeil d'Ulisse* (*The Sleep of Ulysses*)

c. 1721 Bach, *Brandenburg* Concerto No. 5 in D Major

1724 Handel, *Giulio Cesare* (*Julius Caesar*)

1725 Vivaldi, *La Primavera* (*Spring*), Concerto for Violin and Orchestra, Op. 8, No. 1

1731 Bach, Cantata No. 140: *Wachet auf, ruft uns die Stimme*

1741 Handel, *Messiah*

Photos.com/Getty Images

Science History Images/Alamy

The Baroque Style (1600–1750)

Though the word *baroque* has at various times meant bizarre, flamboyant, and elaborately ornamented, modern historians use it simply to indicate a particular style in the arts. An oversimplified but useful characterization of baroque style is that it fills space—canvas, stone, or sound—with action and movement. Painters, sculptors, and architects became interested in forming a total illusion, like a stage setting. Artists such as Caravaggio, Gentileschi, Bernini, Rubens, and Rembrandt exploited their materials to expand the dramatic potential of color, depth, and contrasts of light and dark; they wanted to create totally structured worlds.

Such a style was very well suited to the wishes of the aristocracy, who also thought in terms of completely integrated structures. In France, for example, Louis XIV held court in the palace of Versailles, a magnificent setting that fused baroque painting, sculpture, architecture, and garden design into a symbol of royal wealth and power.

The aristocracy was enormously rich and powerful during the seventeenth and eighteenth centuries. While most of the population barely managed to survive, European rulers surrounded themselves with luxury. There were many such rulers. Germany, for example, was divided into about 300 territories, each governed separately.

Judith Slaying Holofernes (c. 1612–1613) by the Italian painter Artemisia Gentileschi (1593–1652). Baroque artists emphasized motion and drama.

Fine Art Images/Heritage Images/Getty Images

Bernini's *David Slaying Goliath* (1623) fills space with action and movement. It is far more dynamic than Michelangelo's *David* shown on page 64.

Adam Eastland Art + Architecture/Alamy

Kings and princes proclaimed their greatness by means of splendid palaces and magnificent court entertainments like balls, banquets, ballets, operas, and plays. Indeed, entertainment was a necessity; most courtiers did no real work and tried to avoid boredom as much as possible.

The baroque period (1600–1750) is also known as the "age of absolutism" because many rulers exercised absolute power over their subjects. In Germany, for example, the Duke of Weimar could throw his court musician Johann Sebastian Bach into jail for a month because Bach stubbornly asked to leave his job.

Along with the aristocracy, religious institutions powerfully shaped the baroque style. Churches used the emotional and theatrical qualities of art to make worship more attractive and appealing. During the baroque period, Europe was divided into Catholic and Protestant areas: France, Spain, Italy, and the Austrian empire were primarily Catholic; England, Holland, Denmark, Sweden, and parts of Germany were Protestant.

The middle-class, too, influenced the development of the baroque style. In the Netherlands, for example, prosperous merchants and doctors commissioned realistic landscapes and scenes from everyday life.

It is also helpful to think of baroque style against the backdrop of scientific discoveries during the seventeenth and eighteenth centuries. The work of Galileo (1564–1642) and Newton (1642–1727) represented a new approach to science based on the union of mathematics and experiment; they discovered mathematical laws governing bodies in motion. Such scientific advances led to new inventions and the gradual improvement of medicine, mining, navigation, and industry during the baroque era.

The Flemish painter Peter Paul Rubens used sharp contrasts between dark and light to create drama and depth in *Daniel in the Lions' Den* (1614-16). The painting depicts an episode from the Book of Daniel In the Bible. Rubens observed and sketched lions at the Brussels zoo to make his painting as lifelike as possible.
National Gallery of Art, Washington, D.C. Ailsa Mellon Bruce Fund

Self-Portrait (1659) by Rembrandt van Rijn. Rembrandt's use of light and dark contributes to the poetry, drama, and psychological truth of his portraits.
Courtesy National Gallery of Art, Washington

The palace of Versailles, in France, fused baroque architecture, sculpture, and painting into a symbol of royal wealth and power.
Eurasia/robertharding/Getty Images

Las Meninas (1656; "The Ladies-in-Waiting"), by the Spanish painter Diego Velazquez (1599-1660), is recognized as one of the greatest masterpieces of Western art. It portrays Velazquez in his studio working on a large canvas. Shown in the foreground are the king and queen's young daughter, her maids of honor and chaperone, two dwarfs and a dog. Reflected in a mirror in the background, the king and queen enter Velazquez's studio. This enigmatic painting is about viewing and being viewed and claims that painting is not a craft, but a noble art.
Alfredo Dagli Orti/Shutterstock

1 Baroque Music (1600–1750)

In music, the *baroque* style flourished during the period from 1600 to 1750. The two giants of baroque composition were George Frideric Handel and Johann Sebastian Bach. Bach's death in 1750 marks the end of the period. Other baroque masters—Claudio Monteverdi, Henry Purcell, Arcangelo Corelli, Antonio Vivaldi—were largely forgotten until the twentieth century. But the appearance of long-playing records in the late 1940s spurred a "baroque revival" that made these musicians familiar to many music lovers.

The baroque period can be divided into three phases: early (1600–1640), middle (1640–1690), and late (1690–1750). Though the baroque music best known today comes from the latest phase, the earliest was one of the most revolutionary periods in music history. Monteverdi (1567–1643), for instance, strove to create unprecedented passion and dramatic contrast in his works. In Italy, especially, music was composed for texts conveying extreme emotion, and the text ruled the music. With this stress on drama and text, it is not surprising that Italian composers of the early baroque created opera—a drama sung to orchestral accompaniment. Their melodic lines imitated the rhythms and inflections of speech.

Early baroque composers favored homophonic texture over the polyphonic texture typical of Renaissance music. They felt that words could be projected more clearly by using just one main melody with a chordal accompaniment. But note that this new emphasis on homophonic texture characterizes only the *early* baroque; by the *late* baroque period, polyphonic texture returned to favor.

To depict extreme emotions in their texts, early baroque composers used dissonance with a new freedom. Never before were unstable chords so prominent and emphatic. Contrasts of sound were stressed—one or more solo singers against a chorus, or voices against instruments. In Renaissance choral music, instruments—if used at all—duplicated a singer's melody. But in the early baroque, voices were accompanied by melodic lines designed for instruments.

During the middle phase of the baroque (1640–1690), the new musical style spread from Italy to practically every country in Europe. The medieval or church modes—scales that had governed music for centuries—gradually gave way to major and minor scales. By about 1690, major or minor scales were the tonal basis of most compositions. Another feature of the middle baroque phase was the new importance of instrumental music. Many compositions were written for specific instruments, the violin family being most popular.

We focus mainly on the late baroque period (1690–1750), which produced most of the baroque music heard today. Many aspects of harmony—including an emphasis on the attraction of the dominant chord to the tonic—arose in this period. During the late baroque, instrumental music became as important as vocal music for the first time. Early baroque composers had emphasized homophonic texture; late baroque composers gloried in polyphony. Let's look more closely at some features of late baroque style. (From now on the word *baroque* will pertain to the late baroque phase.)

Characteristics of Baroque Music

Unity of Mood A baroque piece usually expresses one basic mood: what begins joyfully will remain joyful throughout. Emotional states like joy, grief, and agitation were represented—at the time, these moods were called *affections.* Composers molded a musical language to depict the affections; specific rhythms or melodic patterns were associated with specific moods. This common language gives a family resemblance to much late baroque music.

The prime exception to this baroque principle of unity of mood occurs in vocal music. Striking changes of emotion in a text may inspire corresponding changes in the music. But even in such cases, one mood is maintained at some length before it yields to another.

Rhythm Unity of mood in baroque music is conveyed, first of all, by continuity of rhythm. Rhythmic patterns heard at the beginning of a piece are repeated throughout it. This rhythmic continuity provides a compelling drive and energy—the forward motion is rarely interrupted. The beat, for example, is emphasized far more in baroque music than in most Renaissance music.

Melody Baroque melody also creates a feeling of continuity. An opening melody will be heard again and again in the course of a baroque piece. And even when a melody is presented in varied form, its character tends to remain constant. There is a continuous expanding, unfolding, and unwinding of melody. This sense of directed motion is frequently the result of a melodic sequence, that is, successive repetition of a musical idea at higher or lower pitches. Many baroque melodies sound elaborate and ornamental, and they are not easy to sing or remember. A baroque melody gives an impression of dynamic expansion rather than of balance or symmetry. A short opening phrase is often followed by a longer phrase with an unbroken flow of rapid notes.

Dynamics Paralleling continuity of rhythm and melody in baroque music is continuity of dynamics: the level of volume tends to stay fairly constant for a stretch of time. When the dynamics do shift, the shift is sudden, like physically stepping from one level to another. This alternation between loud and soft is called **terraced dynamics.** *Gradual* changes through crescendo and decrescendo are *not* prominent features of baroque music. However, singers and instrumentalists no doubt made some subtle dynamic inflections for expressive purposes.

The main keyboard instruments of the baroque period were the organ and harpsichord, both well suited for continuity of dynamics. An organist or harpsichordist could not obtain a crescendo or decrescendo by varying finger pressure, as can pianists today. A third keyboard instrument, the *clavichord,* could make gradual dynamic changes, but only within a narrow range—from about *ppp* to *mp*. (The clavichord produced sound by means of brass blades striking the strings. It was usually not used in large halls because its tone was too weak. But for home use by amateurs it was ideal; its cost was low and its expressive sound satisfying. It had especially wide popularity in Germany.)

Texture We've noted that late baroque music is predominantly polyphonic in texture: two or more melodic lines compete for the listener's attention. Usually, the soprano and bass lines are the most important. Imitation between the various lines, or "voices," of the texture is very common. A melodic idea heard in one voice is likely to make an appearance in the other voices as well.

However, not all late baroque music was polyphonic. A piece might shift in texture, especially in vocal music, where changes of mood in the words demand musical contrast. Also, baroque composers differed in their treatment of musical texture. Bach inclined toward a consistently polyphonic texture, whereas Handel used much more contrast between polyphonic and homophonic sections.

Chords and the Basso Continuo Chords became increasingly important during the baroque period. In earlier times, there was more concern with the beauty of individual melodic lines than with chords formed when the lines were heard together. In a sense, chords were mere by-products of the motion of melodic lines. But in the baroque period, chords became significant in themselves. As composers wrote a melodic line, they thought of chords to mesh with it. Indeed, sometimes they composed a melody to fit a specific chord progression. This interest in chords gave new prominence to the bass part, which served as the foundation of the harmony. The whole musical structure rested on the bass part.

The new emphasis on chords and the bass part resulted in the most characteristic feature of baroque music, an accompaniment called the **basso continuo** (Italian for *continuous bass*). The *continuo*—to use the common abbreviation for basso continuo—is usually played by at least two instruments: a keyboard instrument, such as an organ or a harpsichord, and a low melodic instrument, such as a cello or bassoon. With the left hand the organist or harpsichordist plays the bass part, which is also performed by the cellist or bassoonist. With the right hand the keyboard player improvises chords following the indications of numbers (figures) above the bass part. This bass part with numbers (figures) is called a **figured bass.** The numbers specify only basic chords, not the exact way in which the chords should be played. Thus the performer is given a great deal of freedom. (This shorthand system is similar in principle to the chord indications found on the modern song sheets from which jazz pianists improvise.) Shown here is the beginning of the continuo part of Bach's *Brandenburg* Concerto No. 5, first movement (studied in Chapter 3), and one possible performance or *realization* of this part by a harpsichordist.

The basso continuo offered the advantage of emphasizing the all-important bass part, besides providing a steady flow of chords. Practically, the use of numbers, rather than chords with all their notes written out, saved time for busy baroque composers. It also saved paper during a period when paper was expensive.

Vocal Music   Italy during the 1600s saw the development of three important vocal genres: opera, cantata, and oratorio. Opera is a large-scale, staged sung drama with action and scenery; cantata is a non-staged work in contrasting sections set to a secular or sacred text; and oratorio is a large-scale work in contrasting sections featuring a chorus, usually set to a sacred text. During the seventeenth and eighteenth centuries these vocal genres spread to other parts of Europe, including Germany, France, and England.

Like their predecessors in the Renaissance, baroque composers used music to depict the meaning of specific words. *Heaven* might be set to a high tone, and *hell* to a low tone. Rising scales represented upward motion; descending scales depicted the reverse. Descending chromatic scales were associated with pain and grief. This descriptive musical language was quite standardized: a lament for a lost love might call forth the same descending chromatic scale used to depict suffering in the *Crucifixus* of the mass.

Baroque composers often emphasized words by writing many rapid notes for a single syllable of text; this technique also displayed a singer's virtuosity. The individual words and phrases of a text are repeated over and over as the music continuously unfolds.

The Baroque Orchestra

During the baroque period, the orchestra evolved into a performing group based on instruments of the violin family. By modern standards, the baroque orchestra was small, consisting of from ten to thirty or forty players. Its instrumental makeup was flexible and could vary from piece to piece. At its nucleus were the basso continuo (harpsichord plus cello, double bass, or bassoon) and upper strings (first and second violins and violas). Use of woodwind, brass, and percussion instruments was variable. To the strings and continuo could be added recorders, flutes, oboes, trumpets, horns, trombones, or timpani. One piece might use only a single flute, whereas another would call for two oboes, three trumpets, and timpani. Trumpets and timpani joined the orchestra mainly when the music was festive. This flexibility contrasts with the standardized orchestra of later periods, consisting of four sections: string, woodwind, brass, and percussion.

The baroque trumpet (like the early French horn) had no valves but was given rapid, complex melodic lines to play in a high register. Because the instrument was difficult to play and had a traditional association with royalty, the trumpeter was the aristocrat of the baroque orchestra. When prisoners of war were exchanged, trumpeters, if they had been captured, were treated like military officers.

Bach, Handel, Vivaldi, and others chose their orchestral instruments with care and obtained beautiful effects from specific tone colors. They loved to experiment with different combinations of instruments. However, in the baroque period tone color was distinctly subordinate to other musical elements—melody, rhythm, and harmony. Composers frequently rearranged their own or other composers' works for different instruments. A piece for string orchestra might become an organ solo, losing little in the process. Often, one instrument was treated like another. An oboe would play the same melody as the violins, or the flute and trumpet would imitate each other for extended sections of a piece.

Baroque Forms

It has been noted that a piece of baroque music—particularly instrumental music—usually has unity of mood. Yet many baroque compositions include a set of pieces, or movements, that contrast. A *movement* is a piece that sounds fairly complete and independent but is part of a larger composition. Usually, each movement has its own themes, comes to a definite end, and is separated from the next movement by a brief pause. Thus, a baroque composition in three movements may contain contrasts between a fast and energetic opening, a slow and solemn middle, and a conclusion that is quick, light, and humorous.

All the forms described in Part I, Chapter 9, "Musical Form," appear in baroque music. Three-part form (A B A), two-part form (A B), and continuous or undivided form are all common. We consider examples of these and other forms in the sections that follow.

Regardless of form, baroque music features contrasts between bodies of sound. Often there is a quite regular alternation between a small and a larger group of instruments, or between instruments and voices with instrumental accompaniment. This exploration of contrasting sounds was pursued with great imagination and provides a key to the understanding and enjoyment of baroque music.

2 Music in Baroque Society

Before 1800, most music was written to order, to meet specific demands that came mainly from churches and aristocratic courts. Opera houses and municipalities also required a constant supply of music. In every case, the demand was for *new* music; audiences did not want to listen to pieces in an "old-fashioned" style.

Music was a main source of diversion in the courts of the aristocracy. One court might employ an orchestra, a chapel choir, and opera singers—the size of the musical staff depending on the court's wealth. Bach directed about eighteen players in the orchestra of a small German court in 1717, but a large court might have more than eighty performers, including the finest opera singers of the day. The music director supervised performances and composed much of the music required, including operas, church music, dinner music, and pieces for court concerts. This overworked musician also was responsible for the discipline of the other musicians and for the upkeep of the instruments and the music library.

During the baroque period, musicians often played with amateurs in music clubs or university music societies, getting together in private homes, coffeehouses, and taverns. *The Concert* by Nicholas Tournier (1590–1639) shows one such gathering.
Peter Horree/Alamy

The music director's job had good and bad features. Pay and prestige were quite high, and anything the composer wrote would be performed. But no matter how great, the composer was still a servant who could neither quit nor even take a trip without the patron's permission. Like everyone in baroque society, musicians had to curry favor with the aristocracy.

It is in this light that we must understand dedications like the one Bach addressed to a nobleman along with his *Brandenburg* Concertos: "Begging Your Highness most humbly not to judge their imperfection with the rigor of the fine and delicate taste which the whole world knows Your Highness has for musical pieces; but rather to infer from them in benign Consideration the profound respect and the most humble obedience which I try to show Your Highness." Yet sometimes musicians formed personal friendships with their patrons, as did Arcangelo Corelli, who thus gained a private apartment in a palace.

Some rulers were themselves good musicians. Frederick the Great, king of Prussia during the mid-eighteenth century, was a flutist and good composer, as well as a feared general. At his nightly court concerts, Frederick played his own works and some of the hundreds of pieces supplied by his flute teacher, Johann Quantz. (Quantz was "granted the privilege" of shouting "Bravo!" after a royal performance.)

Churches also needed music, and church music was often very grand. Along with an organ and a choir, many baroque churches had an orchestra to accompany services. Indeed, it was in church that most ordinary citizens heard music. There were few public concerts, and the populace was rarely invited to the palace. The music director of a church, like the music director at a court, had to produce a steady flow of new music and was also responsible for the musical training of choristers in the church school. Fine church music contributed to the prestige of a city, and cities often competed to attract the best musicians.

Still, church musicians earned less and had lower status than court musicians. Their meager income was supplemented by allotments of firewood and grain and by irregular fees for weddings and funerals. They suffered a financial pinch when a "healthy wind" blew and there were fewer funerals than usual, a situation Bach once complained about.

Large towns employed musicians for a variety of functions—to play in churches, in processions, in concerts for visiting dignitaries, and for university graduations. These town musicians often played with amateurs in music clubs or university music societies, getting together at private homes, coffeehouses, and taverns.

Some baroque musicians earned money by writing operas for commercial opera houses; such houses were located mainly in Italy. In Venice, a city of 125,000 people, six opera companies performed simultaneously between 1680 and 1700. In London, Handel became music director of a commercial opera company in 1719. Backed by English nobles, this company was a corporation with shares listed on the London stock exchange. When the company went bankrupt in 1728, Handel formed his own company, for which he wrote operas and served as conductor, manager, and impresario. In filling these many roles, Handel became one of the first great "freelance" musicians.

How did one become a musician in the baroque period? Often the art was handed from father to son; many leading composers—such as Bach, Vivaldi, Purcell, Couperin, and Rameau—were sons of musicians. Sometimes boys were apprenticed to a town musician and lived in his home. In return for instruction, the boys did odd jobs, such as copying music. Many baroque composers began their studies as choirboys, learning music in the choir school. In Italy, music schools were connected with orphanages. (*Conservatory* comes from the Italian for *orphans' home*.) There, orphans, foundlings, and poor children—boys and girls—were given thorough musical training, and some became the most sought-after opera singers and instrumentalists in Europe. Eminent composers such as Vivaldi were hired to teach and direct concerts in these schools. Vivaldi's all-female orchestra in Venice was considered one of the finest ensembles in Italy.

During the baroque period, women were not permitted to be employed as music directors or as instrumentalists in court or opera orchestras. However, women functioned as opera singers and as members of female vocal ensembles in courts. A number of women—including Francesca Caccini (1587–c. 1645), Barbara Strozzi, and Elisabeth Jacquet de La Guerre—succeeded in becoming respected composers. Nuns were given musical instruction, and their performances in convents were often on a high level. Isabella Leonarda (1620–1704), an Italian nun, was one of the most prolific composers of her time.

To get a job, musicians usually had to pass a difficult examination, performing and submitting compositions. Sometimes there were nonmusical job requirements too. An applicant might be expected to make a "voluntary contribution" to the town's treasury, or even to marry the daughter of a retiring musician. Bach and Handel turned down the same job because one of the conditions was marriage to the organist's daughter. Italian musicians held the best posts in most European courts and were frequently paid twice as much as local musicians.

Composers were an integral part of baroque society, working for courts, churches, towns, and commercial opera houses. Though they wrote their music to fit specific needs, its quality is so high that much of it has become standard in today's concert repertoire.

3 The Concerto Grosso and Ritornello Form

We've seen that the contrast between loud and soft sounds—between relatively large and small groups of performers—is a basic principle of baroque music. This principle governs the concerto grosso, an important form of orchestral music in the late baroque period. In a **concerto grosso,** a small group of soloists is pitted against a larger group of players called the **tutti** (*all*). Usually, between two and four soloists play with anywhere from eight to twenty or more musicians for the tutti. The tutti consists mainly of string instruments, with a harpsichord as part of the basso continuo. A concerto grosso presents a contrast of texture between the tutti and the soloists, who assert their individuality and appeal for attention through brilliant and fanciful melodic lines. The soloists were the best and highest-paid members of the baroque orchestra because their parts were more difficult than those of the other players. Concerti grossi were frequently performed by private orchestras in aristocratic palaces.

A concerto grosso consists of *several movements that contrast in tempo and character.* Most often there are three movements: (1) fast, (2) slow, (3) fast. The opening movement is usually vigorous and determined, clearly showing the contrast between tutti and soloists. The slow movement is quieter than the first, often lyrical and intimate. The last movement is lively and carefree, sometimes dancelike.

The first and last movements of concerti grossi are often in **ritornello form,** which is based on alternation between tutti and solo sections. In ritornello form the tutti opens with a theme called the **ritornello** (*refrain*). This theme, always played by the tutti, returns in different keys throughout the movement. But it usually returns in fragments, not complete. Only at the end of the movement does the entire ritornello return in the home key. Although the number of times a ritornello (tutti) returns varies from piece to piece, a typical concerto grosso movement might be outlined as follows:

1. a. Tutti (*f*), ritornello in home key
   b. Solo

2. a. Tutti (*f*), ritornello fragment
   b. Solo

3. a. Tutti (*f*), ritornello fragment
   b. Solo

4. Tutti (*f*), ritornello in home key

In contrast to the tutti's ritornello, the solo sections offer fresh melodic ideas, softer dynamics, rapid scales, and broken chords. Soloists may also expand short melodic ideas from the tutti. The opening movement of Bach's *Brandenburg* Concerto No. 5 is a fine example of ritornello form in the concerto grosso.

Brandenburg Concerto No. 5 in D Major (c. 1721), by Johann Sebastian Bach

With his set of six *Brandenburg* Concertos, Bach brought immortality to a German aristocrat, the Margrave of Brandenburg. Bach and the margrave met in 1718, when Bach was music director for another patron. The margrave loved music and asked Bach to send him some original compositions. About three years later, Bach sent him the *Brandenburg* Concertos with the flattering dedication quoted in Chapter 2, probably hoping for money or favors in return. (We don't know whether he got any.) These concertos had been composed for, and performed by, the orchestra of Bach's employer, the prince of Cöthen. Each of the concertos is written for a different and unusual combination of instruments.

Brandenburg Concerto No. 5 uses a string orchestra and a group of soloists consisting of a flute, a violin, and a harpsichord. This was the first time that a harpsichord had been given the solo role in a concerto grosso. In 1719, the prince of Cöthen bought a new harpsichord; Bach probably wanted to show off this instrument (as well as his own skill as a keyboard player), and so he gave it a solo spot. The tutti is written for violins, violas, cellos, and double bass. During the tutti sections the solo violinist plays along, as does the harpsichordist, who realizes the figured bass.

The *Brandenburg* Concerto No. 5 has three movements: (1) fast, (2) slow, (3) fast. We focus on the first movement.

First Movement: Allegro

The allegro movement opens with the ritornello, which is an almost continuous flow of rapid notes. After the ritornello ends—very definitely—the soloists present short melodic ideas, the flute and violin imitating each other playfully. The appearance of the soloists brings a lower dynamic level and a new tone color—the flute. After a while, the tutti returns loudly with a brief fragment of the ritornello, only to give way again to the soloists. This alternation between brief, relatively loud ritornello fragments in the tutti and longer, softer solo sections continues throughout the movement.

The soloists' music tends to be brilliant, fanciful, and personal as compared with the more vigorous and straightforward tutti sections. Solo sections are also more polyphonic in texture than the tutti and stress imitation between the flute and violin. The soloists play new material of their own or varied fragments from the ritornello. These solo sections build tension and make the listener anticipate the tutti's return. Listen especially for the suspenseful solo section that begins with a new theme in minor and ends with long notes in the flute.

Only the harpsichord plays during the long final solo section. And it is spectacular! Bach builds to a tense high point for the movement through irresistible rhythm and dazzling scale passages that require a virtuoso's skill. His audience must have marveled at this brilliant harpsichord solo within a concerto grosso. Audiences are still dazzled by it.

Listening Outline

BACH, *Brandenburg* Concerto No. 5; c. 1721

First Movement: Allegro

Ritornello form, duple meter (2/2), D major

Flute, violin, harpsichord (solo group); string orchestra, continuo (tutti)

(Duration 9:58)

Listen for the contrast in *tone color* between the tutti sections for strings and the solo sections, which feature *imitation* between flute and violin. Notice the virtuosic solo section for harpsichord alone near the end of the movement.

Tutti

    0:00   **1. a.** Strings, *f*, ritornello.

Solo

    0:20   **b.** Flute, violin, harpsichord, major key.

Tutti

    0:44   **2. a.** Strings, *f*, ritornello fragment.

Solo

    0:49   **b.** Flute, violin, harpsichord, varied ritornello fragment.

Tutti

    1:09   **3. a.** Strings, *f*, ritornello fragment.

Solo

    1:16   **b.** Violin, flute, harpsichord.

Tutti

    1:36   **4. a.** Strings, *f*, ritornello fragment, minor.

Solo

    1:42   **b.** Harpsichord, flute, violin.

Tutti

2:23 **5. a.** Strings, *f*, ritornello fragment, major.

Solo

2:30 **b.** Flute, harpsichord, violin, varied ritornello fragment, ***pp***

2:55 **c.** New theme in minor, ***pp***, tossed between flute and violin.

Flute

pp

Tension mounts, long notes in flute lead to

Tutti

4:11 **6. a.** Strings, *f*, ritornello fragment, major.

Solo

4:16 **b.** Violin, flute, harpsichord.

Tutti

5:01 **7. a.** Strings, *f*, longer ritornello fragment.

Solo

5:12 **b.** Violin, harpsichord, flute, varied ritornello fragment.

Tutti

5:40 **8. a.** Strings, *f*, ritornello fragment.

Solo

5:47 **b.** Violin and flute play carefree idea with rapid harpsichord scales in background.

6:24 **c.** Long harpsichord solo featuring virtuoso display. Mounting tension resolved in

Tutti

9:32 **9. a.** Strings, *f*, ritornello.

4 The Fugue

One cornerstone of baroque music is the fugue, which can be written for a group of instruments or voices, or for a single instrument, such as an organ or harpsichord. A ***fugue*** is a polyphonic composition based on one main theme, called a ***subject.*** Throughout a fugue, different melodic lines, called *voices,* imitate the subject. The top melodic line—whether sung or played—is the soprano voice, and the bottom is the bass. The texture of a fugue usually includes three, four, or five voices. Though the subject remains fairly constant throughout, it takes on new meanings when shifted to different keys or combined with different melodic and rhythmic ideas.

The form of a fugue is extremely flexible; in fact, the only constant feature of fugues is how they begin—the subject is almost always presented in a single, unaccompanied voice. By thus highlighting the subject, the composer tells us what to remember and listen for. In getting to know a fugue, try to follow its subject through the different levels of texture. After its first presentation, the subject is imitated in turn by all the remaining voices.

The opening of a fugue in four voices may be represented as follows:

Soprano	<u>Subject</u> .... etc.		
Alto		<u>Subject</u> .... etc.	
Tenor			<u>Subject</u> .... etc.
Bass			<u>Subject</u> .... etc.

In this case, the top voice announces the subject and then the lower voices imitate it. However, the subject may be announced by *any* voice—top, bottom, or middle—and the order in which the remaining voices imitate it is also completely flexible.

This may seem reminiscent of a round like *Row, Row, Row Your Boat,* but in a fugue the game of follow the leader (exact imitation of the subject) does not continue indefinitely. The dotted lines in the diagram indicate that *after a voice has presented the subject, it is free to go its own way with different melodic material.* The opening of a fugue differs from that of a round in another way: in a round, each voice presents the melody on the same tones. If the melody begins with the tones C–D–E, each voice will begin with these tones, whether at a higher or a lower register. But in the opening of a fugue, *the subject is presented in two different scales.* The first time, it is based on the notes of the *tonic scale.* But when the second voice presents the subject, it is in the *dominant scale*—five scale steps higher than the tonic—and it is then called the ***answer.*** A subject beginning with the notes C–D–E, for example, would be imitated by an answer five steps higher, on G–A–B. This alternation of subject and answer between the two scales creates variety.

In many fugues, the subject in one voice is constantly accompanied in another voice by a different melodic idea called a ***countersubject.*** A constant companion, the countersubject always appears with the subject: sometimes below it, sometimes above it.

After the opening of a fugue, when each voice has taken its turn at presenting the subject, a composer is free to decide how often the subject will be presented, in which voices, and in which keys. Between presentations of the subject, there are often transitional sections called ***episodes,*** which offer either new material or fragments of the subject or countersubject. Episodes do *not* present the subject in its entirety. They lend variety to the fugue and make reappearances of the subject sound fresh. Bach called one composer of fugues "pedantic" because he "had not shown enough fire to reanimate the theme by episodes."

Several musical procedures commonly appear in fugues. One is ***stretto,*** in which a subject is imitated before it is completed; one voice tries to catch the other. Another common procedure is ***pedal point*** (or ***organ point***), in which a single tone, usually in the bass, is held while the other voices produce a series of changing harmonies against it. (The term is taken from organ music, where a sustained low tone is produced by the organist's foot on a key of the pedal keyboard.)

A fugue subject can be varied in four principal ways:

1. It can be turned upside down, a procedure known as *inversion.* If the subject moves *upward* by leap, the inversion will move *downward* the same distance; if the subject moves *downward* by step, the inversion will move *upward* by step. In inversion, each interval in the subject is reversed in direction.

2. The subject may be presented *retrograde,* that is, by beginning with the last note of the subject and proceeding backward to the first.

3. The subject may be presented in *augmentation,* in which the original time values are lengthened.

4. The subject may appear in *diminution,* with shortened time values.

Fugues usually convey a single mood and a sense of continuous flow. They may be written as independent works or as single movements within larger compositions. Very often an independent fugue is introduced by a short piece called a ***prelude.***

Bach and Handel each wrote hundreds of fugues; their fugues represent the peak among works in the form. In the baroque period, as a friend of Bach's observed, "Skill in fugue was so indispensable in a composer that no one could have attained a musical post who had not worked out a given subject in all kinds of counterpoint and in a regular fugue." Fugal writing continued into the nineteenth and twentieth centuries. It is not used as frequently today as in the baroque period; yet to this day, as part of their training, musicians study how to write fugues.

Organ Fugue in G Minor (*Little Fugue*; c. 1709), by Johann Sebastian Bach

One of Bach's best-known organ pieces is the *Little Fugue* in G Minor, so called to differentiate it from another, longer fugue in G minor. The opening section of the *Little Fugue* corresponds to the diagram on page 114. Each of the fugue's four voices takes its turn presenting the tuneful subject, which is announced in the top voice and then appears in progressively lower voices, until it reaches the bass, where it is played by the organist's feet on the pedal keyboard. Like many baroque melodies, the subject gathers momentum as it goes along, beginning with relatively long time values (quarter notes) and then proceeding to shorter ones (eighth and sixteenth notes). Starting with its second appearance, the subject is accompanied by a countersubject that moves in short time values.

After the opening section, the subject appears five more times, each time preceded by an episode. The first episode uses both new material and a melodic idea from the countersubject. This episode contains downward sequences, which are melodic patterns repeated in the same voice but at lower pitches.

For harmonic contrast, Bach twice presents the subject in major keys rather than minor. The final statement of the subject—in minor—exploits the powerful bass tones of the pedal keyboard. Though the fugue is in minor, it ends with a major chord. This was a frequent practice in the baroque period; major chords were thought more conclusive than minor chords.

Listening Outline

BACH, Organ Fugue in G Minor (*Little Fugue*); c. 1709

Fugue, quadruple meter ($\frac{4}{4}$), G minor

Organ

(Duration 4:04)

Listen for the announcement of the fugue subject in the highest voice, followed by *polyphonic imitation* of the subject in successively lower voices. Notice when the subject is presented in a *major key*, instead of a *minor key*, in 3.a. and c.

| 0:00 | **1. a.** Subject, soprano voice alone, minor key. |

Subject

The Camerata wanted to create a new vocal style modeled on the music of ancient Greek tragedy. No actual dramatic music had come down to them from the Greeks, so they based their theories on literary accounts that had survived. It was believed that the Greek dramas had been sung throughout in a style that was midway between melody and speech. The Camerata wanted the vocal line to follow the rhythms and pitch fluctuations of speech. Because it was modeled after speech, the new vocal style became known as *recitative* (*recited*). It was sung by a soloist with only a simple chordal accompaniment. The new music was therefore homophonic in texture. Polyphony was rejected by the Camerata because different words sounding simultaneously would obscure the all-important text.

Euridice by Jacopo Peri is the earliest opera that has been preserved. It was composed for the wedding of King Henri IV of France and Marie de' Medici and was performed in Florence in 1600. Seven years later Monteverdi composed *Orfeo*—the first *great* opera— for the court of the Gonzaga family in Mantua. Both these operas are based on the Greek myth of Orpheus's descent into Hades to bring back his beloved Eurydice.

Much baroque opera was composed for ceremonial occasions at court and was designed as a display of magnificence and splendor. The subject matter was drawn from Greek mythology and ancient history. Not only were aristocratic patrons of the baroque fascinated by the classical civilizations of Greece and Rome, but they identified with Greek and Roman heroes and divinities. Opera did indeed reflect the creative urge of composer and librettist, but it also was a way to flatter the aristocracy. The radiant appearance of Apollo (god of poetry, music, and the sun) might symbolize a prince's enlightened rule.

The first public opera house opened in Venice in 1637; now anyone with the price of admission could attend an opera performance. Between 1637 and 1700 there were seventeen opera houses in Venice alone, as well as many in other Italian cities—ample evidence that opera had been born in the right place at the right time. Hamburg, Leipzig, and London had public opera houses by the early 1700s, but, on the whole, public opera outside Italy took longer to develop.

Venetian opera became a great tourist attraction. An English traveler wrote in 1645 about the opera and its "variety of scenes painted and contrived with no less art of perspective, and machines for flying in the air, and other wonderful motions; taken together, it is one of the most magnificent and expensive diversions the wit of man can invent." The stage machinery of baroque opera bordered on the colossal; stage effects might include gods descending on clouds or riding across the sky in chariots, ships tossing, boulders splitting. And set design was an art in itself. Painters turned backdrops into cities with arches and avenues that stretched into the distant horizon.

Baroque opera marked the rise of virtuoso singers. Chief among these was the *castrato*, a male singer who had been castrated before puberty. (Castration of boy singers was common in Italy from 1600 to 1800; it was usually done with the consent of impoverished parents who hoped their sons would become highly paid opera stars.) A castrato combined the lung power of a man with the vocal range of a woman. His agility, breath control, and unique sound (which was not like a woman's) intrigued listeners. Castrati received the highest fees of any musicians. With their soprano or alto vocal ranges, they played male roles, such as Caesar and Nero. Baroque audiences evidently were more interested in vocal virtuosity than dramatic realism. Today, a castrato part in a baroque opera is often sung by a *countertenor,* a male who sings in a female pitch range using a special kind of voice production.

By combining virtuosity, nobility, and extravagance, baroque opera perfectly expressed the spirit of a grand age.

Much baroque opera was designed to display magnificent extravagance. Pietro Domenico Olivero's painting of the Royal Theater, Turin (1740), shows a performance of Francesco Feo's opera *Arsace*.
Realy Easy Star/Toni Spagone/Alamy

7 Claudio Monteverdi

Claudio Monteverdi (1567–1643), one of the most important composers of the early baroque era, was born in Cremona, Italy. He served at the court of Mantua for twenty-one years, first as a singer and violist, then as music director. For this court Monteverdi created the earliest operatic masterpiece, *Orfeo* (*Orpheus,* 1607). Though widely recognized as a leading composer in Mantua, Monteverdi received little pay or respect: "I have never suffered greater humiliation," he wrote, "than when I had to go and beg the treasurer to obtain what was due me."

Life improved for Monteverdi in 1613, when he was appointed music director at St. Mark's in Venice, the most important church position in Italy. He stayed at St. Mark's for thirty years, until his death in 1643. There he composed not only the required sacred

music but also secular music for the aristocracy. He wrote operas for San Cassiano in Venice, the first public opera house in Europe. At the age of seventy-five, Monteverdi wrote his last opera, *L'incoronazione di Poppea* (*The Coronation of Poppea,* 1642).

Monteverdi is a monumental figure in the history of music. His works form a musical bridge between the sixteenth and seventeenth centuries, and he greatly influenced composers of the time. All his music—madrigals, church music, opera—is for voices, ordinarily supported by a basso continuo and other instruments.

Monteverdi wanted to create music of emotional intensity. He felt that earlier music had conveyed only moderate emotion, and he wanted to extend its range to include agitation, excitement, and passion. To achieve this intensity, he used dissonances with unprecedented freedom and daring. And to evoke the angry or warlike feelings in some of his texts, he introduced new orchestral effects, including pizzicato and tremolo.

Monteverdi was the first composer of operatic masterpieces. Only three of the twelve operas he wrote are preserved, but they truly blend music and drama. His vocal lines respond marvelously to the inflections of Italian while maintaining melodic flow.

Orfeo (*Orpheus*, 1607)

Fittingly enough, Monteverdi's first opera is about Orpheus, the supremely gifted musician of Greek myth. Orpheus, son of the god Apollo, is ecstatically happy after his marriage to Eurydice. But his joy is shattered when his bride is killed by a poisonous snake. Orpheus goes down to Hades hoping to bring her back to life. Because of his beautiful music, he is granted this privilege—on the condition that he not look back at Eurydice while leading her out of Hades. During a moment of anxiety, however, Orpheus does look back, and Eurydice vanishes. Nonetheless, there is a happy ending, of sorts. Apollo pities Orpheus and brings him up to heaven, where he can gaze eternally at Eurydice's radiance in the sun and stars.

Orfeo was composed in 1607 for the Mantuan court, and no expense was spared to make it a lavish production. There were star soloists, a chorus, dancers, and a large orchestra of about forty players. The aristocratic audience was wildly enthusiastic and recognized the historic significance of the performance.

Monteverdi creates variety in *Orfeo* by using many kinds of music—recitatives, arias, duets, choruses, and instrumental interludes. He uses the opera orchestra to establish atmosphere, character, and dramatic situations. With the simplest of musical means, Monteverdi makes his characters come alive. Through vocal line alone he quickly characterizes the hero's joy and despair. Monteverdi sets his text in a very flexible way, freely alternating recitatives with more melodious passages, depending on the meaning of the words.

We now consider one well-known passage from this opera, Orpheus's recitative *Tu se' morta* (*You are dead*).

Act II:
Recitative: *Tu se' morta* (*You are dead*)

Monteverdi's mastery of the then novel technique of recitative is shown in *Tu se' morta,* sung by Orpheus after he is told of Eurydice's death. Orpheus resolves to bring her back from Hades, and he bids an anguished farewell to the earth, sky, and sun.

Orpheus and Euridice (c. 1625), by Jacopo Vignali. The painting depicts Orpheus leading Eurydice out of Hades while a winged demon reaches out to her from behind.
Heritage Images/Getty Images

His vocal line is accompanied only by a basso continuo played by a small portable organ and a bass lute. (In modern performances, other instruments are sometimes substituted.)

The texture is homophonic: the accompaniment simply gives harmonic support to the voice. The vocal line is rhythmically free, with little sense of beat or meter, and its phrases are irregular in length. This flexible setting of text is meant to suggest the passionate speech of an actor declaiming his lines.

Monteverdi frequently uses word painting, the musical representation of poetic images that was favored by baroque composers. For example, words like *stelle* (*stars*) and *sole* (*sun*) are sung to climactic high tones, whereas *abissi* (*abysses*) and *morte* (*death*) are sung to somber, low tones. Three times during the recitative the melodic line rises to a climax and then descends. Through such simple means, Monteverdi expresses Orpheus's passion.

Vocal Music Guide

MONTEVERDI, Recitative: *Tu se' morta (You are dead)*, from *Orfeo (Orpheus)*; 1607

(Duration 2:54)

Listen for the speechlike character of the recitative, and the *homophonic texture* of the recitative and its basso continuo accompaniment. Notice the effect of *word painting* on the low tone for *abissi (abysses)* and the high tone for *stelle (stars)*.

0:00		Tu se' morta, se' morta, mia vita,
		 ed io respiro; tu se' da me partita,
		 se' da me partita per mai più,
		 mai più non tornare, ed io rimango—
		 no, no, che se i versi alcuna cosa
		   ponno,
			You are dead, you are dead, my dearest,
			 And I breathe; you have left me,
			 You have left me forevermore,
			 Never to return, and I remain—
			 No, no, if my verses have any
			   power,

1:12	Low tone on *abissi*.	n'andrò sicuro a' più profondi abissi, e, intenerito il cor del re de l'ombre,	I will go confidently to the deepest abysses, And, having melted the heart of the king of shadows,
1:38	High tone on *stelle*.	meco trarotti a riveder le stelle, o se ciò negherammi empio destino,	Will bring you back to me to see the stars again, Or, if pitiless fate denies me this,
2:00	Low tone on *morte*.	rimarrò teco in compágnia di morte.	I will remain with you in the company of death.
2:17	High tone on *sole*.	Addio terra, addio cielo, e sole, addio.	Farewell earth, farewell sky, and sun, farewell.

8 Henry Purcell

Purcell mastered all the musical forms of late seventeenth-century England. His opera *Dido and Aeneas* was written for students at a girls' boarding school.

The Picture Art Collection/Alamy

Henry Purcell (c. 1659–1695), called the greatest of English composers, was born in London; his father was a musician in the king's service. At about the age of ten, Purcell became a choirboy in the Chapel Royal, and by the time he was in his late teens his extraordinary talents were winning him important musical positions. In 1677, at about eighteen, he became composer to the king's string orchestra; two years later he was appointed organist of Westminster Abbey; and in 1682, he became an organist of the Chapel Royal. During the last few years of his short life, Purcell was also active composing music for plays.

Acclaimed as *the* English composer of his day, Purcell, who died at thirty-six, was buried beneath the organ in Westminster Abbey. He was the last native English composer of international rank until the twentieth century.

Purcell mastered all the musical forms of late seventeenth-century England. He wrote church music, secular choral music, music for small groups of instruments, songs, and music for the stage. His only true opera is *Dido and Aeneas* (1689), which many consider the finest ever written to an English text. His other dramatic works are spoken plays with musical numbers in the form of overtures, songs, choruses, and dances.

Few composers have equaled Purcell's handling of the English language. His vocal music is faithful to English inflection and brings out the meaning of the text. Purcell developed a melodious recitative that seems to grow out of the English language. His music is filled with lively rhythms and has a fresh melodic style that captures the spirit of English folksongs. He treated the chorus with great variety and was able to obtain striking effects through both simple homophonic textures and complex polyphony. His music is spiced with dissonances that seemed harsh to the generation of musicians who followed him. Some of Purcell's finest songs use a variation form found in many baroque works—a ground bass.

Ground Bass

Often in baroque works, a musical idea in the bass is repeated over and over while the melodies above it change. The repeated musical idea is called a ***ground bass,*** or ***basso ostinato*** (*obstinate* or *persistent bass*). The ground bass pattern may be as short as four notes or as long as eight measures. In this type of variation form, the constant repetition of the bass pattern gives unity, while the free flow of the melodic lines above it results in variety.

Composers have used a ground bass in both vocal and instrumental music. We'll hear a ground bass in Purcell's opera *Dido and Aeneas,* as well as in Strozzi's cantata *Che si puòfare (What can be done?),* studied in Chapter 10.

Dido and Aeneas (1689)

Purcell's *Dido and Aeneas,* a masterpiece of baroque opera, was written for students at a girls' boarding school. It lasts only an hour, is scored only for strings and harpsichord continuo, and requires no elaborate stage machinery or virtuoso soloists. Most of its solo roles are for women. Purcell used many dances in *Dido and Aeneas,* because the director of the school was a dancing master who wanted to display the students' accomplishments. The chorus plays a prominent role, both participating in the action and commenting on it.

The libretto of *Dido and Aeneas,* by Nahum Tate, was inspired by the *Aeneid,* an epic poem by the Roman poet Virgil (70–19 BCE). The opera's main characters are Dido, queen of Carthage, and Aeneas, king of the defeated Trojans. After the destruction of his native Troy, Aeneas has been ordered by the gods to seek a site for building a new city. He sets out on the search with twenty-one ships. After landing at Carthage, a north African seaport, Aeneas falls in love with Dido. A sorceress and two witches see this as an opportunity to plot Dido's downfall. (In Purcell's time, people really believed in witches: nineteen supposed "witches" were hanged in Massachusetts in 1692, three years after *Dido*'s first performance.) A false messenger tells Aeneas that the gods command him to leave Carthage immediately and renew his search. Aeneas agrees but is desolate at the thought of deserting Dido.

In the last act, which takes place at the harbor, Aeneas's sailors sing and dance before leaving, and the witches look on in glee. An emotional scene follows between Aeneas and Dido, who enters with her friend Belinda. Dido calls Aeneas a hypocrite and refuses his offer to stay. After he sails, Dido sings a noble, deeply tragic lament and kills herself. The opera concludes with the mourning of the chorus.

Now let's look at *Dido's Lament.*

Act III: *Dido's Lament*

A melodic recitative accompanied only by the basso continuo sets the sorrowful mood for *Dido's Lament,* the climax of the opera. This aria is built on a chromatically descending ground bass that is stated eleven times. (In the baroque period, such chromatic ground basses were commonly used to show grief.) As shown in the music example, Dido's melody moves freely above this repeated bass line, creating touching dissonances with it.

Dido's repeated *Remember me* reaches the highest note of the aria and haunts the listener. The emotional tension is sustained in the orchestral conclusion, where a chromatically descending violin melody movingly expresses the tragedy of Dido's fate.

Vocal Music Guide

PURCELL, *Dido's Lament,* from *Dido and Aeneas;* 1689

(Duration 4:27)

Listen for the *chromatically descending* ground bass (basso ostinato) that appears eleven times in this aria. Notice how the vocal line moves freely above this ground bass and how the *repeated tones* on *Remember me!* create a haunting effect.

0:00

Recitative, descending melody, basso continuo accompanies.

Thy hand, Belinda, darkness shades me,
On thy bosom let me rest;
More I would but Death invades me;
Death is now a welcome guest.

0:46

Dido's Lament (aria), lute introduces chromatically descending ground bass.

Upper strings join.

When I am laid, am laid in earth, may my wrongs create
No trouble, no trouble in thy breast.
Remember me! But ah! forget my fate.

Orchestral conclusion, violin melody descends chromatically.

9 The Baroque Cantata

Along with opera, the cantata was a leading genre of vocal music during the baroque period. The word cantata means a composition that is sung. Developed in Italy during the 1600s, a *cantata* is a work for one or more voices with instrumental accompaniment. Typically, Italian cantatas consisted of an alternation between recitatives and arias. They differed from opera in that they were shorter, did not involve acting or scenery, and were performed in music rooms rather than in theaters. Originally the cantata was a secular genre dealing with love and ancient mythology, but the later 1600s saw the development of the church cantata using texts inspired by the Bible. The composing of cantatas spread from Italy to other areas of Europe, including Germany and France.

10 Barbara Strozzi

Barbara Strozzi was one of the best-known women composers of the seventeenth century.

The Picture Art Collection/Alamy

One of the best-known woman composers of the seventeenth century, Barbara Strozzi (1619–1677) was born in Venice. Her mother was Isabella Garzoni, a long-time servant of Giulio Strozzi, a distinguished Venetian poet and librettist. Giulio adopted Barbara and probably was her biological father. One of Barbara's music teachers was Francesco Cavalli, a leading Venetian opera composer. At age fifteen she was described as "Guilio Strozzi's extraordinarily virtuosic singer." To display his daughter's talents as a singer and hostess when Barbara was eighteen, Giulio Strozzi created the *Accademia degli Unisoni* (*Society of the Harmonious*), a group of philosophers, poets, and scholars.

Barbara Strozzi performed in the setting of a salon, rather than in a theater, court, or convent. Her reputation rested on the eight volumes of her vocal music published between 1644 and 1664. They were dedicated to aristocratic patrons, three of them women. No other composer—male or female—published as much secular vocal music in Venice during this period.

Because it was unusual for women to publish their music, Strozzi was defensive in the preface to her Opus 1 (1644), dedicated to the Grand Duchess of Tuscany: "I must reverently consecrate this first work, which as a woman I publish all too boldly, to the Most August Name of Your Highness...so that it may rest secure against the lightning bolts of slander prepared for it." In the dedications of Strozzi's last three publications, she no longer mentions her gender. Recognition of Strozzi's high status as a composer came in 1656, when her works appeared in two music anthologies together with those of important contemporaries, including her former teacher Francesco Cavalli.

A single mother of four children, Strozzi supported her family partly through gifts from her patrons. She was also a knowledgeable investor in government bonds and occasionally lent money at interest.

Most of her compositions are ariettas, arias, and cantatas for solo soprano and continuo, set to love poems. They were performed in the music rooms of the aristocracy and upper middle class. Her works were known outside Italy and for many decades after her death in 1677. In his *General History of Music* (1776), John Hawkins wrote that Strozzi is thought "to be the inventress of that elegant species of vocal composition the cantata."

Che si può fare (What can be done?; 1664)

Strozzi's last published collection, Opus 8 (1664), includes six cantatas and six arias. This collection was dedicated to Sophia, the Duchess of Brunswick and Lüneburg (in today's Northwestern Germany), who was a musician herself and a patron of poets and composers.

The cantata *Che si può fare,* from Opus 8, consists of five sections: (1) aria (2) recitative (3) recitative and arioso (4) aria (5) recitative. We focus on the opening aria, *Che si può fare (What can be done?).*

Che si può fare is a melancholy aria sung by a woman who blames the heavens and Cupid (god of love) for causing her suffering. In a minor key and in triple meter, the aria is built upon a four-note descending ground bass (basso ostinato) that repeats throughout. The ground bass is played by a lute in our recording.

The singer begins with a poignant melodic phrase that rises and falls on the despairing words *Che si può fare, Che, che* (What can be done, What, what). This soulful phrase recurs several times during the aria.

The expression *Da gl'astri disastri Mi piovano agni hor* (From heavenly stars disasters are raining on me) is depicted by a series of descending rapid notes, an example of word painting.

In this aria, individual words and phrases are often repeated, a characteristic of baroque vocal music.

Vocal Music Guide

STROZZI, *Che si può fare (What can be done?);* 1664

(Duration 3:38)

Listen for the four-note descending ground bass that repeats throughout. Notice the recurring melodic phrase on *Che si può fare, Che, che* (What can be done, What, what) and the word painting on *Da gl'astri disastri Mi piovano agni hor* (From heavenly stars disasters are raining on me).

| 0:00 | Lute introduces four-note descending ground bass. | | |
| 0:09 | Phrase ascends and descends. | | |

	Che si può fare?	What can be done?
	Le stele rubelle	The rebellious stars,
	Non hanno pietà.	Have no mercy on me.
	Che s'el cielo non dà	If heaven cannot bring
	Un influsso di pace al mio penare,	some peace to my suffering
	Che si può fare	What can be done?

1:39	Lute briefly alone.		
1:53			
	Descending rapid notes.		

	Che si può dire?	What can be said?
	Da gl'astri disastri	From heavenly stars
	Mi piovano agni hor;	disasters are raining on me;
	Che le perfido amor	If deceitful Love
	Un respiro diniega al mio martire,	does not relieve my martyrdom,
	Che si può dire?	What can be said?

11 Elisabeth Jacquet de la Guerre

Highly esteemed by King Louis XIV, the virtuoso harpsichordist and composer, Elisabeth Jacquet de la Guerre was the first French woman to have an opera performed.

The Picture Art Collection/Alamy

French composer and harpsichordist Elisabeth Jacquet de la Guerre (1665–1729) was a child prodigy. Born in Paris, she played for King Louis XIV at the French court when only five years old. Her father, an instrument builder and organist, was her first teacher; her sister and two brothers also became professional musicians.

When Jacquet de la Guerre performed at court at age twelve, the Parisian journal *Mercure galant* noted that she "sings at sight the most difficult music. She accompanies herself and others at the harpsichord, which she plays in an inimitable manner. She composes pieces and plays them in all the keys asked of her...The King [Louis XIV] took much pleasure in hearing her play." As a teenager, she spent three years at the court, sponsored by Louis XIV's principal mistress, Madame de Montespan, who took responsibility for Elisabeth's musical education.

At age nineteen she left the court to marry the organist Marin de la Guerre. In Paris, Jacquet de la Guerre taught harpsichord, gave concerts in her home, and published her compositions. Her earliest printed work, *First Book of Harpsichord Pieces* (1687), appeared three years after her marriage. This book, like almost all of her later publications, was dedicated to Louis XIV, her long-time patron.

Jacquet de la Guerre's opera *Cephale and Procris*, the first composed by a French woman, was premiered in Paris in 1694. As in many Baroque operas, the plot of *Cephale and Procris* derives from Greek mythology and is intended to extol the King.

During six years, from 1698 to 1704, Jacquet de la Guerre lost almost all her close family, including her mother, father, husband, and her only child, a musically gifted boy who died when he was ten. She never remarried, remaining a widow for twenty-five years.

Jacquet de la Guerre composed music in variety of genres, including harpsichord pieces, sonatas for violin and basso continuo, an opera, a ballet, and French cantatas, one of which we study. Her last composition, *Te Deum*, a work praising God, written for large chorus, was performed in 1721 in the chapel of the Louvre palace to celebrate the recovery of the child Louis XV—the future king of France—after an attack of smallpox.

Three years after her death, Jacquet de la Guerre was ranked among the leading composers of the time in a biographical dictionary called *French Parnassus*.

Le sommeil d'Ulisse (The Sleep of Ulysses; about 1715)

The early 1700s in France saw a vogue for the chamber cantata, which had developed in Italy during the 1600s. These vocal works were performed in the salons of the aristocracy and upper middle class. Between 1708 and approximately 1715, Jacquet de la Guerre published fifteen French cantatas, twelve on subjects drawn from the Old Testament and three with secular texts. She aimed for a close connection between music and text, writing that "people up till now have flattered me that my music responds very easily to the words upon which I have composed it."

In the secular cantata *Le sommeil d'Ulisse* (*The Sleep of Ulysses*), Neptune, god of the seas, is angry at Ulysses and wants him dead. (Ulysses is Latin for Odysseus, the hero of Homer's ancient Greek epic poem *The Odyssey*.) Neptune whips up a violent storm to cause Ulysses' ship to capsize, but Minerva, goddess of wisdom, saves him and calms him through a deep, magical sleep.

The Sleep of Ulysses is written for soprano, violin, flute, and basso continuo. After an opening instrumental prelude, the cantata alternates between recitatives and arias.

Aria: La Têmpete (The Storm)

In the second aria, *La Têmpete* (*The Storm*), the violin and basso continuo (harpsichord and bass viol) play rapid repeated notes throughout to depict the violent storm. After an extended instrumental introduction, a soprano—the narrator—joins, singing an agitated melody. An instrumental postlude concludes the aria.

Vocal Music Guide

JACQUET DE LA GUERRE, *La Têmpete* (*The Storm*) from *Le sommeil d'Ulisse* (*The Sleep of Ulysses*; about 1715)

(Duration 2:42)

Listen for the depiction of the storm through rapid repeated notes in the violin and continuo. Notice that the word *"disparoit"* (disappeared) is highlighted by a dramatic pause.

0:00	Instrumental introduction: violin, continuo; rapid notes depict storm		
1:11	Soprano	*Pour perdre ce Guerrier,*	To destroy this warrior (Ulysses),
		Il se livre à sa rage.	He (Neptune) gives vent to his anger.

1:17	Instrumental interlude		
1:23	Soprano describes the storm	*De tonnerres bruants*	With loud thunder
		De foudroyants éclairs.	and terrible lightening.
1:28	Instrumental interlude		
1:34	Soprano	*Il fait briller*	He sets ablaze,
		Gronder les Airs	Makes the air rumble
1:41	Brief instrumental interlude		
1:45	Soprano	*L'univers allarmé*	The universe alarmed
		Craint nouveau naufrage,	fears a new shipwreck.
		Tous les vents déchainé	All the winds unleashed
		lutent contre les flots.	struggle against the waves.
2:02	Instrumental interlude		
2:11	Soprano	*Le vaisseau renversé*	The vessel capsized
		cede à l'affreux orage,	giving way to the frightful storm,
2:21	Dramatic pause after "disappeared"	*Disparoit,*	Disappeared,
2:23		*et la Mer*	and the sea
		engloutit ce Héros.	engulfs this Hero (Ulysses).
2:28	Instrumental postlude		

12 The Baroque Sonata

Instrumental music gained importance rapidly and dramatically during the baroque period. One of the main developments in instrumental music was the **sonata,** a composition in several movements for one to eight instruments. (In later periods, the term sonata took on a more restricted meaning.)

Composers often wrote **trio sonatas,** so-called because they had three melodic lines: two high lines and a basso continuo. Yet the word *trio* is misleading, because the "trio" sonata actually involves *four* instrumentalists. There are two high instruments (commonly, violins, flutes, or oboes) and two instruments for the basso continuo—a keyboard instrument (organ or harpsichord) and a low instrument (cello or bassoon).

The sonata originated in Italy but spread to Germany, England, and France during the seventeenth century. Sonatas were played in palaces, in homes, and even in churches—before, during, or after the service. Sometimes composers differentiated between the *sonata da chiesa* (*church sonata*), which had a dignified character and was suitable for sacred performance, and the *sonata da camera* (*chamber sonata*), which was more dancelike and was intended for performance at court.

Trio Sonata in A Minor, Op. 3, No. 10 (1689), Arcangelo Corelli

The most prominent Italian violinist and composer of string music around 1700 was Arcangelo Corelli (1653–1713). Corelli was also an eminent teacher who laid the foundations of modern violin technique. He wrote only instrumental music: sixty sonatas and twelve concertos, all for strings.

court, the king asked for *Spring* as an encore. This posed a problem because the king's orchestra was not present. Rising to the occasion, a group of nobles at the court volunteered to accompany the violin soloist. A Parisian newspaper reported that "this beautiful piece of music was performed perfectly."

Like most of Vivaldi's concertos, *Spring* has three movements: (1) fast, (2) slow, (3) fast. Both the first and last movements are in ritornello form.

First Movement: Allegro

Spring has come, and joyfully,
The birds greet it with happy song.
And the streams, fanned by gentle breezes,
Flow along with a sweet murmur.
Covering the sky with a black cloak,
Thunder and lightning come to announce the season.
When these have quieted down, the little birds
Return to their enchanting song.

The allegro, in E major, opens with an energetic orchestral ritornello depicting the arrival of spring. Each of the ritornello's two phrases is played loudly and then repeated softly, in the terraced dynamics typical of baroque music. After the ritornello, the movement alternates between extended solo sections containing musical tone painting and brief tutti sections presenting part of the ritornello theme. In the first solo section, birdsongs are imitated by high trills and repeated notes played by the violin soloist and two violins from the orchestra. (A *trill* is an ornament consisting of the rapid alternation of two tones that are a whole or half step apart.) In the second descriptive episode, murmuring streams are suggested by soft running notes in the violins. The next solo section contains string tremolos and rapid scales representing thunder and lightning. Following the storm, the ritornello appears in minor instead of in major. All the pictorial passages in this movement provide contrasts of texture and dynamics between returns of the ritornello theme. The allegro's tunefulness, rhythmic vitality, and light, homophonic texture evoke the feeling of springtime.

Listening Outline

VIVALDI, *La Primavera, (Spring),* **Concerto for Violin and String Orchestra, Op. 8, No. 1 from** *The Four Seasons* **(1725)**

First Movement: Allegro

Ritornello form, quadruple meter ($\frac{4}{4}$), E major

Solo violin, string orchestra, harpsichord (basso continuo)

(Duration 3:38)

Listen for the musical imitations of bird song in the first solo section (1.b.), murmuring streams in the second solo section (2.b.), and thunder and lightning in the third solo section (3.b.).

Spring has come

0:00   **1. a.** Tutti, ritornello opening phrase, f, repeated p

closing phrase with syncopations, f, repeated p, major key.

Song of the birds

0:31   **b.** Solo violin joined by two violins from orchestra, high trills and repeated notes.

1:06   **2. a.** Tutti, ritornello closing phrase, f.

Murmuring streams

1:14   **b.** Violins, p, running notes, cellos, p, running notes below sustained tones in violins.

1:38   **3. a.** Tutti, ritornello closing phrase, f.

Thunder and lightning

1:46   **b.** String tremolos, f, upward rushing scales introduce high solo violin, brilliant virtuoso passages answered by low string tremolos.

2:15   **4. a.** Tutti, ritornello closing phrase in minor key, f.

Song of the birds

2:23   **b.** Solo violin joined by two violins from orchestra, high repeated notes and trills, minor key.

2:43   **5. a.** Tutti, ritornello opening phrase varied, f, ends in major key.

2:55   **b.** Solo violin, running notes accompanied by basso continuo.

3:11   **6.** Tutti, ritornello closing phrase, f, repeated p, major key.

Second Movement:
Largo e pianissimo sempre
(very slow and very soft throughout)

And then, on a pleasant meadow covered with flowers,
Lulled by the soft murmuring of leaves and branches,
The goatherd sleeps, his faithful dog at his side.

The peaceful slow movement, in C sharp minor, is much quieter than the energetic opening movement. It uses only the solo violin and the orchestral violins and violas, omitting the cellos, basses, and harpsichord. A tender, expansive melody for the solo violin depicts the goatherd's slumber, while a soft, rocking figure in the violins suggests the rustling of leaves. The violas imitate the barking of the goatherd's "faithful dog" with a repeated-note figure in short-long rhythm. The tranquility of this pastoral scene is evoked by the movement's unchanging texture, rhythm, and dynamic level.

In the performance of this movement on our recordings, the violin soloist Jeanne Lamon decorates the melody with ornaments, or embellishing notes. During the baroque period, performers were often expected to add embellishments not indicated in the printed music. Vivaldi's notated melody and the decorated version of the melody you hear in the recording are shown in the following music examples.

had become in the baroque period. Bach's vocal music—the bulk of his output—was written mostly for the Lutheran church and was often based on familiar hymns. But his personal style was drawn from Italian concertos and French dance pieces, as well as the church music of his native Germany.

Bach's music is unique in its combination of polyphonic texture and rich harmony. His works show an astounding mastery of harmony and counterpoint and are used as models by music students today. Baroque music leans toward unity of mood, and this is particularly true of Bach, who liked to elaborate a single melodic idea in a piece, creating unity of mood by an insistent rhythmic drive. By Bach's time there was little difference in style between secular and sacred music. In fact, he often created sacred music simply by rearranging instrumental pieces or works originally written for secular texts. His church music also uses operatic forms, such as the aria and recitative. Sometimes Bach composed music to demonstrate what he could do with a specific form (his *Art of the Fugue,* for example, displays all the resources of fugue writing), or a particular instrument (for instance his suites for cello solo). His *Well-Tempered Clavier,* a collection of forty-eight preludes and fugues, two in each major key and each minor key, was composed to explain and demonstrate a system of tuning (the title means, roughly, the Well-Tuned Keyboard Instrument).

15 The Baroque Suite

Instrumental music has always been closely linked with dancing; in the past, much of it was written for use in palace ballrooms. During the Renaissance, dances often came in pairs—a dignified dance in quadruple meter was often followed by a lively one in triple meter. In the baroque period and later, music was written that—although meant for listening, not dancing—was related to specific dance types in tempo, meter, and rhythm.

Baroque composers wrote **suites,** which are sets of dance-inspired movements. Whether for solo instruments, small groups, or orchestra, a baroque suite is made up of movements that are all written in the same key but differ in tempo, meter, and character. The dancelike movements also have a variety of national origins: the moderately paced *allemande* (from Germany) might be followed by a fast *courante* and a moderate *gavotte* (from France), a slow and solemn *sarabande* (from Spain), and a fast *gigue* (jig, from England and Ireland). Suites were played in private homes, at court concerts, or as background music for dinner and outdoor festivities.

Dance pieces have a diverse past. Some began as folk dances, and others sprang from aristocratic ballrooms. Even the character of a dance might show dramatic evolution. The slow, solemn sarabande grew out of a sexually suggestive song and dance that a sixteenth-century moralist condemned as "so lascivious in its words, so ugly in its movements, that it is enough to inflame even very honest people." In the seventeenth century, however, the sarabande became respectable enough to be danced by a cardinal at the French court.

The movements of a suite are usually in two-part form with each section repeated; that is, in the form A A B B. The A section, which opens in the tonic key and modulates to the dominant, is balanced by the B section, which begins in the dominant and returns to the tonic key. Both sections use the same thematic material, and so they contrast relatively little except in key.

Suites frequently begin with a movement that is *not* dance-inspired. One common opening is the French overture, which is also the type of piece heard at the beginning of baroque oratorios and operas. Usually written in two parts, the **French overture** first presents a slow section with dotted rhythms that is full of dignity and grandeur. The second section is quick and lighter in mood, often beginning like a fugue. Sometimes part of the opening section returns at the end of the overture.

The suite was an important instrumental form in the baroque. Even compositions not called "suite" often have several dance-inspired movements. Music influenced by dance tends to have balanced and symmetrical phrases of the same length, because formal dancing has a set of steps in one direction symmetrically balanced by a similar motion in the opposite direction.

Bach wrote four suites for orchestra. We don't know exactly when they were composed, but it seems likely that the Collegium Musicum performed them in a coffeehouse in Leipzig.

Suite No. 3 in D Major (1729–1731), by Johann Sebastian Bach

First Movement: Overture

Suite No. 3 in D Major—scored for two oboes, three trumpets, timpani, strings, and basso continuo—opens with a majestic French overture, which exploits the bright sounds of trumpets. After a slow opening section with dotted rhythms, we hear the energetic fast section. This begins like a fugue, with an upward-moving theme introduced by the first violins and then imitated by the other instruments.

The fast section is like a concerto grosso in its alternation of solid tutti passages with lightly scored passages highlighting the first violins. After the fast section, the slow tempo, dotted rhythms, and majestic mood of the opening return.

Air
Section A
0:00
Section B
1:14

Second Movement: Air

The second movement, the Air, contains one of Bach's best-loved melodies. It is scored for only strings and continuo and is serene and lyrical, in contrast to the majestic and then bustling French overture. The title suggests that the movement is written in the style of an Italian aria. Like the opening movement, the Air is not related to dance. It is in A A B B form, with the B section twice as long as the A section. The Air combines a steadily moving bass (which proceeds in upward and downward octave leaps) with a rhapsodic and rhythmically irregular melody in the violins.

Third Movement: Gavotte

All the movements that follow the Overture and the Air are inspired by dance, beginning with the Gavotte, which is written in duple meter and in a moderate tempo and uses the full orchestra again. It may be outlined as follows: gavotte I (A A B B); gavotte II (C C D D); gavotte I (A B). Notice the contrast between the sections for full orchestra and those without trumpets and timpani.

Bourrée
Section A
0:00
Section B
0:16

Fourth Movement: Bourrée

The Bourrée is an even livelier dance, also in duple meter; it is the shortest movement of the suite. Its form is A A B B. Section A uses the full orchestra, including trumpets and timpani. Section B is three times as long as section A and alternates loud tutti passages with softer passages for strings and oboes.

Gigue
Section A
0:00
Section B
0:49

Fifth Movement: Gigue

The suite concludes with a rollicking gigue in $\frac{6}{8}$ time, which is also in the form A A B B. Here, Bach's manner is simple and direct. Listen for the splendid effect when timpani and trumpets periodically join the rest of the orchestra.

At the ritornello's closing cadence the sopranos enter and sing the first phrase of the chorale in long notes. Soon the three lower voices engage in an imitative dialogue based on a new motive in shorter note values. Throughout, the orchestra continues to play still shorter notes.

Thus there are three layers of sound: the chorale phrases in long notes in the soprano; the imitative dialogue in shorter note values in the three lower voices; and the ever-busy orchestra playing motives from the ritornello in even shorter notes. The chorale tune (in the soprano) is presented not as a continuous whole but rather phrase by phrase, with breaks between phrases. After each phrase, the voices pause while the orchestra continues to play interludes made up of either the whole ritornello or sections from it. Sometimes the motives in the three lower voices illustrate the text, as when they have rising scale figures at the word *hoch* (*high*) and exclamations at the repeated *wo* (*where*).

Once during the movement, the three lower voices become emancipated from the soprano and jubilantly sing a melody in rapid notes on *Alleluja*. This, perhaps, is the most exciting moment in the movement.

Vocal Music Guide

BACH, Cantata No. 140: *Wachet auf, ruft uns die Stimme (Awake a Voice Is Calling Us;* 1731)

(Duration 6:06)

Listen for the *dotted rhythms* (long-short, long-short) and *syncopations* in the opening orchestral ritornello. Notice the *polyphonic texture* of three simultaneous layers of sound: choral phrases in long notes in the soprano, imitative dialogue in shorter notes in three lower voices, and the orchestra playing in even shorter notes.

First Movement			
Orchestral ritornello.	**0:00**		
Brief orchestral interlude.	**0:28**	*Wachet auf, ruft uns die Stimme*	"Awake," the voice of watchmen
Rising scales in lowervoices depict *hoch (high).* Brief orchestral interlude.	**0:49**	*der Wächter sehr hoch auf der Zinne*	calls us from high on the tower,
Orchestral ritornello.	**1:32**	*wach auf, du Stadt Jerusalem!*	"Awake, you city of Jerusalem!"
Brief orchestral interlude.	**2:00**	*Mitternacht heisst diese Stunde;*	Midnight is this very hour;
Brief orchestral interlude.		*sie rufen uns mit hellem Munde:*	they call to us with bright voices:
Long orchestral interlude.	**3:04**	*wo seid ihr klugen Jungfrauen?*	"Where are you, wise virgins?"
Brief orchestral interlude.		*Wohl auf, der Bräut'gam kömmt,*	Take cheer, the Bridegroom comes,
Altos, jubilant melody in rapid notes. Imitation by tenors, then basses.	**3:56**	*steht auf, die Lampen nehmt! Alleluja!*	arise, take up your lamps! Hallelujah!
Sopranos, chorale in long notes. Orchestral interlude.	**4:22**	*Alleluja!*	Hallelujah!
Orchestral interlude.		*Macht euch bereit*	Prepare yourselves
Brief orchestral interlude.		*zu der Hochzeit*	for the wedding,
Orchestral ritornello.	**5:14**	*ihr müsset ihm entgegen gehn.*	you must go forth to meet him.

1:48	Long repeated tones against quick exclamations; phrases repeated at higher pitches.	{ King of Kings, and Lord of Lords, for ever and ever, Hallelujah, Hallelujah!
2:28	Polyphonic, imitation.	and He shall reign for ever and ever,
2:40	Long repeated tones against quick exclamations. Polyphonic.	King of Kings, and Lord of Lords, for ever and ever, Hallelujah! and He shall reign for ever and ever,
2:55	Homophonic. Polyphonic.	King of Kings, and Lord of Lords, and He shall reign for ever and ever.
3:10	Quick exclamations.	{ King of Kings, and Lord of Lords, for ever and ever, for ever and ever, Hallelujah, Hallelujah, Hallelujah, Hallelujah!
3:20	Pause. Sustained chords, homophonic.	Hallelujah!

The Baroque Period: Summary

Music in Society

- Music was composed to order for specific events.
- The primary areas of employment for musicians were in aristocratic courts, the church, and the opera house. Composers working in aristocratic courts were considered servants.
- Some aristocrats became accomplished musicians.
- Large towns employed musicians for a variety of functions.

Important Style Features

Mood and Emotional Expression

- In instrumental music, a section or entire movement will express one basic mood throughout ("unity of mood").
- In vocal music, changes of mood in the text are often accompanied by changes in the music.

Rhythm

- Rhythmic patterns heard at the beginning of a piece are often repeated throughout.
- The rhythmic pulse is regular, consistent, and strong, typically featuring a constantly moving bass line, even when the music is in a slow tempo.
- The unity of rhythm provides compelling drive and energy that are characteristic of baroque music.

Dynamics

- Terraced dynamics change suddenly rather than gradually and are a major feature of baroque music.

Tone Color

- The basso continuo—consisting of a bass melodic instrument, such as the cello or bassoon; and a keyboard instrument, such as the organ or harpsichord—is one of the most distinctive instrumental features of baroque music.
- The instruments of baroque orchestras, typically ten to forty players, vary from piece to piece.
- Stringed instruments predominate, along with the basso continuo. Woodwind, brass, and percussion instruments are optional and variable in number when used.
- Purely instrumental music grows in importance as a genre throughout the baroque period.

Melody and Harmony

- Melodies are often complex and are not easy to remember on one hearing.
- Melodies recur as a whole or in part throughout a movement or aria.
- Melodies give an impression of continuous expansion, even within a slow tempo.
- Vocal melodies frequently use wide leaps and contain striking chromatic intervals.
- Harmony is based on major and minor scales but may contain passages of striking chromaticism.

IMPORTANT TERMS

Baroque, p. 104
Affections, p. 104
Terraced dynamics, p. 105
Clavichord, p. 105
Basso continuo, p. 106
Figured bass, p. 106
Movement, p. 107
Tutti, p. 110
Ritornello form, p. 110
Ritornello, p. 110
Subject, p. 113
Answer, p. 114
Countersubject, p. 114
Episode, p. 114
Stretto, p. 114
Pedal point (organ point), p. 114
Prelude, p. 114
Libretto, p. 117
Librettist, p. 117
Voice categories of opera, p. 118
Aria, p. 118
Recitative, p. 118
Ensemble, p. 119
Chorus, p. 119
Prompter, p. 119
Overture (prelude), p. 119
Camerata, p. 119
Castrato, p. 120
Countertenor, p. 120
Ground bass, p. 125
Basso ostinato, p. 125
Trill, p. 134
Improvisation, p. 137
French overture, p. 138
Chorale, p. 140
Chorale prelude, p. 140
Da capo aria, p. 147
Da capo, p. 147

FEATURED GENRES

Concerto grosso, p. 110
Fugue, p. 113
Opera, p. 116
Sonata, p. 131
Trio sonata, p. 131
Solo concerto, p. 133

Texture

- In late baroque music, the texture is predominantly polyphonic, with an emphasis on the lowest and highest melodic lines.
- The bass line provides a harmonic foundation for the music, often written as a figured bass that encouraged improvisation.
- Imitation between the individual melodic lines of music is very common.

Baroque Performance Practice

- Performers of baroque music face numerous choices about how they are going to play the music written on the page. Their decisions greatly affect the music you hear.
- Baroque musical scores often do not specify either the instruments to be used in a performance or the exact numbers of performers required, especially in early baroque music. Pay careful attention to the types and number of instruments or voices you hear.
- Improvisation and virtuosity by instrumentalists and vocalists were both expected and greatly prized by baroque audiences. Performing or "realizing" a basso continuo line relies heavily on this practice. Listen carefully for the distinctive sound of the basso continuo, or note if the soloist embellishes the music if a section is repeated.
- Performers of baroque music must choose to perform on either "authentic" period instruments that are typical of those used during the baroque era, or modern instruments that utilize technological advances made since the music was composed.

Design Elements: (Listening Icon): McGraw Hill Education; (Baroque violin): McGraw Hill Education

Alfredo Dagli Orti/Shutterstock

Mozart playing a duet with his sister, Maria Anna, while their father Leopold, listens. A portrait of their late mother, Anna Maria, is seen in the background.

PART IV

I am never happier than when I have something to compose, for that, after all, is my sole delight and passion.

—Wolfgang Amadeus Mozart

The Classical Period

LEARNING OBJECTIVES

- Compare and contrast the classical style and the late baroque style.

- Trace the gradual emancipation of the composer through the careers of Haydn, Mozart, and Beethoven.

- Explain the main elements of sonata form, theme and variations, minuet and trio, and rondo.

- Distinguish the sonata form from the *sonata*.

- Describe a typical symphony of the classical period.

- List the ways in which the classical concerto differs from the classical symphony.

- Discuss the key features of classical chamber music.

- Explain some of the innovative features in Beethoven's music.

Classical Period 1750–1820

1750-1770	1770-1820

Historical and Cultural Events

1756–1763 Seven Years' War

1769 Watt invents steam engine

DEA/A. DAGLI ORTI/De Agostini via Getty Images

1774–1792 Louis XVI reigns in France

1776 American Declaration of Independence

1780–1790 Joseph II reigns in Austria

1789 French Revolution begins

1799 Napoleon becomes first consul of France

1803–1815 Napoleonic Wars

1814–1815 Congress of Vienna

VCG Wilson/Corbis/Getty Images

Arts and Letters

1751 Publication of the French *Encyclopedia* begins

1759 Voltaire, *Candide*

1762 Rousseau, *The Social Contract*

1776 Fragonard, *The Swing*

1784 David, *Oath of Horatii*

1800 David, *Napoleon at St. Bernard*

1808 Goethe, *Faust*

1813 Austen, *Pride and Prejudice*

1814 Goya, *The Third of May, 1808*

1819 Scott, *Ivanhoe*

DEA PICTURE LIBRARY/De Agostini via Getty Images

Music

c. 1757 Haydn, String Quartets, Op. 1

1759 Haydn, Symphony No. 1 in D Major

1764 Mozart, Symphony No. 1 in E Flat Major, K. 16

1772 Haydn, Symphony No. 45 in F Sharp Minor (*Farewell*)

1787 Mozart, *Don Giovanni* and *Eine kleine Nachtmusik*

1788 Mozart, Symphony No. 40 in G Minor, K. 550

1791 Haydn, Symphony No. 94 (*Surprise*)

1796 Haydn, Trumpet Concerto in E Flat Major

1798 Beethoven, Piano Sonata in C Minor, Op. 13 (*Pathétique*)

1808 Beethoven, Symphony No. 5 in C Minor

1824 Beethoven, Symphony No. 9 in D Minor (*Choral*)

Fine Art Images/Heritage Images/Getty Images

Universal History Archive/UIG/Shutterstock

The Classical Era
(1750–1820)

In looking at the baroque era, we found that the scientific methods and discoveries of geniuses like Galileo and Newton vastly changed people's view of the world. By the middle of the eighteenth century, faith in the power of reason was so great that it began to undermine the authority of the social and religious establishment. Philosophers and writers—especially Voltaire (1694–1778) and Denis Diderot (1713–1784)—saw their time as a turning point in history and referred to it as the "age of enlightenment." They believed in progress, holding that reason, not custom or tradition, was the best guide for human conduct. Their attacks on the privileges of the aristocracy and clergy reflected the outlook of the middle class, which was struggling for its rights.

The ideas of enlightenment thinkers were implemented by several rulers during the eighteenth century. For example, Emperor Joseph II of Austria, who reigned from 1780 to 1790, abolished serfdom, closed monasteries and convents, and eliminated the nobility's special status in criminal law. He discouraged elaborate religious ceremonies and decreed that burials be simple; though this decree was soon revoked, modest funerals became customary in Vienna. In 1791, Wolfgang Amadeus Mozart—one of the greatest composers of the classical period—was buried in a sack in an unmarked communal grave.

Violent political and social upheaval marked the seventy-year period from 1750 to 1820. These years were convulsed by the Seven Years' War, the American and French revolutions, and the Napoleonic Wars. Political and economic power shifted from the aristocracy and church to the middle class. Social mobility increased to a point that Napoleon could become emperor of France by his own genius rather than as a birthright. "Subversive" new slogans like *Liberty, equality, fraternity!* sprang from the people's lips. All established ideas were being reexamined, including the existence of God.

Revolutions in thought and action were paralleled by shifts in style in the visual arts. During the early eighteenth century, the heavy, monumental baroque style gave way to the more intimate *rococo* style, with its light colors, curved lines, and graceful ornaments. The painters Antoine Watteau (1684–1721) and Jean-Honoré Fragonard (1732–1806) depicted an enchanted world peopled by elegant men and women in

The rococo painter Jean-Honoré Fragonard portrayed the game of love in *The Swing* (1776).
The Print Collector/Getty Images

In the *Oath of the Horatii* (1784), the neoclassical painter Jacques-Louis David depicted Romans swearing loyalty to their cause.

VCG Wilson/Corbis via Getty Images

Monticello, Thomas Jefferson's home, shows the influence of ancient Greek and Roman architecture.

PhotoLink/Photodisc/Getty Images

constant pursuit of pleasure. But by the later eighteenth century there was yet another change in taste, and rococo art was thought frivolous, excessively ornamented, and lacking in ethical content. The rococo style was superseded by the *neoclassical* style, which attempted to recapture the "noble simplicity and calm grandeur" of ancient Greek and Roman art. Neoclassical artists emphasized firm lines, clear structure, and moralistic subject matter. The painter Jacques-Louis David (1748–1825), who took part in the French Revolution, sought to inspire heroism and patriotism through his scenes of ancient Rome.

The artistic response to the decline of traditional power is evidenced further by the English painter William Hogarth (1697–1764), whose socially conscious paintings satirized the manners and morals of the British aristocracy and middle class; and by the Spanish painter Francisco Goya (1746–1828), who used his highly personal vision to create art that lashed out against hypocrisy, oppression, and inhumanity.

Napoleon at St. Bernard (1800) by Jacques-Louis David. Beethoven originally planned to name his Third Symphony (*Eroica,* 1803–1804) "Bonaparte," because he saw Napoleon as an embodiment of heroism; but when he learned that Napoleon had proclaimed himself emperor, Beethoven tore out the title page and later renamed the symphony "Heroic Symphony composed to celebrate the memory of a great man."
VCG Wilson/Corbis/Getty Images

The Third of May, 1808 by the Spanish artist Francisco Goya. The classical period was a time of violent political and social upheaval, witnessing the American Revolution, the French Revolution, and the Napoleonic wars. In 1814 Goya painted this vivid scene of the execution of Spanish hostages by Napoleon's soldiers.
Universal History Archive/UIG/Shutterstock

1 The Classical Style (1750–1820)

In music history, the transition from the baroque style to the full flowering of the classical is called the *preclassical* period; it extends from roughly 1730 to 1770. The shift in musical taste parallels the similar, earlier trend in the visual arts. It was developing even as Bach and Handel were creating baroque masterpieces. Among the important pioneers in this new style were Bach's sons Carl Philipp Emanuel (1714–1788) and Johann Christian (1735–1782). Around the middle of the eighteenth century, composers concentrated on simplicity and clarity, discarding much that had enriched late baroque music. Polyphonic texture was neglected in favor of tuneful melody and simple harmony. Carl Philipp Emanuel Bach described music with strict polyphonic imitation as "dry and despicable pieces of pedantry." Mid-eighteenth-century composers entertained their listeners with music offering contrasts of mood and theme. The term *style galant* (*gallant style*) was applied to this light, graceful music. The *style galant* in music is comparable to the rococo style in art.

The term *classical* is confusing because it has so many meanings. It may refer to Greek or Roman antiquity, or it may be used for any supreme accomplishment of lasting appeal (as in the expression *movie classic*). Many people take *classical music* to mean anything that is not rock, jazz, folk, or popular music.

Music historians have borrowed the term *classical* from art history, where it is more appropriate. The painting, sculpture, and architecture of the late eighteenth century and the early nineteenth century were often influenced by Greek and Roman models. But the music of this period shows little direct relation to antiquity. The significant parallel between "classical" music and "neoclassical" art is a common stress on balance and clarity of structure. These traits can be found in the fully developed *classical style* in music, which is our focus. That style flourished from about 1770 to 1820, and its master composers were Joseph Haydn (1732–1809), Wolfgang Amadeus Mozart (1756–1791), and Ludwig van Beethoven (1770–1827). First, we study the characteristics of their work.

Characteristics of the Classical Style

Contrast of Mood Great variety and contrast of mood received new emphasis in classical music. Whereas a late baroque piece may convey a single emotion, a classical composition fluctuates in mood. Dramatic, turbulent music might lead into a carefree dance tune. Not only are there contrasting themes within a movement, but there may also be striking contrasts within a single theme.

Mood in classical music may change gradually or suddenly, expressing conflicting surges of elation and depression. But such conflict and contrast are under the firm control of the classical composer. Masters like Haydn, Mozart, and Beethoven were able to impart unity and logic to music of wide emotional range.

Rhythm Flexibility of rhythm adds variety to classical music. A classical composition has a wealth of rhythmic patterns, whereas a baroque piece contains a few patterns that are reiterated throughout. Baroque works convey a sense of continuity and perpetual motion, so that after the first few bars one can predict pretty well the rhythmic character of an entire movement. But the classical style also includes unexpected pauses, syncopations, and frequent changes from long notes to shorter notes. And the change from one pattern of note lengths to another may be either sudden or gradual.

Texture In contrast to the polyphonic texture of late baroque music, classical music is basically homophonic. However, texture is treated as flexibly as rhythm. Pieces shift smoothly or suddenly from one texture to another. A work may begin homophonically with a melody and simple accompaniment but then change to a more complex polyphonic texture that features two simultaneous melodies or melodic fragments imitated among the various instruments.

Melody Classical melodies are among the most tuneful and easiest to remember. The themes of even highly sophisticated compositions may have a folk or popular flavor. Occasionally, composers simply borrowed popular tunes. (Mozart did, in his variations on the French song *Ah, vous dirai-je, maman,* which we know as *Twinkle, Twinkle, Little Star.*) More often, however, they wrote original themes with a popular character.

Classical melodies tend to sound balanced and symmetrical because they are frequently made up of two phrases of the same length. The second phrase in such melodies may begin like the first, but it ends more conclusively. Such a melodic type, which may be diagrammed a a', is easy to sing. (It is frequently found in nursery tunes such as *Mary Had a Little Lamb.*) Baroque melodies, in contrast, tend to be less symmetrical, more elaborate, and harder to sing.

Dynamics and the Piano Classical composers' interest in expressing shades of emotion led to the widespread use of gradual dynamic change—crescendo and decrescendo. These composers did not restrict themselves to the terraced dynamics (abrupt shifts from loud to soft) characteristic of baroque music. Crescendos and decrescendos were an electrifying novelty; audiences sometimes rose excitedly from their seats.

During the classical period, the desire for gradual dynamic change led to the replacement of the harpsichord by the piano. By varying the finger pressure on the keys, a pianist can play more loudly or softly. Although the piano was invented around 1700, it began to replace the harpsichord only around 1775. Most of the mature keyboard compositions of Haydn, Mozart, and Beethoven were written for the piano, rather than for harpsichord, clavichord, and organ, which had been featured in baroque music. The late eighteenth-century piano—called a *fortepiano*—weighed much less than the modern piano and had thinner strings held by a frame made of wood rather than metal. Its pitch range was smaller, and its tone was smaller and lasted a shorter time.

The End of the Basso Continuo The basso continuo was gradually abandoned during the classical period. In Haydn's or Mozart's works, a harpsichordist did not need to improvise an accompaniment. One reason the basso continuo became obsolete was that more and more music was written for amateurs, who could not master the difficult art of improvising from a figured bass. Also, classical composers wanted more control; they preferred to specify an accompaniment rather than trust the judgment of improvisers.

The Classical Orchestra

A new orchestra evolved during the classical period. Unlike the baroque orchestra, which could vary from piece to piece, it was a standard group of four sections: strings, woodwinds, brass, and percussion. In the late instrumental works of Mozart and Haydn, an orchestra might consist of the following:

> *Strings:* 1st violins, 2d violins, violas, cellos, double basses
> *Woodwinds:* 2 flutes, 2 oboes, 2 clarinets, 2 bassoons
> *Brass:* 2 French horns, 2 trumpets
> *Percussion:* 2 timpani

Notice that woodwind and brass instruments are paired and that clarinets have been added. Trombones were also used by Haydn and Mozart, but only in opera and church music, not in solely instrumental works.

The number of musicians was greater in a classical orchestra than in a baroque group, though practice varied considerably from place to place. Haydn directed a private orchestra of only twenty-five players from 1761 to 1790. But for public concerts in London in 1795, he led an orchestra of sixty.

Classical composers exploited the individual tone colors of orchestral instruments. Unlike baroque composers, they did not treat one instrument like another. Classical composers would not let an oboe duplicate the violin melody for the entire length of a movement. A classical piece has greater variety—and more rapid changes—of tone color. A theme might begin in the full orchestra, shift to the strings, and then continue in the woodwinds.

Each section of the classical orchestra had a special role. The strings were the most important section, with the first violins taking the melody most of the time and the lower strings providing an accompaniment. The woodwinds added contrasting tone colors and were often given melodic solos. Horns and trumpets brought power to loud passages and filled out the harmony, but they did not usually play the main melody. Timpani were used for rhythmic bite and emphasis. As a whole, the classical orchestra had developed into a flexible and colorful instrument to which composers could entrust their most powerful and dramatic musical conceptions.

Classical Forms

Instrumental compositions of the classical period usually consist of several movements that contrast in tempo and character. There are often four movements, arranged as follows:

1. Fast movement
2. Slow movement
3. Dance-related movement
4. Fast movement

Classical symphonies and string quartets usually follow this four-movement pattern, whereas classical sonatas may consist of two, three, or four movements. A *symphony* is written for orchestra; a *string quartet* for two violins, viola, and cello; and a *sonata* for one or two instruments. (The classical symphony, string quartet, and sonata are more fully described in Chapters 3 to 7 and 9.)

In writing an individual movement of a symphony, string quartet, or sonata, a classical composer could choose from several forms. One movement of a composition might be in A B A form, whereas another might be a theme and variations. The sections that follow describe some forms used in classical movements, but now let's look at a few general characteristics of classical form.

Classical movements often contrast themes vividly. A movement may contain two, three, or even four or more themes of different character. This use of contrasting themes distinguishes classical music from baroque music, which often uses only one main theme. The classical composer sometimes uses a brief pause to signal the arrival of a new theme.

The larger sections of a classical movement balance each other in a satisfying and symmetrical way. Unstable sections that wander from the tonic key are balanced by stable sections that confirm it. By the end of a classical movement, musical tensions have been resolved.

Though we speak of the classical style, we must remember that Haydn, Mozart, and Beethoven were three individuals with dissimilar personalities. Although Haydn's and Mozart's works may sound similar at first, deeper involvement reveals striking personal styles. Beethoven's music seems more powerful, violent, and emotional when compared with the apparently more restrained and elegant works of the earlier masters. But Haydn and Mozart also composed music that is passionate and dramatic. We'll see that all three composers used similar musical procedures and forms, yet their emotional statements bear the particular stamp of each.

2 Composer, Patron, and Public in the Classical Period

Haydn, Mozart, and Beethoven—three of the world's greatest composers—worked during a period of violent political and social upheaval, as we have seen in the opening of Part IV. Like everyone else, musicians were strongly affected by changes in society, and in the careers of the three classical masters we can trace the slow emancipation of the composer. First came Joseph Haydn (1732–1809), who was content to spend most of his life serving a wealthy aristocratic family. His contract of employment (1761) shows that he was considered a skilled servant, like a gardener or gamekeeper. He had to wear a uniform and "compose such music as His Highness shall order"—and was warned to "refrain from vulgarity in eating, drinking, and conversation." Wolfgang Amadeus Mozart (1756–1791), born just twenty-four years later, could not bear being treated as a servant; he broke from his court position and went to Vienna to try his luck as a freelance musician. For several years he was very successful, but then his popularity declined; he died in debt. Ludwig van Beethoven (1770–1827) fared better than Mozart. Only a few years after Mozart's death, Beethoven was able to work as an independent musician in Vienna. His success was gained through a wider middle-class market for music and a commanding personality that prompted the nobility to give him gifts and treat him as an equal.

As the eighteenth century advanced, more people made more money. Merchants, doctors, and government officials could afford larger homes, finer clothes, and better food. But the prospering middle class wanted more than material goods; it also sought aristocratic luxuries such as theater, literature, and music. In fact, during the classical period, the middle class had a great influence on music. Because palace concerts were usually closed to them, townspeople organized public concerts, where, for the price of admission, they could hear the latest symphonies and concertos. During the second half of the eighteenth century, public concerts mushroomed throughout Europe. In London, a concert series ran from 1765 to 1781, codirected by one of Bach's sons, Johann Christian Bach, who had settled in England. In Paris, around the same time, a concert organization called the *Concert des Amateurs* assembled a large orchestra, conducted during the 1770s by the Chevalier de Saint-Georges (1739–1799), a Black composer and violinist who was a champion fencer as well.

But merchants and lawyers were not content to hear music only in concerts. They wanted to be surrounded by music at home. They felt that their sons and daughters deserved music lessons as much as the children of aristocrats did. Indeed, if middle-class children played instruments well enough, they might be invited to palaces and

During the classical period, many members of the aristocracy and the wealthy middle class were good musicians. Johann Zoffany (1733–1810), *George, Third Earl Cowper with the Family of Charles Gore* (c. 1775).
Fine Art Images/Heritage Images/Getty Images

eventually marry into the aristocracy. In any event, the demand for printed music, instruments, and music lessons had vastly increased.

Composers in the classical period took middle-class tastes into account. They wrote pieces that were easy for amateur musicians to play and understand. They turned from serious to comic opera, from the heroic and mythological plots dear to the nobility to middle-class subjects and folklike tunes. Their comic operas sometimes even ridiculed the aristocracy, and their dance movements became less elegant and courtly, more vigorous and rustic.

Serious composition was flavored by folk and popular music. The classical masters sometimes used familiar tunes as themes for symphonies and variations. Mozart was delighted that people danced to waltzes arranged from melodies in his operas. Haydn, Mozart, and Beethoven all wrote dance music for public balls in Vienna.

Vienna

Vienna was one of the music centers of Europe during the classical period, and Haydn, Mozart, and Beethoven were all active there. As the seat of the Holy Roman Empire (which included parts of modern Austria, Germany, Italy, Hungary, and the Czech Republic), it was a bustling cultural and commercial center with a cosmopolitan character. Its population of almost 250,000 (in 1800) made Vienna the fourth largest city in Europe. All three classical masters were born elsewhere, but they were drawn to Vienna to study and to seek recognition. In Vienna, Haydn and Mozart became close friends and influenced each other's musical style. Beethoven traveled to Vienna at sixteen to play for Mozart; at twenty-two, he returned to study with Haydn.

Most of Haydn's music was composed for a wealthy aristocratic family. Shown here is a performance of a comic opera by Haydn in 1775 at the palace Eszterhaza.
akg-images/Newscom

Aristocrats from all over the empire would spend winters in Vienna, sometimes bringing their private orchestras. Music was an important part of court life, and a good orchestra was a symbol of prestige. Many of the nobility were excellent musicians. For instance, Empress Maria Theresa had sung in palace musicales when she was young, Emperor Joseph II was a competent cellist, and Archduke Rudolf was Beethoven's longtime student of piano and composition.

Much music was heard in private concerts, where aristocrats and wealthy commoners played alongside professional musicians. Mozart and Beethoven often earned money by performing in these intimate concerts. The nobility frequently hired servants who could double as musicians. An advertisement in the *Vienna Gazette* of 1789 reads: "Wanted, for a house of the gentry, a manservant who knows how to play the violin well."

In Vienna there was also outdoor music, light and popular in tone. Small street bands of wind and string players played at garden parties or under the windows of people likely to throw down money. A Viennese almanac reported that "on fine summer nights you may come upon serenades in the streets at all hours." Haydn and Mozart wrote many outdoor entertainment pieces, which they called *divertimentos* or *serenades*. Vienna's great love of music and its enthusiastic demand for new works made it the chosen city of Haydn, Mozart, and Beethoven.

3 Sonata Form

An astonishing amount of important music from the classical period to the twentieth century was composed in sonata form (sometimes called *sonata-allegro form*). The term **sonata form** refers to the form of a *single* movement. It should not be confused with the term *sonata,* which is used for a whole composition made up of *several* movements. The opening fast movement of a classical symphony, sonata, or string quartet is usually in sonata form. This form is also used in slow movements and in fast concluding movements.

A sonata-form movement consists of three main sections: the exposition, where the themes are presented; the development, where themes are treated in new ways; and the recapitulation, where the themes return. These three main sections are often followed by a concluding section, the coda (Italian for *tail*). Remember that these sections are all within *one movement.* A *single* sonata-form movement may be outlined as follows:

Exposition
First theme in tonic (home) key
Bridge containing modulation from home key to new key
Second theme in new key
Closing section in key of second theme

Development
New treatment of themes; modulations to different keys

Recapitulation
First theme in tonic key
Bridge
Second theme in tonic key
Closing section in tonic key

Coda
In tonic key

A fast movement in sonata form is sometimes preceded by a slow introduction that creates a strong feeling of expectancy.

5 Minuet and Trio

The form known as **minuet and trio,** or **minuet,** is often used as the third movement of classical symphonies, string quartets, and other works. Like the movements of the baroque suite, the minuet originated as a dance. It first appeared at the court of Louis XIV of France around 1650 and was danced by aristocrats throughout the eighteenth century. The minuet was a stately, dignified dance in which the dancing couple exchanged curtsies and bows.

The minuet movement of a symphony or string quartet is written for listening, not dancing. It is in triple meter ($\frac{3}{4}$) and usually in a moderate tempo. The movement is in A B A form: minuet (A), trio (B), minuet (A). The trio (B) is usually quieter than the minuet (A) section and requires fewer instruments. It often contains woodwind solos. The trio section got its name during the baroque period, when a set of two dances would be followed by a repetition of the first dance. The second dance was known as a "trio" because it was usually played by three instruments. Classical composers did not restrict themselves to three instruments in the B sections of their minuets, but the name *trio* remained.

The A (minuet) section includes smaller parts a, b, and a′ (variation of a). In the opening A (minuet) section, all the smaller parts are repeated, as follows: a (repeated) ba′ (repeated). (In the musical score, the repeat sign ⦙ indicates each repetition.) The B (trio) section is quite similar in form: c (repeated) dc′ (repeated). At the close of the B (trio) section, the repetition of the entire A (minuet) section is indicated by the words **da capo** (*from the beginning*). This time, however, the minuet is played straight through without the repetitions: a ba′. The whole movement can be outlined like this:

Minuet	Trio	Minuet
A	B	A
a (repeated) ba′ (repeated)	c (repeated) dc′ (repeated)	a ba′

With its A B A form and its many repeated parts, the minuet is structurally the simplest movement of a symphony or string quartet.

In many of Beethoven's compositions, the third movement is not a minuet but a related form called a *scherzo*. Like a minuet, a **scherzo** is usually in A B A form and triple meter, but it moves more quickly, generating energy, rhythmic drive, and rough humor. (*Scherzo* is Italian for *joke*.)

Eine kleine Nachtmusik (A Little Night Music; 1787), K. 525, by Wolfgang Amadeus Mozart

Third Movement:
Minuet (Allegretto)

Mozart's *Eine kleine Nachtmusik* is a **serenade,** a work that's usually light in mood, meant for evening entertainment. It is written for a small string orchestra or for a string quartet plus a double bass. (The double bass plays the cello part an octave lower.) The third movement is a courtly minuet in A B A form. The A (minuet) section is stately, mostly loud and staccato, with a clearly marked beat. In contrast, the B (trio) section is intimate, soft, and legato. Its murmuring accompaniment contributes to the smooth flow of the music.

Listening Outline

MOZART, *Eine kleine Nachtmusik (A Little Night Music; 1787), K. 525*

Third Movement: Minuet (Allegretto)

A B A form, triple meter ($\frac{3}{4}$), G major

1st violins, 2d violins, violas, cellos, double basses

(Duration 2:03)

Listen for the *A B A form* and *triple meter* of this minuet and trio for string orchestra. Notice the contrast in *dynamics* and *melody* between the stately minuet section, which is loud and *staccato*, and the intimate trio section, which is soft and *legato*.

Minuet (A)

0:00   1. Stately melody, *f*, predominantly staccato. Repeated.

Legato phrase, *p*, leads to stately staccato phrase, *f*. Repeated.

Trio (B)

0:42   2. Gracious legato melody, *p*, murmuring accompaniment. Repeated.

Climbing legato phrase, *f*, leads to legato melody, *p*. Repeated.

Minuet (A)

1:39   3. Stately melody, *f*, predominantly staccato. Legato phrase, *p*, leads to stately staccato phrase, *f*.

6 Rondo

Many classical movements are in rondo form. A **rondo** features a tuneful main theme (A) that returns several times in alternation with other themes. Common rondo patterns are A B A C A and A B A C A B A. The main theme is usually lively, pleasing, and simple to remember, and the listener can easily recognize its return. Because the main theme is usually stated in the tonic key, its return is all the more welcome. The rondo can be used either as an independent piece or as one movement of a symphony, string quartet, or sonata. It often serves as a finale, because its liveliness, regularity, and buoyancy bring a happy sense of conclusion.

Rondo form is often combined with elements of sonata form to produce a sonata-rondo. The **sonata-rondo** contains a development section like that in sonata form and is outlined A B A—development section—A B A.

The popularity of the rondo did not end with the classical period. It was used by twentieth-century composers, such as Igor Stravinsky and Arnold Schoenberg.

String Quartet in C Minor, Op. 18, No. 4 (1798–1800), by Ludwig van Beethoven

Fourth Movement: Rondo (Allegro)

The exciting rondo movement from Beethoven's String Quartet in C Minor, Op. 18, No. 4, may be outlined A B A C A B A. Its lively main theme, A, in the style of a Gypsy dance, is made up of two repeated parts: a a b b. An unexpected held tone in part b suggests the improvisatory playing of a Gypsy fiddler. The main theme, in minor, contrasts with the other themes, which are in major. Theme B is a lyrical legato melody. Theme C is playful, with quick upward rushes. At its final return, the main theme (A) has a faster tempo, prestissimo, and leads into a frenzied concluding section.

Listening Outline

BEETHOVEN, String Quartet in C Minor, Op. 18, No. 4 (1798–1800)

Fourth Movement: Rondo (Allegro)

Duple meter (²₂), C minor

1st violin, 2d violin, viola, cello

(Duration 4:08)

Listen for the rondo form—A B A C A B A—in this concluding movement of a string quartet. Notice the contrast between the energetic main theme (A), in *minor,* and the lyrical *legato* theme B and playful theme C, both in *major keys.*

A

0:00   **1.** Lively main theme in 1st violin, minor key.

B

0:29   **2.** Lyrical melody, legato, major key.

A

1:14   **3.** Lively main theme, minor key. Theme becomes more agitated.

C

1:42   **4.** Upward rushes in each instrument, playful downward phrase in 1st violin, major key.

A

2:05   **5.** Lively main theme, minor key. Crescendo to held chord, *ff*.

B

2:43   **6.** Lyrical melody, legato, major key. Melody repeated an octave higher. Playful phrases in violins, crescendo to *f*, sustained tones in 1st violin.

A

3:26   **7.** Lively main theme, *ff*, faster tempo (prestissimo), minor key. Concluding section builds, downward staccato scale, high repeated tones, *p*. Upward rushes, *ff*, at end.

7 The Classical Symphony

The great contribution of the classical period to orchestral music is the symphony. Haydn wrote at least 104 symphonies, Mozart more than 40, and Beethoven 9. Most of Haydn's symphonies were composed for his employers, who required a steady flow of works for their palace concerts. Beethoven, on the other hand, wrote a symphony only when inspired. His symphonies are longer than Haydn's or Mozart's and were conceived for performance in large concert halls.

A *symphony* is an extended, ambitious composition typically lasting between twenty and forty-five minutes, exploiting the expanded range of tone color and dynamics of the classical orchestra. A classical symphony usually consists of four movements that evoke a wide range of emotions through contrasts of tempo and mood. A typical sequence is (1) a vigorous, dramatic fast movement; (2) a lyrical slow movement; (3) a dancelike movement (minuet or scherzo); and (4) a brilliant or heroic fast movement.

The opening movement is almost always fast and in sonata form. It is usually the most dramatic movement and stresses an exciting development of short motives. Sometimes a slow introduction leads to the opening fast movement and creates a feeling of anticipation.

It is in the slow second movement that we are most likely to find broad, song-like melodies. This movement, by and large, is in either sonata form, A B A form, or theme-and-variations form. Unlike the other movements in the symphony, the slow movement is generally *not* in the tonic key. For example, if the first, third, and fourth movements are in the tonic key of C major, the second movement may be in F major. The new key points up the expressive contrast of the slow movement.

In the symphonies of Haydn and Mozart, the third movement is generally a minuet and trio, which may be in a moderate or fairly quick tempo. This movement varies in character from a courtly dance to a peasant romp or a vigorous piece that is hardly dancelike. Beethoven liked fast, energetic scherzos for his third movements.

The fourth, concluding movement of a symphony by Haydn or Mozart is fast, lively, and brilliant, but somewhat lighter in mood than the opening movement. (The agitated final movement of Mozart's Symphony No. 40 in G Minor is not typical.) Beethoven's concluding movement tends to be more triumphant and heroic in character and is sometimes meant as the climax of the whole symphony. The final movement of a classical symphony is most often in sonata or sonata-rondo form.

In most classical symphonies, each movement is a self-contained composition with its own set of themes. A theme in one movement will only rarely reappear in a later movement. (Beethoven's Fifth and Ninth Symphonies are exceptions.) But a symphony is unified partly by the use of the same key in three of its movements. More important, the movements balance and complement each other both musically and emotionally.

The importance of the symphony lasted throughout the twentieth century and into the twenty-first. Its great significance is reflected in such familiar terms as *symphonic music, symphony hall,* and *symphony orchestra.*

8 The Classical Concerto

A classical ***concerto*** is a three-movement work for an instrumental soloist and orchestra. It combines the soloist's virtuosity and interpretive abilities with the orchestra's wide range of tone color and dynamics. Emerging from this encounter is a contrast of ideas and sound that is dramatic and satisfying. The soloist is very much the star, and all of his or her musical talents are needed in this challenging dialogue.

The classical love of balance can be seen in the concerto, because soloist and orchestra are equally important. Between them, there's an interplay of melodic lines and a spirit of give-and-take. One moment the soloist plays the melody while the orchestra accompanies. Then the woodwinds may unfold the main theme against rippling arpeggios (broken chords) played by the soloist. Mozart and Beethoven—the greatest masters of the classical concerto—often wrote concertos for themselves to play as piano soloists; the piano is their favored solo instrument. But other solo instruments used in classical concertos include violin, cello, horn, trumpet, clarinet, and bassoon.

Like symphonies, concertos can last anywhere from twenty minutes to forty-five minutes. But instead of the symphony's four movements, a classical concerto has three: (1) fast, (2) slow, and (3) fast. A concerto has no minuet or scherzo.

In the first movement and sometimes in the last movement, there is a special unaccompanied showpiece for the soloist, the ***cadenza*** (Italian for *cadence*). Near the end of the movement, the orchestra suspends forward motion by briefly sustaining a dissonant chord. This is indicated in the score by a *fermata* (⌢), a sign meaning *pause,* which is placed over the chord. The suspense announces the entry of the soloist's cadenza. For several minutes, the soloist, *without orchestra,* displays virtuosity by playing dazzling scale passages and broken chords. Themes of the movement are varied and presented in new keys. At the end of a cadenza, the soloist plays a long trill followed by a chord that meshes with the reentrance of the orchestra.

In the classical era, the soloist, who was often the composer, generally improvised the cadenzas. In this case, the score contained only the fermata, indicating where the cadenza should be inserted. But after the eighteenth century, the art of improvisation declined, and composers began to write cadenzas directly into the score. This gave them more control over their compositions.

Today, performers of eighteenth-century concertos may have a choice of cadenzas. For some concertos, composers wrote cadenzas for their own performance or for that of a student. Also, many nineteenth-, twentieth-, and early twenty-first-century musicians later provided cadenzas for classical concertos. These are best when their style matches that of the concerto. For example, the cadenzas Beethoven composed for Mozart's D Minor Piano Concerto are so strong and so much in the spirit of the work that pianists still use them today.

A classical concerto begins with a movement in sonata form of a special kind, containing *two* expositions. The first is played by the orchestra, which presents several themes in the home key. This opening section sets the mood for the movement and leads us to expect the soloist's entrance. The second exposition begins with the soloist's first notes. Music for the solo entry may be powerful or quiet, but its effect is dramatic because suspense has been built. Together with the orchestra, the soloist explores themes from the first exposition and introduces new ones. After a modulation from the home key to a new key, the second exposition then moves to a development section, followed by the recapitulation, cadenza, and coda. The slow middle movement may take any one of several forms, but the finale is usually a quick rondo or sonata-rondo.

9 Classical Chamber Music

Classical *chamber music* is designed for the intimate setting of a room (chamber) in a home or palace, rather than for a public concert hall. It is performed by a small group of two to nine musicians, with one player to a part. Chamber music is lighter in sound than classical orchestral music. During the classical period, it was fashionable for an aristocrat or a member of the well-to-do middle-class to play chamber music with friends and to hire professional musicians to entertain guests after dinner.

Chamber music is subtle and intimate, intended to please the performer as much as the listener. A chamber music group is a team. Each member is essential, and each may have an important share of the thematic material. Therefore much give-and-take is called for among the instruments. Classical chamber music does not need a conductor; instead, each musician must be sensitive to what goes on and must coordinate dynamics and phrasing with the other musicians. In this respect, a chamber ensemble is like a small jazz group.

The most important form in classical chamber music is the *string quartet,* written for two violins, a viola, and a cello. Haydn, Mozart, and Beethoven wrote some of their most important music in this form. The string quartet can be compared to a conversation among four lively, sensitive, and intelligent people. It's not surprising that the string quartet evolved when conversation was cultivated as a fine art.

Like a symphony, a string quartet usually consists of four movements: (1) fast, (2) slow, (3) minuet or scherzo, (4) fast. (Sometimes the second movement is a minuet or a scherzo, and the slow movement is third.)

Other popular forms of classical chamber music are the sonata for violin and piano; the piano trio (violin, cello, and piano); and the string quintet (two violins, two violas, and cello).

Today, as in the eighteenth century, much chamber music is performed by amateurs. By consulting the Internet or the directory *Amateur Chamber Music Players,* one can find partners for chamber music almost anywhere in the United States.

10 Joseph Haydn

Joseph Haydn (1732–1809) was born in a tiny Austrian village called Rohrau. Until he was six, his musical background consisted of folksongs and peasant dances (which later had an influence on his style). Haydn's eager response to music was recognized, and he was given training. At the age of eight, he went to Vienna to serve as a choirboy in the Cathedral of St. Stephen. When his voice changed, Haydn was dismissed, penniless, from St. Stephen's. He gave music lessons to children, struggled to teach

Haydn was a pathfinder for the classical style, a pioneer in the development of the symphony and string quartet.
DEA PICTURE LIBRARY/De Agostini via Getty Images

himself composition, and took odd jobs, including playing violin in street bands. Gradually, aristocratic patrons of music began to notice Haydn's talent. In 1761, when he was twenty-nine, his life changed for the better, permanently: he entered the service of the Esterházys, the richest and most powerful of the Hungarian noble families. For almost thirty years, most of his music was composed for performance in the palaces of the family, especially Eszterháza, which contained an opera house, a theater, two concert halls, and 126 guest rooms.

As a highly skilled servant, Haydn was to compose all the music requested by his patron, conduct the orchestra, coach singers, and oversee the instruments and the music library. This entailed a staggering amount of work; there were usually two concerts and two opera performances weekly, as well as daily chamber music. Though today this sort of patronage seems degrading, it was taken for granted at the time and had definite advantages for composers. They received a steady income and their works were performed. Haydn was conscientious about his professional duties, concerned about his musicians' interest, and—despite an unhappy marriage—good-humored and unselfish. Word spread about the Esterházys' composer, and Haydn's music became immensely popular all over Europe. In 1791–1792 and again in 1794–1795, Haydn went to London. Reports of the time say that his appearances were triumphs. (The twelve symphonies he composed for these visits are now known as the *London Symphonies*.) A servant had become a celebrity. Haydn was wined and dined by the aristocracy, given an honorary doctorate at Oxford, and received by the royal family.

In 1795, he returned to Vienna rich and honored. In his late sixties, he composed six masses and two oratorios, *The Creation* (1798) and *The Seasons* (1801). They were so popular that choruses and orchestras were formed for the sole purpose of performing them.

He died in 1809, at the age of seventy-seven.

Haydn's Music

Haydn was a pathfinder for the classical style, a pioneer in the development of the symphony and string quartet. Both Mozart and Beethoven were influenced by his style. Haydn's music, like his personality, is robust and direct; it radiates a healthy optimism. Much of it has a folk flavor, and *The Creation* and *The Seasons* reflect his love of nature. Haydn was a master at developing themes. He could build a whole movement out of a single main theme, creating contrasts of mood through changes in texture, key, rhythm, dynamics, and orchestration. The contagious joy that springs from his lively rhythms and vivid contrasts makes it clear why London went wild.

"I prefer to see the humorous side of life," Haydn once said. He produced comic effects from unexpected pauses and tempo changes and from sudden shifts in dynamics and pitch. We've heard one of his musical jokes in the second movement of the *Surprise* Symphony, where a soft theme is suddenly punctuated by a loud chord.

Haydn's 104 symphonies—along with his 68 string quartets—are considered the most important part of his enormous output. Many of them have nicknames, such as *Surprise* (No. 94), *Military* (No. 100), *Clock* (No. 101), and *Drum Roll* (No. 103).

Some scholars believe that Haydn invented the string quartet form. He began writing string quartets for a good reason—only three other musicians (two violinists and a cellist, in addition to Haydn as a violinist) were on hand during the summer of 1757, when he was invited to take part in chamber music performances at a castle.

Haydn's output also includes piano sonatas, piano trios, divertimentos, concertos, operas, and masses. The variety in his works is astounding. He was a great innovator and experimenter who hated arbitrary "rules" of composition. "Art is free," he said. "The educated ear is the sole authority . . . and I think that I have as much right to lay down the law as anyone."

Trumpet Concerto in E Flat Major (1796)

Haydn's Trumpet Concerto in E Flat Major has a remarkable history. After its premiere in 1800, it was forgotten for almost 130 years. It was first published only in 1929, and in the 1930s a phonograph recording brought it to a wide audience. Now, it may well be Haydn's most popular work.

Haydn wrote the concerto in 1796 for a friend, a trumpeter at the Viennese court who had recently invented a keyed trumpet that could produce a complete chromatic scale. The keyed trumpet was intended to replace the natural trumpet, which could produce only a restricted number of tones. But the keyed trumpet had a dull sound and was supplanted by the valve trumpet around 1840. Today, the concerto is performed on a valve trumpet. Like most concertos, it has three movements: (1) fast, (2) slow, (3) fast. We examine the third movement.

Third Movement: Allegro

The third movement is a dazzling sonata-rondo in which Haydn gives the trumpeter's virtuosity free rein. The movement combines the recurring main theme characteristic of rondo form with the development section found in sonata form. It may be outlined as A B A B′ A—development section—A B″—coda.

Themes A and B are introduced by the orchestra and are then presented mainly by the trumpet, with orchestral support. The main theme (A) is a high-spirited melody that is well suited to the trumpet. Theme B is playful; it contains a short, downward-moving phrase that is repeated several times. Haydn's fondness for musical surprises is reflected in the coda, which contains sudden changes of dynamics, unexpected harmonic twists, and a suspenseful long pause.

Listening Outline

HAYDN, Trumpet Concerto in E Flat Major (1796)

Third Movement: Allegro

Sonata-rondo form, duple meter ($\frac{2}{4}$), E flat major

Solo trumpet, 2 flutes, 2 oboes, 2 bassoons, 2 French horns, 2 trumpets, timpani, 1st violins, 2d violins, violas, cellos, double basses

(Duration 4:35)

Listen for the contrast in *tone color* between the orchestra, dominated by strings, and the brilliance of the virtuosic solo trumpet. Notice the musical surprises in the coda, which contains sudden changes of *dynamics,* unexpected *harmonies,* and a suspenseful long pause.

A

0:00   **1. a.** Main theme in violins, **_p_**.

    b. Main theme in full orchestra, **_f_**, violins, running notes and rising scale lead to

B

0:23   **c.** Violins, **_f_**, downward short phrase, repeated **_p_**,

orchestra, **_f_**, brass fanfares, cadence, pause.

A

0:38   **2.** Main theme in trumpet, strings accompany, trumpet repeats main theme, orchestra, **_f_**, violins, **_p_**, lead to

B′

1:08   **3.** Trumpet, held tone, ushers in downward short phrases, upward phrases with trills, downward legato phrases, trumpet trill to cadence, trumpet fanfares, orchestra, **_f_**.

A

1:48   **4. a.** Trumpet, held tone, ushers in main theme.

    b. Main-theme phrase in full orchestra, **_f_**.

Development

2:06   **5.** Trumpet, main-theme phrases, **_p_**, violins, **_p_**, main-theme phrases in minor with trumpet fanfares, running notes in violins, **_f_**, trumpet and brasses join, suddenly soft, violins introduce

A

2:40   **6. a.** Trumpet, held tone, ushers in main theme.

    b. Orchestra, **_f_**, running notes and rising scale lead to

B″

2:58   **7. a.** Trumpet, downward short phrases, downward broken chords, octave leaps, trill to cadence.

    b. Violins, **_p_**, high woodwinds, **_p_**, trumpet fanfares, violins, **_p_**, lead to

Coda

3:33   **8. a.** Trumpet, main-theme phrase, strings, **_p_**, trumpet, downward chain of trills.

    b. Suddenly loud, full orchestra, sudden **_pp_**, string tremolos, suddenly loud, full orchestra, repeated notes in trumpet, long pause.

    c. Trumpet, main-theme phrases, orchestra, **_p_**, crescendo to **_ff_**, repeated notes in trumpet, closing chords in orchestra.

Performance Perspectives

Wynton Marsalis, Trumpeter, Playing the Third Movement of Haydn's Trumpet Concerto in E Flat Major

Wynton Marsalis is a highly acclaimed trumpeter, composer, educator, author, and the Artistic Director of Jazz at Lincoln Center, New York City. He grew up in a family of musicians in a suburb of New Orleans, Louisiana, the second of six sons of jazz pianist-educator Ellis Marsalis Jr. and social worker Delores Marsalis. In 2011, the Jazz Master Award of the National Endowment for the Arts, America's highest honor in jazz, was given to musicians of the Marsalis family: Ellis Jr. and sons Branford (saxophonist), Wynton, Delfeayo (trombonist), and Jason (drummer).

At age six, Wynton began playing the trumpet, and at eight he played jazz in a children's marching band. At fourteen, Wynston performed the Haydn Trumpet Concerto with the New Orleans Philharmonic Orchestra. He first learned the Haydn Concerto from listening to a record, without the written notes, and later described it as "such a beautiful piece of music, so lyrical and so logical . . ."

Hiroyuki Ito/Getty Images

While in high school, Marsalis also attended the New Orleans Center for the Creative Arts, a new arts magnet school where his father taught jazz. Marsalis later recalled that "every teacher loved the arts and cherished the opportunity to teach young people. The foundation of my knowledge and love of the arts comes from the education in classical music, jazz, and vocal music that I got there."

At seventeen, Marsalis was the youngest person to attend the Berkshire Music Center at Tanglewood, Massachusetts, where he won an award as the most outstanding brass student. The following year he moved to New York City to study at the Juilliard School of Music, but in 1980 left to join the legendary group Art Blakey and his Jazz Messengers. In early 1982, Wynton and his brother Branford formed their own band, performing with such jazz greats as Sarah Vaughan, Sonny Rollins, and Herbie Hancock.

In 1983, Marsalis became the first and only musician to win Grammy awards both for classical and jazz recordings. These included trumpet concertos by Haydn, Hummel, and Leopold Mozart (Mozart's father), and his trumpet performance on the album *Think of One*. He repeated this feat the following year by winning Grammy awards for *Baroque Music for Trumpet* and *Hot House Flowers*. He is the only artist to have won a Grammy in five consecutive years (1983–1987). Marsalis has made ten classical recordings and played solo with such leading orchestras as the New York Philharmonic and the Los Angeles Philharmonic.

A high point of Marsalis's classical career was his collaboration with famed opera singer Kathleen Battle, soprano, on their recording of *Baroque Duets* (1992), which included music by Bach and Handel. While preparing this recording Marsalis observed that "we instrumentalists are always trying to get the kind of clarity that the vocalists have. It's like the early jazz musicians; when they played trumpets and saxophones they would try to sound like singers in the church and the blues singers. And then when the instrumentalists get to that level of expression, the vocalists imitate them."

Through his countless concerts and more than 80 recordings, Marsalis has brought new, young audiences to jazz. His educational activities have been equally impressive, and he has been awarded honorary doctorates from more than 30 universities, including Harvard, Yale, and Howard. In 1995, he wrote and hosted the PBS television series *Marsalis on Music*, later published as a book.

In 1997, Marsalis was the first jazz musician ever to win the Pulitzer Prize for Music for his oratorio *Blood on the Fields*, which deals with a couple moving from slavery to freedom. He has written music for the New York City Ballet, the Alvin Ailey American Dance Theater, the Lincoln Center Chamber Music Society, and the New York and Berlin Philharmonic Orchestras. He has performed and taught every year since 1991 in Marciac, France, where a life-size statue of Marsalis sits in the town square. In 2011 he was given France's highest distinction for his commitment to the transmission of culture from one generation to the next, the French Legion of Honor award.

Marsalis has said, "Jazz is the sound of democracy," and has described music as "so connected to memory. We learn how to speak though music. Music teaches us teamwork. It teaches us individuality. It teaches us discipline. It deals with everything that's invisible . . . thoughts and emotions."

11 Wolfgang Amadeus Mozart

Wolfgang Amadeus Mozart (1756–1791), one of the most amazing child prodigies in history, was born in Salzburg, Austria. By the time he was six, he could play the harpsichord and violin, improvise fugues, write minuets, and read music perfectly at first sight. At the age of eight, he wrote a symphony; at eleven, an oratorio; at twelve, an opera.

Mozart's father, Leopold, a court musician, was eager to show him off. Between the ages of six and fifteen, Mozart was continually on tour. He played for Empress Maria Theresa in Vienna, Louis XV at Versailles, George III in London, and innumerable aristocrats along the way. On his trips to Italy he was able to master the current operatic style, which he later put to superb use.

When he was fifteen, Mozart returned to Salzburg, which was ruled by a new prince-archbishop. The archbishop was a tyrant who did not appreciate Mozart's music and refused to grant him more than a subordinate seat in the court orchestra. With his father's help, Mozart tried repeatedly over the next decade to find a suitable position elsewhere, but with no success.

The tragic irony of Mozart's life was that he won more acclaim as a boy wonder than as an adult musician. Having begun his professional life as an international celebrity, he could not tolerate being treated like a servant. He became insubordinate when the prince-archbishop forbade him to give concerts or perform at the houses of the aristocracy, and his relationship with his patron went from bad to worse. Moreover, his complete dependence on his father had given him little opportunity to develop initiative, and a contemporary observed that he was "too good-natured, not active enough, too easily taken in, too little concerned with the means that may lead him to good fortune."

When he was twenty-five, Mozart could stand it no longer. He broke free of provincial Salzburg and traveled to Vienna, intending to be a freelance musician. Indeed, Mozart's first few years in Vienna were successful. His German opera *Die Entführung aus dem Serail* (*The Abduction from the Seraglio,* 1782) was acclaimed. Concerts of his own music were attended by the emperor and the nobility. Pupils paid him high fees, his compositions were published, and his playing was heard in palace drawing rooms. Contributing to the brightness of these years was Mozart's friendship with Haydn, who told Leopold, "Your son is the greatest composer that I know, either personally or by reputation; he has taste and, what is more, the most profound knowledge of composition."

In 1786 came Mozart's opera *Le Nozze di Figaro* (*The Marriage of Figaro*). Vienna loved it, and Prague was even more enthusiastic. "They talk about nothing but *Figaro,*" Mozart joyfully wrote.

This success led an opera company in Prague to commission *Don Giovanni* (*Don Juan*) the following year. Although *Don Giovanni* was a triumph in Prague, its dark qualities and dissonance did not appeal to the Viennese, and Mozart's popularity in Vienna began to decline. It was a fickle city in any case, and it found Mozart's music complicated and hard to follow. His pupils dwindled, and the elite snubbed his concerts.

During his last year, Mozart was more successful. He received a commission for a German comic opera, *Die Zauberflöte* (*The Magic Flute*), and, while working on it,

Mozart was among the most versatile of all composers; he wrote masterpieces in all the musical forms of his time.

DEA/A. DAGLI ORTI/De Agostini via Getty Images

was visited by a stranger who carried an anonymous letter commissioning a requiem, a mass for the dead. As Mozart's health grew worse, he came to believe that the requiem was for himself and rushed to finish it while on his deathbed. (In fact, the stranger was the servant of a nobleman who intended to claim the requiem as his own composition.) *The Magic Flute* was premiered to resounding praise in Vienna, but its success came too late. Mozart died of rheumatic fever on December 5, 1791, shortly before his thirty-sixth birthday, leaving the requiem unfinished. (It was completed by his friend and pupil Franz Süssmayer.)

Mozart's Music

Mozart was among the most versatile of all composers. He wrote masterpieces in all the musical forms of his time—symphonies, string quartets, piano concertos, and operas. His music sings and conveys a feeling of ease, grace, and spontaneity, as well as balance, restraint, and perfect proportion. Yet mysterious harmonies bring dark moods that contrast with the lyricism. Mozart fuses power and elegance in a unique way.

His compositions sound effortless and were created with miraculous rapidity. For example, he completed his last three symphonies in only six weeks!

Many of Mozart's concertos are among his greatest works. His piano concertos—composed mainly for his own performances—are particularly important. He also wrote concertos for violin, horn, flute, bassoon, oboe, and clarinet.

He was a master of opera with a supreme ability to coordinate music and stage action, a keen sense of theater, an inexhaustible gift of melody, and a genius for creating characters through tone. Most of his operas are comedies, composed to German or Italian librettos. Mozart's three masterpieces of Italian comic opera are *The Marriage of Figaro* (1786), *Don Giovanni* (1787), and *Così fan tutte* (*All Women Behave Like This,* 1790); they were all composed to librettos by Lorenzo da Ponte. Mozart's finest opera in German is *The Magic Flute* (1791). The comic operas contain both humorous and serious characters. The major characters are not mere stereotypes but individual human beings who think and feel. Emotions in his arias and ensembles continuously evolve and change.

"I am never happier," Mozart once wrote his father, "than when I have something to compose, for that, after all, is my sole delight and passion." Mozart's "delight and passion" are communicated in his works, which represent late eighteenth-century musical style at its highest level of perfection.

Don Giovanni (1787)

Don Giovanni (*Don Juan*) is a unique blend of comic and serious opera, combining seduction and slapstick with violence and the supernatural. The old tale of Don Juan, the legendary Spanish lover, had attracted many playwrights and composers before Mozart. Mozart's Don Giovanni is a seductive but ruthless nobleman who will stop at nothing to satisfy his sexual appetite. Don Giovanni's comic servant, Leporello, is a grumbling accomplice who dreams of being in his master's place.

The Don attempts to rape a young noblewoman, Donna Anna; she pursues and struggles with Don Giovanni—who conceals his face—trying to determine his identity. Her father, the Commendatore (Commandant), challenges him to a duel. Don Giovanni kills the old man, causing Donna Anna and her fiancé, Don Ottavio, to swear revenge. Pursued by his enemies, Don Giovanni seeks sexual pleasure in a series of adventures. During one of them, he hides in a cemetery, where he sees a marble statue of the dead Commandant. The unearthly statue utters threatening words, but Don Giovanni brazenly invites it to dinner. When the statue appears at the banquet hall, it orders the Don to repent. Don Giovanni defiantly refuses and is dragged down to hell.

Act I:
Introduction

The overture leads directly into the action-packed opening scene. In breathless succession we witness Leporello keeping guard, Don Giovanni struggling with Donna Anna, the Commandant dueling with the Don, and the Commandant's agonized last gasps. Mozart's music vividly depicts the characters and pushes the action forward. (In the Vocal Music Guide, braces indicate that characters sing at the same time. *Etc.* indicates that previous lines of text are repeated.)

Vocal Music Guide

MOZART, *Don Giovanni* (1787)

Act I: Excerpt from Opening Scene
(Duration 5:48)

Listen for the music characterizing each phase of the action: Leporello's comic complaints, Anna's struggle with Giovanni, and the Commandant's duel and tragic death. Notice the upward string sweeps in the dueling music, the *dissonant held chord* at Giovanni's fatal sword thrust, and the *slow tempo* and *minor key* as the Commandant dies.

0:00

Orchestral introduction, molto allegro; sudden fortes suggest pacing and abrupt turns.

(Late evening outside the Commandant's palace in Seville. Don Giovanni, concealing his identity, has stolen into Donna Anna's room. Leporello paces back and forth.)

Leporello

Time	Italian	English
0:15	*Notte e giorno faticar,*	Night and day I slave
	Per chi nulla sa gradir;	For one who does not appreciate it.
	Piova e vento sopportar,	I put up with wind and rain,
0:29	*Mangiar male e mal dormir!*	Eat and sleep badly.
	Voglio far il gentiluomo,	I want to be a gentleman
	E non voglio più servir,	And to give up my servitude.
	No, no, no, no, no, no,	No, no, no, no, no, no,
	Non voglio più servir!	I want to give up my servitude.
0:46	*Oh che caro galantuomo!*	Oh, what a fine gentleman!
	Voi star dentro colla bella	You stay inside with your lady
0:58	*Ed io far la sentinella!*	And I must play the sentinel!
	Voglio far il gentiluomo, ecc.	Oh, what a fine gentleman, etc.
1:24	*Ma mi par che venga gente . . .*	But I think someone is coming!
	Non mi voglio far sentir, ecc.	I don't want them to hear me, etc.

1:41

Orchestral crescendo.

(Leporello hides to one side. Don Giovanni and Donna Anna come down the palace stairs struggling. The Don hides his face to prevent her from recognizing him.)

Donna Anna

1:47

Non sperar, se non m'uccidi.
Ch'io ti lasci fuggir mai!

There's no hope, unless you kill me
That I'll ever let you go!

Don Giovanni

Donna folle, indarno gridi:
Chi son io tu non saprai.

Idiot! You scream in vain.
Who I am you'll never know!

Donna Anna

Non sperar, ecc.

There's no hope, etc.

Don Giovanni

1:58

Donna folle! ecc.

Idiot! etc.

Leporello

Che tumulto! Oh ciel, che gridi! Il
padron in nuovi guai.

What a racket! Heavens, what screams!
My master in another scrape.

Donna Anna

2:07

Gente! Servi! Al traditore!

Help! Everyone! The betrayer!

Don Giovanni

Taci, e trema al mio furore!

Keep quiet! Beware my wrath!

Donna Anna

Scellerato!

Scoundrel!

Don Giovanni

Sconsigliata!

Fool!

Donna Anna

Scellerato!

Scoundrel!

Don Giovanni

Sconsigliata!

Fool!

Leporello

Sta a veder che il malandrino Mi farà
precipitar.

We will see if this rascal
Will be the ruin of me!

Donna Anna

Gente! Servi!

Help! Everyone!

Don Giovanni

Taci, e trema!

Keep quiet!

Donna Anna

Come furia disperata
Ti saprò perseguitar! ecc.
Scellerato! Gente! Servi!
Come furia disperata, ecc.

Like a desperate fury
I'll know how to pursue you! etc.
Scoundrel! Help! Everyone!
Like a desperate fury, etc.

2:18

Don Giovanni

Questa furia disperata
Mi vuol far precipitar! ecc.
Sconsigliata! Taci, e trema!
Questa furia disperata, ecc.

This desperate fury
Is aimed at destroying me!
Fool! Keep quiet!
This desperate fury, etc.

Leporello

Che tumulto! Oh ciel, che gridi!
Sta a veder che il malandrino, ecc.

What a racket! Heavens, what screams!
We will see if this rascal, etc.

3:02

String tremolo, **ff**, shift to minor key.

(Donna Anna hears the Commandant; she leaves Don Giovanni and goes into the house. The Commandant appears.)

Commandant

3:10

Lasciala, indegno! Battiti meco!

Leave her alone, wretch, and defend yourself.

Don Giovanni

Va, non mi degno di pugnar teco.

Go away! I disdain to fight with you.

Commandant

Così pretendi da me fuggir?

Thus you think to escape me?

Leporello

Potessi almeno di qua partir.

If I could only get out of here!

3:23

Don Giovanni

Va, non mi degno, no!

Go away! I disdain you!

Commandant

Così pretendi da me fuggir?

Thus you think to escape me!

Leporello

Potessi almeno di qua partir!

If I could only get out of here!

Commandant

3:31

Battiti!

Fight!

Don Giovanni

Misero! Attendi, se vuoi morir!

So be it, if you want to die!

3:47

Dueling music, upward sweeps in strings. Death blow, suspenseful, held chord.

(They duel. The Commandant is fatally wounded.)

4:06

andante, **pp** pathetic minor phrases.

Commandant

Ah, soccorso! son tradito!
L'assassino m'ha ferito,
E dal seno palpitante
Sento l'anima partir.

Help! I've been betrayed!
The assassin has wounded me!
And from my heaving breast
I feel my soul escaping!

Don Giovanni

Ah! già cade il sciagurato!
Affannosa e agonizzante
Già dal seno palpitante
Veggo l'anima partir, ecc.

Ah, already the wretch has fallen,
And he gasps for air.
From his heaving breast I already
See his soul escaping, etc.

Leporello

Qual misfatto! Qual eccesso!
Entro il sen dallo spavento
Palpitar il cor mi sento!
Io non sò che far, che dir, ecc.

What a misdeed! What a crime!
I can feel my heart
Beating hard from fright!
I don't know what to do or say, etc.

(The Commandant dies.)

Recitative,
harpsichord
accompanies.

Don Giovanni

Leporello, dove sei?	Leporello, where are you?

Leporello

Son qui, per mia disgrazia. E voi?	I'm here, unfortunately, and you?

Don Giovanni

Son qui.	Over here.

Leporello

Chi è morto, voi, o il vecchio?	Who's dead, you or the old man?

Don Giovanni

Che domanda da bestia! Il vecchio.	What an idiotic question! The old man.

5:29

Leporello

Bravo! Due imprese leggiadre, *Sforzar la figlia, ed ammazzar il padre!*	Well done! Two misdeeds! First you raped the daughter, then murdered the father!

Don Giovanni

L'ha voluto, suo danno.	He asked for it; too bad for him.

Leporello

Ma Donn' Anna cosa ha voluto?	And Donna Anna, did she ask for it too?

Don Giovanni

Taci, non mi seccar! *Vien meco, se non vuoi qualche cosa ancor tu.*	Keep quiet and don't bother me. Now come along, unless you're anxious for something for yourself.

Leporello

Non vo' nulla, signor, non parlo più.	I have no desires, sir, and no more to say.

Act I:
Duet: *Là ci darem la mano*
(*There you will give me your hand*)

The Don's seduction technique is put to use in the lovely duet *Là ci darem la mano*. Don Giovanni persuades the pretty peasant girl Zerlina to come to his palace, promising to marry her and change her life. The music magically conveys his persuasiveness and her gradual surrender, as the voices become more and more intertwined. Forgetting her fiancé, Masetto, Zerlina throws herself into the Don's arms and they sing together, "Let us go, my beloved."

As they go off together, they are suddenly intercepted by Donna Elvira, a woman whom Don Giovanni had earlier seduced and deserted. She denounces Don Giovanni as a liar, and protectively leads Zerlina away. During the opera, all of Don Giovanni's attempts at seduction or rape are frustrated.

Uruguayan tenor Erwin Schrott as Don Giovanni and American mezzo-soprano Isabel Leonard as Zerlina sing the duet *Là ci darem la mano* at the Metropolitan Opera House, Lincoln Center, New York.

Jack Vartoogian/Getty Images

Vocal Music Guide

MOZART, *Là ci darem la mano*, from *Don Giovanni* (1787)

(Duration 3:10)

Listen to the musical depiction of Don Giovanni's persuasiveness and Zerlina's surrender as their voices increasingly intertwine in this duet. Notice that in the Andante opening section in *duple meter* ($\frac{2}{4}$) the voices of Don Giovanni and Zerlina alternate, whereas in the second section, in *sextuple meter* ($\frac{6}{8}$), they sing together, signifying her agreement to come to his palace.

0:00		**Don Giovanni**	
Andante, $\frac{2}{4}$, legato melody.	Là ci darem la mano,	There you will give me your hand,	
	Là mi dirai di sì.	There you will tell me "yes."	
	Vedi, non è lontano;	You see, it is not far;	
	Partiam, ben mio, da qui.	Let us leave, my beloved.	
		Zerlina	
0:20			
Legato melody repeated.	Vorrei e non vorrei;	I'd like to, but yet I would not.	
	Mi trema un poco il cor.	My heart trembles a little.	
	Felice è ver, sarei,	It's true I would be happy,	
	Ma può burlarmi ancor.	But he may just be tricking me.	
		Don Giovanni	
0:45			
Quicker interchange between voices.	Vieni, mio bel diletto!	Come, my dearly beloved!	
		Zerlina	
	Mi fa pietà Masetto!	I'm sorry for Masetto	
		Don Giovanni	
	Io cangierò tua sorte.	I will change your life!	

	Zerlina
Presto, non son più forte!	Soon I won't be able to resist.
	Don Giovanni
Vieni! Vieni!	Come! Come!
1:14 *Là ci darem la mano!*	There you will give me your hand.
Legato melody now shared by both voices.	
	Zerlina
Vorrei, e non vorrei!	I'd like to, but yet I would not.
	Don Giovanni
Là mi dirai di sì.	There you will tell me "yes."
	Zerlina
Mi trema un poco il cor!	My heart trembles a little.
	Don Giovanni
Partiam, mio ben, da qui!	Let us leave, my beloved.
	Zerlina
Ma può burlarmi ancor!	But he may just be tricking me.
	Don Giovanni
1:41 *Vieni, mio bel diletto!*	Come, my dearly beloved!
	Zerlina
Voices overlap. *Mi fa pietà Masetto!*	I'm sorry for Masetto.
	Don Giovanni
Io cangierò tua sorte.	I will change your life.
	Zerlina
Presto, non son più forte!	Soon I won't be able to resist.
	Don Giovanni
1:58 *Andiam! Andiam!*	Let us go!
	Zerlina
Andiam!	Let us go!
	Don Giovanni and Zerlina
2:09 *Andiam, andiam, mio bene,*	Let us go, let us go, my beloved,
Allegro, ⁶⁄₈; together they *A ristorar le pene*	To soothe the pangs
sing a new joyous tune. *D'un innocente amor! ecc.*	Of an innocent love, etc.

Symphony No. 40 in G Minor, K. 550 (1788)

Symphony No. 40 in G Minor is the most passionate and dramatic of Mozart's symphonies. Although the work is classical in form and technique, it is almost romantic in emotional intensity. It staggers the imagination that Mozart could compose the G Minor and two other great symphonies—No. 39 in E Flat and No. 41 in C (*Jupiter*)—during the short period of six weeks. They are his last three symphonies.

Like most classical symphonies, Symphony No. 40 in G Minor has four movements: (1) fast, (2) slow, (3) minuet, (4) fast.

First Movement: Molto allegro

Mozart opens his Symphony No. 40 in G Minor with the agitated movement already described in Chapter 3.

Second Movement: Andante

Exposition
0:00

Development
3:39

Recapitulation
5:03

The mood of the andante hovers between gentleness and longing. The andante is written in sonata form and is the only movement of this symphony in major (it is in E flat). This movement develops from a series of gently pulsating notes in the opening theme.

As the theme continues, the violins introduce an airy two-note rhythmic figure that will appear—with changes of dynamics and orchestration—in almost every section of the andante. The rhythmic figure will be, at different times, graceful, insistent, and forceful.

Later, Mozart uses the airy figures as a delicate countermelody to the repeated-note idea. Floating woodwinds interwoven with strings reveal Mozart's sensitivity to tone color as an expressive resource.

Third Movement: Menuetto (Allegretto)

The minuet, in G minor, is serious and intense; it does not sound like an aristocratic dance. The form of the minuet is A B A:

Minuet	Trio	Minuet
A	B	A
a (repeated) ba' (repeated)	c (repeated) dc' (repeated)	a ba'

Section A
0:00

Powerful syncopations give a fierce character to the A section (the minuet), which is predominantly loud and in minor.

Later, Mozart increases the tension through polyphonic texture and striking dissonances. At the end of the A section, there is a sudden drop in dynamics; the flute, supported by oboes and a bassoon, softly recalls the opening melody of the minuet.

The trio section (B) brings a shift from minor to major, from fierce energy to graceful relaxation.

Section B
1:54

Return to Section A
3:57

This change of mood is underscored by a soft dynamic level and pastoral woodwind interludes. After the trio, a sudden forte announces the return of the fierce A section.

Fourth Movement:
Allegro assai (very fast)

The very fast finale, in sonata form, is unusually tense. Its opening theme, in the tonic key of G minor, offers brusque contrasts of dynamics and rhythm. A soft upward arpeggio (broken chord) alternates repeatedly with a loud rushing phrase.

First theme
0:00

Bridge
0:27

Excitement is maintained throughout the long bridge, which is based on the loud rushing phrase of the first theme. The bridge ends clearly with a brief pause, as do other sections in this movement.

Second theme
1:00

The tender second theme, in the new key of B flat major, is a lyrical contrast to the brusque opening theme. It is softer, flows more smoothly, and uses longer notes.

Closing section
1:29

Development
1:49

The exposition closes with a loud passage of continuously rushing notes in the strings.

Mozart weaves almost the entire development section from the upward arpeggio of the first theme. During the opening few seconds, there is an eruption of violence as the orchestra in unison plays a variation of the arpeggio and a series of jagged downward leaps.

Recapitulation
First theme
3:03

Second theme
3:38

As the development continues, the texture becomes polyphonic and contrasts with the homophony of the exposition. Arpeggios press upon each other in quick imitation. Rapid shifts of key create restless intensity.

In the recapitulation, both the first and the second theme are in the tonic key, G minor. This minor key now adds a touch of melancholy to the tender second theme, which was heard in major before. The passion and violence of this movement foreshadow the romantic expression to come during the nineteenth century.

Piano Concerto No. 23 in A Major, K. 488 (1786)

Mozart's Piano Concerto in A Major—completed on March 2, 1786—dates from a very productive and successful period in his life. Between October 1785 and May 1786, he taught piano and composition; conducted operas; performed in concerts; and composed *The Marriage of Figaro,* the comic one-act opera *The Impresario,* two other great piano concertos (K. 482 in E Flat and K. 491 in C Minor), Quartet for Piano and Strings (K. 478), and *Masonic Funeral Music* (K. 477).

Mozart thought highly of the A Major piano concerto. In a letter to the court chamberlain of a prospective patron, he included it among "the compositions which I keep for myself or for a small circle of music-lovers and connoisseurs." Today, it is one of the best-known of his piano concertos.

Like all classical concertos, this one has three movements. The grace of the opening movement and the high spirits of the finale contrast with the melancholy of the middle movement. This concerto stresses poetry and delicacy rather than pianistic virtuosity or orchestral power. It is scored for an orchestra without trumpets or timpani and highlights the clarinets, flute, and bassoon. Mozart associated its key—A major—with tenderness, lyricism, and elegance. (He also used this key for the Clarinet Concerto and the duet between Don Giovanni and Zerlina in *Don Giovanni*.)

First Movement: Allegro

The gentle opening movement blends lyricism with a touch of sadness, owing to many shifts between major and minor. Two main lyrical themes introduced by the orchestra in the first exposition are restated by the piano and orchestra in the second exposition. The development section is based on a new legato theme that is unexpectedly introduced by the orchestra after a dramatic pause. (In the Listening Outline, this is called the *development theme.*) Mozart creates a dramatic confrontation by juxtaposing fragments of this new theme, played by the woodwinds, with restless ideas in the piano and orchestra.

Toward the end of the allegro is a cadenza—an unaccompanied showpiece for the soloist. Exceptionally, Mozart notated the cadenza directly into the score, instead of leaving it to be improvised by the soloist. With its rapid sweeps up and down the keyboard, its alternation between brilliant and tender passages, and its concluding trill, this cadenza gives us some idea of how Mozart himself must have improvised.

Listening Outline

MOZART, Piano Concerto No. 23 in A Major (1786)

First Movement: Allegro

Sonata form, quadruple meter (4/4), A major

Solo piano, flute, 2 clarinets, 2 bassoons, 2 French horns, 1st violins, 2d violins, violas, cellos, double basses

(Duration 11:36)

Listen for the two lyrical themes introduced softly by the strings in the first exposition and restated by the piano and orchestra in the second exposition. Notice the *legato* development theme presented by the strings and elaborated by the piano, and the cadenza for unaccompanied solo piano near the end of the movement.

First exposition

First theme

0:00   **1. a.** Strings, ***p***, gracious main melody, legato, major key,

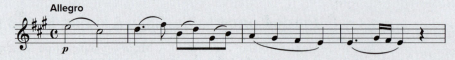

staccato ascent.

  b. Winds, *p*, repeat opening of main melody an octave higher. Strings, *f*, answered by winds; cadence to

Bridge

0:34   **2.** Full orchestra, *f*, vigorous bridge theme,

running notes in violins, *f*. Brief pause.

Second theme group

0:58   **3. a.** Violins, *p*, tender second theme, repeated notes in dotted rhythm.

  b. Violins and bassoon, *p*, repeat second theme, flute joins.

  c. Agitated rhythms in minor lead to

1:33   **d.** Full orchestra, *f*, major; winds alternate with violins, minor, crescendo to

  e. Full orchestra, *f*, major, cadence. Brief pause.

  f. High woodwind phrase, *p*, orchestral chords, *f*. Brief pause.

Second exposition

First theme

2:08   **1. a.** Piano solo, main melody, low strings join, violins introduce

  b. Piano, varied repetition of main melody, rapid downward and upward scales.

Bridge

2:37   **2. a.** Full orchestra, *f*, bridge theme.

  b. Piano, running notes, with string accompaniment. High staccato violins, high staccato winds, downward scale in piano. Brief pause.

Second theme group

3:07   **3. a.** Piano solo, second theme, dolce.

  b. Violins and flute repeat second theme, piano joins.

3:38   **c.** Piano and orchestra.

3:49   **d.** Violins alternate with piano, minor.

  e. Piano, major. Long passage of running notes in piano culminating in short trill closing into

4:21   **4.** Full orchestra, opening of bridge theme. Sudden pause.

Development

4:33   **1. a.** Strings, *p*, legato development theme.

  b. Piano solo, development theme embellished by rapid notes.

came to him while he walked through the Viennese countryside. His Sixth Symphony, the *Pastoral,* beautifully expresses his recollections of life in the country.

As Beethoven's hearing weakened, so did his piano playing and conducting. By the time he was forty-four, this once brilliant pianist was forced to stop playing in public. But he insisted on conducting his orchestral works long after he could do it efficiently. His sense of isolation grew with his deafness. Friends had to communicate with him through an ear trumpet, and during his last years he carried notebooks in which people would write questions and comments.

Despite this, and despite mounting personal problems, Beethoven had a creative outburst after 1818 that produced some of his greatest works: the late piano sonatas and string quartets, the *Missa solemnis,* and the Ninth Symphony—out of total deafness, new realms of sound.

Beethoven's Music

For Beethoven, music was not mere entertainment, but a moral force, "a higher revelation than all wisdom and philosophy." His music directly reflects his powerful, tortured personality.

Beethoven's demand for perfection meant long and hard work. Sometimes he worked for years on a single symphony, writing other works during the same period of time. He carried music sketchbooks everywhere, jotting down new ideas, revising and refining old ones. The final versions of his works were often hammered out through great labor.

Beethoven mostly used classical forms and techniques, but he gave them new power and intensity. The musical heir of Haydn and Mozart, he bridged the classical and romantic eras. Many of his innovations were used by composers who came after him.

In his works, great tension and excitement are built up through syncopations and dissonances. The range of pitch and dynamics is greater than ever before, so that contrasts of mood become more pronounced. Accents and climaxes seem titanic. Greater tension called for a larger musical framework, so Beethoven expanded his forms. Beethoven was a musical architect who was unsurpassed in his ability to create large-scale structures in which every note seems inevitable. But not all his music is stormy and powerful; much is gentle, humorous, noble, or lyrical.

More than his predecessors, Beethoven tried to unify the contrasting movements by means of musical continuity. Sometimes one movement leads directly into the next, without the traditional pause. He also greatly expanded the development section and coda of sonata-form movements and made them more dramatic. His works often have climactic, triumphant finales, toward which the previous movements seem to build. Beethoven's finales mark an important departure from the light, relaxed ending movement favored by Haydn and Mozart.

Beethoven's most popular works are the nine symphonies, written for larger orchestras than Haydn's or Mozart's. Each is unique in character and style. There is a curious alternation of mood between his odd-numbered symphonies, which tend to be forceful and assertive, and his even-numbered ones, which are calmer and more lyrical. In the finale of the Ninth Symphony (*Choral*), Beethoven took the unprecedented step of using a chorus and four solo vocalists who sing the text of Schiller's *Ode to Joy.*

His thirty-two piano sonatas are far more difficult than the sonatas of Haydn and Mozart and exploit the stronger, tonally improved piano of Beethoven's time, drawing many new effects from it. In these sonatas, he experimented with compositional techniques that he would later expand in the symphonies and string quartets. The sixteen string quartets are among the greatest music composed, and each of the five superb piano concertos is remarkable for its individuality.

Most of Beethoven's important works are for instruments, but his sense of drama was also expressed in vocal music, including two masses and his only opera, *Fidelio.*

Beethoven's total output is usually divided into three periods: early (up to 1802), middle (1803–1814), and late (1815–1827). The music of Haydn and Mozart influenced some works of the early period, but other pieces clearly show Beethoven's personal style. The compositions of the middle period are longer and tend to be heroic in tone. And the sublime works of the last period well up from the depths of a man almost totally deaf. During this period Beethoven often used the fugue to express new musical concepts. The late works contain passages that sound surprisingly harsh and "modern." When a violinist complained that the music was very difficult to play, Beethoven reportedly replied, "Do you believe that I think of a wretched fiddle when the spirit speaks to me?"

Piano Sonata in C Minor, Op. 13 (*Pathétique;* 1798)

The title *Pathétique,* coined by Beethoven, suggests the tragically passionate character of his famous Piano Sonata in C Minor, Op. 13. Beethoven's impetuous playing and masterful improvisational powers are mirrored in the sonata's extreme dynamic contrasts, explosive accents, and crashing chords. At the age of twenty-seven, during his early period, Beethoven had already created a powerful and original piano style that foreshadowed nineteenth-century romanticism.

First Movement:
Grave (solemn, slow introduction);
Allegro molto e con brio (very fast and brilliant)

Slow introduction
0:00

The *Pathétique* begins in C minor with an intense, slow introduction, dominated by an opening motive in dotted rhythm: long-short-long-short-long-long.

This six-note idea seems to pose a series of unresolved questions as it is repeated on higher and higher pitch levels. The tragic mood is intensified by dissonant chords, sudden contrasts of dynamics and register, and pauses filled with expectancy. The slow introduction is integrated in imaginative and dramatic ways into the allegro that follows it.

First theme
1:41

The tension of the introduction is maintained in the allegro con brio, a breathless, fast movement in sonata form. The opening theme, in C minor, begins with a staccato idea that rapidly rises up a two-octave scale. It is accompanied by low broken octaves, the rapid alternation of two tones an octave apart.

Texture

- Texture is predominantly homophonic.
- Fluctuations of texture occur to provide contrasts; a piece may shift gradually or suddenly from one texture to another.

Performance Practice

- During the classical era, the use of the characteristic baroque basso continuo was gradually abandoned.
- The piano, able to create subtle dynamic changes through varied finger pressure on the keys, became favored over the harpsichord.
- An increase in the number of amateur musicians, unable to improvise an accompaniment at the keyboard from a figured bass, led to simpler accompaniments written out by the composer.
- Audiences were keenly aware of differences in musical style, and they expected music to be composed for specific performers to capitalize on their musical strengths.
- When performing cadenzas in concertos for solo instrument by Mozart, soloists must choose among using one composed by Mozart (if one exists), using one by another composer, or creating one.

Design Elements: (Listening Icon): McGraw Hill Education; (Baroque violin): McGraw Hill Education

■ Musicians, artists, and writers of the romantic period put an unprecedented emphasis on individuality of style. *Paganini* (1831) by the French painter Eugène Delacroix (1798–1863) conveys the intensity of a performance by the most famous violinist of the 19th century.

PART V

The Romantic Period

The prevailing qualities of my music are passionate expressiveness, inner fire, rhythmic drive, and unexpectedness.

—Hector Berlioz

LEARNING OBJECTIVES

- Describe the characteristics of romantic music considering individuality of style, expressive aims and subjects, nationalism, program music, tone color, harmony, range of dynamics and pitch, and form.

- Explain how the composer's role in society changed during the nineteenth century.

- Analyze the relationship between words and music in Schubert's song *Erlkönig* (*The Erlking*).

- Discuss the relationship among the three instruments in Clara Schumann's Piano Trio in G Minor.

- Compare and contrast piano pieces by Robert Schumann and Chopin.

- Define program music and compare and contrast orchestral works by Berlioz, Tchaikovsky, and Smetana.

- Discuss the relationship between music and drama in scenes from operas by Bizet, Verdi, Puccini, and Wagner.

Romantic Period (1820–1900)

| 1820–1850 | 1850–1900 |

Historical and Cultural Events

1823 Monroe Doctrine

1830 Revolutions in France, Belgium, Poland

1837–1901 Queen Victoria reigns in England

1848 Revolutions in Europe

1848 Marx and Engels, *The Communist Manifesto*

1859 Darwin, *Origin of Species*

1861–1865 American Civil War

1870 Franco-Prussian War

1876 Bell invents telephone

1898 Spanish-American War

Arts and Letters

1819 Keats, *Ode to a Nightingale*

1822 Delacroix, *Dante and Virgil in Hell*

1830 Delacroix, *Liberty Leading the People*

1831 Hugo, *The Hunchback of Notre Dame*

1835 Friedrich, *The Evening Star*

1837 Dickens, *Oliver Twist*

1840 Turner, *The Slave Ship*

1844 Dumas, *The Three Musketeers*

1845 Poe, *The Raven*

1857 Millet, *The Gleaners*

1866 Dostoevsky, *Crime and Punishment*

1870 Degas, *The Orchestra of the Opéra*

1874 Monet, *Impression, Sunrise*

1877 Cézanne, *Still Life with Apples*

1877 Tolstoy, *Anna Karenina*

1884 Twain, *The Adventures of Huckleberry Finn*

1889 van Gogh, *The Starry Night*

1893 Munch, *The Scream*

Barney Burstein/Corbis/VCG via Getty Images

Music

1815 Franz Schubert, *Erlkönig*

1830 Berlioz, *Symphonie fantastique*

1831 Chopin, Nocturne in E♭ Major, Op. 9, No. 2

1831 Chopin, Étude in C Minor, Op. 10, No. 12 (*Revolutionary*)

1834 Fanny Mendelssohn Hensel, String Quartet in E♭ Major

1837 Robert Schumann, *Fantasiestücke,* Op. 12

1842 Chopin, Polonaise in A♭ Major, Op. 53

1844 Mendelssohn, Violin Concerto in E Minor, Op. 64

1846 Clara Wieck Schumann, Piano Trio in G Minor, Op. 17

1851 Liszt, *Transcendental* Étude in F Minor

1851 Verdi, *Rigoletto*

1856 Wagner, *Die Walküre*

1868 Brahms, *German Requiem*

1870 Tchaikovsky, *Romeo and Juliet*

1874 Smetana, *The Moldau*

1875 Bizet, *Carmen*

1893 Dvořák, Symphony No. 9 in E Minor (From the *New World*)

1896 Puccini, *La Bohème*

DEA/A. DAGLI ORTI/De Agostini via Getty Images

Romanticism
(1820–1900)

The early nineteenth century brought the flowering of romanticism, a cultural movement that stressed emotion, imagination, and individuality. In part, romanticism was a rebellion against the neoclassicism of the eighteenth century and the age of reason. Romantic writers broke away from time-honored conventions and emphasized freedom of expression. Romantic painters used bolder, more brilliant colors and preferred dynamic motion to gracefully balanced poses.

But romanticism was too diverse and complex to be defined by any single formula. It aimed to broaden horizons and encompass the totality of human experience. The romantic movement was international in scope and influenced all the arts.

Emotional subjectivity was a basic quality of romanticism in art. "All good poetry is the spontaneous overflow of powerful feelings," wrote William Wordsworth, the English romantic poet. And "spontaneous overflow" made much romantic literature autobiographical; authors projected their personalities in their work. Walt Whitman, the American poet, expressed this

Nineteenth-century musicians and painters often saw political revolution as a reflection of their own struggle for artistic freedom. *In Liberty Leading the People* (1830), the French painter Eugène Delacroix (1798–1863) combined a realistic depiction of street fighting in Paris in the July Revolution of 1830 with a symbolic representation of liberty.
Fine Art Images/Heritage Images/Getty Images

Self Portrait (1837), by Eugène Delacroix (1798–1863). Emotional subjectivity was a basic characteristic of romanticism.

Photo Josse/Leemage/Getty Images

Wanderer above the Sea of Fog (1818), by the German painter Caspar David Friedrich (1774–1840). The romantics were particularly drawn to the realms of fantasy, the unconscious, the irrational, and the world of dreams.

UniversalImagesGroup/Getty Images

subjective attitude beautifully when he began a poem, "I celebrate myself, and sing myself."

In exploring their inner lives, the romantics were especially drawn to the realm of fantasy: the unconscious, the irrational, the world of dreams. Romantic fiction includes tales of horror and the supernatural, such as *The Cask of Amontillado,* by Edgar Allan Poe, and *Frankenstein,* by Mary Wollstonecraft Shelley. The writer Thomas De Quincey vividly describes his drug-induced dreams in *Confessions of an English Opium-Eater:* "I was buried, for a thousand years, in stone coffins, with mummies and sphinxes. I was kissed, with cancerous kisses, by crocodiles." The visual arts also depict nightmarish visions. In an etching called *The Sleep of Reason Breeds Monsters,* the Spanish

painter Francisco Goya shows batlike monsters surrounding a sleeping figure. The realm of the unknown and the exotic also interested the French artist Eugène Delacroix, who often depicted violent scenes in far-off lands.

The romantic fascination with fantasy was paired with enthusiasm for the Middle Ages, that time of chivalry and romance. Whereas neoclassicists had thought of the medieval period as the "dark ages," the romantics cherished it. They were inspired by medieval folk ballads and by tales of fantasy and adventure. Romantic novels set in the Middle Ages include *Ivanhoe* (1819), by Walter Scott, and *The Hunchback of Notre Dame* (1831), by the French writer Victor Hugo. Gothic cathedrals, which had long gone unappreciated, now seemed picturesque and mysterious. A "gothic revival" in

architecture resulted in the construction of buildings such as the houses of Parliament in London (1836–1852) and Trinity Church in New York (1839–1846).

Of all the inspirations for romantic art, none was more important than nature. The physical world was seen as a source of consolation and a mirror of the human heart. Wordsworth, for example, thought of nature as "the nurse,/the guide, the guardian of my heart, and soul." One of his poems begins:

There was a time when meadow,
    grove, and stream,
The earth, and every common
    sight,
        To me did seem
    Apparelled in celestial light,
The glory and the freshness of a
    dream.

Wivenhoe Park (1816), by the English painter John Constable (1776–1837). Of all the inspirations for romantic art, none was more important than nature.
Courtesy National Gallery of Art, Washington

Slave Ship (Slavers Throwing Overboard the Dead and Dying, Typhoon Coming On) (1840) by the English painter J. M. W. Turner. In Turner's seascapes, the sweep of waves expresses not only the power of nature but also human passion.
Barney Burstein/Corbis/VCG via Getty Images

The Gleaners (1857), by the French painter Jean-François Millet. The industrial revolution caused vast social and economic changes and awakened interest in the poor. Millet portrayed the labor of peasant women picking up left over grain in the fields.
Gianni Dagli Orti/Shutterstock

The romantic sensitivity to nature is revealed in landscape painting, which attained new importance. Artists such as John Constable and J. M. W. Turner in England were masters at conveying movement in nature: rippling brooks, drifting clouds, stormy seas. In Turner's seascapes, the sweep of waves expresses not only the grandeur of nature but human passion as well.

Romanticism coincided with the industrial revolution, which caused vast social and economic changes. Many writers and painters recorded the new social realities of their time. The novels of Charles Dickens and the paintings of Honoré Daumier reflect an interest in the working class and the poor.

Subjectivity, fantasy, and enthusiasm for nature and the Middle Ages are only a few aspects of romanticism in literature and painting. We now focus on romanticism in music.

1 Romanticism in Music (1820–1900)

The *romantic period* in music extended from about 1820 to 1900. Among the most significant musicians of the period were Franz Schubert, Robert Schumann, Clara Wieck Schumann, Frédéric Chopin, Franz Liszt, Felix Mendelssohn, Fanny Mendelssohn Hensel, Hector Berlioz, Peter Ilyich Tchaikovsky, Bedřich Smetana, Antonin Dvořák, Johannes Brahms, Georges Bizet, Giuseppe Verdi, Giacomo Puccini, and Richard Wagner. The length of this list—and some important composers have not been included—testifies to the richness and variety of romantic music and its continued impact on today's concert and operatic repertoire.

Composers of the romantic period continued to use the musical forms of the preceding classical era. The emotional intensity associated with romanticism was already present in the work of Mozart and particularly in that of Beethoven, who greatly influenced composers after him. The romantic preference for expressive, songlike melody also grew out of the classical style.

Nonetheless, there are many differences between romantic and classical music. Romantic works tend to have greater ranges of tone color, dynamics, and pitch. Also, the romantic harmonic vocabulary is broader, with more emphasis on colorful, unstable chords. Romantic music is linked more closely to the other arts, particularly to literature. New forms developed, and in all forms there was greater tension and less emphasis on balance and resolution. But romantic music is so diverse that generalizations are apt to mislead. Some romantic composers, such as Mendelssohn and Brahms, created works that were deeply rooted in classical tradition; other composers, such as Berlioz, Liszt, and Wagner, were more revolutionary.

Characteristics of Romantic Music

Individuality of Style Romantic music puts unprecedented emphasis on self-expression and individuality of style. There is "not a bar which I have not truly felt and which is not an echo of my innermost feelings," wrote Tchaikovsky of his Fourth Symphony. A "new world of music" was the goal of the young Chopin. Many romantics created music that sounds unique and reflects their personalities. As Robert Schumann observed, "Chopin will soon be unable to write anything without people crying out at the seventh or eighth bar, 'That is indeed by him.'" And today, with some listening experience, a music lover can tell within a few minutes—sometimes within a few seconds—whether a piece is by Schumann or Chopin, Tchaikovsky or Brahms.

Expressive Aims and Subjects The romantics explored a universe of feeling that included flamboyance and intimacy, unpredictability and melancholy, rapture and longing. Countless songs and operas glorify romantic love; often, the lovers are unhappy and face overwhelming obstacles. Fascination with the fantastic and diabolical is expressed in music like the *Dream of a Witches' Sabbath* from Berlioz's *Symphonie fantastique* (*Fantastic Symphony*). All aspects of nature attracted romantic musicians. In different sections of **Part V** we study music that depicts shepherds' pipes and distant thunder (Berlioz's *Fantastic Symphony*), a wild horseback ride on a stormy night (Schubert's *Erlkönig*, or *Erlking*), and the flow of a river (Smetana's *Moldau*). Romantic composers also dealt with subjects drawn from the Middle Ages and from Shakespeare's plays.

Nationalism and Exoticism Nationalism was an important political movement that influenced nineteenth-century music. Musical **nationalism** was expressed when romantic composers deliberately created music with a specific national identity, using the folksongs, dances, legends, and history of their homelands. This national flavor of romantic music—whether Polish, Russian, Bohemian (Czech), or German—contrasts with the more universal character of classical music.

Fascination with national identity also led composers to draw on colorful materials from foreign lands, a trend known as musical *exoticism.* For instance, some composers wrote melodies in an Asian style or used rhythms and instruments associated with distant lands. The French composer Georges Bizet wrote *Carmen,* an opera set in Spain; the Italian Giacomo Puccini evoked Japan in his opera *Madame Butterfly;* and the Russian Rimsky-Korsakov suggested an Arabian atmosphere in his orchestral work *Scheherazade.* Musical exoticism was in keeping with the romantics' attraction to things remote, picturesque, and mysterious.

Program Music The nineteenth century was the great age of *program music,* instrumental music associated with a story, poem, idea, or scene. The nonmusical element is usually specified by a title or by explanatory comments called a *program.* A programmatic instrumental piece can represent the emotions, characters, and events of a particular story, or it can evoke the sounds and motion of nature. For example, in Tchaikovsky's *Romeo and Juliet,* an orchestral work inspired by Shakespeare's play, agitated music depicts the feud between the rival families, a tender melody conveys young love, and a funeral-march rhythm suggests the lovers' tragic fate. And in *The Moldau,* an orchestral work glorifying the main river of Bohemia, Smetana uses musical effects that call to mind a flowing stream, a hunting scene, a peasant wedding, and the crash of waves.

Program music in some form or another has existed for centuries, but it became particularly prominent in the romantic period, when music was closely associated with literature. Many composers—Berlioz, Schumann, Liszt, and Wagner, for example—were prolific authors as well. Artists in all fields were intoxicated by the concept of a "union of the arts." Poets wanted their poetry to be musical, and musicians wanted their music to be poetic.

Expressive Tone Color Romantic composers reveled in rich and sensuous sound, using tone color to obtain a variety of moods and atmosphere. Never before had timbre been so important.

In both symphonic and operatic works, the romantic orchestra was larger and more varied in tone color than the classical orchestra. Toward the end of the romantic era, an orchestra might include close to one hundred musicians. (There were twenty to sixty players in the classical ensemble.) The constant expansion of the orchestra reflected composers' changing needs as well as the growing size of concert halls and opera houses. The brass, woodwind, and percussion sections of the orchestra took on a more active role. Romantic composers increased the power of the brass section to something spectacular, calling for trombones, tubas, and more horns and trumpets. In 1824, Beethoven had broken precedent by asking for nine brasses in the Ninth Symphony; in 1894, the Austrian composer Gustav Mahler demanded twenty-five brass instruments for his Second Symphony. The addition of valves had made it easier for horns and trumpets to cope with intricate melodies.

The woodwind section took on new tone colors as the contrabassoon, bass clarinet, English horn, and piccolo became regular members of the orchestra. Improvements in the construction of instruments allowed woodwind players to perform more flexibly and accurately. Orchestral sounds became more brilliant and sensuously appealing through increased use of cymbals, the triangle, and the harp.

New sounds were drawn from all instruments of the nineteenth-century orchestra. Flutists were required to play in the breathy low register, and violinists were asked to strike the strings with the wood of their bows. Such demands compelled performers to attain a higher level of technical virtuosity.

Composers sought new ways of blending and combining tone colors to achieve the most poignant and intense sound. In 1844, Hector Berlioz's *Treatise on Modern Instrumentation and Orchestration* signaled the recognition of orchestration as an art in itself.

The piano, the favorite instrument of the romantic age, was vastly improved during the 1820s and 1830s. A cast-iron frame was introduced to hold the strings under greater tension, and the hammers were covered with felt. Thus the piano's tone became more "singing." Its range was also extended. With a stronger instrument, the pianist could produce more sound. And use of the damper ("loud") pedal allowed a sonorous blend of tones from all registers of the piano.

Colorful Harmony In addition to exploiting new tone colors, the romantics explored new chords and novel ways of using familiar chords. Seeking greater emotional intensity, composers emphasized rich, colorful, and complex harmonies.

There was more prominent exploitation of *chromatic harmony,* which uses chords containing tones not found in the prevailing major or minor scale. Such chord tones come from the chromatic scale (which has twelve tones), rather than from the major or minor scales (which have seven different tones). Chromatic chords add color and motion to romantic music. Dissonant, or unstable, chords were also used more freely than during the classical era. By deliberately delaying the resolution of dissonance to a consonant, or stable, chord, romantic composers created feelings of yearning, tension, and mystery.

A romantic piece tends to have a wide variety of keys and rapid modulations, or changes from one key to another. Because of the nature and frequency of these key shifts, the tonic key is somewhat less clear than in classical works. The feeling of tonal gravity tends to be less strong. By the end of the romantic period, even more emphasis was given to harmonic instability and less to stability and resolution.

Expanded Range of Dynamics, Pitch, and Tempo Romantic music also calls for a wide range of dynamics. It includes sharp contrasts between faint whispers and sonorities of unprecedented power. The classical dynamic extremes of *ff* and *pp* didn't meet the needs of romantics, who sometimes demanded *ffff* and *pppp*. Seeking more and more expressiveness, nineteenth-century composers used frequent crescendos and decrescendos, as well as sudden dynamic changes.

The range of pitch was expanded too, as composers reached for extremely high or low sounds. In search of increased brilliance and depth of sound, the romantics exploited instruments such as the piccolo and contrabassoon, as well as the expanded keyboard of the piano.

Changes of mood in romantic music are often underlined by accelerandos, ritardandos, and subtle variations of pace: there are many more fluctuations in tempo than there are in classical music. To intensify the expression of the music, romantic performers made use of *rubato,* the slight holding back or pressing forward of tempo.

Form: Miniature and Monumental The nineteenth century was very much an age of contradictions. Romantic composers characteristically expressed themselves both in musical miniatures and in monumental compositions. On one hand are piano pieces by Chopin and songs by Schubert that last but a few minutes. Such short forms were meant to be heard in the intimate surroundings of a home; they met the needs of the growing number of people who owned pianos. The romantic genius for creating an intense mood through a melody, a few chords, or an unusual tone color found a perfect outlet in these miniatures. On the other hand, there are gigantic works by Berlioz and Wagner that call for a huge number of performers, last for several hours, and were designed for large opera houses or concert halls.

Romantic composers continued to write symphonies, sonatas, string quartets, concertos, operas, and choral works, but their individual movements tended to be longer than Haydn's and Mozart's. For example, a typical nineteenth-century symphony might last about forty-five minutes, in contrast to twenty-five minutes for an eighteenth-century symphony. And as the romantic period drew to a close, compositions tended to become even more extended, more richly orchestrated, and more complex in harmony.

New techniques were used to unify such long works. The same theme or themes might occur in several movements of a symphony. Here composers followed the pioneering example of Beethoven's Fifth Symphony, in which a theme from the scherzo is quoted within the finale. When a melody returns in a later movement or section of a romantic work, its character may be transformed by changes in dynamics, orchestration, or rhythm—a technique known as *thematic transformation.* A striking use of thematic transformation occurs in Berlioz's *Symphonie fantastique* (*Fantastic Symphony,* 1830), in which a lyrical melody from the opening movement becomes a grotesque dance tune in the finale.

Different movements or sections of a romantic work also can be linked through transitional passages; one movement of a symphony or concerto may lead directly into the next. Here, again, Beethoven was the pioneer. And nineteenth-century operas are unified by melodic ideas that reappear in different acts or scenes, some of which may be tied together by connecting passages.

In dealing with an age that so prized individuality, generalizations are especially difficult. The great diversity found in romantic music can best be appreciated, perhaps, by approaching each piece as its composer did—with an open mind and heart.

2 Romantic Composers and Their Public

The composer's role in society changed radically during Beethoven's lifetime (1770–1827). In earlier periods, part of a musician's job had been the composition of works for a specific occasion and audience. Thus Bach wrote cantatas for weekly church services in Leipzig, and Haydn composed symphonies for concerts in the palaces of the Esterházy family. But Beethoven, as we have seen, was one of the first great composers to work as a freelance musician outside the system of aristocratic or church patronage.

The image of Beethoven as a "free artist" inspired romantic musicians, who often composed to meet an inner need rather than fulfill a commission. Romantic composers were interested not only in pleasing their contemporaries but also in being judged favorably by posterity. The young Berlioz wrote to his father, "I want to leave on this earth some trace of my existence." It became common for romantics to create extended works with no immediate prospects for performance. For example, Wagner wrote *Das Rheingold* (*The Rhine Gold*), a two and a half hour opera, and then had to wait fifteen years before seeing its premiere.

Sometimes the romantic composer was a "free artist" by necessity rather than choice. Because of the French Revolution and the Napoleonic wars (1789–1814), many aristocrats could no longer afford to maintain private opera houses, orchestras, and "composers in residence." Musicians lost their jobs when many of the tiny princely states of Germany were abolished as political units and merged with neighboring territories. (In Bonn, Germany, the court and its orchestra were disbanded; Beethoven could not have returned to his position there even if he had wanted to.) Many composers who would have had modest but secure incomes in the past had to fight for their livelihood and sell their wares in the marketplace.

Romantic composers wrote primarily for a middle-class audience whose size and prosperity had increased because of the industrial revolution. During the nineteenth century, cities expanded dramatically, and a sizable number of people wanted to hear and play music.

The needs of this urban middle-class led to the formation of many orchestras and opera groups during the romantic era. Public concerts had developed during the eighteenth century, but not until the nineteenth century did regular subscription concerts become common. The London Philharmonic Society was founded in 1813, the Paris Société des Concerts du Conservatoire was founded in 1828, and the Vienna Philharmonische Konzerte and the New York Philharmonic were founded in 1842.

The first half of the nineteenth century also witnessed the founding of music conservatories throughout Europe. In the United States, conservatories were founded in Chicago, Cleveland, Boston, Oberlin (Ohio), and Philadelphia during the 1860s. More

During the nineteenth century, a piano could be found in many middle-class homes. *Young Girls at the Piano* (1892), by the French painter Auguste Renoir (1841–1919).
The Metropolitan Museum of Art, New York, Robert Lehman Collection, 1975

young men and women than ever before studied to be professional musicians. At first women were accepted only as students of performance, but by the late 1800s they could study musical composition as well.

The nineteenth-century public was captivated by virtuosity. Among the musical heroes of the 1830s were the pianist Franz Liszt and the violinist Niccolò Paganini (1782–1840), who toured Europe and astonished audiences with their feats. Never before had instrumental virtuosity been so acclaimed. After one concert by Liszt in Budapest, Hungarian nobles presented him with a jeweled sword, and a crowd of thousands formed a torchlight parade to escort him to his dwelling. Following Liszt's example, performers such as pianist Clara Wieck Schumann and violinist Joseph Joachim began to give solo recitals in addition to their customary appearances with orchestras.

Private music making also increased during the romantic era. The piano became a fixture in every middle-class home, and there was great demand for songs and solo piano pieces. Operas and orchestral works were transcribed, or arranged, so that they could be played on a piano in the home.

Romantic composers came from the social class that was their main audience. Berlioz was the son of a doctor; Schumann was the son of a bookseller; and Felix Mendelssohn and his sister, Fanny Mendelssohn Hensel, were children of a wealthy

The desire of the urban middle class for access to music performance led to the formation of many orchestras during the romantic era. This engraving shows Louis Jullien conducting an orchestra and four military bands at Covent Garden Theater in London.

Lebrecht Music & Arts/Alamy

banker. This was a new situation. In earlier periods, music, like cabinetmaking, had been a craft passed from one generation to another. Bach, Mozart, and Beethoven were all children of musicians. But the romantics often had to do a great deal of persuading before their parents permitted them to undertake a musical career. Berlioz wrote to his reluctant father in 1824: "I am voluntarily driven toward a magnificent career (no other term can be applied to the career of an artist) and I am not in the least headed toward damnation. . . . This is the way I think, the way I am, and nothing in the world will change me."

Middle class parents had reason for concern when their children wanted to be musicians. Few romantic composers were able to support themselves through composition alone. Only a very successful opera composer such as Verdi could become wealthy by selling music to opera houses and publishers. Most composers were forced to work in several areas at once. Some were touring virtuosos, such as Paganini and Liszt. Many taught; Chopin charged high fees for giving piano lessons to rich young women in Paris. Music criticism was a source of income for Berlioz and Schumann. (And Berlioz bitterly resented having to waste time reviewing compositions by nonentities.) Some of the finest conductors of the romantic period were composers, among them Mendelssohn and Mahler. Only a few fortunates, such as Tchaikovsky and Wagner, had wealthy patrons to support them while they created.

3 The Art Song

One of the most distinctive forms in romantic music is the *art song,* a composition for solo voice and piano. Here, the accompaniment is an integral part of the composer's concept, and it serves as an interpretive partner to the voice. Although they are now performed in concert halls, romantic songs were written to be sung and enjoyed at home.

Poetry and music are intimately fused in the art song. It is no accident that this form flowered with the emergence of a rich body of romantic poetry in the early nineteenth century. Many of the finest song composers—Schubert, Schumann, and Brahms, for example—were German or Austrian and set poems in their native language. Among the poets favored by these composers were Johann Wolfgang von Goethe (1749–1832) and Heinrich Heine (1797–1856). The German word *lied* (*song*) is commonly used for a song with German text. (*Lied* is pronounced *leet;* its plural, *lieder,* is pronounced *leader.*)

Yearning—inspired by a lost love, nature, a legend, or other times and places— haunted the imagination of romantic poets. Thus art songs are filled with the despair of unrequited love; the beauty of flowers, trees, and brooks; and the supernatural happenings of folktales. There are also songs of joy, wit, and humor. But by and large, romantic song was a reaching out of the soul.

Song composers would interpret a poem, translating its mood, atmosphere, and imagery into music. They created a vocal melody that was musically satisfying and perfectly molded to the text. Important words were emphasized by stressed tones or melodic climaxes.

The voice shares the interpretive task with the piano. Emotions and images in the text take on an added dimension from the keyboard commentary. Arpeggios in the piano might suggest the splashing of oars or the motion of a mill wheel. Chords in a low register might depict darkness or a lover's torment. The mood is often set by a brief piano introduction and summed up at the end by a piano section called a *postlude.*

Song Forms

Composers have used many methods to set music to poems made up of several stanzas. They may employ strophic form, repeating the same music for each stanza of the poem. **Strophic form** makes a song easy to remember and is used in almost all folksongs. Or composers might use **through-composed form,** writing new music for each stanza. (*Through-composed* is a translation of the German term *durchkomponiert*.) Through-composed form allows music to reflect a poem's changing moods.

Songs are not restricted to strophic or through-composed form. There are many techniques by which music can be molded to the structure and feeling of a poem. We will consider other song forms when discussing specific songs.

The Song Cycle

Romantic art songs are sometimes grouped in a set, or **song cycle.** A cycle may be unified by a story line that runs through the poems, or by musical ideas linking the songs. Among the great romantic song cycles are *Winterreise* (*Winter's Journey,* 1827) by Schubert, and *Dichterliebe* (*Poet's Love,* 1840) by Schumann.

In many of their art songs, romantic composers achieved a perfect union of music and poetry. They created an intensely personal world with a tremendous variety of moods. These miniatures contain some of the most haunting melodies and harmonies in all music.

4 Franz Schubert

The career of Franz Schubert (1797–1828), the earliest master of the romantic art song, was unlike that of any great composer before him. He never held an official position and was neither a conductor nor a virtuoso. His income came entirely from musical composition. "I have come into the world for no other purpose but to compose," he told a friend. The full measure of his genius was recognized only years after his tragically early death.

Schubert was born in Vienna, the son of a schoolmaster. Even as a child, he had astounding musical gifts. "If I wanted to instruct him in anything new," recalled his amazed teacher, "he knew it already." At eleven, he became a choirboy in the court chapel and won a scholarship to the Imperial Seminary.

Schubert managed to compose an extraordinary number of masterpieces in his late teens while teaching at his father's school, a job he hated. His love of poetry led him to the art song; he composed his first great song, *Gretchen am Spinnrade* (*Gretchen at the Spinning Wheel*), when he was seventeen. The next year he composed 143 songs, including *The Erlking*. When he was nineteen, his productivity rose to a peak: he composed 179 works, including two symphonies, an opera, and a mass.

At twenty-one, he gave up teaching school to devote himself entirely to music. He associated with a group of Viennese poets and artists who led a bohemian existence. Often he lived with friends because he did not have money to rent a room of his own. Working incredibly fast, from seven in the morning until early afternoon, he turned out one piece after another. He spent his afternoons in cafés, and many of his evenings at "Schubertiads," parties where only his music was played. Most of his works were composed for performances in the homes of Vienna's cultivated middle-class. Unlike Beethoven, Schubert did not mingle with the aristocracy. The publication and performance of his songs brought him some recognition, but his two most important symphonies—the *Unfinished* and the *Great* C Major—were not performed in public during his lifetime.

Franz Schubert did not mingle with the aristocracy, preferring instead the company of poets, painters, and other musicians.
Imagno/Getty Images

Fantasiestücke for Piano, Op. 12
(*Fantasy Pieces* for Piano; 1837)

Fantasiestücke (*Fantasy Pieces*) is a cycle of eight short pieces, each with its own particular character, mood, and evocative title, including *Des Abends* (*In the Evening*), *Aufschwung* (*Soaring*), *Warum?* (*Why?*), and *Grillin* (*Whims*). The pieces alternate between the inwardness associated with Eusebius and the impulsive exuberance associated with Florestan. Like many other romantics, Schumann was especially drawn to the world of fantasy, linking his works to definite images or poetic ideas. Schumann chose the titles of individual pieces only *after* the music was composed. The title *Fantasy Pieces* was borrowed from the title of a collection of stories and essays by romantic author E. T. A. Hoffmann.

Schumann composed *Fantasiestücke* (*Fantasy Pieces*) in 1837, toward the end of an eighteen-month separation period from Clara that was enforced by her father. Around the time that Schumann finished *Fantasy Pieces*, he proposed marriage to Clara. She replied, "So all you desire is a simple 'yes.' . . . Shouldn't a heart as full of inexpressible love as mine be able to utter this tiny word? I say it and my innermost being whispers it to you, eternally."

We focus on two of the best known of the Fantasy Pieces: No. 2, *Aufschwung* (*Soaring*), and No. 3, *Warum?* (*Why?*), which, respectively, represent the impulsive and introverted sides of Schumann's musical personality.

Aufschwung (*Soaring;* 1837)

Soaring is passionate and impulsive with a very fast tempo, driving rhythms, and lyric interludes. It may be outlined as A B A C A B A. The brief main theme (A) is agitated, with powerful accents and dotted rhythms. Its melody appears in a middle register.

Theme B is songlike and flowing with a long-short-long-short rhythmic pattern.

The extended middle section (C) brings a calm melody and subtle changes of tempo.

Near the end of section C, a crescendo creates tension and prepares for the return of the agitated main theme.

Listening Outline

SCHUMANN, *Aufschwung (Soaring;* 1837)

Piano

Sehr rasch (Very Fast), ⁶⁄₈ (sextuple) meter, F minor

A B A C A B A form

(Duration 3:04)

Listen for the contrast between the agitated main theme (A) and the more lyrical sections B and C. Notice that in theme A the melody shifts from the middle voice to the highest voice.

A	0:00	**1.** Agitated theme, *f*, in middle register, mostly staccato, soars to melodic high point and descends to cadence in major. Agitated theme repeated.
B	0:18	**2. a.** Songlike melody, *p*, legato, long-short-long-short rhythm, major key
	0:38	**b.** Songlike melody repeated, *mf*, leads into
A′	0:45	**3.** Agitated theme, *f*, repeats at higher pitch, *ff*, leads into
C	1:00	**4. a.** Calm melody, legato, descends in even rhythm, major key, contrasts between legato and staccato
	1: 40	**b.** Calm melody leads to gradual crescendo, held chords, agitated theme fragments lead to
A	2:16	**5.** Agitated theme, *ff*, soars to melodic high point and descends to cadence in major.
B	2:26	**6. a.** Songlike melody, *p*, legato, long-short-long-short rhythm.
	2:43	**b.** Songlike melody repeated, *mf*, leads into
A″	2:52	**7.** Agitated theme leads to abrupt concluding cadence in minor.

Warum? (Why?; 1837)

Marked "slowly and tenderly," Why? evokes yearning though a songful motive that recurs throughout this very short piece. This six-note idea in dotted rhythm (long-long-short-long) ends with a questioning upward leap.

The tender melodic lines are enhanced by an accompaniment of gently syncopated chords.

Why? has the form *A BA′ BA′*, in which *A′* is an abridged variant of A. In part A, the highest melodic line is freely imitated by the one below it. Part B becomes more intense as the bass line joins the conversation. In A' the soft questioning motive alternates between the highest two melodic lines; *Why?* ends softly with an unanswered question.

Listening Outline

SCHUMANN, *Warum?* (*Why?*; 1837)

Langsam und Zart (Slowly and tenderly)
Piano
(Duration 2:48)

Listen for the pervasive questioning motive ending with an *upward leap*. Notice that the questioning motive appears in different *registers,* first in the highest two voices, and then in the bass.

A	0:00	**1.** Questioning motive in two highest melodic lines, syncopated chords accompany.
BA'	0:43	**2.** Questioning motive in middle voice answered in bass, crescendo to *f*; questioning motive, *p*, alternates between highest two melodic lines.
BA'	1:40	**3.** Questioning motive in middle voice answered in bass, crescendo to *f*; questioning motive, *p*, alternates between highest two melodic lines ending *Why?*, with the question unanswered.

6 Clara Wieck Schumann

One of the leading concert pianists of the nineteenth century, Clara Wieck Schumann (1819–1896) premiered many works by her husband, Robert Schumann, and by her close friend Johannes Brahms. Born in Leipzig, Germany, she was the daughter of Marianne Wieck, a singer and pianist; and Friedrich Wieck, a well-known piano pedagogue. Her father trained her to be a child prodigy who would both earn money and demonstrate the superiority of his teaching methods. Between the ages of twelve and twenty she performed throughout Europe to great acclaim, usually programming one or more of her own compositions.

Clara Wieck married Robert Schumann the day before her twenty-first birthday, despite her father's opposition. During their fourteen-year marriage she continued to concertize and compose—though on a reduced scale—while caring for seven children (one of the Schumanns' children had died in infancy) and catering to the needs of her hypersensitive husband. The year 1853 was particularly important for Clara Schumann. The twenty-year-old composer Johannes Brahms came to play his works for the Schumanns, beginning a friendship with Clara that would last until her death in 1896. In the same year, she also met the famous violinist Joseph Joachim, with whom she would often give chamber music concerts.

After her husband's death, Clara Schumann expanded her performing activities, became renowned as a teacher, and edited his collected works. She helped refine the tastes of concert audiences by performing serious works by earlier composers, such as Bach, Mozart, and Beethoven, as well as works by her late husband and her friend Brahms.

Clara Wieck was already a well-known concert pianist at age fifteen.

DEA/A. DAGLI ORTI/De Agostini via Getty Images

Clara Schumann considered herself primarily a performing artist. "I feel I have a mission to perform beautiful works, Robert's above all," she once wrote. "The practice of my art . . . is the very air I breathe." She was less confident about her creative ability and stopped composing when she was thirty-six, after she had become a widow. Her self-doubt was perhaps influenced by the predominantly negative attitude toward women composers and by her relationship with overwhelming geniuses such as Robert Schumann and Brahms.

Until recently, Clara Schumann was known mainly as a famous pianist who had been the wife of one great composer and the close friend of another. But in the past decade, her compositions have been increasingly recorded and performed. These include a piano concerto, piano pieces, songs, and a trio for violin cello, and piano, which is studied here.

Trio for Violin, Cello, and Piano in G Minor, Op. 17 (1846)

The piano trio (usually piano, violin, and cello) is a type of chamber music developed in the Classical period by Haydn, Mozart, and Beethoven and continued in the early Romantic period by Schubert. Clara Schumann's Trio for Violin, Cello, and Piano in G minor, Op. 17, often considered her finest work, was composed in 1846. Robert arranged to have her Trio published, and he presented the printed copy to Clara on her twenty-eighth birthday in 1847. Creating this Trio gave Clara much pleasure. "There is no greater joy than composing something oneself and then listening to it," she wrote in her diary. Clara's Trio inspired Robert to compose his own Piano Trio No. 1 in D minor (1847), and during the nineteenth century, both pieces were often performed on the same program. We focus on the Andante, the third of its four movements.

The Andante is in A B A′ (shortened) Coda form, with each instrument given an equal share of the melodic material. The A section, in major, conveys lyricism and warmth. The piano introduces a tender melody that is repeated and expanded by the violin and cello.

The highly contrasting B section, in minor, is forceful and animated, with louder dynamics, faster tempo, and agitated dotted (long-short) rhythms.

The A′ section and coda bring a return to the pensive mood and soft dynamics of the opening.

Listening Outline

WIECK SCHUMANN, Trio for Violin, Cello, and Piano in G Minor, Op. 17 (1846)

Third movement: Andante

A B A′ coda form, sextuple meter ($^6_8$), G major

Violin, cello, piano

(Duration 5:24)

Listen for the contrast between the lyrical A section and the agitated B section. Notice that each of the three instruments is given an equal share of the melodic material.

A

0:00	**1. a.**	Piano alone, *p*, tender main theme in major.
0:32	**b.**	Violin, *p*, main theme, piano and cello accompany.
1:03	**c.**	Cello, *p*, new melody, violin countermelody, piano accompanies, crescendo to

B

1:40	**2. a.**	Violin, *f*, agitated theme in minor, dotted rhythm, faster tempo; piano and cello accompany.
1:53	**b.**	Cello, *f*, agitated theme, piano and violin accompany.
2:07	**c.**	Violin, *p*, variation of agitated theme in major, piano and cello accompany, flowing melody in violin.
2:28	**d.**	Piano, dotted rhythm, *p*, violin rising melody, crescendo, piano and violin dotted rhythms.
2:47	**e.**	Piano, *f*, agitated theme in minor, violin and cello *f*, decrescendo, ritardando, long cello tones.

A′

3:17	**3. a.**	Cello, *p*, tender main theme, piano flowing accompaniment, violin pizzicato.
3:49	**b.**	Cello leads, violin countermelody, piano accompanies.

Coda

4:19	**4. a.**	Conversation among violin, piano and cello, *p*; violin, descent to cadence.
5:00	**b.**	Rising piano arpeggio, *pp*, violin and cello pizzicato conclusion.

7 Frédéric Chopin

Frédéric Chopin (1810–1849) was the only great composer who wrote almost exclusively for the piano. The son of a Polish mother and a French father, he was brought up in Warsaw and graduated from the Warsaw Conservatory.

At twenty-one he arrived in Paris, then the center of romanticism and the artistic capital of Europe. In Paris he met such writers as Victor Hugo, Balzac, and Heine. The painter Delacroix was a close friend of Chopin, as were Liszt and Berlioz. His playing soon gained him access to aristocratic salons. He was a shy, reserved man who preferred salons to concert halls, and it was for such intimate gatherings that he conceived short pieces such as the nocturnes, preludes, and waltzes. He earned a good living by teaching piano to the daughters of the rich, and lived in luxury.

Chopin had a well-known love affair with Aurore Dudevant, a novelist whose pen name was George Sand. A frail man, he thrived on her care and composed many of his greatest works during the years they lived together. After they separated, his health declined rapidly and he composed very little. He died of tuberculosis at thirty-nine.

Chopin's Music

By the age of eighteen, Chopin had evolved an utterly personal and original style. Most of his pieces are exquisite miniatures; they evoke an infinite variety of moods and are always elegant, graceful, and melodic. Unlike Schumann, Chopin did not attach literary programs or titles to his pieces. The mazurkas and the polonaises—stylized dances—capture a Polish spirit without actually using folk tunes.

No composer has made the piano sound as beautiful as Chopin. His unique melodic gift creates the illusion that the piano is singing. He uses delicate and graceful ornamental tones and exploits the pedal sensitively. His colorful treatment of harmony was highly original and influenced later composers.

Nocturne in E Flat Major, Op. 9, No. 2 (1830–1831)

Chopin composed his popular Nocturne in E Flat Major, Op. 9, No. 2, when he was about twenty. A **nocturne,** or *night piece,* is a slow, lyrical, intimate composition for piano. Like much of Chopin's music, this nocturne is tinged with melancholy.

Nocturne in E Flat Major opens with a legato melody containing graceful upward leaps, which become increasingly wide as the line unfolds. This melody is heard again three times during the piece. With each repetition, it is varied by ever-more elaborate decorative tones and trills. The nocturne also includes a subordinate melody, which is played with rubato—slight fluctuations of tempo.

A sonorous foundation for the melodic line is provided by the widely spaced notes in the accompaniment, connected by the damper pedal. The waltzlike accompaniment gently emphasizes the $\frac{12}{8}$ meter, 12 beats to the measure subdivided into four groups of 3 beats each.

The nocturne is reflective in mood until it suddenly becomes passionate near the end. The new concluding melody begins softly but then ascends to a high register and is played forcefully in octaves. After a brilliant trill-like passage, the excitement subsides; the nocturne ends calmly.

Chopin was a shy, reserved man who disliked crowds and preferred to play in salons rather than in public concert halls. Photograph of Chopin by L. A. Bisson, Paris, 1849.
DeAgostini/Getty Images

Listening Outline

CHOPIN, Nocturne in E Flat Major, Op. 9, No. 2 (1830–1831)

Andante, $\frac{12}{8}$ meter
Piano
(Duration 4:05)

Listen for the songful main *melody* repeated three times, each time with ever-more elaborate decorative tones and trills. Notice the *homophonic texture* and the widely spaced notes of the accompaniment connected by the damper pedal.

0:00   **1. a.** Main melody, dolce, espressivo, waltzlike accompaniment.

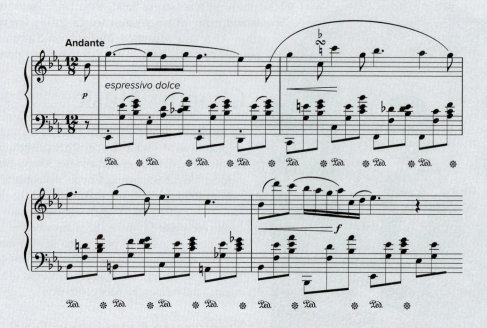

0:25   **b.** Main melody, **p**, embellished with decorative notes and trills.

0:51   **2. a.** Subordinate melody, **p**, played with rubato;

crescendo to

1:18   **b.** Main melody, with more elaborate decorative notes and trills; chromatic descent leads to cadence.

1:44   **c.** Subordinate melody, **p**, played with rubato; crescendo to

2:11   **d.** Main melody with more elaborate decorative notes and trills; chromatic descent leads to cadence.

2:39   **3. a.** Concluding melody, **p**, then **pp**.

3:10   **b.** Concluding melody varied, crescendo with ascent to high register, melody played forcefully in octaves, **ff**; high trill-like figure, decrescendo and descent to gentle, rocking close, **pp**, then **ppp**.

Étude in C Minor, Op. 10, No. 12 (*Revolutionary;* 1831?)

The Russian takeover of Warsaw in 1831 may have inspired Chopin to compose the blazing and furious *Revolutionary* Étude in C Minor, Op. 10, No. 12. An **étude** is a study piece designed to help a performer master specific technical difficulties. The *Revolutionary* Étude, for example, develops speed and endurance in the pianist's left hand, which must play rapid passages throughout. Chopin's études reach beyond mere exercises in technique to become masterpieces of music, exciting to hear as well as to master.

The *Revolutionary* Étude, in A A'—coda form, begins with a dramatic outburst. High, dissonant chords and downward rushing passages lead to the main melody, marked *appassionato (impassioned)*, which is played in octaves by the right hand. Tension mounts because of the melody's dotted rhythms and its tempestuous accompaniment. After a climax at the end of section A', the coda momentarily relaxes the tension. Then a torrential passage sweeps down the keyboard to come to rest in powerful closing chords.

Listening Outline

CHOPIN, Étude in C Minor, Op. 10, No. 12 (*Revolutionary;* 1831?)

Allegro con fuoco (allegro with fire), duple meter ($\frac{2}{2}$)
Piano
(Duration 2:31)

Listen for the continuous rapid notes in the pianist's left hand and the *dotted rhythm* of the passionate main *melody.*

A

0:00	**1. a.**	High accented chords, *f*, answered by downward rushing passages; low running notes introduce
0:15	**b.**	Passionate main melody in octaves, *f*, dotted rhythm, minor,

decrescendo to

0:32	**c.**	Repetition of main melody, *p*, with different continuation, syncopated chords, crescendo to cadence in major.
0:46	**d.**	Lyrical melody in dotted rhythm, minor, crescendo and downward running notes; very high descending phrases lead to return of

A'

1:07	**2. a.**	High accented chords, *f*, answered by downward rushing passages; low running notes introduce
1:22	**b.**	Passionate main melody intensified, *f*, decrescendo; low running notes introduce
1:40	**c.**	Repetition of intensified main melody leading to
1:47	**d.**	Majestic downward phrases in major, *ff*, decrescendo, *p*, return to minor, low running notes rise and fall, ritardando to

Coda

2:10	**e.**	Gentle upward phrase repeated with ritardando. Sudden *ff*, downward rushing passage, powerful closing chords, *fff*.

Polonaise in A Flat Major, Op. 53 (1842)

The *polonaise,* a piece in triple meter, originated as a stately processional dance for the Polish nobility. Chopin's heroic polonaises evoke the ancient splendor of the Polish people.

His Polonaise in A Flat Major is majestic and powerful, with moments of lyrical contrast. It may be outlined as follows: introduction—A B A'—coda. Its main theme makes a grand entrance.

Introduction

0:00

Section A

0:28

The majesty of this theme is enhanced by intervals of thirds in the right hand and by the resonant, wide-ranging accompaniment. After the main theme is repeated twice with an even richer texture, Chopin offers the contrasting middle section (B). This is a marchlike melody accompanied by relentlessly repeated rapid octaves in the left hand. This section tests a pianist's strength and endurance. Powerful crescendos bring mounting excitement. Then Chopin gradually relaxes the mood to prepare for the final return of the heroic main theme (A').

Section B

2:48

Section A'

5:17

8 Franz Liszt

Franz Liszt (1811–1886) was handsome, magnetic, an incredible showman, irresistible to women, and a pacesetter in musical history. During the 1840s, he performed superhuman feats at the piano, overwhelming the European public and impressing musicians as much as the concertgoing public.

Chopin wished he could play his own piano études the way Liszt played them. Robert Schumann wrote that Liszt "enmeshed every member of the audience with his art and did with them as he willed." Brahms later said, "Whoever has not heard Liszt cannot speak of piano playing."

Liszt was born in Hungary. His father was an administrator for the same Esterházy family that Haydn had served. As a boy of eleven, Liszt studied in Vienna, where he met Schubert and Beethoven. During his teens and twenties, he lived in Paris, a city where romanticism flourished and that was a mecca for virtuosos. When he was nineteen and already acclaimed as a brilliant pianist, Liszt was awed by the great violinist Paganini, who drove audiences into a frenzy and was half suspected of being in league with the devil. Young Liszt was determined to become the Paganini of the piano. He withdrew from the concert stage for a few years, practiced from eight to twelve hours a day, and emerged as probably the greatest pianist of his time.

Franz Liszt—handsome, long-haired, magnetic—performed superhuman feats at the piano and overwhelmed the European musical public.
Imagno/Getty Images

To display his own incomparable piano mastery, Liszt composed his *Transcendental* Études and made piano transcriptions of Paganini's violin pieces. "My piano," he wrote, "is my very self. . . . A man's ten fingers have the power to reproduce the harmonies which are created by hundreds of performers." Once, after an orchestral performance of a movement from Berlioz's *Fantastic Symphony,* Liszt played his own piano arrangement and made a more powerful effect than the entire orchestra. He toured Europe tirelessly between 1839 and 1847, playing mainly his own piano music and receiving unprecedented public adulation.

But Liszt also wanted recognition as a serious composer. At thirty-six, he abandoned his career as a traveling virtuoso to become court conductor in Weimar, where he composed many orchestral pieces (developing a new and influential form of program music) and conducted works by such contemporaries as Berlioz, Schumann, and Wagner. Unselfish and generous, he taught hundreds of gifted pianists free of charge and provided musical and financial support crucial to Wagner's success. He also wrote music criticism and books on Chopin and Gypsy music. His literary efforts were aided by two aristocratic women writers: Countess Marie d'Agoult and, later, the Russian Princess Carolyne Sayn-Wittgenstein. (Marie d'Agoult left her husband to live with Liszt; she and Liszt had three children, one of whom, Cosima, later left her own husband to marry Richard Wagner.)

Liszt went to Rome to pursue religious studies in 1861, and, in 1865 he took minor holy orders, becoming Abbé Liszt. Contemporaries were stunned by the seeming incongruity: a notorious Don Juan and diabolical virtuoso had become a churchman. In Rome, he composed oratorios and masses.

During his last years, Liszt traveled between Rome, Weimar, and Budapest, where he was president of the new Academy of Music. Now he began to write curious, experimental piano pieces that foreshadowed some features of twentieth-century music. Though these late works went unappreciated, Liszt had become a living legend. The grand duke of Weimar said, "Liszt *was* what a prince *ought* to be."

Liszt's Music

Liszt's music is controversial. Some consider it vulgar and bombastic; others revel in its extroverted romantic rhetoric. Yet few would deny Liszt's originality, his influence, or his importance as the creator of the symphonic poem.

Liszt found new ways to exploit the piano; his melodies are sometimes surrounded by arpeggios that create the impression of three hands playing; and in the *Hungarian Rhapsodies,* which influenced a generation of nationalist composers, he makes the piano sound at times like an entire Gypsy band. His piano works contain daring leaps, rapid octaves and runs, and an unprecedented range of dynamics. Before the age of recordings and frequent concerts, Liszt's transcriptions made it possible for people to play operas and symphonies on their own pianos.

Breaking away from classical sonata form and the standard four-movement symphony, Liszt created the **symphonic poem,** or **tone poem,** a one-movement orchestral composition based to some extent on literary or pictorial ideas (see **Chapter 11**). Among his favorite inspirations were the works of Goethe (on which he based his *Faust* Symphony, 1854) and Dante (which inspired the *Dante* Symphony, 1856). Many of his compositions are concerned with the devil or death and bear titles such as *Mephisto Waltz, Totentanz* (*Dance of Death*), or *Funérailles* (*Funeral Ceremony*). Continual changes of tempo and mood and alternations between diabolical fury and semireligious meditation contribute to a feeling of improvisation; but in his symphonic poems and other orchestral works, contrasting moods are often unified through thematic transformations of a single, recurring musical idea.

Liszt's music influenced many composers, including Wagner, who admitted to him: "When I compose and orchestrate, I always think only of you." As a stupendous performer, innovative composer, and charismatic personality, Liszt typified the romantic movement.

Transcendental Étude No. 10 in F Minor (1851)

As dazzling, passionate, and poetic as Liszt himself, the *Transcendental* Étude No. 10 in F Minor is one of the finest virtuoso pieces of the romantic era. Liszt had written an early, simpler version of this piece in 1824, when he was only thirteen, and included it in a group of twelve studies. Fifteen years later, at the peak of his career as a virtuoso, he published a revised version that demanded transcendent, almost superhuman technical skill from the pianist. (Schumann was so overwhelmed by Liszt's études that he described them as "studies in storm and dread meant to be played by, at most, ten or twelve players in the world.") In 1851, after retiring from the concert stage, Liszt dedicated a third and final version—which we study—to his piano teacher Carl Czerny (1791–1857) "as a token of esteem, gratitude, and friendship."

0:00 The étude taxes the player with left-hand passages that require rapid skips and changes of hand position. Though written in A B A'—coda form, it almost seems like an improvisation, owing to its frequent alternations between brilliant virtuoso passages and more melodic ideas. Section A contains three themes. The first, in minor, is fragmentary and syncopated.

0:42 The second, in major, is more lyrical and in a high register, with dotted rhythms, and with rapid notes in the accompaniment.

1:14 The third, which has a processional character, is a transformation of the second. A melody that was introduced in major in a high register is now presented in minor, in a low register set against higher arpeggios.

1:26
2:04
4:05
The brief section B develops and transforms the syncopated main theme. All three themes return in section A', which is introduced by a decrescendo and ritardando. The étude ends with a furious coda based on a speeded-up transformation of the main theme.

9 Felix Mendelssohn

Besides his musical achievements, Felix Mendelssohn was a talented painter, a fine writer, and a brilliant conversationist in four languages.
DeAgostini/Getty Images

Felix Mendelssohn (1809–1847), a romantic whose music was rooted in classical tradition, was born in Hamburg, Germany, to a wealthy and distinguished Jewish family. (He was, however, raised as a Protestant.) By the age of nine, he was a brilliant pianist; by thirteen, he had written symphonies, concertos, sonatas, and vocal works of astounding quality. As a teenager, he performed his works at home with a private orchestra for the intellectual and artistic elite of Berlin, where the Mendelssohns had settled.

In 1829, at twenty, he conducted Bach's *St. Matthew Passion* in its first performance since the composer's death. This historic concert rekindled interest in Bach's music and earned Mendelssohn an international reputation. He often performed as a pianist, an organist, and a conductor in Germany and in England, where his music was especially popular.

He often visited and played for Queen Victoria, and the high point of his career was the triumphant premiere of his oratorio *Elijah* in Birmingham, England, in 1846.

When only twenty-six, he became conductor of the Leipzig Gewandhaus Orchestra, and he founded the Leipzig Conservatory at age thirty-three.

Mendelssohn's personal life was more conventional than that of many romantics. He was happily married and had four children. But constant travel and exhausting work sapped Mendelssohn's strength, and he died, after a stroke, at thirty-eight.

Mendelssohn's Music

Mendelssohn's music radiates the elegance and balance of his personality. It evokes a variety of moods but avoids emotional extremes and typically conveys an elfin quality through rapid movement, lightness, and transparent orchestral texture.

He wrote an enormous amount of music in all the genres of his day except opera. Today, only a few of his works are in the concert repertoire, but these are very popular. They include the Violin Concerto—which we study—the *Midsummer Night's Dream* and *Hebrides* overtures, the *Italian* and *Scotch* symphonies (1833, 1842), the oratorio *Elijah,* and a number of chamber works.

Concerto for Violin and Orchestra in E Minor, Op. 64 (1844)

Mendelssohn's Violin Concerto in E Minor, Op. 64, was inspired by his friendship with the concertmaster of his orchestra, the famous violinist Ferdinand David. "I should like to make a violin concerto for you next winter," Mendelssohn wrote. "One in E minor runs in my head and its beginning gives me no rest." With David as soloist, the Violin Concerto met with great success at its premiere in 1845. Ever since, its unique fusion of lyricism and virtuosity has made it one of the best-loved concertos.

The concerto's three movements are played without pause, in a characteristic linking technique used by romantic composers. Mendelssohn's love of balance is reflected in the cooperation and interplay between soloist and orchestra. Themes pass from one to another, producing a beautiful contrast of tone color and expression. At one moment, the violinist plays a melody while the orchestra discreetly accompanies; at another, the woodwinds present thematic fragments while the soloist has dazzling running passages.

Performance Perspectives

Hilary Hahn, Violinist, Playing the First Movement of Mendelssohn's Violin Concerto in E Minor, Op. 64

Hilary Hahn is one of the most prominent concert violinists of our time. When she was nineteen, *Time* magazine called her "America's best" young classical musician.

As with most concert artists, Hahn's extraordinary musical talent was recognized at a very early age. When not quite four, she began studying violin, and at age ten she was accepted at the Curtis Institute of Music in Philadelphia. At sixteen, she signed a recording contract, made her debut at Carnegie Hall with the Philadelphia Orchestra, and completed the requirements for her bachelor of music degree. However, she chose to delay her graduation from Curtis for three years: "I loved the school, so I stayed as long as I could. There were a lot of classes that interested me that I hadn't taken yet; for extra electives, I enrolled in poetry and fiction-writing workshops and several literature classes, in addition to continuing with German." One of her teachers at Curtis, Jennifer Higdon (studied in **Part VI**, **Chapter 22**), wrote a violin concerto for Hilary Hahn.

Hiroyuki Ito/Getty Images

For Hahn, "communicating music to people is something that I feel very lucky to be able to do." She writes her own liner notes for her recordings and maintains an online journal (on her website, **HilaryHahn.com**) of her experiences in cities where she performs. To expand children's musical horizons, Hahn often plays in grade schools. "I always play solo Bach, a slow and a fast movement. The music casts a spell. They really like it."

Hahn enjoys music in a wide range of styles, from blues and world music to hip-hop and classical. Her prize-winning recordings include works by Mendelssohn, Bach, Beethoven, and Bernstein, and she performs on the sound track of the M. Night Shyamalan film *The Village*, as well as on an album by Austin alt-rockers . . . *And You Will Know Us by the Trail of Dead.*

Hahn learned the Mendelssohn Violin Concerto when she was eleven and performed excerpts with the Curtis Orchestra the following year. (Her performance of the first movement of the concerto is included in the recordings.) "Not long after, I performed the entire concerto with a chamber orchestra in Florida, and since then the Mendelssohn concerto has been a staple of my repertoire." For Hahn, the first movement of the concerto is full of "lyricism, fire, drama, and contrast."

Hahn observes that performing a concerto requires close cooperation with the conductor and members of the orchestra. "Sometimes the conductor and I will disagree about something and meet in the middle. There's a system of give-and-take, opinions, and compromise—though as a musician, you try to never be compromised or compromise someone else's interpretation. Musicians inevitably interact with each other, so we have to be aware of what the others are doing. For example, if I share a solo line with the flute, I will pay attention to how the flutist plays the line so that it sounds like a duet. The conductor coordinates some of that, but in a concerto, the minutiae are really decided by the musicians, by listening to each other and reacting to the musical ideas that we hear."

For Hahn, playing before a live audience is very different from recording in a studio. "The audience influences performing to a large extent because the presence of people affects the way the concert hall sounds. The energy in the hall is hard to describe, but there is a different feeling when you know people are there to absorb the music (both acoustically and psychologically). It's quite energizing and inspiring. In recording, you have a limited time and an empty hall—any tiny noise can ruin a take, so no audience is allowed in the studio—and you have to get it right, so that situation takes a different approach. I try to keep the feeling as similar as possible, though, by imagining an audience listening in the hall, or in their car, or to their stereo."

10 | Fanny Mendelssohn Hensel

Fanny Mendelssohn Hensel was very prolific, composing over 450 works including songs, piano pieces, oratorios, and chamber music.
The Picture Art Collection/Alamy

Fanny Mendelssohn Hensel (1805–1847), older sister of Felix Mendelssohn, was a composer whose compositions were known only to a select few during her lifetime. Since the 1980s, her works have been rediscovered, published, performed, and recorded. Like her brother, Felix, she was born in Hamburg Germany to a wealthy and distinguished family of Jewish origin, and was raised in the Protestant faith. In 1811, the family moved to Berlin, where later Fanny and Felix studied piano and composition with the finest teachers in the city.

At thirteen, in honor of her father's birthday, Fanny played from memory all the twenty-four Preludes from Bach's *The Well-Tempered Clavier*, and at fourteen, composed songs and piano pieces. However, her father limited Fanny's musical ambitions by saying that as an upper-class young woman she could never aspire to be a professional musician like her brother Felix: "Music will perhaps be his profession, whilst for you it can only be an ornament, never the root of your being and doing." Even her beloved brother Felix agreed with their father and discouraged Fanny from publishing her compositions.

In 1826, two of her songs were published together with four songs by Felix under *his* name. Years later Felix visited Queen Victoria at Buckingham Palace and accompanied her as she sang a song she thought was by him. After the Queen praised the song, Felix admitted to her that it was composed by his sister.

When she was twenty-three, Fanny married Wilhelm Hensel, painter at the court in Berlin, who encouraged her musical activities. The couple's only child was named Sebastian Ludwig Felix Hensel after Fanny's favorite composers, Johann Sebastian Bach, Ludwig van Beethoven, and Felix Mendelssohn. In 1831, Fanny became music director and performer at Sunday concerts in the Mendelssohn family mansion, reviving the musicales her parents had hosted years before. Fanny's concerts were attended by up to 200 invited guests from Berlin's elite.

The works heard included compositions ranging from Bach to Chopin, and guest performers included such famous virtuosos as Clara Schumann and Franz Liszt.

In 1846, persuaded by praise from musicians, Fanny wrote in her diary, "I have made up my mind to publish my things." To Felix she wrote: "I am as afraid of you my brother at age 40 as I was of Father at age 14...I hope I won't disgrace all of you through my publishing." Felix replied giving Fanny his "professional blessing on your decision to join our guild." Several of her works finally appeared in print under her name, but less than a year later, in 1847 at age forty-one, Fanny died of a stroke.

Fanny Mendelssohn Hensel was extremely prolific, composing over 450 works. Her works include *Das Jahr* (*The Year*; 1841), a cycle of twelve piano pieces, each named after a month of the year, two cantatas for soloists, chorus and orchestra, a piano trio, and a String Quartet, which is studied here.

String Quartet in E Flat Major (1834)

The String Quartet in E Flat major, composed in 1834, but first published only in 1988, is one of Fanny's most important works, and one of the earliest string quartets composed by a woman. This String Quartet started out as a sonata for piano. In 1829, Fanny wrote three movements of a piano sonata but abandoned the work without its projected fourth movement. Five years later she arranged the first two movements, Adagio ma non troppo and Allegretto, for string quartet and added two new movements: Romanza (a songlike movement) and Allegro molto vivace. We focus on the Allegretto.

Second Movement: Allegretto

The Allegretto, a lively scherzo in C minor, was Felix Mendelssohn's favorite movement in the Quartet. The movement is in A B A′ form and sextuple meter (*1*-2-3-*4*-5-6). The hushed A section is dark and driven in mood. The opening theme moves down the scale with repeated notes.

There are many alternations between pizzicato notes and those played with the bow.
The highly energetic and extended middle section is in C major and alternates between loud and soft passages. It opens with a loud C-major chord and an ascending theme in rapid notes played by the viola.

This theme is imitated in turn, fugue-like, by the second violin, cello, and first violin. This recalls the C-major opening of the middle section in the Scherzo of Beethoven's Fifth Symphony, studied on page 208. In this section each instrument is given an equal share of the melodic material. The rapid-note theme appears in different forms, including moving downward instead of upward. Fragments of the opening theme help drive the Allegretto to its *ff* climax. A sudden *p* and slowing of tempo prepare the return of the opening theme of the movement, which begins the hushed A′ section. The Allegretto ends with two pizzicato chords in C major, recalling the many pizzicato tones heard earlier and the C-major key of the middle section.

Listening Outline

MENDELSSOHN HENSEL, String Quartet in E-flat Major (1834)

Second Movement: Allegretto
A B A′ form, sextuple meter ($\frac{6}{8}$), C minor
1st violin, 2nd violin, viola, cello
(Duration 3:30)

Listen for the difference between bowed and pizzicato string sounds in the A section. Notice the contrast between the minor key, homophonic texture and relatively soft dynamics of the A section, and the major key, polyphonic texture and loud dynamics of the B section.

A

0:00	**1. a.**	Violin, *p*, short opening motive in minor. Repeated.
0:09	**b.**	Strings, *p*, pizzicato, cadence, *f*.
0:19	**c.**	High violin, *p*, opening motive, legato chromatic descent.
0:29	**2. a.**	Violin, *p*, return of opening motive, climb to
0:43	**b.**	Legato downward chromatic phrases, *pp*, cadence to

B

0:57	**3. a.**	Major chord, *f*, viola alone, rushing theme, imitated by 2nd violin, cello. 1st violin, *f*, rushing motive; sudden *p*, rise to *f*.
1:20	**b.**	Cello, rushing motive, *f*, imitated by 1st violin, motive passed among the strings; diminuendo to
1:37	**c.**	Mysterious high chords, *p*. above solo cello, *p*, rushing motive expanded, crescendo to
1:46	**d.**	Rushing motive in violins, *f*, alternating with opening motive in long polyphonic passage; all strings join rushing motive and rise to
2:22	**e.**	High 1st violin downward arpeggios, *ff*, sudden *p*, tempo slows gradually.

A′

2:43	**5. a.**	Violin, *p*, short opening motive in minor. Repeated.
2:51	**b.**	Strings, *p*, pizzicato.
3:00	**c.**	1st violin then 2nd violin, *p*, tender legato phrases, rise to high sustained tone.
3:15	**d.**	1st violin, *pp*, varied opening motive, strings descend to low register, pizzicato chords, *pp*, at end.

11 Program Music

Romantic composers were particularly attracted to program music—instrumental music associated with a story, poem, idea, or scene. Programmatic works such as Berlioz's *Fantastic Symphony,* Tchaikovsky's *Romeo and Juliet,* and Smetana's *Moldau* depict emotions, characters, and events, or the sounds and motions of nature. Such nonmusical ideas are usually specified by the title or by the composer's explanatory comments (the program).

Program music draws on the capacity of music to suggest and evoke. Music can, of course, imitate certain sounds—birdsongs, thunder, bells, wind. But "sound effects" are only part of the descriptive resources of music. A composer can also exploit the correspondence between musical rhythm and objects in motion. A continuous flow of rapid notes, for example, can evoke waves or a stream. Most important is the ability of music to create mood, emotion, and atmosphere. An agitated theme may represent conflict; a lyrical melody may symbolize love. However, music alone makes no definite reference to ideas, emotions, and objects. Music cannot identify anything. It is the title or a verbal explanation that lets us fully grasp a composer's source of inspiration.

The aim of most program music is expression more than mere description. Beethoven, for example, referred to his *Pastoral* Symphony (Symphony No. 6) as "an expression of feeling rather than painting." Even the most "realistic" episodes in program music can also serve a purely musical function; and one can generally appreciate a descriptive piece as pure music, without knowing its title or program. (We can enjoy the lyrical theme of Tchaikovsky's *Romeo and Juliet,* for example, without associating it with young love.) The forms used for program music are similar to those used for nonprogram music, or *absolute music.* A programmatic work can be heard simply as an example of rondo, fugue, sonata form, or theme and variations. But our pleasure may be greater when we can relate music to literary or pictorial ideas, and romantic composers were well aware of this. Occasionally, they even added titles or programs to finished works. Both musicians and audiences in the romantic period liked to read stories into all music, whether intended by the composer or not.

Most romantic program music was written for piano or for orchestra. The main forms of orchestral program music are the program symphony, the concert overture, the symphonic poem (tone poem), and incidental music.

A *program symphony* is a composition in several movements—as its name implies, a symphony with a program. Usually, each movement has a descriptive title. For example, Berlioz's *Fantastic Symphony* has five movements: (1) *Reveries, Passions,* (2) *A Ball,* (3) *Scene in the Country,* (4) *March to the Scaffold,* and (5) *Dream of a Witches' Sabbath.* (This work is discussed in **Chapter 1**2.)

A *concert overture* has one movement, usually in sonata form. The romantic concert overture was modeled after the opera overture, a one-movement composition that establishes the mood of an opera. But the concert overture is *not* intended to usher in a stage work; it is an independent composition. Well-known concert overtures include Mendelssohn's *Hebrides* Overture and Tchaikovsky's *Overture 1812* and *Romeo and Juliet* Overture, which is studied in **Chapter 14**.

A symphonic poem, or *tone poem,* is also in one movement. Symphonic poems take many traditional forms—sonata form, rondo, or theme and variations—as well as irregular forms. This flexibility of form separates the symphonic poem from the concert overture, which is usually in sonata form. Franz Liszt developed the symphonic poem in the late 1840s and 1850s, and it became the most important type of program music after 1860. Well-known tone poems include *Les Préludes* (1854) and *Hamlet* (1858), by Liszt; *Danse macabre* (1874), by Camille Saint-Saëns (1835–1921); and *The Sorcerer's Apprentice* (1897), by Paul Dukas (1865–1935). A leading composer of tone poems at the end of the nineteenth century was Richard Strauss (1864–1949). His tone poems—characterized by brilliant orchestration—include *Don Juan* (1889), *Till Eulenspiegel's Merry Pranks* (1895), and *Also sprach Zarasthustra* (*So Spoke Zoroaster;* 1896), which was used in the film *2001: A Space Odyssey.* During the late nineteenth century, symphonic poems became an important means of expression for nationalism in music. In **Chapter 1**3, we consider a nationalistic tone poem, Smetana's *Moldau,* depicting the longest river of Bohemia (a region that became part of the modern Czech Republic) as it winds through the countryside.

Incidental music is music to be performed before and during a play. It is "incidental" to the staged drama, but it sets the mood for certain scenes. Interludes, background music, marches, and dances are all incidental music (as are today's movie scores). Mendelssohn's incidental music for *A Midsummer Night's Dream* includes his famous *Wedding March.*

12 Hector Berlioz

Hector Berlioz (1803–1869), one of the first French romantic composers and a daring creator of new orchestral sounds, was born in a small town near Grenoble. His father, a physician, sent him to Paris to study medicine, but Berlioz was "filled with horror" by the dissecting room and shocked his parents by abandoning medicine to pursue a career in music. He studied at the Paris Conservatory, haunted the opera house, and composed.

When he was twenty-three, Berlioz was overwhelmed by the works of Shakespeare and also fell madly in love with a Shakespearean actress, Harriet Smithson, to whom

The French composer Hector Berlioz was a daring creator of new orchestral sounds and one of the first great orchestra conductors.

Tony Evans/Getty Images

he wrote such wild, impassioned letters that she thought he was a lunatic and refused to see him. To depict his "endless and unquenchable passion," Berlioz wrote the *Symphonie fantastique* (*Fantastic Symphony*) in 1830, which startled Parisians by its sensationally autobiographical program, its amazingly novel orchestration, and its vivid depiction of the weird and diabolical.

In 1830, too, Berlioz won the Prix de Rome (Rome Prize), subsidizing two years' study in Rome. When he returned to Paris, Berlioz met and married Harriet Smithson—after she had attended a performance of the *Fantastic Symphony* and realized that it depicted her. (They separated, however, after only a few years.)

Berlioz's unconventional music irritated the opera and concert establishment. To get a hearing for his works, he had to arrange concerts at his own expense—an enormous undertaking that drained him financially, physically, and emotionally. Although he had a following of about 1,200 who faithfully bought tickets to his concerts, this was not enough support for a composer of difficult, monumental works requiring hundreds of performers. Berlioz turned to musical journalism, becoming a brilliant and witty music critic who tried to convince the Parisian public that music was not merely entertainment but dramatic emotional expression.

Outside France, Berlioz's stock was higher. After 1840, he was in demand throughout Europe, conducting his own and others' music. As one of the first great conductors, he influenced a whole generation of musicians. But his last years were bitter. He was repeatedly passed over for important positions and honors and composed very little during the six years before his death at sixty-five.

Berlioz's Music

"The prevailing qualities of my music," wrote Berlioz, "are passionate expressiveness, inner fire, rhythmic drive, and unexpectedness." Above all, Berlioz's music sounds unique. It includes abrupt contrasts, fluctuating dynamics, and many changes in tempo.

As an orchestrator, Berlioz was extraordinarily imaginative and innovative. At a time when the average orchestra had about sixty players, he often assembled hundreds of musicians to achieve new power, tone colors, and timbres. His melodies are often long, irregular, and asymmetrical, taking unexpected turns. Most of his works are for orchestra, or orchestra with chorus and vocal soloists; all are dramatic and programmatic. He invented new forms: his "dramatic symphony" *Romeo and Juliet* (1839) is for orchestra, chorus, and vocal soloists; and his "dramatic legend" *The Damnation of Faust* (1846) combines opera and oratorio. He also wrote three operas and a grandiose, monumental Requiem (1837).

He knew he was a pioneer. He wrote of the Requiem, "I have seen one man listening in terror, shaken to the depths of his soul, while his next neighbor could not catch an idea, though trying with all his might to do so."

Symphonie fantastique (*Fantastic Symphony;* 1830)

The astonishing *Symphonie fantastique* (*Fantastic Symphony*), a five-movement program symphony (we study its fourth and fifth movements), is a romantic manifesto. Both the symphony and Berlioz's program reflect the twenty-six-year-old composer's unrequited passion for the actress Harriet Smithson:

A young musician of extraordinary sensibility and abundant imagination, in the depths of despair because of hopeless love, has poisoned himself with opium. The drug is too feeble to kill him but plunges him into a heavy sleep accompanied by weird visions. His sensations, emotions, and memories, as they pass through his affected mind, are transformed into musical images and ideas. The beloved one herself becomes to him a melody, a recurrent theme (*idée fixe*) which haunts him continually.

A single melody, which Berlioz called the **idée fixe,** or *fixed idea,* is used to represent the beloved. When introduced in the first movement—*Reveries, Passions*—it sounds, in Berlioz's description, "passionate but at the same time noble and shy."

Allegro agitato e appassionato assai

It appears in all five movements and unifies the contrasting episodes of the symphony. This recurrence of the same theme in every movement of a symphony was a striking novelty in Berlioz's day. The theme changes in character during the work. For example, in the second movement—*A Ball*—it is transformed into a waltz, and in the third movement—*Scene in the Country*—it is played against an agitated countermelody.

Another innovation in the symphony is its use of a very large and colorful orchestra: piccolo, 2 flutes, 2 oboes, English horn, 2 clarinets, 4 bassoons, 4 French horns, 2 cornets, 2 trumpets, 3 trombones, 2 tubas, 4 timpani, bass drum, snare drum, cymbals, bells, 2 harps, and strings. (Beethoven, for one, had not used the English horn, tuba, bells, cornet, or harp in his symphonies.) Berlioz saves the heaviest orchestration for the last two movements, where he depicts the fantastic and diabolical. Though the macabre and supernatural had long been dealt with in opera (for example, in Mozart's *Don Giovanni*), this is its first expression in an important symphony.

Fourth Movement: *March to the Scaffold*
Allegretto non troppo

> He dreams that he has murdered his beloved, that he has been condemned to death and is being led to the scaffold. The procession moves forward to the sounds of a march that is now somber and fierce, now brilliant and solemn, in which the muffled sounds of heavy steps give way without transition to the noisiest outbursts. At the end, the *idée fixe* returns for a moment, like a last thought of love interrupted by the death blow.

"The *March to the Scaffold* is fifty times more frightening than I expected," Berlioz gleefully observed after the first rehearsals of the *Fantastic Symphony*. It is not until this fiendish fourth movement that all the brass and percussion instruments enter the action. Berlioz creates a menacing atmosphere with the opening orchestral sound, a unique combination of muted French horns, timpani tuned a third apart, and basses playing pizzicato chords.

Two contrasting themes alternate within *March to the Scaffold*. The first theme, described as "somber and fierce" in Berlioz's program, is introduced by cellos and basses and moves down the scale for two octaves. This scalewise melody appears both in minor and in major and is combined with countermelodies. It is also inverted, moving upward rather than downward. The second theme, described as "brilliant and solemn" in the program, is a syncopated march tune blared by the brasses and woodwinds. At the end of the march a solo clarinet begins to play the *idée fixe* but is savagely interrupted by a very loud chord representing the fall of the guillotine's blade. The following string pizzicato may well have been intended to suggest the bouncing of the severed head.

Listening Outline

BERLIOZ, *Symphonie fantastique (Fantastic Symphony; 1830)*

Fourth Movement: *March to the Scaffold*

Allegretto non troppo

2 flutes, 2 oboes, 2 clarinets, 4 bassoons, 2 trumpets, 2 cornets, 4 French horns, 3 trombones, 2 tubas, timpani, bass drum, snare drum, cymbals, 1st violins, 2d violins, violas, cellos, double basses
(Duration 4:48)

Listen for the *downward scale theme* in the strings, often combined with *countermelodies,* and the *syncopated march theme.* Notice near the end of the *March to the Scaffold* that the *idée fixe* (fixed idea) in the solo clarinet is interrupted by an abrupt, loud *chord* representing the fall of the guillotine's blade.

0:00	**1.**	Timpani, pizzicato basses, $\boldsymbol{pp}$; syncopations in muted French horns, $\boldsymbol{p}$, crescendo to $\boldsymbol{ff}$ chord.
0:27	**2. a.**	Basses and cellos alone, $\boldsymbol{ff}$, downward scalewise melody, minor, decrescendo.

0:41	**b.**	Downward melody repeated with countermelody in high bassoons.
0:54	**c.**	High violins, $\boldsymbol{f}$, downward melody, major, accompanied by staccato lower strings. Sudden $\boldsymbol{ff}$. Melody repeated by violins, $\boldsymbol{f}$.
1:19	**d.**	Staccato bassoons, $\boldsymbol{p}$, together with pizzicato strings, minor, decrescendo to $\boldsymbol{pp}$, quick crescendo to
1:39	**3.**	Brasses and woodwinds, $\boldsymbol{f}$, syncopated march tune, major. March tune repeated.

2:04	**4. a.**	Very loud brass and woodwind fanfare introduces
2:11	**b.**	Splintered downward melody, pizzicato and bowed strings, staccato winds, minor. Pizzicato violins and timpani, crescendo to
2:22	**c.**	Brasses, woodwinds, $\boldsymbol{f}$, syncopated march tune, major, active string accompaniment. March tune repeated.
2:46	**d.**	Very loud brass and woodwind fanfare introduces
2:54	**e.**	Splintered downward melody, pizzicato and bowed strings, staccato winds, minor.
3:02	**f.**	Brasses, $\boldsymbol{mf}$, shortened downward melody repeated on higher pitches, active string accompaniment, crescendo.
3:16	**5. a.**	Whole orchestra, downward melody, $\boldsymbol{ff}$, timpani, cymbals, minor, decrescendo to $\boldsymbol{pp}$.
3:27	**b.**	Sudden $\boldsymbol{ff}$, whole orchestra, upward scalewise melody, major, timpani, cymbals.

Staccato strings alone, orchestral punctuation, *ff*, excited dotted rhythm in strings, repeated figure in brasses and woodwinds; downward staccato strings, *ff*, lead to

4:01 **c.** Wind and string chords alternate, *f*, decrescendo to *pp*. Sudden *ff*, full orchestra.

4:14 **d.** Solo clarinet, *idée fixe,*

interrupted by

4:24 **e.** Short orchestral chord, *ff* (fall of guillotine blade), and string pizzicato (bouncing of severed head), powerful timpani roll, *ff*, brasses and woodwinds *f*, repeated major chord, strings, *ff*, cymbals, ending chord by full orchestra, *ff*.

Fifth Movement: *Dream of a Witches' Sabbath*
Larghetto; Allegro

> He sees himself at a witches' sabbath in the midst of a hideous crowd of ghouls, sorcerers, and monsters of every description, united for his funeral. Strange noises, groans, shrieks of laughter, distant cries, which other cries seem to answer. The melody of the loved one is heard, but it has lost its character of nobleness and timidity; it is no more than a dance tune, ignoble, trivial, and grotesque. It is she who comes to the sabbath! . . . A howl of joy greets her arrival. . . . She participates in the diabolical orgy. . . . The funeral knell, burlesque of the *Dies irae*. Witches' dance. The dance and the *Dies irae* combined.

0:00 *Dream of a Witches' Sabbath* is the most "fantastic" movement of the symphony; it depicts a series of grotesque events. Its slow, hushed introduction (larghetto) immediately draws the listener into the realm of the macabre and supernatural, evoking "strange noises, groans, shrieks of laughter" and "distant cries." Eerie tremolos in high muted strings and menacing low tones of cellos and basses begin a succession of fragmentary ideas in starkly contrasting tone colors, registers, and dynamics. In the exploratory spirit of his romantic age, Berlioz dared to create sounds that are weird rather than conventionally pleasing.

1:39 In the allegro section, the beloved is revealed to be a witch. Her theme, the once "noble and timid" *idée fixe,* is transformed into a dance tune that is "trivial and grotesque." Played shrilly by a high-pitched clarinet, the tune moves in quick notes decorated by trills.

3:22   A "funeral knell" of sonorous bells lends an awesome atmosphere to the next part of the movement. Tubas and bassoons intone a solemn low melody in long, even notes.

3:54   This melody is the medieval chant *Dies irae (Day of wrath),* traditionally sung in the mass for the dead. Berlioz quotes it here as a symbol of eternal damnation. Soon the chant melody is shifted up to a high register and played by woodwinds and pizzicato strings in a quick dancelike rhythm.

Thus Berlioz dared to parody a sacred chant by transforming it into a trivial tune, as he had just done moments earlier with the *idée fixe.*

5:14   Berlioz conveys the frenzy of a witches' dance in a fuguelike section. The fugue subject (the witches' dance) is introduced by the lower strings and then imitated by other instruments.

7:52   A crescendo builds to a powerful climax in which the rapid witches' dance, played in the strings, is set against the slower-moving Dies irae, proclaimed by the brasses and woodwinds. This musical nightmare ends in an orgy of orchestral power.

13 Nationalism in Nineteenth–Century Music

During the nineteenth century, Europeans felt strongly that their homelands merited loyalty and self-sacrifice. These nationalistic feelings were awakened during the upheavals of the French Revolution and the Napoleonic wars (1789–1814), when French armies invaded much of Europe. In many countries, military resistance to Napoleon aroused the citizens' sense of national identity. Common bonds of language, culture, and history were strengthened as battles now were fought by soldiers drawn from the general population—not by mercenaries, as in the past. These patriotic feelings were intensified by romanticism, which glorified love for one's national heritage.

As a revolutionary political movement, nationalism led to the unification of lands—such as Germany and Italy—that had previously been divided into tiny states. It spurred revolts in countries under foreign rule, such as Poland and Bohemia (later part of the Czech Republic).

Nationalism was a potent cultural movement as well, particularly regarding language. In lands dominated by foreign powers, the national language was used increasingly in textbooks, newspapers, and official documents. For example, Bohemia saw a revival of the Czech language, which before 1800 had lost ground to the German spoken by its Austrian rulers. By the 1830s and 1840s, important textbooks on astronomy and chemistry were written in Czech, and there were many collections of Czech folk poetry. In every land, the "national spirit" was felt to reside in the "folk," the peasantry. The national past became a subject of intense historical investigation, and there was new enthusiasm for folksongs, dances, legends, and fairytales.

Nationalism influenced romantic music, as composers deliberately gave their works a distinctive national identity. They used folksongs and dances and created original melodies with a folk flavor. Nationalist composers wrote operas and program music inspired by the history, legends, and landscapes of their native lands. Their works bear titles like *Russian Easter* Overture (Rimsky-Korsakov), *Finlandia* (Sibelius), and *Slavonic Dances* (Dvořák). But a genuine feeling of national style does not come merely through the use of folksongs or patriotic subjects. A piece of music will *sound* French, Russian, or Italian when its rhythm, tone color, texture, and melody spring from national tradition. There were regional traits in music before the romantic period, but never had differences of national style been emphasized so strongly or so consciously.

In these revolutionary times, musical compositions could symbolize nationalist yearnings and sometimes stirred audiences to violent political demonstrations. The Italian opera composer Giuseppe Verdi deliberately chose librettos that fanned public hatred for the Austrian overlords; censors constantly pressured him to change scenes that might be interpreted as anti-Austrian or antimonarchical. A twentieth-century parallel occurred when the Nazis banned performances of Smetana's symphonic poem *The Moldau* in Prague, the composer's home city.

The strongest impact of nationalism was felt in lands whose own musical heritage had been dominated by the music of Italy, France, Germany, or Austria. During the romantic period, Poland, Russia, Bohemia, the Scandinavian countries, and Spain produced important composers whose music had a national flavor. Early in the nineteenth century, Chopin transformed his native Polish dances into great art. After about 1860, groups or "schools" of composers consciously declared their musical independence and established national styles. Among the leading musical nationalists were Mussorgsky, Rimsky-Korsakov, and Borodin from Russia; Smetana and Dvořák from Bohemia; Edvard Grieg (1843–1907) from Norway; Jean Sibelius (1865–1957) from Finland; and Isaac Albéniz (1860–1909) from Spain.

An important national school is the Russian, which created highly distinctive music. The opera *A Life for the Tsar,* by Mikhail Glinka (1804–1857), laid the groundwork for a national style, and in the 1860s five young men—now known as the *Russian Five*—formed a true national school. They were Mily Balakirev (1837–1910), César Cui (1835–1918), Alexander Borodin (1833–1887), Nikolai Rimsky-Korsakov (1844–1908), and Modest Mussorgsky (1839–1881). Remarkably, all but Balakirev began as amateurs, and most of them held nonmusical jobs. Mussorgsky was the most original of the Russian five, and his opera *Boris Godunov* is a masterpiece of musical nationalism.

The Moldau (1874), by Bedřich Smetana

Bedřich Smetana (1824–1884) was the founder of Czech national music. His works are steeped in the folk music and legends of his native Bohemia. But he grew up when Bohemia was under Austrian domination, and in this repressive atmosphere, his musical nationalism could make little headway. He emigrated to Sweden in 1856.

In 1862, when Austria had made some liberal concessions, Smetana returned to Prague. He was active as a composer, pianist, conductor, and teacher and wrote the *Bartered Bride,* his most famous opera. At age fifty, he became completely deaf, but some of his finest works followed, including *Má Vlast* (*My Country;* 1874–1879), a cycle of six symphonic poems. His last years were blighted by syphilis, and he died in an insane asylum at age sixty.

"Today I took an excursion to the St. John Rapids where I sailed in a boat through huge waves. . . . The view of the landscape was both beautiful and grand." Smetana's trip inspired his famous symphonic poem *The Moldau,* which depicts Bohemia's main river as it flows through the countryside. This orchestral work, part of the cycle *Má Vlast* (*My Country*), is both a romantic representation of nature and a display of Czech nationalism. *The Moldau* was written in three weeks shortly after Smetana became deaf, but its fresh, optimistic mood gives no hint of the composer's anguish and despair.

The Moldau River and Charles Bridge in the city of Prague, Czech Republic. Smetana's famous symphonic poem The Moldau (1874) musically evokes the flow of the Moldau River and scenes along its banks.

Efrain Padro/Alamy

Smetana wrote the following program to preface his score:

The composition depicts the course of the river, beginning from its two small sources, one cold the other warm, the joining of both streams into one, then the flow of the Moldau through forests and across meadows, through the countryside where merry feasts are celebrated; water nymphs dance in the moonlight; on nearby rocks can be seen the outline of ruined castles, proudly soaring into the sky. The Moldau swirls through the St. John Rapids and flows in a broad stream toward Prague. It passes Vyšehrad [where an ancient royal castle once stood], and finally the river disappears in the distance as it flows majestically into the Elbe.

The Moldau falls into contrasting musical sections that represent different scenes and episodes described in the program. Hunting along the riverbank is suggested by horn fanfares; a peasant wedding by a rustic polka, the Bohemian dance; and a moonlit night by shimmering woodwinds and a serene melody in high muted strings. An expansive folklike theme that recurs several times symbolizes the river. Smetana unifies the symphonic poem with running notes evoking the movement of water, sometimes rippling, sometimes turbulent.

Listening Outline

SMETANA, *The Moldau* (1874)

Allegro commodo non agitato (unhurried allegro, not agitated), sextuple meter (§), E minor
Piccolo, 2 flutes, 2 oboes, 2 clarinets, 2 bassoons, 4 French horns, 2 trumpets, 3 trombones, tuba, timpani, bass drum, triangle, cymbals, harp, 1st violins, 2d violins, violas, cellos, double basses
(Duration 11:35)

Listen for the contrasting musical sections that represent different scenes described in the program, such as "Two springs," "The river," "Forest hunt," and "Peasant wedding." Notice that this symphonic poem is unified by a recurring "river" theme, and by running notes representing the flow of water.

Two springs

0:00　　　**1. a.** Flutes, ***p***, running notes. Harp, pizzicato violins.

　　　Clarinets, ***p***, join, running notes.
　　　b. Lower strings, ***p***, running notes lead to

The river

1:10　　　**2.** Violins, songlike river theme, minor key. Running-note accompaniment in strings.

1:39　　　River theme extended.

Forest hunt

3:00　　　**3. a.** French horns and trumpets, ***f***, hunting calls. Strings, running notes. Crescendo to ***ff***.
　　　b. Decrescendo to ***ppp***.

Peasant wedding

3:57   **4. a.** Strings, *p*, polka.

mf

Crescendo to *f*, triangle strokes.
   b. Decrescendo to *ppp*, melody descends.

Moonlight: dance of water nymphs

5:19   **5. a.** Woodwinds, *pp*, sustained tones. Flutes, *p*, running notes lead to
5:42   **b.** High muted violins, *pp*, serene legato melody, flutes and harp accompany, *p*.
6:58   **c.** Brasses, *pp*. Gentle staccato chords join accompaniment to violin melody.
7:36   **d.** Crescendo. Woodwinds, running notes lead to

The river

7:59   **6.** Violins, river theme. Running-note accompaniment in strings.

The rapids

8:40   **7. a.** Full orchestra, *ff*. Brasses, timpani roll, piccolo, cymbal crashes.
   b. Strings, *pp*. Quick crescendo.

The river at its widest point

9:53   **8.** Full orchestra, *ff*, river theme in major key. Faster tempo.

Vyšehrad, the ancient castle

10:21   **9. a.** Brasses and woodwinds, *ff*, hymnlike melody. Cymbal crashes.
   b. Decrescendo. Violins, *ppp*. Full orchestra, *ff*, closing chords.

14 Peter Ilyich Tchaikovsky

Peter Ilyich Tchaikovsky (1840–1893), the most famous Russian composer, started his career as a government clerk and began to study music theory at the relatively late age of twenty-one. His progress in music was rapid, however. After graduating from the St. Petersburg Conservatory, he became professor of harmony at the new Moscow Conservatory, and composed furiously: a symphony, an opera, a tone poem, and by the age of thirty, his first great orchestral work, *Romeo and Juliet*.

The year 1877 was dramatic for Tchaikovsky. He married, disastrously and apparently only to conceal his homosexuality, attempted suicide two weeks later, and had a nervous collapse. (He separated from his wife and never saw her again.) But in 1877 he also acquired a wealthy benefactress, Nadezhda von Meck, with whom he had a curious but intimate friendship—they corresponded but did not meet. She gave him an annuity that allowed him to quit his conservatory position and devote himself to composition.

Peter Ilyich Tchaikovsky was the most famous Russian composer of the nineteenth century.

Maxim Anisimov/Getty Images

Fourteen years later, Tchaikovsky was deeply hurt when she abruptly cut off the annuity and stopped writing to him.

During these years, Tchaikovsky achieved success conducting his own works throughout Europe (and, in 1891, in the United States). Yet success did not bring spiritual peace. In 1893, nine days after conducting the premiere of his Symphony No. 6 (*Pathétique*), which ends unconventionally with a slow, despairing finale, he died at the age of fifty-three.

Tchaikovsky's Music

Tchaikovsky thought of himself as "*Russian* in the fullest sense of the word," but his style was influenced by French, Italian, and German music as well as Russian folksong. His works are much more in the western tradition than those of his contemporaries, the Russian five. He fused national and international elements to produce intensely subjective and passionate music.

Among his most popular orchestral compositions are the Fourth, Fifth, and Sixth (*Pathétique*) Symphonies (1877, 1888, and 1893); Piano Concerto No. 1 in B Flat Minor (1875); the Violin Concerto (1878); and the overture-fantasy *Romeo and Juliet* (1869), which we study. He wrote some of his best music for ballet: *Swan Lake* (1876), *Sleeping Beauty* (1889), and *The Nutcracker* (1892). The spirit of ballet permeates much of Tchaikovsky's music. He also wrote eight operas and the orchestral showpieces *Marche slave* and *Overture 1812*.

Romeo and Juliet, Overture–Fantasy (1869)

Romantic composers felt an artistic kinship with Shakespeare because of his passionate poetry, dramatic contrasts, and profound knowledge of the human heart. Shakespeare's plays inspired some of the finest nineteenth-century compositions. Among these were *Macbeth* and *Othello,* set as operas by Verdi; and *A Midsummer Night's Dream,* depicted in incidental music by Mendelssohn. *Romeo and Juliet* inspired both a "dramatic symphony" by Berlioz and a concert overture by Tchaikovsky.

Tchaikovsky composed *Romeo and Juliet* at twenty-nine, near the beginning of his musical career. Although it is now one of the best-loved works, *Romeo and Juliet* was a dismal failure at its premiere in 1870. "After the concert we dined. . . . No one said a single word to me about the overture the whole evening. And yet I yearned so for appreciation and kindness." Tchaikovsky decided to revise the overture. He composed a new theme to represent Friar Laurence, adopting a suggestion made by his friend Balakirev. Despite this, the work remained unappreciated. Only about twenty years later, after further revisions, did it achieve worldwide popularity.

Like Shakespeare's play, Tchaikovsky's *Romeo and Juliet* glorifies a romantic love powerful enough to triumph over death. Tchaikovsky captures the essential emotions of Shakespeare's play without defining the characters or the exact course of events. Highly contrasted themes are used to express the conflict between family hatred and youthful love. Tchaikovsky also depicts the gentle and philosophical Friar Laurence, intermediary between the lovers and the harsh outside world.

Romeo and Juliet is a concert overture consisting of a slow introduction followed by a fast movement in sonata form. (Tchaikovsky's title—Overture-Fantasy—implies that he treated the musical material in a free and imaginative way.) We can enjoy *Romeo and Juliet* as an exciting orchestral piece without knowing the play. However, a new dimension is added to our listening experience when we associate the music with the drama.

Tchaikovsky opens the overture with the Friar Laurence theme, a solemn, hymnlike melody.

First theme
5:16

As the slow introduction unfolds, brooding strings set an atmosphere of impending tragedy. The clash of swords and the anger of the feud between the Montagues and the Capulets are suggested by the violent first theme of the allegro.

Bridge
6:38

Syncopations, rushing strings, and massive sounds create enormous excitement. The exposition continues with a bridge section that brings a sudden **pp**, a calmer mood, and a slower rhythm.

Second theme
7:28

The second theme of the exposition, a tender love theme, is expressively scored for English horn and muted violas.

Pulsating Melody
7:48

It is followed by a gently pulsating melody in the muted violins.

Development
10:32

Recapitulation
12:35

The development section focuses mainly on the feud theme and the Friar Laurence theme. In the recapitulation, the gently pulsating melody precedes the love theme, which now has a new exultant character as Tchaikovsky envelops the listener in opulent sound. There are long crescendos as the melody is led higher and higher to ever-more passionate orchestral climaxes.

Pulsating Melody
12:57

Love theme
13:34

In the coda, Tchaikovsky transforms the love theme into a song of mourning, while timpani softly beat the rhythm of a funeral march.

Coda
16:24

Then, a new hymn and a tender reminiscence of the love theme suggest that Romeo and Juliet are reunited in death.

1:01

Apostrophes, cris et tapage	Yells, shouts and noises
Poussés jusques à la fureur!	Push to the breaking point!
Car c'est la fête du courage!	For it is the celebration of courage!
C'est la fête des gens de cœur!	It is the celebration of the brave of heart!
Allons! en garde!	Let's go! On guard! Let's go!
Allons! allons! Ah!	Let's go! Let's go! Ah!

1:28

Toreador melody,
major key.

Toréador, en garde! Toréador!
Toréador!

Toreador, on guard! Toreador!
Toreador!

Et songe bien, oui,	And contemplate well, yes contemplate
songe en combattant	as you fight
Qu'un œil noir te regarde,	that a dark eye is watching you,
Et que l'amour t'attend,	and that love awaits you,
Toréador, l'amour, l'amour t'attend!	Toreador, love, love awaits you!

1:59

Toreador melody re-
peated, other voices
join Escamillio

Toréador, en garde! Toréador!	Toreador, on guard! Toreador!
Toréador!	Toreador!
Et songe bien, oui,	And contemplate well,
songe en combattant	yes think as you fight
Qu''un œil noir te regarde,	that a dark eye is watching you,
Et que l'amour t'attend,	and that love awaits you,
Toréador, l'amour, l'amour t'attend!	Toreador, love, love awaits you!

2:25

Orchestra, opening
melody, minor key.

2:45

Escamillo

Tout d'un coup, on fait silence,	All at once, we are silent,
On fait silence, . . . ah! que se passe-t-il?	we are silent, . . . Oh, what is happening?
Plus de cris, c'est l'instant!	No more shouts, this is the moment!
Plus de cris, c'est l'instant!	No more shouts, this is the moment!

3:05

Le taureau s'élance	The bull is rushing
en bondissant hors du toril!	while jumping out of its fence! . . .
Il s'élance! Il entre, il frappe! . . .	He is rushing in! He's entering, he strikes!
un cheval roule,	A horse is falling,
entraînant un picador,	Dragging down a picador.
"Ah! Bravo! Toro! " hurle la foule,	"Ah! Bravo! Toro! " the crowd roars,
le taureau va . . . il vient . . .	The bull goes on . . . he comes . . .
il vient et frappe encore!	he comes, and strikes again!

En secouant ses banderilles,	While shaking his banderillas,
plein de fureur, il court!	full of rage, he rushes!
Le cirque est plein de sang!	The arena is full of blood!
On se sauve . . . on franchit les grilles!	We flee . . . we jump the gates!
C'est ton tour maintenant!	It's your turn now!
Allons! en garde! allons! allons! Ah!	Let's go! On guard! Let's go! Let's go! Ah!

3:54

Toreador melody,
major key.

Toréador, en garde! Toréador!	Toreador, on guard! Toreador!
Toréador!	Toreador!
Et songe bien, oui, songe en combattant	And think well, yes think as you are fighting
Qu'un œil noir te regarde,	that a dark eye is looking at you,
Et que l'amour t'attend,	and that love awaits you!
Toréador, l'amour, l'amour t'attend!	Toreador, love, love awaits you!

4:24

Toreador melody
repeated.

Other voices join
Escamillio.

Toréador, en garde! Toréador!	Toreador, on guard! Toreador!
Toréador!	Toreador!
Et songe bien, oui, songe en combattant	And think well, yes think as you are fighting
Qu'un œil noir te regarde,	that a dark eye is looking at you,
Et que l'amour t'attend,	and that love awaits you,
Toréador, l'amour, l'amour t'attend!	Toreador, love, love awaits you!

4:52

Solo voices.

Chorus, crescendo.

L'amour! L'amour! L'amour!	Love! Love! Love!
Toréador, Toréador,	Toreador, Toreador,
Toreador! L'amour t'attend!	Toreador! Love awaits you!

5:22

Orchestral ending, *ff*.
Toreador theme
fragment.

18 Giuseppe Verdi

Giuseppe Verdi (1813–1901), the most popular of all opera composers, was born in a tiny Italian village. He began studying music in a nearby town, Busseto, where he was taken into the home of a wealthy patron who later also supported Verdi's education in Milan. When he completed his studies, he became municipal music director in Busseto and was able to marry his patron's daughter. Three years later he returned to Milan with the score of his first opera, *Oberto* (1839).

Oberto was produced at La Scala (Milan's opera house), had a modest success, and brought Verdi a contract for more operas. Then disaster struck: his wife and their two children died. Verdi managed to complete his next opera, but it was a failure and, in despair, he vowed to compose no more.

He changed his mind after reading a libretto about the ancient Jews exiled from their homeland. Verdi was an ardent nationalist who yearned for a free and unified Italy and saw the Jews as a symbol of the oppressed Italians. He quickly composed *Nabucco* (*Nebuchadnezzar*, king of Babylon, 1842), which was an enormous success. From then on, Verdi and his operas symbolized Italian independence. (The cry *Viva*

Giuseppe Verdi was one of the greatest opera composers and an ardent Italian nationalist.

PALM/RSCH /Redferns/Getty Images

Verdi also stood for the patriotic slogan, "*Vittorio Emmanuele, Re D'Italia*"—*Victor Emmanuel, king of Italy.*)

In his late thirties, Verdi composed *Rigoletto* (1851), *Il Trovatore* (1853), and *La Traviata* (1853). Although the public loved them, critics were often scandalized by their subject matter. *Rigoletto* seemed to condone rape and suicide, and *La Traviata* apparently glorified free love and made a heroine out of a kept woman. But Verdi was fiercely independent and himself lived openly with his second wife for ten years before marrying her.

After these successes had made him wealthy, Verdi bought an estate at Busseto. In 1861 he was elected deputy to the first Italian parliament to convene after Italy had become a nation. In his later years he wrote *Aïda* (1871), *Otello* (1887), and—at the age of seventy-nine—his final opera *Falstaff* (1893).

Verdi's Music

Verdi composed not for the musical elite, but for a mass public whose main entertainment was opera. He wanted subjects that were "original, interesting . . . and passionate; passions above all!" Almost all of his mature works are serious and end unhappily. The operas move quickly and involve extremes of hatred, love, jealousy, and fear. His powerful music underlines the dramatic situations.

Expressive vocal melody is the soul of a Verdi opera. There are many duets, trios, and quartets; and the chorus plays an important role. Verdi's style became less conventional as he grew older. His later works have greater musical continuity, less difference between aria and recitative, more imaginative orchestration, and richer accompaniments. His last three operas—*Aïda, Otello,* and *Falstaff*—are perhaps his greatest. *Falstaff,* his final work, is a comic masterwork with a carefree fugue to the words *All the world's a joke!*

Rigoletto (1851)

Verdi dared to create an operatic hero out of a hunchbacked court jester—Rigoletto—whose only redeeming quality is an intense love for his daughter, Gilda. Rigoletto's master, the licentious Duke of Mantua, has won Gilda's love while posing as a poor student. When the Duke seduces the innocent girl, Rigoletto plots his death. Gilda loves the Duke even after learning about his dissolute character, and she ultimately sacrifices her own life to save his. Vice triumphs in this powerful drama.

Act III: *La donna è mobile* and Quartet

Act III of *Rigoletto* contains two of the most popular pieces in opera, the Duke's aria *La donna è mobile* and the Quartet. The scene is a run-down inn where the Duke has come to meet Maddalena, the voluptuous sister of the cutthroat Sparafucile.

The carefree and tuneful *La donna è mobile* (*Woman is fickle*) perfectly expresses the Duke's pleasure-loving personality. Its melody is easy to remember because the opening rhythmic pattern for *La don-ne è mo-bi-le*, long-long-long-long-short-long, appears throughout. The aria is in strophic form: the same melody is sung for each stanza of the text. Even before the premiere of *Rigoletto,* which was to take place in Venice, Verdi knew that *La donna è mobile* would be a hit. Afraid that his catchy tune would leak out during rehearsals and be sung by every Venetian gondolier, he waited until the last possible moment before giving the manuscript to the tenor who was to sing the aria.

The Quartet is sung as Rigoletto and Gilda peer through a crack in the wall of the inn, observing the Duke flirting with Maddalena. Verdi projects four conflicting emotions at one time, characterizing each singer with an appropriate melodic line. The Duke attempts to seduce Maddalena with a suave and ardent legato melody. Maddalena coquettishly repels his advances with quick, staccato laughs. Outside the inn, Gilda laments her fate with anguished sobs punctuated by rests, while Rigoletto curses and mutters threats of vengeance in repeated notes. Verdi lets us hear each of the four voices separately before combining them in a glorious ensemble.

Vocal Music Guide

VERDI, *Rigoletto* (1851)

(Duration 8:06)

Listen for the pervasive *rhythmic pattern* long-long-long-long-short-long and the strophic form of *la donna è mobile*. In the quartet, four conflicting emotions are projected simultaneously as the Duke, Maddalena, Gilda, and Rigoletto each sing different melodic lines.

La donna è mobile and **Quartet**

0:00
Aria. Orchestra
introduces
Duke's melody.

Duke

La donna è mobile	Woman is fickle
Qual piuma al vento,	Like a feather in the wind,
Muta d'accento	She changes her words
E di pensiero.	And her thoughts.

La   don - na ë   mo - bi - le   qual   piu - ma al   ven - to,

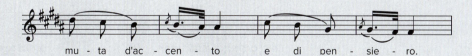

mu - ta   d'ac - cen - to   e   di   pen - sie - ro.

Sempre un amabile	Always a lovable
Leggiadro viso,	And lovely face,
In pianto o in riso,	Weeping or laughing,
È menzognero.	Is lying.
La donna è mobile	Woman is fickle
Qual piuma al vento	Like a feather in the wind,
Muta d'accento	She changes her words
E di pensier.	And her thought.

Orchestra.
Duke's melody
repeated with
different
words.

È sempre misero	The man's always wretched
Chi a lei s'affida,	Who believes in her,
Chi le confida	Who recklessly entrusts
Mal cauto il core!	His heart to her!
Pur mai non sentesi	And yet one who never
Felice appieno	Drinks love on that breast
Chi su quel seno	Never feels
Non liba amore!	Entirely happy!
La donna è mobile, ecc.	Woman is fickle, etc.

2:04

Duke's melody
in orchestra,
decrescendo.

(Sparafucile comes back in with a bottle of wine and two glasses, which he sets on the table; then he strikes the ceiling twice with the hilt of his long sword. At this signal, a laughing young girl, in a Gypsy dress—Maddalena—leaps down the stairs: the Duke runs to embrace her, but she escapes him. Meanwhile Sparafucile has gone out into the road, where he says softly to Rigoletto:)

Sparafucile

È là vostr'uomo . . .	Your man is there . . .
viver dee o morire?	Must he live or die?

Rigoletto

Più tardi tornerò l'opra a compire.	I'll return later to complete the deed.

Brief pause.

(Sparafucile goes off behind the house toward the river. Gilda and Rigoletto remain in the street, the Duke and Maddalena on the ground floor.)

2:47

Allegro

Duke

Un dì, se ben rammentomi,	One day, if I remember right,
O bella, t'incontrai . . .	I met you, O beauty . . .
Mi piacque di te chiedere,	I was pleased to ask about you,
E intesi che qui stai.	And I learned that you live here.
Or sappi, che d'allora	Know then, that since that time
Sol te quest'alma adora!	My soul adores only you!

Gilda

Iniquo!	Villain!

Maddalena

Ah, ah! . . . e vent'altre appresso	Ha, ha! . . . And does it now perhaps
Le scorda forse adesso?	Forget twenty others?
Ha un'aria il signorino	The young gentleman looks like
Da vero libertino . . .	A true libertine . . .

Duke

(starting to embrace her)

Si . . . un mostro son . . .	Yes . . . I'm a monster . . .

Gilda

Ah padre mio!	Ah, Father!

Maddalena

Lasciatemi, stordito.	Let me go, foolish man!

Duke

Ih, che fracasso!   Ah, what a fuss!

Maddalena

Stia saggio.   Be good.

Duke

E tu sii docile,   And you, be yielding,
Non fare tanto chiasso.   Don't make so much noise.
Ogni saggezza chiudesi   All wisdom concludes
Nel gaudio e nell'amore.   In pleasure and in love.
                                            (He takes her hand.)
La bella mano candida!   What a lovely, white hand!

Maddalena

Scherzate voi, signore.   You're joking, sir.

Duke

No, no.   No, no.

Maddalena

Son brutta.   I'm ugly.

Duke

Abbracciami.   Embrace me.

Gilda

Iniquo!   Villain!

Maddalena

Ebro!   You're drunk!

Duke

D'amor ardente!   With ardent love!

Maddalena

Signor l'indifferente,   My indifferent sir,
Vi piace canzonar?   Do you enjoy teasing?

Duke

No, no, ti vo'sposar.   No, no, I want to marry you.

Maddalena

Ne voglio la parola.   I want your word.

Duke
(ironic)
Amabile figliuola!   Lovable maiden!

Rigoletto
(to Gilda, who has seen and heard all)
E non ti basta ancor?   Isn't that enough for you yet?

Rhythm slows.

Quick rhythm
resumes.

Gilda

Iniquo traditor!	Villainous betrayer!

Maddalena

Ne voglio la parola.	I want your word.

Duke

Amabile figliuola!	Lovable maiden!

Rigoletto

E non ti basta ancor?	Isn't that enough for you yet?

Characters sing simultaneously

Short pause.

4:14

Quartet, andante.

Duke

Bella figlia dell'amore,	Beautiful daughter of love,
Schiavo son de' vezzi tuoi;	I am the slave of your charms;
Con un detto sol tu puoi	With a single word you can
Le mie pene consolar.	Console my sufferings.

Bel - la Æ- glia del - l'a - - mo - re, schia-vo son de'

vez - zi tuo - i; con un det-to, un det - to sol tu

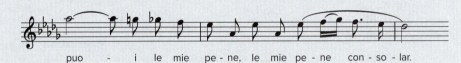

puo - i le mie pe - ne, le mie pe - ne con - so - lar.

Vieni, e senti del mio core	Come, and feel the quick beating
Il frequente palpitar . . .	Of my heart . . .
Con un detto sol tu puoi	With a single word you can
Le mie pene consolar.	Console my sufferings.

Maddalena

Ah! ah! rido ben di core,	Ha! Ha! I laugh heartily,
Chè tai baie costan poco.	For such tales cost little.

Ah! ah! ri - do ben di co - re, chë tai ba - ie cos-tan po - co;

Gilda

Ah! così parlar d'amore . . .	Ah! To speak thus of love . . .

Ah! _____ co s!___ par-lar _ d'a - mo-re!

Maddalena

Quanto valga il vostro gioco,	Believe me, I can judge
Mel credete, so apprezzar.	How much your game is worth.

Gilda

. . . a me pur l'infame ho udito!	. . . I too have heard the villain so!

Rigoletto
(to Gilda)

Taci, il piangere non vale.	Hush, weeping is of no avail.

Ta - ci, il pian-ge-re non va - le;

Gilda

Infelice cor tradito,	Unhappy, betrayed heart.
Per angoscia non scoppiar. Ah, no!	Do not burst with anguish. Ah, no!

Maddalena

Characters sing simultaneously.

Son avvezza, bel signore,	I'm accustomed, handsome sir,
Ad un simile scherzare.	To similar joking.
Mio bel signor!	My handsome sir!

Duke

Bella figlia dell'amore, ecc.	Beautiful daughter of love, etc.
Vieni!	Come!

Rigoletto

Ch'ei mentiva sei sicura.	You are sure that he was lying.
Taci, e mia sarà la cura	Hush, and I will take care
La vendetta d'affrettar.	To hasten vengeance.
Sì, pronto fia, sarà fatale,	Yes, it will be swift and fatal,
Io saprollo fulminar.	I will know how to strike him down.
Taci taci . . .	Hush, hush . . .

19 Giacomo Puccini

Giacomo Puccini.
Bettmann/Getty Images

Giacomo Puccini (1858–1924), who created some of the best-loved operas, came from a long line of composers and church organists. During his student years at the Milan Conservatory, he lived a hand-to-mouth existence. The success of his first opera, shortly after his graduation, brought him commissions and an annual income from Italy's leading music publisher. In 1893, he became well known throughout Italy for his opera *Manon Lescaut;* after 1896, he was wealthy and world famous from the enormous success of *La Bohème. Tosca* (1900) and *Madame Butterfly* (1904) were also very popular. He died before completing his last opera, *Turandot,* which was completed by a friend.

Puccini's marvelous sense of theater has given his operas lasting appeal. His melodies have short, remembered phrases and are intensely emotional. He used the orchestra to reinforce the vocal melody and to suggest mood. To achieve unity and continuity, he minimized the difference between aria and recitative and used the same material in different acts. Puccini was very much concerned with the literary and dramatic qualities of his librettos; he spent as much time polishing them as composing the music and often demanded endless changes from the librettists. Some of his operas, notably *Tosca,* reflect an artistic trend of the 1890s known as *verismo—realism,* or the quality of being "true to life." But they also feature exoticism: *Madame Butterfly* is set in Japan and *Turandot* in China, and both have melodic and rhythmic elements derived from the music of those countries.

La Bohème (1896)

La Bohème (*Bohemian Life*) takes place in the Latin Quarter of Paris around 1830. Its hero is Rodolfo, a young poet who shares a garret with Marcello, a painter; Colline, a philosopher; and Schaunard, a musician. Mimi, the heroine, is a poor, tubercular seamstress who lives in the same building. The simple, touching plot has been aptly summarized as "boy meets girl, boy loses girl, boy and girl are reunited as girl dies of consumption in boy's arms and curtain falls." Everyone can relate to the characters and emotions of this enchanting opera. Though there are many realistic touches in this picture of bohemian life, it is seen through a romantic haze.

Act I:
Scene between Rodolfo and Mimi

Mimi and Rodolfo meet and fall in love toward the end of Act I, which takes place on a cold Christmas eve. Her candle has blown out, and she knocks on his door asking for a light. At Rodolfo's insistence, Mimi enters, but she suddenly has a coughing fit and faints in his arms. She revives after Rodolfo sprinkles water on her face. She then leaves, her candle lit, but she returns immediately, for she has lost her key. They must search for the key in the dark—a gust of wind has extinguished their candles. When their hands touch, Rodolfo sings the aria *Che gelida manina* (*How cold your little hand is!*). He sings about himself, his dreams, and his fantasies. Mimi responds with a poetic description of her simple life in the aria *Mi chiamano Mimì* (*They call me Mimì*). Under the spell of their newfound love, they join in a duet that closes the act.

Puccini's sensuous melody casts a glow over the entire scene. His music has an improvisatory quality, with many fluctuations of tempo that reflect changes of mood and dramatic action. In the musical dialogue between Mimi and Rodolfo, Puccini easily alternates between speechlike and melodic phrases. When Mimi enters, the orchestra murmurs a touching phrase—Mimi's theme—that suggests her fragility and tenderness. Mimi's coughing fit is evoked by agitated music and her fainting by a poignant oboe solo. When Mimi returns to get her key, she introduces a new melody in a faster tempo. Each of the two arias begins simply, almost conversationally. Then the melody grows warmer until it reaches a climax in a broad, passionate phrase. The climactic phrase of Rodolfo's aria, sung to the words *Talor dal mio forziere* (*My hoard of treasure is robbed by two thieves: a pair of beautiful eyes*), is the love theme of the whole opera. Mimi's emotional high point is reached when she dreams about the end of winter (*ma quando vien la sgelo*), when "the first kiss of April" is hers. Returning to reality at the end of her aria, she sings in conversational repeated tones.

The mood changes momentarily as Rodolfo goes to the window and has a brief exchange with his friends in the courtyard—an example of Puccini's theatrical timing, for he provides a moment of relaxation before the lovers join in the closing duet. First, Rodolfo sings alone; then both voices unite beautifully in a declaration of love.

Vocal Music Guide

PUCCINI, *La Bohème* (1896)

(Duration 17:37)

Listen for the alternation between speechlike and *melodic phrases* in the musical dialogue between Mimi and Rodolfo. Notice that both Rodolfo's aria *Che gelida manina* and Miml's aria *Mi chiamano Mimi* begin simply, almost conversationally, and then build to a climax in a broad, passionate phrase.

Excerpt from Act I

0:00

Flute melody.

(Rodolfo closes the door, sets his light on the table, and tries to write. But he tears up the paper and throws the pen down.)

	Rodolfo	
	Non sono in vena.	I'm not in the mood.

(A timid knock at the door.)

Speechlike.

	Chi è la?	Who's there?

	Mimi	
	Scusi.	Excuse me.

	Rodolfo	
	Una donna!	A woman!

	Mimi	

Mimi's theme, *pp*, in orchestra.

	Di grazia, me si è spento	I'm sorry . . . my light
	Il lume.	Has gone out.

	Rodolfo	
	(opens the door)	
	Ecco.	Here.

Mimi	
Importuna è la vicina . . .	You've a bothersome neighbor . . .
Rodolfo	
Cosa dice, ma le pare!	What do you mean? Not at all!
Mimi	
Cerchi.	Search.
Rodolfo	
Cerco.	I'm searching.
	(They both grope on the floor for the key.)
Mimi	
Ove sarà?	Where can it be?
Rodolfo	
	(finds the key, pockets it)
Ah!	Ah!
Mimi	
L'ha trovata?	Did you find it?
Rodolfo	
No.	No.
Mimi	
Mi parve . . .	I thought . . .
Rodolfo	
In verità!	Truthfully!
Mimi	
Cerca?	Are you hunting?
Rodolfo	
Cerco.	I'm hunting for it.

3:40

Orchestra alone, tempo slows.

(Guided by her voice, Rodolfo pretends to search as he draws closer to her. Then his hand meets hers, and he holds it.)

Mimi	
	(surprised)
Ah!	Ah!
	(They rise. Rodolfo continues to hold Mimi's hand.)

4:01

Rodolfo's aria.

Rodolfo	
Che gelida manina,	How cold your little hand is!
Se la lasci riscaldar.	Let me warm it for you.

Harp.

Cercar che giova? Al buio	What's the use of searching?
Non si trova. Ma per fortuna	We'll never find it in the dark.
È una notte di luna,	But luckily there's a moon,
E qui la luna l'abbiamo vicina.	And she's our neighbor here.
Aspetti, signorina,	Just wait, my dear young lady,
Le dirò con due parole chi son,	And meanwhile I'll tell you

Chi son, e che faccio, come vivo.	In a word who and what I am.
Vuole?	Shall I?
	(Mimi is silent.)
Chi son? Chi son? Son un poeta.	Who am I? I'm a poet.
Che cosa faccio? Scrivo.	My business? Writing.
E come vivo? Vivo.	How do I live? I live.
In povertà mia lieta	In my happy poverty
Scialo da gran signore	I squander like a prince
Rime ed inni d'amore.	My poems and songs of love.
Per sogni e per chimere	In hopes and dreams
E per castelli in aria	And castles in air,
L'anima ho milionaria.	I'm a millionaire in spirit.

6:22

Love theme.

Talor dal mio forziere	My hoard of treasure
Ruban tutti i gioielli	Is stolen by two thieves:
Due ladri: gli occhi belli.	A pair of beautiful eyes.

V'entrar con voi pur ora	They came in now with you
Ed i miei sogni usati,	And all my lovely dreams,
Ed i bei sogni miei	My dreams of the past,
Tosto si dileguar!	Were soon stolen away.
Ma il furto non m'accora	But the theft doesn't upset me,
Poichè, poichè v'ha preso stanza	Since the empty place was filled
La speranza.	With hope.
Or che mi conoscete	Now that you know me,
Parlate voi, deh! parlate.	It's your turn to speak.
Chi siete? Vi piaccia dir?	Who are you? Will you tell me?

8:23

Mimi's aria.

Mimi

Sì.	Yes.
Mi chiamano Mimì,	They call me Mimi,
Ma il mio nome è Lucia.	But my real name is Lucia.

La storia mia è breve.	My story is brief.
A tela o a seta	I embroider silk and satin
Ricamo in casa e fuori.	At home or outside.
Son tranquilla e lieta,	I'm tranquil and happy,
Ed è mio svago	And my pastime
Far gigli e rose.	Is making lilies and roses.
Mi piaccion quelle cose	I love all things
Che han si dolce malia,	That have a gentle magic,

Che parlano d'amor, di primavere,	That talk of love, of spring,
Che parlano di sogni e di chimere,	That talk of dreams and fancies—
Quelle cose che han nome poesia . . .	The things called poetry . . .
Lei m'intende?	Do you understand me?

Rodolfo

Sì.	Yes.

10:13

Mimi

Mi chiamano Mimì—	They call me Mimi—
Il perchè non so.	I don't know why.
Sola, mi fo il pranzo	I live all by myself
Da me stessa.	And I eat all alone.
Non vado sempre a messa,	I don't often go to church,
Ma prego assai il Signor.	But I like to pray.
Vivo sola, soletta,	I stay all alone
Là in una bianca cameretta;	In my tiny white room,
Guardo sui tetti e in cielo.	I look at the roofs and the sky.
Ma quando vien lo sgelo	But when the thaw comes
Il primo sole è mio,	The first sunshine is mine,
Il primo bacio	The first kiss
Dell'aprile è mio!	Of April is mine!
Il primo sole è mio!	The first sunshine is mine!
Germoglia in un vaso una rosa.	A rose blossoms in my vase,
Foglia a foglia l'aspiro.	I breathe in its perfume,
Così gentil è il profumo d'un fior.	Petal by petal. So lovely,
Ma i fior ch'io faccio, ahimè,	So sweet is the flower's perfume.
I fior ch'io faccio,	But the flowers I make,
Ahimè non hanno odore.	Alas, have no scent.
Altro di me non le saprei narrare.	What else can I say?
Sono la sua vicina	I'm your neighbor,
Che la vien fuori d'ora a importunare.	Disturbing you at this impossible hour.

Schaunard
(from below)

13:02

Friends in the courtyard.

Eh! Rodolfo!	Hey! Rodolfo!

Colline

Rodolfo!	Rodolfo!

Marcello

Olà! Non senti?	Hey! Can't you hear?
Lumaca!	You snail!

Colline

Poetucolo!	You fake!

Schaunard

Accidenti al pigro!	To hell with that lazy one!

(Rodolfo, impatient, goes to the window to answer. When the window is opened, the moonlight comes in, lighting up the room.)

Rodolfo

Scrivo ancora tre righe a volo.	I've a few more words to write.

Mimi

Chi son?	Who are they?

Rodolfo

Amici. | Friends.

Schaunard

Sentirai le tue. | You'll hear about this.

Marcello

Che te ne fai lì solo? | What are you doing there alone?

Rodolfo

Non son solo. Siamo in due. | I'm not alone. There's two of us.
Andate da Momus, tenete il posto. | Go to Momus and get a table.
Ci saremo tosto. | We'll be there soon.

Marcello, Schaunard, Colline

Momus, Momus, Momus, | Momus, Momus, Momus.
Zitti e discreti audiamocene via. | Quietly, discreetly, we're off.
Momus, Momus, Momus. | Momus, Momus, Momus.
Trovò la poesia. | He's found his poem at last.
(Turning, Rodolfo sees Mimi wrapped in a halo of moonlight. He contemplates her, in ecstasy.)

13:40

Duet.

Rodolfo

O soave fanciulla, o dolce viso | Oh! lovely girl, oh! sweet face
Di mite circonfuso alba lunar, | Bathed in the soft moonlight.
In te, ravviso il sogno | I see in you the dream
Ch'io vorrei sempre sognar! | I'd dream forever!

14:18

Voices unite, love theme.

Fremon già nell'anima | Already I taste in spirit
Le dolcezze estreme, | The heights of tenderness!
Amor nel bacio freme! | Love trembles in our kiss!

Mimi

Ah, tu sol comandi, amore. . . . | Ah! Love, you rule alone. . . .
Oh! come dolci scendono | How sweet his praises
Le sue lusinghe al core. . . . | Enter my heart. . . .
Tu sol comandi, amore! | Love, you alone rule!

(Rodolfo kisses her.)

Mimi

No, per pietà! | No, please!

Rodolfo

Sei mia! | You're mine!

Mimi

V'aspettan gli amici. . . . | Your friends are waiting.

Rodolfo

Già mi mandi via? | You send me away already?

Mimi

Vorrei dir . . . ma non oso. | I daren't say what I'd like . . .

Rodolfo

Di'. | Tell me.

Mimi

Se venissi con voi? | If I came with you?

Rodolfo	
Che? Mimì!	What? Mimi!
Sarebbe così dolce restar qui.	It would be so fine to stay here.
C'è freddo fuori.	Outside it's cold.
Mimi	
Vi starò vicina!	I'd be near you!
Rodolfo	
E al ritorno?	And when we come back?
Mimi	
Curioso!	Who knows?
Rodolfo	
Dammi il braccio, o mia piccina . . .	Give me your arm, my little one . . .
Mimi	
Obbedisco, signor!	Your servant, sir . . .
Rodolfo	
Che m'ami . . . di' . . .	Tell me you love me!
Mimi	
Io t'amo.	I love you.
Rodolfo	
Amor!	My love!
Mimi	
Amor!	My love!
Rodolfo and Mimi	
Amor!	Beloved!

16:15
Melody from
Rodolfo's aria.

20 Richard Wagner

Few composers have had so powerful an impact on their time as Richard Wagner (1813–1883). His operas and artistic philosophy influenced not only musicians, but also poets, painters, and playwrights. Such was his preeminence that an opera house of his own design was built in Bayreuth, Germany, solely for performances of his music dramas.

Wagner was born in Leipzig into a theatrical family. His boyhood dream was to be a poet and playwright, but at fifteen he was overwhelmed by Beethoven's music and he decided to become a composer. He taught himself by studying scores and had almost three years of formal training in music theory, but he never mastered an instrument. As a student at Leipzig University, he dueled, drank, and gambled. A similar pattern persisted throughout his life; Wagner shamelessly lived off other people and accumulated enormous debts that he never repaid.

During his early twenties, Wagner conducted in small German theaters and wrote several operas. In 1839 he decided to try his luck in Paris, then the center of grand opera. He and his wife, Minna, spent two miserable years there, during which he was unable to get an opera performed and was reduced to musical hackwork. Wagner returned to

Richard Wagner's operas and artistic philosophy had a powerful impact on musicians, poets, painters, and playwrights.
Hulton-Deutsch Collection/ CORBIS/Corbis via Getty Images

Germany in 1842 to supervise the production of his opera *Rienzi* in Dresden. The work was immensely successful, and Wagner was appointed conductor of the Dresden Opera. Wagner spent six years at this post, becoming famous both as an opera composer and as a conductor.

When the revolutions of 1848 were sweeping across Europe, Wagner's life in Dresden had become difficult because of accumulated debts. Hoping that a new society would wipe out his debts and produce conditions favorable to his art, he participated in the insurrection and then had to flee to Switzerland. For several years Wagner did no composing; instead he worked out theories of art in several essays and completed the librettos to *Der Ring des Nibelungen* (*The Ring of the Nibelung*), a set of four operas based on Nordic myth, which would occupy him for twenty-five years. He interrupted his work on the music for *The Ring* to compose *Tristan and Isolde* (1857–1859).

Wagner had several bad years after finishing *Tristan*. His opera *Tannhäuser* was a failure at the Paris Opera; *Tristan* was abandoned by the Vienna Opera; and he was hounded by creditors. In 1864, however, he was rescued by King Ludwig of Bavaria, an eighteen-year-old fanatical Wagnerian who put all the resources of the Munich Opera at Wagner's disposal. At this time, Wagner fell in love with Cosima von Bülow, who was Liszt's daughter and the wife of Hans von Bülow, Wagner's close friend and favorite conductor. Cosima gave birth to two of Wagner's children while still married to von Bülow. Shortly after Wagner's first wife died, he married Cosima.

In Wagner, towering musical genius was allied with selfishness, ruthlessness, rabid German nationalism, and absolute self-conviction. He forged an audience for his complex music dramas from a public accustomed to conventional opera. The performance of the *Ring* cycle in 1876 was perhaps the single most important musical event of the century. Though some critics still found his music too dissonant, heavily orchestrated, and long-winded, Wagner was generally acclaimed the greatest composer of his time. A year after completing *Parsifal* (1877–1882), his last opera, he died in Venice, at age sixty-nine.

Wagner's Music

For Wagner, an opera house was a temple in which the spectator was to be overwhelmed by music and drama. He wrote his own librettos, which he based on medieval Germanic legends and myths. His characters are usually larger than life—heroes, gods, demigods. He called his works *music dramas* rather than operas, but today many people find Wagner's music more exciting than his rather static drama.

Within each act, there is a continuous musical flow (Wagner called this "unending melody") instead of traditional arias, recitatives, and ensembles; and there are no breaks where applause can interrupt. His vocal line, which he conceived as "speech song," is inspired by the rhythms and pitch of the German text. Wagner revolutionized opera by shifting the focus from voice to orchestra and treating the orchestra symphonically. His expanded and colorful orchestration expresses the drama and constantly develops, transforms, and intertwines musical ideas. (And the orchestral sound is so full that only very powerful voices can cut through it.) In the orchestra—and sometimes in the vocal parts—he uses brief, recurrent musical ideas called *leit motifs,* or *leading motives.* A **leitmotif** is a short musical idea associated with a person, an object, or a thought in the drama.

The tension of Wagner's music is heightened by chromatic and dissonant harmonies. Wagner's chromatic harmony ultimately led to the breakdown of tonality and to the new musical language of the twentieth century.

Die Walküre (The Valkyrie; 1856)

Die Walküre (*The Valkyrie*) is the second and most widely performed of the four music dramas in Wagner's gigantic cycle *Der Ring des Nibelungen* (*The Ring of the Nibelung*). Despite its gods, giants, dwarfs, and magic fire, the *Ring* is really about Wagner's view of nineteenth-century society. He uses Nordic mythology to warn that society destroys itself through lust for money and power. It is fitting that Wagner first sketched the plot of the *Ring* in 1848, the year that brought Marx's *Communist Manifesto* and revolutions throughout Europe.

Act I:
Love scene (conclusion)

Wagner builds the first act of *Die Walküre* to an overwhelming climax in the passionate love scene that concludes it. To grasp this scene fully, it's helpful to know what has happened earlier in the *Ring*.

A Nibelung dwarf, Alberich, has stolen gold belonging to the Rhine maidens, mermaids in the Rhine River. From this gold, the dwarf fashions a ring that can bestow immense power on anyone who wears it and is willing to renounce love. The dwarf, in turn, is robbed of his prize by Wotan, king of the gods. (*Wednesday* comes from *Wotan's day*.) Soon Wotan himself is forced to give up the ring; he then lives in fear that Alberich will get it back and use it to destroy him. Hoping to protect himself, he surrounds his castle, Valhalla, with a bodyguard of heroes. His daughters, goddesses called *Valkyries*, swoop over battlefields on horseback and bear away the dead bodies of the bravest warriors. The Valkyrie of the opera's title is Brünnhilde, Wotan's favorite daughter.

Eva-Maria Westbroek and Jonas Kaufmann in a scene from Wagner's *Die Walküre* at the Metropolitan Opera in New York.

ANDREA MOHIN/The New York Times/Redux

Seeking to create a hero who can help him regain the ring, Wotan takes a human wife and fathers the Volsung twins—a son, Siegmund; and a daughter, Sieglinde. The twins know their father as Wälse, unaware that he is the god Wotan. They are separated as children when a hostile clan kidnaps Sieglinde and kills their mother. Siegmund becomes an outlaw and Sieglinde is eventually forced to marry the warrior-chief Hunding, whom she hates. During the wedding feast in Hunding's home, Wotan appears, disguised as an old man dressed in gray. He thrusts a magic sword into the tree around which the house is built, and proclaims that the weapon belongs to the one who can draw it out. Hunding and his followers try but are unable to withdraw the sword.

The first act of *Die Walküre* begins as Siegmund, weaponless and pursued by enemies, unwittingly takes refuge in the house of Hunding, who is away hunting. Sieglinde and Siegmund almost immediately fall in love, unaware that they are brother and sister. Hunding returns and soon realizes that the stranger—who identifies himself as *Wehwalt* (*Woeful*)—is an enemy of his clan. He says that Siegmund is his guest for the night, but the next day they must do battle. Sieglinde gives her husband a sleeping potion and tells Siegmund that her shame and misery will be avenged by the hero who can withdraw the sword from the tree. As they embrace passionately, the door of the hut suddenly opens, allowing the moonlight of a beautiful spring night to shine on them.

The following excerpt occurs at the end of the love scene, when Siegmund and Sieglinde gradually become aware of their amazing resemblance to each other and finally realize that they are brother and sister. Since her beloved no longer wants to be called *Wehwalt*, Sieglinde renames him *Siegmund* (*Victor*). With a powerful effort, Siegmund withdraws the sword from the tree and the lovers rapturously embrace. (The offspring of this unlawful union will be Siegfried, the human hero of the *Ring* cycle. In the mythology and folklore of many lands, heroes are often born of incestuous love.)

In the excerpt we study, Wagner creates a continuous musical flow that depicts the surging passions of the lovers through frequent changes of tempo, dynamics, and orchestral color. Typically, the vocal lines range from speechlike to highly melodic and closely reflect the inflections and meaning of the text. For example, the word *Notung* (*Needy*)—the name of the sword—is powerfully emphasized when it is sung to the downward leap of an octave.

Several leitmotifs are heard, sometimes together. In this excerpt, the leitmotif *Valhalla*—Wotan's castle—is first presented when Sieglinde looks at Siegmund and later the leitmotif returns when she recalls how their father (Wotan disguised as the old man) gazed at her during her marriage feast. The very important *sword* leitmotif is barely noticeable when it first appears, as Sieglinde refers to the fire in Siegmund's eyes. It is presented ***pp***, in combination with the leitmotif *Volsung* (the people to which Siegmund and Sieglinde belong). Later, the sword motif is very prominent when it is proclaimed by the brasses as Siegmund draws the sword out of the tree and as the lovers embrace during the orchestral conclusion of the act. Other leitmotifs heard in our excerpt are *love* and *spring*.

Vocal Music Guide

WAGNER, *Die Walküre* (*The Valkyrie*; 1856)

(Duration 8:12)

Listen for the continuous musical flow, the powerful and colorful orchestra, and the vocal lines that range from speechlike to highly melodic. Notice the leitmotifs *Valhalla* (Wotan's castle), *sword*, *love*, and *spring* in the orchestra and voices.

Act I, Love Scene, Conclusion

(Sieglinde pushes Siegmund's hair back from his brow and looks at him with astonishment.)

Sieglinde

0:00	*Wie dir die Stirn so offen steht,*	Look how your forehead broadens out,
	der Adern Geäst in den Schläfen sich schlingt!	and the network of veins winds into your temples.
	Mir zagt es vor der Wonne, die mich entzückt!	I tremble with the delight that enchants me.

0:19

Valhalla,
French horns, *p*.

Valhalla

Ein Wunder will mich gemahnen:	It brings something strange to my mind:
den heut zuerst ich erschaut,	though I first saw you today,
mein Auge sah dich schon!	I've set eyes on you before.

Siegmund

0:45

| Ein Minnetraum gemahnt auch mich: | A dream of love comes to my mind as well: |
| in heissem Sehnen sah ich dich schon! | burning with longing I have seen you before. |

Sieglinde

1:04

Im Bach erblickt' ich mein eigen Bild	In the stream I've seen my own likeness;
und jetzt gewahr ich es wieder:	and now I see it again.
wie einst dem Teich es enttaucht,	As once it appeared in the water
bietest mein Bild mir nun du!	so now you show me my likeness.

Siegmund

1:28

Du bist das Bild, das ich in mir barg.   You are the likeness that I hid in myself.

Love, voice.

Sieglinde

Love, French horn, **p**.

| O still! Lass mich der Stimme lauschen: | Hush! let me listen to your voice. |
| mich dünkt, ihren Klang hört' ich als Kind. | Its sound, I fancy, I heard as a child, |

2:00

Doch nein! Ich hörte sie neulich,	but no! I heard it recently—
als meiner Stimme Schall	when the echo of my voice sounded
mir widerhallte der Wald.	back through the forest.

Siegmund

| O lieblichste Laute, denen ich lausche! | O loveliest sound for me to hear! |

2:24

Volsung, low strings, **pp**, together with *Sword,* bass trumpet, **pp**.

Sieglinde

| Deines Auges Glut erglänzte mir schon: | The fire in your eyes has blazed at me before: |

2:34

Valhalla. French horns, **pp**, then strings, **pp**.

| so blickte der Greis grüssend auf mich, | So the old man gazed at me in greeting |
| als der Traurigen Trost er gab. | when to my sadness he brought comfort. |

| An dem Blick erkannt' ihn sein Kind. | By his look his child recognized him, |
| schon wollt' ich beim Namen ihn nennen! | I even wanted to call him by name. |

Pause.

3:04

Wehwalt heisst du fürwahr?   Are you really called Woeful?

Siegmund

Nicht heiss ich so, seit du mich liebst:	I am not called that since you love me:
nun walt ich der hehrsten Wonnen!	Now I am full of purest rapture.

Sieglinde

3:23

Und Friedmund darfst du froh dich nicht nennen?	And "Peaceful" may you not, being happy, be named?

Siegmund

Nenne mich du, wie du liebst, dass ich heisse:	Name me what you love to call me.
den Namen nehm ich von dir!	I take my name from you.

Sieglinde

3:42

Doch nanntest du Wolfe den Vater?	But did you name Wolf as your father?

Siegmund

Ein Wolf war er feigen Füchsen!	A Wolf he was to craven foxes!
Doch dem so stolz strahlte das Auge,	But he whose proud eyes shone
wie, Herrliche, hehr dir es strahlt,	as grandly as yours, you marvel,
der war: Wälse genannt.	his name was "Volsa."

Sieglinde

4:03

War Wälse dein Vater, und bist du ein Wälsung,	If "Volsa" was your father and you are a "Volsung,"
stiess er für dich sein Schwert in den Stamm,	it was for you he thrust his sword into the tree—
so lass mich dich heissen, wie ich dich liebe: Siegmund: so nenn ich dich!	so let me call you by the name I love: Siegmund (Victor)—so I name you.

Siegmund

4:27

Siegmund heiss ich und Siegmund bin ich!	Siegmund I am called and Siegmund I am,
Bezeug es dies Schwert, das zaglos ich halte!	let this sword, which I fearlessly hold, bear witness.

4:42

Wälse verhiess mir, in höchster Not fänd' ich es einst: ich fass es nun!	Volsa promised me that in deepest distress I should one day find it. Now I grasp it.
Heiligster Minne höchste Not,	Holiest love's deepest distress,
sehnender Liebe sehrende Not	yearning love's scorching desire,
brennt mir hell in der Brust,	burn bright in my breast,
drängt zu Tat und Tod.	urge me to deeds and death.

5:20

Voice, downward octave leaps.

Notung! Notung! so nenn ich dich,	"Needy," "Needy," I name you,
Schwert.	sword.
Notung, Notung! neidlicher Stahl!	"Needy," "Needy," precious blade,
Zeig deiner Schärfe schneidenden Zahn:	show your sharpness and cutting edge:
heraus aus der Scheide zu mir!	come from your scabbard to me!

5:50

Sword, the trumpets, ***ff***.

(With a powerful effort, Siegmund pulls the sword from the tree, showing it to astonished and delighted Sieglinde.)

6:07

Volsung,
trumpets, **pp**.

*Siegmund, den Wälsung, siehst du,
Weib!
Als Brautgabe bringt er dies Schwert:
so freit er sich
die seligste Frau;
dem Feindeshaus entführt er dich so.
Fern von hier folge mir nun,*

You see Siegmund, the Volsung,
woman!
As wedding gift he brings this sword;
so he weds
the fairest of women;
he takes you away from the enemy's house.
Now follow me far from here,

6:41

Spring, voice.

fort in des Lenzes lachendes Haus:

out into springtime's smiling house.

fort   in   des   Len   -   zes   la - chen-des   Haus;

*dort schützt dich Notung, das
Schwert,
wenn Siegmund dir liebend erlag!*

For protection you'll have "Needy" the
sword,
even if Siegmund expires with love.

Sieglinde

7:10

*Bist du Siegmund, den ich hier sehe,
Sieglinde bin ich, die dich ersehnt:
die eig'ne Schwester
gewannst du zu eins mit dem Schwert!*

Are you Siegmund whom I see here?
I am Sieglinde who longed for you:
your own sister
you have won and the sword as well.

Siegmund

*Braut und Schwester bist du dem
Bruder,
so blühe denn Wälsungen-Blut!*

Wife and sister you'll be to your brother.

So let the Volsung blood increase!

7:39

Sword,
brasses, **ff**.
Passionate
orchestral
conclusion.

(He draws her to him with passionate fervor.)

The Romantic Period: Summary

Music in Society

- A large and growing urban middle-class wanted to hear and play music; this trend resulted in the formation of numerous orchestras, opera companies, and music societies.
- Subscription concerts became common.
- The nineteenth-century musical public was captivated by virtuoso performers.
- Numerous music conservatories were founded in Europe and the United States.
- Women assumed greater roles as performers, composers, and patrons in professional music making.
- Music making in the home took on great importance.
- The piano became a regular fixture in middle-class and upper-class homes, used both for entertainment and for educating children, particularly girls.

Important Style Features

Mood and Emotional Expression
- Music of the romantic era is closely related to the other arts, particularly literature.
- Art forms, including music, exhibited extreme interest in subjects related to nature, death, the fantastic, the macabre, and the diabolical.
- Unprecedented emphasis was placed on self-expression and the development of a uniquely personal musical style.
- Music explored a universe of feeling that included flamboyance and intimacy, unpredictability and melancholy, rapture and longing, the mysterious and the remote.
- Some composers wrote music evoking a specific national identity ("nationalism") or an exotic location ("exoticism").

Rhythm
- Rhythm is extremely diverse.
- Tempos are flexible and may change frequently.
- Tempo rubato permitted greater expressivity and freedom in performance.

Dynamics
- Dynamic changes can be sudden or gradual.
- Extremely wide dynamic ranges, from very soft to very loud, add considerably to emotional excitement and intensity.

Tone Color
- Romantic music exhibits a wide range of expressive tone color and sensuous sound.
- The addition of new instruments and the increased size of the orchestra led to new and varied timbres.
- Woodwinds, brass, and percussion instruments played prominent roles in orchestral and operatic works. Composers experimented with timbre through unusual combinations of instruments or by having instruments play in unusual ways.

IMPORTANT TERMS

Romantic period, p. 221
Nationalism, p. 221
Exoticism, p. 222
Program music, p. 222
Program, p. 222
Chromatic harmony, p. 223
Rubato, p. 223
Thematic transformation, p. 223
Postlude, p. 226
Strophic form, p. 227
Through-composed form, p. 227
Absolute music, p. 250
Idée fixe, p. 252
Pentatonic scale, p. 262
Leitmotif, p. 291

FEATURED GENRES

Art song, p. 226
Song cycle, p. 227
Piano trio, p. 235
Nocturne, p. 237
Étude, p. 239
Polonaise, p. 240
Concerto, p. 243
String quartet, p. 248
Symphonic poem (tone poem), p. 250
Program symphony, p. 250
Concert overture, p. 250
Incidental music, p. 250
Symphony, p. 262
Opera, pp. 269, 276, 282, 291

Twentieth Century and Beyond (1900–2020)

Historical and Cultural Events

1900 Freud, *Interpretation of Dreams*

1905 Einstein, special theory of relativity

1914–1918 First World War

1917 Russian Revolution begins

1929 Great Depression begins

1929–1953 Stalin dictator of Soviet Union

1933 Franklin D. Roosevelt inaugurated

1933 Hitler appointed chancellor of Germany

1939–1945 Second World War

1945 Atomic bomb destroys Hiroshima

1950–1953 Korean War

1953 Crick and Watson discover the structure of DNA

1955–1975 Vietnam War

1959 Fidel Castro becomes premier of Cuba

1963 President Kennedy assassinated

1969 American astronauts land on the moon

1974 President Nixon resigns

1981 Ronald Reagan inaugurated

1990 Reunification of Germany

1991 Dissolution of the Soviet Union

1994 Mandela elected president of South Africa

2001 Terrorist attacks in United States on September 11

2003 War in Iraq begins

2004 Tsunami in Asia

2005 New Orleans flooded

2007 Worldwide recession

2009 Barack Obama inaugurated

2012 Barack Obama reelected

2015 USA and Cuba resume diplomatic relations

2016 Donald Trump elected president

2017 Me Too movement begins

2018 Parkland school shooting

2019 Pro-democracy movement in Hong Kong

2020 Covid-19 pandemic

Arts and Letters

VG-Bild-Kunst Bonn/Age Fotostock

PRISMA ARCHIVO/Alamy

1907 Picasso, *Les Demoiselles d'Avignon*

1913 Kirchner, *Street, Berlin*

1914 Kandinsky, *Panels for Edward R. Campbell*

1915 Kafka, *The Metamorphosis*

1922 Eliot, *The Waste Land*

1922 Joyce, *Ulysses*

1929 Faulkner, *The Sound and The Fury*

1932 Picasso, *Girl before a Mirror*

1940–1941 Lawrence, *The Migration Series*

1942 Camus, *The Stranger*

1946 Sartre, *Existentialism and Humanism*

1948 Mailer, *The Naked and the Dead*

1950 Pollock, *One*

1951 Salinger, *Catcher in the Rye*

1955 Baldwin, *Notes of a Native Son*

1962 Warhol, *Campbell's Soup Cans*

1964 Riley, *Hesitate*

1967 Frankenthaler, *Flood*

1974 Solzhenitsyn, *The Gulag Archipelago*

1988 Morrison, *Beloved*

1990 Hockney, *Thrusting Rocks*

1996 Larson, *Rent*

2002 Kiefer, *The Sky Palace*

2002 Parks, *Topdog/Underdog*

2003 Gehry, Walt Disney Concert Hall

2005 Rowling, *Harry Potter and the Half-Blood Prince*

2007 Richter, *4900 Colors*

2012 Morrison, *Home*

2015 Ai Weiwei's *Bicycle Chandelier*

2016 Bob Dylan awarded Nobel Prize in Literature

2019 Margaret Atwood, *The Testaments*

2020 Mantel, *The Mirror and the Light*

Music

1894 Debussy, *Prelude to the Afternoon of a Faun*

1912 Schoenberg, *Pierrot lunaire*

1913 Stravinsky, *The Rite of Spring*

1916 Boulanger, *Psalm 24*

1917 Prokofiev, *Classical* Symphony

1922 Berg, *Wozzeck*

1924 Gershwin, *Rhapsody in Blue*

1926 Smith, *Lost Your Head Blues*

1927 Armstrong, *Hotter Than That*

1928 Ravel, *Boléro*

1930 Stravinsky, *Symphony of Psalms*

1931 Still, *Afro-American Symphony*

1941 Ginastera, *Estancia* Suite

1942 Ellington, *C-Jam Blues*

1943 Bartók, Concerto for Orchestra

1943–1944 Copland, *Appalachian Spring*

1945 Parker, *KoKo*

1946 Britten, *Young Person's Guide to the Orchestra*

1946–1948 Cage, *Sonatas and Interludes*

1947 Schoenberg, *A Survivor from Warsaw*

1957 Bernstein, *West Side Story*

1958 Varèse, *Poème électronique*

1960 Penderecki, *Threnody: To the Victims of Hiroshima*

1961 Carter, Double Concerto

1967 The Beatles, *Sgt. Pepper's Lonely Hearts Club Band*

1970 Crumb, *Ancient Voices of Children*

1976 Glass, *Einstein on the Beach*

1986 Adams, *Short Ride in a Fast Machine*

2000 Saariaho, *L'amour de loin*

2002 Higdon, *City Scape*

2004 Reich, *You Are (Variations)*

2005 Adams, *Dr. Atomic*

2006 Beyoncé, *Irreplaceable*

2009 León, *Inura*

2013 Whitacre, *Sainte-Chapelle*

2015 Lin Manuel Miranda, *Hamilton: An American Musical*

2017 Kendrick Lamar, *Damn*

2019 Taylor Swift, *Lover*

2020 Bob Dylan, *Rough and Rowdy Ways*

picture-alliance/Newscom

Jeff Vespa/WireImage/Getty Images

Twentieth–Century Developments (1900–1945)

Extremes of violence and progress marked the twentieth century. During the first half of the century, two world wars—from 1914–1918 and from 1939–1945—unleashed new weapons of unprecedented destructive force. Between the wars, dictatorships and a global depression caused massive hardship. The second half of the century saw the breakup of colonial empires, an extended cold war between the United States and the Soviet Union (a nation that later dissolved), and armed conflicts around the world. At the same time, rapid economic growth propelled prosperity for many. The principle of equal rights gained ground after protracted struggles by women, Black Americans, and others.

Extraordinarily accelerated developments in technology and science transformed politics and society. The Wright brothers made the first powered flight in 1903; sixty-six years later, humans walked on the moon. A flood of new technologies including sound recordings, movies, radio, satellites, computers, and the Internet triggered a continuous revolution in communications. Albert Einstein reshaped our understanding of the universe with his theory of relativity, Sigmund Freud probed the unconscious, and Francis Crick and James Watson discovered the structure of DNA, the basic material of heredity.

Rapid changes and radical breaks with earlier traditions characterized the arts. Shock as a goal was a twentieth-century phenomenon.

In the decade before World War I, Isadora Duncan's modern dance clashed with conventions of classical ballet; Pablo Picasso's cubist paintings distorted figures and objects, showing them from several angles at one time; and Wassily Kandinsky's abstract paintings no longer tried to represent the visual world at all.

In the arts, as in other aspects of life, there was an increased emphasis on pluralism and diversity.

Dance (1910), by the French painter Henri Matisse (1869–1954), conveys the fierce energy of a tribal rite. The red dancers are flattened and shown against areas of bright green and sky blue. During the early 1900s, many artists, composers, and writers were fascinated by so-called "primitive" or preliterate cultures.
Images & Stories/Alamy Stock Photo

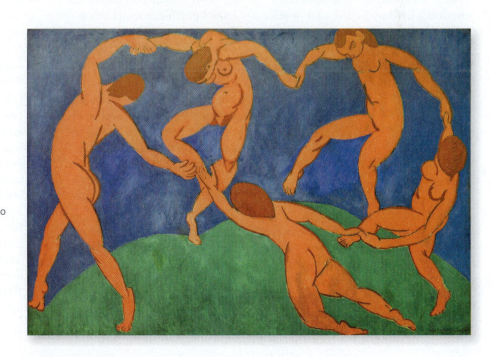

In the cubist painting of 1910, *Girl with a Mandolin (Fanny Tellier),* by Pablo Picasso (1881–1973), the musical instrument and female figure are fragmented into squares, cubes, and other geometric shapes.
VG-Bild-Kunst Bonn/Age Fotostock

In the neoclassical painting *Woman in White* (1923) by Pablo Picasso, the idealized woman's face reflects the artist's love of classical art. After the turbulence of World War I (1914–1918), many artists and composers reacted by creating emotionally restrained works incorporating stylistic features of earlier periods.
Edward Westmacott/Alamy

Contradictory styles and tendencies coexisted, as conservative and avant-garde works appeared at the same time. Moreover, individual artists, such as Picasso and the composer Igor Stravinsky, often alternated between radical and more traditional styles.

Summarizing such an incredibly diverse cultural landscape is difficult, yet any overview must include the following developments:

1. The United States powerfully shaped world culture and entertainment, as well as politics and economics. Paris and Vienna, cities that had so dominated nineteenth-century and early twentieth-century culture, were supplanted by New York and Hollywood.

2. Nonwestern cultures and thought had wide and profound effects on all the arts. Examples include the impact of African sculpture on Picasso, of Japanese design on the architect Frank Lloyd Wright, and of Indian philosophy on the composer John Cage.

3. New technologies stimulated many artists. Sculptors used such materials as plastic, fluorescent lights, and television monitors; architects called for reinforced concrete and steel girders; and musicians exploited audiotape, electric guitars, and computers.

4. Artists explored the varieties of human sexuality with extraordinary frankness.

5. The concerns of women, Black Americans, and other minorities were more powerfully represented in the arts than ever before.

6. Many artists expressed alienation, antirationality, nihilism, and dehumanization in their works, partly in reaction against catastrophic wars and massacres. The antihero became a prominent feature of novels, plays, and musical compositions.

7. Since the 1960s, many painters, architects, writers, and musicians have rejected the seriousness of modernism in favor of more pluralistic approaches. "Postmodern" artists have combined different styles, blurred the boundaries between elite and popular culture, and used preexisting images and texts from history, advertising, and the media. The pop artist Andy Warhol, for example, painted multiple Campbell's soup cans and heads of Marilyn Monroe.

The semi-abstract painting *Composition IV* (1911) by Russian artist Wassily Kandinsky (1866–1944), has vivid contrasting colors and references to a rainbow and three red-capped cavalrymen with spears. A pioneer of abstraction, Kandinsky stated that his paintings were a "graphic representation of a mood."

Album/Alamy

Street, Berlin (1913) by the German painter Ernst Ludwig Kirchner (1880–1938). Expressionist painters, such as Kirchner, used deliberate distortion and violent colors to communicate the tension and anguish of the human psyche. Expressionist composers include Arnold Schoenberg, Alban Berg, and Anton Webern.

incamerastock/Alamy

The Builders (1947), by the American painter Jacob Lawrence (1917–2000). This painting, which hangs in the White House, shows busy workers on a construction site. Lawrence was influenced by the Harlem Renaissance, a cultural movement of the 1920s and 1930s that included writers, artists and musicians. An important musical voice of this movement was William Grant Still, who often made use of spirituals, ragtime, and blues.
Susan Biddle/*The Washington Post* via Getty Images

1 Musical Styles: 1900–1945

In music, as in the other arts, the early twentieth century was a time of revolt. The years following 1900 saw more fundamental changes in the language of music than any time since the beginning of the baroque era. There were entirely new approaches to the organization of pitch and rhythm and a vast expansion in the vocabulary of sounds, especially percussive sounds. Some compositions broke with tradition so sharply that they were met with violent hostility. The most famous riot in music history occurred in Paris on May 29, 1913, at the premiere of Igor Stravinsky's ballet *Le Sacre du printemps* (*The Rite of Spring*). Police had to be called in as hecklers booed, laughed, made animal noises, and actually fought with those in the audience who wanted to hear Stravinsky's evocation of primitive rites. One music critic complained that *The Rite of Spring* produced a "sensation of acute and almost cruel dissonance" and that "from the first measure to the last, whatever note one expects is never the one that comes." Another wrote, "To say that much of it is hideous in sound is a mild description . . . . It has no relation to music at all as most of us understand the word."

Today, we are amused by the initial failure of some music critics to understand this composition, now recognized as a masterpiece. Chords, rhythms, and percussive sounds that were baffling in 1913 are now commonly heard in jazz, rock, and music for movies and television. But the hostile critics of the early 1900s were right in seeing that a great transformation in musical language was taking place.

From the late 1600s to about 1900, musical structure was governed by certain general principles. As different as the works of Bach, Beethoven, and Brahms may be, they share fundamental techniques of organizing pitches around a central tone. Since 1900, however, no single system has governed the organization of pitch in all musical compositions. Each piece is more likely to have its own unique system of pitch relationships.

In the past, composers depended on the listener's awareness—conscious or unconscious—of the general principles underlying the interrelationship of tones and chords. For example, they relied on the listener's expectation that a dominant chord would normally be followed by a tonic chord. By substituting another chord for the expected one, the composer could create a feeling of suspense, drama, or surprise. Twentieth-century music relies less on preestablished relationships and expectations. Listeners are guided primarily by musical cues within an individual composition. This new approach to the organization of sound makes twentieth-century music fascinating. When we listen openly, with no assumptions about how tones "should" relate, modern music is an adventure.

1900–1945: An Age of Musical Diversity

The range of musical styles during the first half of the twentieth century was vast. The stylistic diversity in the works of Claude Debussy, Maurice Ravel, Lili Boulanger, Igor Stravinsky, Sergei Prokofiev, Arnold Schoenberg, Alban Berg, Béla Bartók, Charles Ives, George Gershwin, William Grant Still, Aaron Copland, and Alberto Ginastera— to name only composers studied here—is a continuation and intensification of the diversity we've seen in romantic music. During the twentieth century, differences among styles were so great that it seems as though composers used different musical languages, not merely different dialects of the same musical language. Radical changes of style occur even within the works of individual composers.

Modern orchestral and chamber works often sound transparent; individual tone colors are heard clearly. To bring out the individuality of different melodic lines that are played simultaneously, a composer will often assign each line to a different timbre. In general, there is less emphasis on blended sound than there was during the romantic period. Many twentieth-century works are written for nonstandard chamber groups made up of instruments with sharply contrasting tone colors. Stravinsky's *L'Histoire du soldat* (*The Soldier's Tale,* 1918), for example, is scored for violin, double bass, clarinet, bassoon, cornet, trombone, and percussion. Even orchestral works often sound as though they are scored for a group of soloists.

Harmony

Consonance and Dissonance The twentieth century brought fundamental changes in the way chords are treated. Up to about 1900, chords were divided into two opposing types: consonant and dissonant. A consonant chord was stable; it functioned as a point of rest or arrival. A dissonant chord was unstable; its tension demanded onward motion, or resolution to a stable, consonant chord. Traditionally, only the triad, a three-tone chord, could be consonant. All others were considered dissonant. In the nineteenth century, composers came to use ever-more dissonant chords, and they treated dissonances with increasing freedom. By the early twentieth century, the traditional distinction between consonance and dissonance was abandoned in much music. A combination of tones that earlier would have been used to generate instability and expectation might now be treated as a stable chord, a point of arrival. In Stravinsky's words, dissonance "is no longer tied down to its former function" but has become an entity in itself. Thus "it frequently happens that dissonance neither prepares nor anticipates anything. Dissonance is thus no more an agent of disorder than consonance is a guarantee of security."

This "emancipation of dissonance" does not prevent composers from differentiating between chords of greater or lesser tension. Relatively mild-sounding chords may be goals of motion, and harsher chords are used for transitional sounds. But no longer is there a general principle that determines whether a chord is stable or not. It is now entirely up to the composer's discretion. "We find ourself confronted with a new logic of music that would have appeared unthinkable to the masters of the past," wrote Stravinsky. "This new logic has opened our eyes to riches whose existence we never suspected."

New Chord Structures Before 1900, there were general principles governing chord construction: certain combinations of tones were considered chords, and others were not. At the core of traditional harmony is the triad. A triad might be made up of alternate tones of a major scale, such as the first (*do*), third (*mi*), and fifth (*sol*). Within a triad, there are two intervals of a third:

Although the triad often appears in twentieth-century music, it is no longer so fundamental.

Some twentieth-century composers create fresh harmonies by placing one traditional chord against another. Such a combination of two chords heard at the same time is called a *polychord*.

Copland, *Appalachian Spring*

E major chord

A major chord

A polychord can be heard either as a single block of sound or as two distinct layers, depending on whether the two combined chords contrast in tone color and register.

Another development in twentieth-century music was the use of chordal structures *not* based on triads. One used commonly is the ***fourth chord***, in which the tones are a fourth apart, instead of a third. (From *do* to *fa*, or from *re* to *sol*, is an interval of a fourth.)

Ives, *The Cage*

Harmonic resources were also extended through the ***tone cluster***, a chord made up of tones only a half step or a whole step apart. A tone cluster can be produced on a piano by striking a group of adjacent keys with the fist or forearm.

Ives, *The Majority*

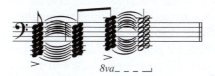

Alternatives to the Traditional Tonal System In addition to creating new chord structures, twentieth-century composers explored alternatives to the traditional tonal system. This system of tonal gravity, known as *tonality* or *key,* governed the organization of pitch from the 1600s to about 1900. By the late nineteenth century, the gravitational pull of a central tonality had been weakened by rapid and frequent key shifts. After 1900, some composers continued to use the traditional system, but others modified it greatly and still others discarded it entirely.

Before looking at new approaches to pitch organization, recall the basic principles of the traditional tonal system. As we saw in Part I ("Elements"), *tonality,* or *key,* refers to the use of a central tone, scale, and chord within a composition. The central tone, called the *tonic* or *keynote* (*do*), is the composition's resting point. The tonic major or minor scale and the tonic triad are built on this tone. Because the tonic triad is stable and restful, compositions almost always ended with it. Next in importance to the tonic triad is the *dominant chord,* which is built on the fifth tone (*sol*) of the tonic scale. There is a special gravitational pull from the dominant chord toward the tonic chord, and the motion from dominant to tonic is the essential chord progression of the tonal system. This cadence provides a strong sense of conclusion, and traditionally it was used to round off melodies, sections, and entire pieces. In summary, the tonal system is based on a central tone, a major or minor scale, and a triad; and there is a special relationship between the tonic and dominant chords.

After 1900, this system was modified in many ways. The new techniques of pitch organization are so varied as to resist easy generalization. Some compositions have a central tone but are missing other traditional elements, such as the tonic triad, the central major or minor scale, or the dominant-tonic relationship.

To create fresh sounds, composers used scales other than major or minor. For example, they breathed new life into the church modes—scales that had been used widely before 1600 as well as in folk songs of every period. Other scales were borrowed from the musical tradition of lands outside western Europe, and still others were invented by composers.

Twentieth-century compositions are often organized around a central chord other than the triad. Thus, the basic chord may well be one that was considered a dissonance earlier. In some works, the traditional relationship between dominant and tonic triads is replaced by other chord relationships. Melodies, sections, or entire pieces are rounded off not by the usual dominant-tonic cadence, but by other chord progressions.

Another twentieth-century approach to pitch organization is the use of two or more keys at one time: *polytonality*. When only two keys are used at once—as is most common—the technique is called *bitonality*. A famous bitonal passage occurs in Stravinsky's ballet *Petrushka,* when one clarinet plays in C major and another plays in F sharp major:

In general, the greater the contrast of tone color, register, and rhythm between the different layers of sound, the more we can hear the different keys.

A further departure from tradition is *atonality*, the absence of tonality or key. Atonality was foreshadowed in nineteenth-century works such as Wagner's *Tristan and Isolde,* in which the pull of a central key is weakened by frequent modulations and by liberal use of all twelve tones in the chromatic scale. Arnold Schoenberg wrote the first significant atonal pieces around 1908. He avoided traditional chord progressions in these works and used all twelve tones without regard to their traditional relationship to major or minor scales. But atonality is not a specific technique of composition; each atonal work is structured according to its own needs. (Though the word *atonality* is imprecise and negative, no other term has yet come into general use.)

Before long, Schoenberg felt the need for a more systematic approach to atonal composition, and during the early 1920s he developed the *twelve-tone system*, a new technique of pitch organization. This system gives equal prominence to each of the twelve chromatic tones, rather than singling out one pitch, as the tonal system does. For about twenty years, only Schoenberg and a few disciples used the twelve-tone system, but during the 1950s it came to be used by composers all over the world.

Rhythm The new techniques of organizing pitch were accompanied by new ways of organizing rhythm. The rhythmic vocabulary of music was expanded, with increased emphasis on irregularity and unpredictability. Rhythm is one of the most striking elements of twentieth-century music; it is used to generate power, drive, and excitement.

In the twentieth century, new rhythmic procedures were drawn from many sources, including jazz, folk music from all over the world, and European art music from the Middle Ages through the nineteenth century. The syncopations and complex rhythmic combinations of jazz fired the imagination of Stravinsky and Copland. Béla Bartók used the "free and varied rhythmic structures" of east European peasant music. And irregular phrase structures in Brahms's music inspired rhythmic innovations in Schoenberg's works.

Rapidly changing meters are characteristic of twentieth-century music, whereas baroque, classical, or romantic music maintains a single meter throughout a movement or section. Before the twentieth century, beats were organized into regularly recurring groups; the accented beat came at equal time intervals. Rhythmic irregularities such as syncopations or accents on weak beats were heard against a pervasive meter. But in many twentieth-century compositions, beats are grouped irregularly, and the accented beat comes at unequal time intervals. In some modern music the meter changes with almost every bar, so that we might count *1–2–3, 1–2–3–4–5, 1–2–3–4–5, 1–2–3, 1–2–3–4, 1–2–3–4–5, 1–2–3–4–5–6, 1–2–3–4–5, 1–2, 1–2–3–4–5–6.*

Stravinsky, *Ritual of Abduction from The Rite of Spring*

Count this again quickly and experience some of the rhythmic excitement of twentieth-century music, which often has a rapid and vigorous beat with jolting accents at unexpected times.

The rhythmic resources of twentieth-century music were also expanded through unconventional meters. Along with traditional meters such as duple and triple, modern composers use meters with five or seven beats to the measure. The pulses within a measure of any length may be grouped in irregular, asymmetrical ways. For example, eight quick pulses in a measure may be subdivided 3 + 3 + 2, or **1**–2–3–**4**–5–6–**7**–8, **1**–2–3–**4**–5–6–**7**–8.

Twentieth-century music often has two or more contrasting, independent rhythms at the same time; this is called ***polyrhythm***. Each part of the musical texture goes its own rhythmic way, often creating accents that are out of phase with accents in the other parts. Different meters are used at the same time. For example, one instrument may play in duple meter (*1–2, 1–2*) while another plays in triple meter (*1–2–3, 1–2–3*). Although polyrhythm occasionally occurs in classical and romantic music, it became more common and more complex after 1900. The polyrhythms of jazz strongly influenced composers in the 1920s and 1930s.

Rhythmic repetition of a group of pitches is a unifying technique widely used in twentieth-century music. Many modern compositions contain an ***ostinato***, a motive or phrase that is repeated persistently at the same pitch throughout a section. The ostinato may occur in the melody or in the accompaniment. Ostinatos can be found in music from various periods and cultures. In twentieth-century music, they usually serve to stabilize particular groups of pitches.

Melody The new techniques of pitch and rhythmic organization that we've surveyed had a strong impact on twentieth-century melody. Melody is no longer necessarily tied to traditional chords or to major and minor keys. It may be based on a wide variety of scales, or it may freely use all twelve chromatic tones and have no tonal center. Melody often contains wide leaps that are difficult to sing. Rhythmic irregularity and changing meters tend to make twentieth-century melodies unpredictable. They often consist of a series of phrases that are irregular in length. In general, twentieth-century music relies less than classical and romantic music on melodies that are easy to sing and remember. Melody is as rich and varied as twentieth-century music itself; neither can be classified easily.

2 Music and Musicians in Society since 1900

The twentieth and early twenty-first centuries have seen dramatic changes in how music reaches its listeners. To experience music before the 1890s—that is, before phonographs and recordings first became commercially available—you had to listen to live performers, or sing or play an instrument yourself. Since 1900, recordings, radio, film, television, the Internet, smartphones, and portable digital music players have brought a wider variety of music to more people than ever before.

Early recordings were relatively poor in sound quality and limited to about three minutes per side of a 78-rpm record. During the later twentieth century, such technological advances as long-playing records, audiotape, multichannel recording, and compact discs brought higher-fidelity sound reproduction and increased the potential playing time per recording to about seventy-five minutes. In the twenty-first century, you can carry an entire music library in your pocket: digital devices such as the iPod and Mp3 players have the capacity for hundreds of hours of music.

Radio broadcasts of live and recorded music began to reach a large audience during the 1920s and 1930s. Very popular in the mid-1930s were live performances by the Benny Goodman band broadcast on NBC's *Let's Dance*. In 1937, the National Broadcasting Company established the NBC Symphony Orchestra, directed by Arturo Toscanini (1867–1957), which was heard weekly over the radio until 1954. In addition, regular radio broadcasts of the Saturday matinee performances of the Metropolitan Opera in New York made opera available to millions of people nationwide.

The first pairing of music and film took place in Paris in 1895, when short silent movies were accompanied by a pianist. In the late 1920s, films with synchronized sound tracks began to be screened. Since then, film music has been composed in a variety of styles. Most movie music functions as a discreet background to the events on-screen, but some, such as John Williams's score for *Star Wars* (1977), is enjoyed apart from the film, on recordings and in concert halls.

With the advent of commercial television in the early 1950s, broadcast music performances could be seen as well as heard. Christmas eve, 1951, brought the premiere of the first opera created for television, *Amahl and the Night Visitors,* by the Italian American composer Gian-Carlo Menotti (1911–2007). Other television highlights included Leonard Bernstein (1918–1990) conducting the New York Philharmonic orchestra. Public television brought a wide range of music to home viewers, including *Live from Lincoln Center* and *Live from the Met.* The 1980s saw the development of MTV, a cable television network broadcasting rock videos. An innovator in the use of rock video was the singer Michael Jackson (1958–2009), whose *Thriller* (1983) was one of the most widely viewed videos ever made.

Owing to advances in communication, transportation, and technology during the twentieth century, leading musicians come not only from Europe—as in the past—but from almost everywhere in the world. The music world also has become more inclusive as women and Black Americans have become prominent as composers, soloists, and music educators.

Like all people, musicians were affected by the political, economic, and social upheavals of the twentieth century. Adolf Hitler's rise to power in Germany in 1933 had an especially dramatic impact on musicians. Avant-garde, socialist, Jewish, and anti-Nazi musicians were abruptly ousted from their jobs, and their works were no longer performed. Dictatorship, persecution, and the onset of World War II led to the largest migration of artists and intellectuals in history. Many composers, including Stravinsky, Bartók, Schoenberg, and Hindemith, left Europe for the United States. Such distinguished immigrants made enormous contributions to American musical culture. Schoenberg and Hindemith are examples of émigrés who taught in universities and helped train young American composers. Since the early twentieth century, American music has been performed worldwide. By 1918, ragtime and jazz were often heard in Paris, played by Black American musicians. Leading composer Igor Stravinsky said, "I know little about American music except that of the music hall, but I consider that unrivaled. It is veritable art and I can never get enough of it to satisfy me." American musical theater and popular song also swept the world. In 1937, Italian composers in Rome elected the American composer George Gershwin—famous for his musicals, popular songs, and orchestral work *Rhapsody in Blue*—to be included as an honorary member of the prestigious Academy of Santa Cecilia. Music in America is explored further in Chapter 15.

3 Impressionism and Symbolism

Many different musical styles coexisted around the beginning of the twentieth century. Among the most important was *impressionism,* best represented by the music of the French composer Claude Debussy (1862–1918). We look closely at musical impressionism in Chapter 4; but first, two related, though slightly earlier, artistic movements in France demand our attention: impressionist painting and symbolist poetry.

French Impressionist Painting

In 1874, a group of French painters including Claude Monet (1840–1926), Auguste Renoir (1841–1919), and Camille Pissarro (1830–1903) had an exhibition in Paris. One painting by Monet titled *Impression: Sunrise*—a misty scene of boats in port—particularly annoyed an art critic, who wrote, "Wallpaper in its embryonic state is more finished than that seascape." Using Monet's title, the critic mockingly called the entire show "the exhibition of the impressionists." The term *impressionist* stuck, but it eventually lost its derisive implication.

Impression: Sunrise (1874) by Claude Monet. At an exhibition in Paris in 1874, this painting annoyed a critic who saw it as a formless collection of tiny colored patches. Using Monet's own title, he mockingly called the entire show the "exhibition of the impressionists." Like the impressionist painters, the French composer Claude Debussy was a master at evoking a fleeting mood and misty atmosphere.
PRISMA ARCHIVO/Alamy

Today most of us appreciate impressionist paintings, which colorfully depict the joys of life and the beauties of nature. But during the 1870s, they were seen as formless collections of tiny colored patches—which they are when viewed closely. From a distance, however, the brushstrokes blend and merge into recognizable forms and shimmering colors. Impressionist painters were concerned primarily with effects of light, color, and atmosphere—with impermanence, change, and fluidity. Monet created a series of twenty paintings (1892–1894) showing Rouen Cathedral at different times of the day, from dawn to dusk. In this series, the cathedral's stone facade is desolidified and looks like colored mist. Many impressionist painters preferred to work in the open air rather than in a studio. They were fascinated by outdoor scenes from contemporary life, picnics in the woods, and crowds on Parisian boulevards. But most of all, the impressionists were obsessed with water. Using light pastel colors, they depicted the ripples and waves of the ocean and sailboats on the river Seine.

French Symbolist Poetry

As impressionist painters broke from traditional depictions of reality, writers called *symbolists* rebelled against the conventions of French poetry. Like the painters, poets such as Stéphane Mallarmé (1842–1898), Paul Verlaine (1844–1896), and Arthur Rimbaud (1854–1891) emphasized fluidity, suggestion, and the purely musical, or sonorous, effects of words. "To *name* an object," insisted Mallarmé, "is to suppress three-quarters of the enjoyment of a poem, which is made up of gradually guessing; the dream is to *suggest* it."

Claude Debussy was a close friend of many symbolist poets, especially Mallarmé, whose poem *L'Après-midi d'un faune* (*The Afternoon of a Faun*) inspired Debussy's most famous orchestral work. Many poems by Verlaine became texts for Debussy's songs. (And, more personally, Verlaine's mother-in-law was Debussy's first piano teacher.) Impressionist painting and symbolist poetry were an impetus for many developments during the twentieth century. Chapter 4 describes their effect on music.

4 Claude Debussy

The French impressionist composer Claude Debussy (1862–1918) linked the romantic era with the twentieth century. From the early age of ten until he was twenty-two, he studied at the Paris Conservatory, where his teachers regarded him as a talented rebel. In 1884, he won the prestigious Prix de Rome, which subsidized three years of study in Rome. But he left Italy after only two years because he lacked musical inspiration away from his beloved Paris.

Influences on Debussy's work included several visits to Russia, where he worked as a pianist for Tchaikovsky's patroness, Nadezhda von Meck, and formed a lifelong interest in Russian music. He was also influenced by the Asian music performed at the Paris International Exposition of 1889, and by the ideas and music of Richard Wagner, which were having a profound effect in France and both attracted and repelled him.

For years, Debussy led an unsettled life, earning a small income by teaching piano. His friends were mostly writers, such as Stéphane Mallarmé, whose literary gatherings he attended regularly. He was little known to the musical public and not completely sure of himself, though he composed important work, including his String Quartet

(1893) and the tone poem *Prelude to the Afternoon of a Faun* (1894). But his opera *Pelléas et Mélisande* (1902) marked a turning point in his career. Although the critics were sharply divided over it, the opera soon caught on, and Debussy was recognized as the most important living French composer.

Debussy led a life filled with financial and emotional crises, constantly borrowing money (he had a craving for luxuries) and having tempestuous love affairs. He was not gifted as a conductor and hated appearing in public, but to maintain his high standard of living he undertook concert tours and presented his music throughout Europe. He died in Paris in 1918.

Debussy's Music

Like the impressionist painters and symbolist poets, Debussy evoked fleeting moods and misty atmosphere, as the titles of his works suggest: *Reflets dans l'eau* (*Reflections in the Water*), *Nuages* (*Clouds*), and *Les Sons et les parfums tournent dans l'air du soir* (*Sounds and Perfumes Swirl in the Evening Air*).

Debussy was often inspired by literary and pictorial ideas, and his music sounds free and spontaneous, almost improvised. His stress on tone color, atmosphere, and fluidity is characteristic of **impressionism** in music.

Tone color truly gets unprecedented attention in Debussy's works. They have a sensuous, beautiful sound and subtle but crucial changes of timbre. The entire orchestra seldom plays together to produce massive sound. Instead, there are brief but frequent solos. Woodwinds are prominent; strings and brasses are often muted.

In his music for piano—which includes some of the finest piano works of the twentieth century—he creates hazy sonorities and uses a rich variety of bell and gonglike sounds.

Debussy's treatment of harmony was a revolutionary aspect of musical impressionism. He tends to use a chord more for its special color and sensuous quality than for its function in a standard harmonic progression. He uses successions of dissonant chords that do not resolve. (As a young man, Debussy was once asked which harmonic rules he followed; he replied, simply, "My pleasure.") He freely shifts a dissonant chord up or down the scale; the resulting parallel chords characterize his style:

Debussy, *La Cathédrale engloutie* (*The Sunken Cathedral*)

Debussy's harmonic vocabulary is large. Along with traditional three- and four-note chords, he uses five-note chords with a lush, rich sound. Chord progressions that were highly unorthodox when Debussy wrote them soon came to seem mild and natural.

"One must drown the sense of tonality," Debussy wrote. Although he never actually abandoned tonality, Debussy weakened it by avoiding chord progressions that would strongly affirm a key and by using scales in which the main tone is not emphasized. He turned to the medieval church modes and the **pentatonic**, or five-tone, **scales** heard

The impressionist Claude Debussy was a master at evoking a fleeting mood and misty atmosphere.
Time Life Pictures/Mansell/The LIFE Picture Collection/Getty Images

in Javanese music. A pentatonic scale is produced by five successive black keys of the piano—for example, F♯–G♯–A♯–C♯–D♯.

Debussy's most unusual and tonally vague scale is the ***whole-tone scale***, made up of six different notes each a whole step away from the next (C–D–E–F♯–G♯–A♯–C).

Unlike major or minor, the whole-tone scale has no special pull from *ti* to *do* because its tones are all the same distance apart. And because no single tone stands out, the whole-tone scale creates a blurred, indistinct effect.

Debussy, *Voiles* (*Sails*)

The pulse in Debussy's music is sometimes as vague as the tonality. This rhythmic flexibility reflects the fluid, unaccented quality of the French language, and in fact he set French to music very sensitively. He composed fifty-nine art songs, many of which are set to symbolist poems. His only opera, *Pelléas et Mélisande,* is an almost word-for-word setting of a symbolist play by Maurice Maeterlinck. It is the essence of musical impressionism: nebulous, mysterious, dreamlike, with a discreet, understated orchestral accompaniment.

Although not large, Debussy's output is remarkably varied. In addition to his opera and art songs, it includes works for piano, orchestra, and chamber ensembles. Echoes of his music can be heard in the works of many composers during the first two decades of the twentieth century; but no other important musician can so fairly be described as an impressionist. Even the composer most similar to him, his younger French contemporary Maurice Ravel (1875–1937), wrote music with greater clarity of form. Debussy's style was both a final expression of romanticism and the beginning of a new era.

Prélude à l'Après–midi d'un faune (*Prelude to the Afternoon of a Faun;* 1894)

"The music of this Prelude," wrote Debussy of his *Prelude to the Afternoon of a Faun,* "is a very free illustration of the beautiful poem by Stéphane Mallarmé, *The Afternoon of a Faun.*" This poem evokes the dreams and erotic fantasies of a pagan forest creature who is half man, half goat. While playing a "long solo" on his flute, the intoxicated faun tries to recall whether he actually carried off two beautiful nymphs or only dreamed of doing so. Exhausted by the effort, he falls back to sleep in the sunshine.

Debussy intended his music to suggest "the successive scenes through which pass the desires and dreams of the faun in the heat of this afternoon." The subtle, sensuous timbres of this miniature tone poem were new in Debussy's day. Woodwind solos, muted horn calls, and harp glissandos create a rich variety of delicate sounds. The dynamics are usually subdued, and only rarely does the entire orchestra—from which trombones, trumpets, and timpani are excluded—play at one time. The music often swells sensuously and then subsides in voluptuous exhaustion.

The prelude begins with an unaccompanied flute melody; its vague pulse and tonality make it dreamlike and improvisatory. This flute melody is heard again and again, faster, slower, and against a variety of lush chords. Though the form of the prelude may be thought of as A B A′, one section blends with the next. It has a continuous ebb and flow. The fluidity and weightlessness typical of impressionism are found in this music. We are never tempted to beat time to its subtle rhythms. The prelude ends magically with the main melody, played by muted horns, seeming to come from far off.

The bell-like tones of antique cymbals finally evaporate into silence. With all its new sounds and musical techniques, the piece has aptly been described as a "quiet revolution" in the history of music.

Listening Outline

DEBUSSY, *Prélude à l'Après-midi d'un faune (Prelude to the Afternoon of a Faun; 1894)*

At a very moderate tempo, A B A′ form, E major

3 flutes, 2 oboes, 1 English horn, 2 clarinets, 2 bassoons, 4 French horns, 2 harps, antique cymbals, 1st violins, 2d violins, violas, cellos, double basses

(Duration 9:40)

Listen for the dreamlike atmosphere of the opening *solo flute melody,* which recurs in different instrumental *tone colors* and *tempos.* Notice the prominent use of the harp.

A

0:00   **1. a.** Solo flute, ***p***, main melody.

       Harp glissando; soft horn calls. Short pause. Harp glissando; soft horn calls.

0:43   **b.** Flute, ***p***, main melody; tremolo strings in background. Oboe, ***p***, continues melody. Orchestra swells to ***f***. Solo clarinet fades into

1:35   **c.** Flute, ***p***, main melody varied and expanded; harp and muted strings accompany. Flute melody comes to quiet close.

2:48   **2. a.** Clarinet; harp and cellos in background.

3:16   **b.** New oboe melody.

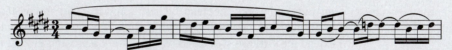

       Violins take up melody, crescendo and accelerando to climax. Excitement subsides. Ritardando. Clarinet, ***p***, leads into

B

4:33   **3. a.** Woodwinds, ***p***, legato melody in long notes. Crescendo.

5:16   **b.** Strings repeat melody; harps and pulsating woodwinds in background, crescendo. Decrescendo. Horns, ***p***, solo violin, ***p***, clarinet, oboe.

A'

6:21	**4. a.** Harp accompanies flute, *p*, main melody in longer notes. Oboe, staccato woodwinds.
6:56	**b.** Harp accompanies oboe, *p*, main melody in longer notes. English horn, harp glissando.
7:39	**5. a.** Antique cymbals, bell-like tones. Flutes, *p*, main melody. Solo violins, *pp*, in high register.
8:16	**b.** Flute and solo cello, main melody; harp in background.
8:45	**c.** Oboe, *p*, brings melody to close. Harps, *p*.
9:10	**d.** Muted horns and violins, *ppp*, beginning of main melody sounding far off. Flute, antique cymbals, and harp; delicate tones fade into silence.

5 Maurice Ravel

The French composer Maurice Ravel (1875–1937) was a master of orchestral and pianistic tone color. Like his older contemporary Debussy, Ravel grew up in Paris and studied piano and composition for many years at the Paris Conservatory. But unlike Debussy, Ravel never succeeded in winning the Prix de Rome, despite five attempts. His last failure—at age thirty, when he was already a recognized composer—caused a scandal that led to a change of administration at the Conservatory. It was perhaps owing to his lingering resentment of the musical establishment that he refused the Legion of Honor when it was offered to him, as France's most famous living composer, in 1920.

Though he is often described as an impressionist and paired with Debussy, Ravel does not fit neatly into any stylistic category. It is true that some of his music—such as the piano piece *Jeux d'eaux* (*Fountains*, 1901) and the ballet *Daphnis and Chloé* (1909–1912)—has the fluid, misty, atmospheric quality associated with impressionism. And subtle changes of tone color are indeed extremely important in Ravel's works, as in the impressionist music of Debussy. Yet much music by Ravel is too clearly defined in form and tonality and classically balanced in phrase structure to be considered impressionist. His lyrical melodic lines, though individual in style, are closely related to melodies by nineteenth-century French composers, such as Georges Bizet. However, Ravel's melodies are often based on modes, which sometimes make them suggest music from a foreign land or from the distant past. His music is often characterized by a clear beat, and rhythmic patterns are often obsessively repeated.

Above all, Ravel was a master craftsman; he once said, "My objective is technical perfection." He worked unceasingly to produce a relatively small number of vocal and instrumental works (for piano, orchestra, and chamber groups) that are almost all widely performed and recorded. His highly original piano pieces contain novel sonorities and extend the virtuoso style of Liszt. They were a proving ground for compositional procedures he later used in orchestral compositions. In fact, a considerable proportion of his orchestral works—including *Alborada del gracioso* (*Jester's Dawn Song*) and *Le Tombeau de Couperin* (*The Tomb of Couperin*)—are orchestrations of piano pieces; and his orchestral transcription of Mussorgsky's piano piece *Pictures at an Exhibition* is very popular. Ravel was extremely sensitive to the technical and expressive capacities of orchestral instruments and created many fresh combinations of tone colors.

Ravel had a taste for exotic musical idioms. Many of his works have a Spanish flavor; examples are the one-act opera *L'Heure espagnole* (*The Spanish Hour*, 1907–1909) and the orchestral works *Rhapsodie espagnole* (*Spanish Rhapsody*, 1908) and *Boléro*. He exploited the rhythms and tone colors of American jazz in such works of the 1920s as Piano Concerto in G major, Piano Concerto for the Left Hand (commissioned by the one-armed pianist Paul Wittgenstein), and the *Blues* movement of Sonata for Violin and Piano. Ravel was also fascinated by dance and wrote several ballets, including *Daphnis and Chloé*, which he later arranged as two concert suites for orchestra. Stylized dance rhythms pervade much of his music: the Renaissance pavane in *Pavane pour une infante défunte* (*Pavane for a Dead Princess*, 1899); the baroque forlane, rigaudon, and minuet in *Le Tombeau de Couperin* (1914–1917); the Viennese waltz in *Valses nobles et sentimentales* (*Noble and Sentimental Waltzes*, 1911) and *La Valse* (*The Waltz*, 1919–1920); and the Spanish boléro in *Boléro*.

Boléro (1928)

One of the best-known of all orchestral works, *Boléro* reflects Ravel's fascination with tone color, Spanish music, and obsessive rhythmic repetition. It originated as a ballet commissioned by the dancer Ida Rubinstein and was introduced by her at the Paris Opera in 1928. Set in a dimly lit Spanish café, the ballet centers on a young Gypsy woman dancing a boléro on a table surrounded by men. Her movements become increasingly lively, and the excitement and tension of the onlookers culminate in violence. The ballet was a success, but soon *Boléro* became more famous internationally as a concert piece. After its American premiere by Arturo Toscanini and the New York Philharmonic in 1929, a critic wrote that "*Boléro* brought shouts and cheers from the audience."

Ravel modestly described *Boléro* as an "experiment" consisting of "one long, very gradual crescendo." Its theme and rhythm "were deliberately given a Spanish character" and "repeated to the point of obsession." *Boléro* is unusual in form, consisting of an extended, exotic-sounding theme that is heard over and over with increasingly rich and brilliant orchestration. Ravel creates movement and growth through changes of tone color, as Stravinsky does in the *Firebird* Suite and *The Rite of Spring*. The theme is first presented by solo woodwind instruments, including the unusual oboe d'amore, which is lower than the oboe but higher than the English horn. As the volume gradually increases, brass instruments and tenor and sopranino saxophones—rare in a symphony orchestra—are given the theme. Novel tone colors result from unusual doublings, such as muted trumpet and flute, as though Ravel were inventing new instruments. Sometimes the melody is doubled at different pitch levels, a device that results in sliding parallel chords.

Only after the dynamic level has reached f is the melody presented by the violins and doubled by woodwinds and brasses.

Boléro's accompaniment is even more obsessive than its melody. From beginning to end, a two-bar boléro rhythmic pattern is repeated in the snare drum, which is progressively doubled by more and more instruments. Moreover, in the bass of virtually every bar we hear a three-note ostinato played pizzicato by the lower strings. Also contributing to the hypnotic effect is the insistence on the key of C major, which persists until an electrifying climax—resulting from a sudden, momentary upward shift to the brighter key of E major—and a violently dissonant ending.

The theme of *Boléro* is made up of two extended parts, each heard twice with varied orchestration: A A B B. This A A B B pattern is presented four times, gradually building in power. Finally, Ravel compresses the theme to A B. Thus *Boléro* can be outlined A A B B—A A B B—A A B B—A A B B—A B. The boléro rhythmic pattern and the accompanying bass ostinato are presented alone—without the melody—as an introduction to each A and B, with gradually increasing volume and richness of sound.

In part A, the melody is fairly narrow in range and uses only the notes of the C major scale. It has two phrases, the first ending with a questioning upward skip to an incomplete cadence, and the second ending with a complete cadence as if giving an answer.

Part B of the theme is also made up of two phrases, but it is wider in range and darker in mood because it combines elements of major, minor, and modal scales. After ascending to a climactic tone that is repeated with hypnotic insistence, the melody gradually moves downward a long distance until it reaches a cadence.

Listening Outline

RAVEL, *Boléro* (1928)

Tempo di boléro, moderato assai (tempo of a boléro, very moderate), triple meter ($\frac{3}{4}$)

2 piccolos, 2 flutes, 2 oboes (one doubling on oboe d'amore), English horn, E flat clarinet, 2 B flat clarinets, bass clarinet, 3 saxophones (sopranino, soprano, tenor), 2 bassoons, contrabassoon, 4 French horns, 1 small trumpet in D, 3 trumpets, 3 trombones, tuba, harp, 3 timpani, cymbals, tam-tam, celesta, 2 snare drums, 1st violins, 2d violins, violas, cellos, double basses

(Duration 15:05)

Listen for changing *tone colors* as the extended theme repeats over and over again with increasingly rich and brilliant orchestration. Notice that the theme is accompanied throughout by the boléro *rhythm* in the snare drum and six-note ostinato (**long**-long-long, **long**-long-short-short) in pizzicato strings.

0:00	**1. a.**	Boléro rhythm in snare drum, *pp*, accompanied by ostinato in pizzicato violas and cellos.
0:10	**b.**	Part A, flute, *pp*, extended melody with two phrases. Boléro rhythm in flute, *pp*, introduces
0:58	**c.**	Part A repeated, clarinet, *p*. Boléro rhythm in flute, *pp*, introduces
1:46	**d.**	Part B, bassoon, *mp*, enters in high register, extended exotic-sounding melody with two phrases. Harp, *pp*, and boléro rhythm in flute, *pp*, introduce
2:35	**e.**	Part B, repeated an octave higher, high (E flat) clarinet, *p*. Boléro rhythm in high bassoon, *mp*, introduces
3:24	**2. a.**	Part A, oboe d'amore, *mp*. Boléro rhythm in French horn, *p*, introduces
4:13	**b.**	Part A repeated, muted trumpet, *mp*, doubled an octave higher by flute, *p*. Pizzicato violins, boléro rhythm in muted trumpet, *mp*, introduce
5:00	**c.**	Part B, tenor saxophone, *mp*, melody decorated by slides. Pizzicato violins, boléro rhythm in muted trumpet, *mp*, introduce
5:48	**d.**	Part B repeated an octave higher, sopranino saxophone, *mf*. Harp, boléro rhythm in French horn, *mf*, introduce
6:37	**3. a.**	Part A, French horn, *mf*, doubled at higher pitches by piccolos. Pizzicato strings, boléro rhythm in muted trumpets, *mf*, introduce
7:24	**b.**	Part A repeated in woodwinds, *mf*. Harp, boléro rhythm in violas and French horns, *mf*, introduce
8:10	**c.**	Part B, trombone, *mf*, melody decorated by slides. Boléro rhythm in trumpets, *f*, introduces
8:59	**d.**	Part B repeated in high woodwinds, *mf*, with melody in parallel chords, *f*. Boléro rhythm in French horns, *f*, introduces
9:46	**4. a.**	Part A, violins, *f*, and woodwinds. Boléro rhythm in French horns, *f*, introduces
10:33	**b.**	Part A, repeated in violins, *f*, and woodwinds, with melody in parallel chords. Boléro rhythm in French horns, *f*, introduces
11:20	**c.**	Part B, violins, woodwinds, and trumpet, *f*. Boléro rhythm in strings, woodwinds, and French horns, *f*, introduces
12:02	**d.**	Part B repeated in strings, woodwinds, and trombone, *f*, with melody in parallel chords. Boléro rhythm in strings, woodwinds, and French horns, *ff*, introduces
12:56	**5. a.**	Part A, violins, trumpets, and woodwinds, *ff*, with melody in parallel chords. Boléro rhythm in strings, woodwinds, and French horns, *ff*, introduces
13:44	**b.**	Part B, violins, woodwinds, and brasses, *ff*, with melody in parallel chords; melody changes with shift to new key, closes with return to original key. Boléro rhythm in whole orchestra; percussion, *ff*, cymbal crashes, dissonant concluding chords.

6 Lili Boulanger

The French composer Lili Boulanger (on right) , the first woman to win the Rome Prize, with her older sister Nadia (on left), who became a famous teacher of composition, in 1913.

The History Collection/Alamy

French composer Lili Boulanger (1893–1918) was the first woman to win the prestigious Rome Prize in composition (in 1913), a scholarship that allowed young musicians to live in Rome for several years at the expense of the French government. Lili was born in Paris into a family of musicians: her grandmother, a well-known singer; her grandfather, a cellist; her father Ernest, who won the Rome Prize in music composition in 1835, taught voice at the Paris Conservatory; her mother Raissa had studied singing with Ernest, who became her husband; her older sister Nadia Boulanger came to be one of the most important teachers of composition in the twentieth century.

At age two, Lili contracted bronchial pneumonia that weakened her immune system. Throughout her short life she was often ill. As a child she had private music lessons and audited classes at the Paris Conservatory. She could read complex music at sight and perform on piano, violin, cello, organ, and harp. At eighteen she entered the Paris Conservatory determined to win the Rome Prize that her sister Nadia had failed to do a few years earlier.

Winning the Rome Prize at nineteen made Lili an international celebrity. She was awarded a contract with the important music publisher Ricordi, which gave her a monthly income and regular publication of her works. After listening to her prize-winning cantata in a concert, Claude Debussy—the leading French composer of the time—wrote that Lili Boulanger "is only nineteen years old. Her experience in the techniques of writing music seems much older!"

In March 1914, Lili Boulanger arrived in Rome but was obliged to return to Paris only several months later due to the outbreak of World War I. During 1915, Lili and Nadia were the secretaries of a Franco-American organization that sent food, clothing, and money to Paris Conservatory students serving in the French army. In 1916, Lili returned to Rome and began working on an opera based on *Princess Maleine*, a war drama by Belgian symbolist poet and playwright Maurice Maeterlinck. Sadly, Lili Boulanger died in Paris at age twenty-four, eight months before the end of the war, never finishing the opera.

Though she wrote instrumental music, her most important compositions are. for voices. These include *Vielle prière bouddhique* (*Old Buddhist Prayer*), for chorus and orchestra, the song cycle *Clairières dans le ciel* (*Rifts in the Sky*), *Pie Jesu* (*Loving Jesus*), for mezzo-soprano, string quartet, harp, and organ, and settings of psalms 129, 130, and 24, the last of which we study here.

Psaume 24 (Psalm 24; 1916)

The text of *Psalm 24* praises the creator of the world. After posing the question "Qui" ("Who"), the Psalmist replies that only the righteous can ascend the Lord's holy mountain.

Composed in Rome in 1916, *Psalm 24* is scored for the unusual combination of tenor soloist, chorus, four French horns, three trumpets, four trombones, tuba, timpani, harp, and organ. There are no woodwinds or strings. Though lasting only three-and-a-half minutes, *Psalm 24* includes sharp contrasts of sound and mood.

The energetic opening section begins with brass and organ fanfares alternating with passages for unaccompanied male voices. The words "Ce sera l'homme qui a les mains pures" (" He that hath clean hands") bring a meditative, softer section in which the male voices are accompanied only by the organ. The French text is sung with one note per syllable, so that each word is projected clearly. The full choir—including sopranos and altos—appears only in the final section of *Psalm 24*, creating a climactic ending.

Vocal Music Guide

BOULANGER, *Psaume 24* (*Psalm 24*; 1916)

(Duration 3:30)

Listen for the contrast between the loud and energetic opening section and the meditative softer section that reflects the words "Ce sera l'homme qui a les mains pures" ("He that hath clean hands")

0:00	Lively and decisive. Brasses, organ, timpani, *ff*, introduce		
0:05	Tenors, basses, *ff*	*La terre appartient à l'Eternel, et tout ce qui s'y trouve la terre habitable et ceux qui l'habitent.*	The earth is the Lord's and the fullness thereof, the world and they that dwell therein.
0:13	Brasses, organ, *ff*		
0:16	Tenors, basses, *ff*	*Car il l'a fondé sur les mers, etablie sur les fleuves.*	For he has founded it on the seas established it upon the floods.
0:22	Brasses, organ, *ff*		
0:27	Tenors, basses, *f*	*Qui est-ce qui montera à la montagne de l'Eternel et qui est-ce qui demeura au lieu de sa sainteté*	Who shall ascend into the hill of the Lord? and who shall stand in his holy place?
0:38	Brasses, organ, timpani, *ff*		
0:42	Tenors, basses, *mf* organ, *pp*	*Ce sera l'homme qui a les mains pures et le coeur net, dont l'âme n'est point portée à la fausseté Et qui ne jure point pour tromper.*	He that hath clean hands, and a pure heart; who has not lifted up his soul unto vanity nor sworn in deceitfully.
1:09	Slower tempo, Tenor solo, *p* Harp, horns, organ accompany	*Il recevra la bénédiction de l'Eternel* *et la justice de Dieu son sauveur.*	He shall receive the blessing from the Lord. And righteousness from God his salvation.

1:35	Tenors, basses, harp, organ, *p*, long held chord	*Telle est la génération de ceux* *Qui Le cherchent* *Qui cherchent Ta face en Jacob.*	This is the generation of those that seek Him that see thy face O Jacob.
2:02	Lively, unaccompanied chorus, *f*, joined by brass fanfares	*Portes, élevez vos têtes,* *Portes éternelles,* *haussez vous* *et le Roi de gloire entrera.*	Lift up your heads, O ye gates, and be lift up, ye everlasting doors and the King of glory shall come in.
2:13	Brasses, organ, *ff*		
2:19	Basses, tenors join	*Qui est ce Roi de gloire?* *C'est l'Eternel fort et puissant* *dans les combats.*	Who Is this King of glory? The Lord strong and mighty in battle.
2:28	Brasses, organ, timpani, *f*, introduce		
2:30	Unaccompanied chorus	*Portes, élevez vos têtes* *élevez vous aussi* *Portes éternelles*	Lift up your heads, O ye gates and be ye lift up ye everlasting doors;
2:39	Brasses, organ join full chorus, *ff*	*Et le Roi de Gloire entrera.*	And the King of glory shall come in.
2:43	Brasses, organ, harp, timpani, *ff*		
2:48	Chorus	*Qui est ce Roi de gloire?*	Who Is this King of glory?
2:54	Faster tempo, full chorus and orchestra	*C'est l'Eternel des armées* *C'est Lui* *qui est le Roi,*	The Lord of strong and mighty. It is Him who is this King of glory?
3:06	Tempo accelerates to sudden pause	*Eternel, Eternel, Eternel!*	Everlasting!
3:15	Held final tone, *fff*, in chorus and orchestra	*Ah!*	Ah!

7 Primitivism

During the early 1900s, many artists, scholars, and musicians were fascinated by so-called primitive cultures—those without a written language. An important influence on twentieth-century primitivism in art was the French painter Paul Gauguin (1848–1903), who found inspiration in far-off Tahiti and the Marquesas Islands. Before one of his voyages he told an interviewer, "I'm leaving so that I can rid myself of civilization's influence." Many early twentieth-century artists, including Matisse and Picasso, collected African masks and statues. In 1907, Picasso's violent and pathbreaking painting *Les Demoiselles d'Avignon* (*The Young Women of Avignon*) reflected the impact of

African sculpture. Contact with tribal art led modern painters and sculptors to emphasize simplicity, crudeness, intense colors, and forceful outlines, disregarding conventional Western ideas of beauty.

In music, *primitivism*—the deliberate evocation of primitive power through repetitive rhythms, harsh dissonances, and percussive sounds—had a significant impact on several works composed between 1910 and 1915. In Chapter 8 we study the most important example of musical primitivism, *Le Sacre du Printemps* (*The Rite of Spring*; 1913), ballet music by the Russian Igor Stravinsky. Other works inspired by primitivism are *Sythian Suite* for orchestra (1915), by the Russian Sergei Prokofiev, and the piano piece *Allegro barbaro* (1911) by the Hungarian Béla Bartók.

8 Igor Stravinsky

Even during his lifetime, Igor Stravinsky (1882–1971) was a legendary figure. His once revolutionary works had already become modern classics, and he influenced three generations of composers and other artists. Cultural giants, such as Picasso and T. S. Eliot, were his friends. President John F. Kennedy honored him at a White House dinner in his eightieth year.

Stravinsky, who was born in Russia, near St. Petersburg, grew up in a musical atmosphere and studied with Nikolai Rimsky-Korsakov. He had his first important opportunity in 1909, when the great impresario Sergei Diaghilev heard his music. Diaghilev was the director of the Russian Ballet, an extremely influential troupe that employed great painters as well as dancers, choreographers, and composers. Diaghilev first asked Stravinsky to orchestrate some piano pieces by Chopin as ballet music and then, in 1910, commissioned an original ballet, *The Firebird*, which was immensely successful. A year later (1911) Stravinsky's second ballet, *Petrushka*, was performed, and Stravinsky was hailed as a modern master. His orchestral colors delighted sophisticated Parisians. When his third ballet, *The Rite of Spring*, had its premiere in Paris in 1913, a riot erupted in the audience—spectators were shocked and outraged by its pagan primitive, harsh dissonance, percussiveness, and pounding rhythms. But it too was recognized as a masterpiece and influenced composers all over the world.

Igor Stravinsky (on right) with the impresario Sergei Diaghilev in 1921.

Hulton Archive/Stringer/Getty Images

During World War I, Stravinsky sought refuge in Switzerland. After the armistice, he moved to France, his home until the onset of World War II, when he came to the United States. In the 1920s and 1930s, he was an international celebrity, constantly touring in Europe and the United States; and his compositions—which had originally been inspired by Russian folk music—became cooler and more objective. During his years in the United States (he lived outside Los Angeles), his young musical assistant Robert Craft familiarized him with the works of Schoenberg and Berg. In the 1950s, Stravinsky astonished his followers by adopting Schoenberg's twelve-tone system. Unlike Schoenberg and Bartók, Stravinsky got well-paying commissions for his work and was an astute businessman. He also loved order and discipline and said that he composed "every day, regularly, like a man with banking hours." In his seventies and eighties, he was still touring, conducting his rich and intense late works. He also, for the first time in fifty years, returned to Russia and bared his soul to a group of Soviet composers: "The smell of the Russian earth is different . . . . A man has one birthplace, one fatherland, one country."

Stravinsky's Music

Stravinsky's extensive output includes compositions of almost every kind, for voices, instruments, and the stage; and his innovations in rhythm, harmony, and tone color had an enormous influence.

Stravinsky's development shows dramatic changes of style. His three early ballets—*The Firebird* (1910), *Petrushka* (1911), and *The Rite of Spring* (1913)—call for very large orchestras and draw on Russian folklore and folk tunes. During World War I, he wrote for chamber groups using unconventional combinations of instruments and incorporating ragtime rhythms and popular dances (an example is *The Soldier's Tale,* 1918). From about 1920 to 1951 (his "neoclassical" period), he was inspired largely by eighteenth-century music. His ballet *Pulcinella* (1920) was based partly on the music of Giovanni Battista Pergolesi (1710–1736). His opera *The Rake's Progress* (1951) was modeled on Mozart. Stravinsky's neoclassical works emphasize restraint, balance, and wit, and are far removed from the violence of *The Rite of Spring.* But his shift to the twelve-tone system in the 1950s was an even more dramatic change of approach because until then, all his music had a clear tonal center. Inspired by Anton Webern (1883–1945), Stravinsky now wrote brief works in which melodic lines were "atomized" into short fragments in continually changing tone colors and registers.

Despite such stylistic changes, all his music has an unmistakable "Stravinsky sound." Tone colors are dry and clear, and the beat is strong. His music abounds in changing and irregular meters; sometimes several meters are heard at once. Ostinatos, or repeated rhythmic and melodic patterns, frequently unify sections of a piece. His treatment of musical form is also unique: rather than connecting themes with bridge passages, he makes abrupt shifts, but his music nevertheless sounds unified and continuous. The effectiveness of his rhythms, chords, and melodies often depends largely on his orchestration, in which highly contrasting tone colors are frequently combined.

Stravinsky's music has rich, novel harmonies—he makes even conventional chords sound unique through spacing, doubling, and the orchestration of their tones.

Stravinsky drew on a wide range of styles, from Russian folk songs to baroque melodies, from Renaissance madrigals to tango rhythms. He sometimes used existing music to create original compositions, but more often the music is entirely his own while vaguely suggesting a past style.

Le Sacre du printemps (The Rite of Spring; 1913)

Few compositions have had so powerful an impact on twentieth-century music as *Le Sacre du printemps* (*The Rite of Spring*), Stravinsky's third ballet score for the Russian Ballet. Its harsh dissonances, percussive orchestration, rapidly changing meters, violent offbeat accents, and ostinatos fired the imagination of many composers. The idea for *The Rite of Spring* came to Stravinsky as a "fleeting vision" while he was completing *The Firebird* in St. Petersburg in 1910. "I saw in imagination a solemn pagan rite: wise elders, seated in a circle, watching a young girl dance herself to death. They were sacrificing her to propitiate the god of spring." Later in life, Stravinsky remarked that the "most wonderful event" of every year of his childhood was the "violent Russian spring that seemed to begin in an hour and was like the whole earth cracking."

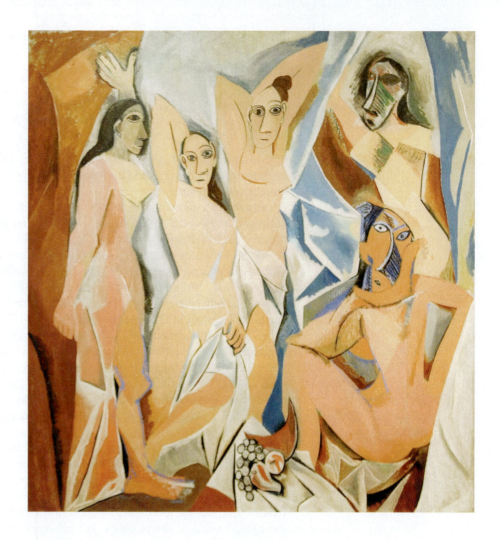

Les Demoiselles d'Avignon (1907) by Picasso reflects the influence of African sculpture.
Alfonso Vicente/Alamy

Stravinsky's interest in so-called primitive or preliterate culture was shared by many artists and scholars in the early 1900s. In 1907, Picasso's violent and path-breaking painting *Les Demoiselles d'Avignon* reflected the influence of African sculpture. In 1913—the same year as *The Rite of Spring*—Freud published *Totem and Taboo,* a study of "resemblances between the psychic lives of savages and neurotics." *Primitivism*—the deliberate evocation of primitive power through insistent rhythms and percussive sounds—had a significant impact on early twentieth-century music.

The Rite of Spring has two large parts, which are subdivided into sections that move at various speeds. These subsections follow each other without pause. The titles of the dances suggest their primitive subject matter. Part I, *The Adoration of the Earth,* consists of (1) *Introduction;* (2) *Omens of Spring: Dances of the Youths and Maidens;* (3) *Ritual of Abduction;* (4) *Spring Rounds;* (5) *Games of the Rival Tribes;* (6) *Procession of the Wise Elder;* (7) *Adoration of the Earth;* (8) *Dance of the Earth.* Part II, *The Sacrifice,* consists of (1) *Introduction;* (2) *Mysterious Circles of the Young Girls;* (3) *Glorification of the Chosen Maiden;* (4) *Evocation of the Ancestors;* (5) *Ritual of the Ancestors;* (6) *Sacrificial Dance.* Each of the two large parts begins with a slow introduction and ends with a frenzied, climactic dance.

The Rite of Spring is written for an enormous orchestra including eight horns, four tubas, and a very important percussion section made up of five timpani, bass drum, tambourine, tam-tam, triangle, antique cymbals, and a guiro (a notched gourd scraped with a stick). The melodies of *The Rite of Spring* are folklike. Like ancient Russian folk tunes, they have narrow ranges, and they are made up of fragments that are repeated with slight changes in rhythm and pitch. Many individual chords are repeated, and each change of harmony produces a great impact. This melodic and harmonic repetition gives the music a ritualistic, hypnotic quality. Rhythm is a vital structural element in *The Rite of Spring;* it has a life of its own, almost independent of melody and harmony. Today, *The Rite of Spring* is performed more frequently as a concert piece than as a ballet.

We now take a closer look at four sections of *The Rite of Spring: Introduction, Omens of Spring—Dances of the Youths and Maidens,* and *Ritual of Abduction,* which open Part I; and *Sacrificial Dance,* which concludes Part II.

Part I:
Introduction

For Stravinsky, the *Introduction* to Part I represented "the awakening of nature, the scratching, gnawing, wiggling of birds and beasts." It begins with the strangely penetrating sound of a solo bassoon straining at the top of its register. As though improvising, the bassoon repeats a fragment of a Lithuanian folk tune in irregular ways.

Soon, other woodwind instruments join the bassoon with repeated fragments of their own. The impression of improvisation is strengthened by the absence of a clearly defined pulse or meter. Dissonant, unconventional chord structures are used. Toward the end of the *Introduction,* different layers of sounds—coming mostly from woodwinds and brasses—are piled on top of each other, and the music builds to a piercing climax. But suddenly, all sound is cut off; only the solo bassoon forlornly repeats its opening melody. Then the violins, playing pizzicato, introduce a repeated four-note "ticking" figure. This figure later serves as an ostinato in *Omens of Spring—Dances of the Youths and Maidens,* which immediately follows the *Introduction.*

Part I:
Omens of Spring—Dances of the Youths and Maidens

Sounding almost like drums, the strings pound out a dissonant chord. There are unexpected and irregular accents whose violence is heightened by jabbing sounds from the eight horns. This is the way the passage might be counted (with a rapid pulse): 1–2–3–4, 1–2–3–4, 1–**2**–3–**4**, 1–2–3–4, 1–**2**–3–4, **1**–2–3–4, **1**–2–3–4, 1–**2**–3–4. The unchanging dissonant harmony is a polychord that combines two different traditional chords. Successive melodic fragments soon join the pounding chord and other repeated figures. The melodic fragments, played by brass and woodwind instruments, are narrow in range and are repeated over and over with slight variations. The rhythmic activity is ceaseless and exciting, and gradually more and more instruments are added.

It's interesting to contrast Stravinsky's musical techniques in *Dances of the Youths and Maidens* with those of a classical movement in sonata form. A classical movement grows out of conflicts between different keys; this section of *The Rite of Spring* is based almost entirely on repetition of a few chords. Themes in a classical movement are developed through different keys, varied, and broken into fragments that take on new emotional meanings. In *Dances of the Youths and Maidens,* Stravinsky simply repeats melodic fragments with relatively slight variation. To create movement and growth, he relies instead on variations of rhythm and tone color—a technique that can be traced back to nineteenth-century Russian musical tradition.

Part I:
Ritual of Abduction

The frenzied *Ritual of Abduction* grows out of the preceding section and is marked by violent strokes on the timpani and bass drum. Enormous tension is generated by powerful accents and rapid changes of meter (see the music example on page 331). This section of *The Rite of Spring* closes with high trills in the strings and flutes.

Listening Outline

STRAVINSKY, *Le Sacre du printemps* (*The Rite of Spring;* 1913)

Part I: *Introduction, Omens of Spring—Dances of the Youths and Maidens, Ritual of Abduction*

2 piccolos, 3 flutes, alto flute, 4 oboes, English horn, E flat clarinet, 3 clarinets, 2 bass clarinets, 4 bassoons, 2 contrabassoons, 8 French horns, small trumpet in D, 4 trumpets, 3 trombones, 3 tubas, timpani, bass drum, triangle, antique cymbals, 1st violins, 2d violins, violas, cellos, double basses
(Duration 7:24)

Listen, in the *Introduction*, for the high solo bassoon repeating melodic fragments with slight changes of *pitch* and *rhythm*. In Omens of Spring—Dances of the Youths and Maidens, notice the "ticking" four-note ostinato and pulsating *dissonant* polychord punctuated by irregular *accents*.

Introduction

0:00	**1. a.**	High solo bassoon, repeated folksong fragment in changing meters, joined by French horn, ***mp***, then clarinets and bass clarinets, ***p***.

0:43	**b.**	English horn, new melodic fragment; high bassoon; English horn, melodic fragment, bassoons accompany in faster rhythm.
1:12	**c.**	Pizzicato strings, oboe, repeated notes introduce high clarinet melody.
1:24	**d.**	Oboe phrase, ***f***, high flutes accompany; English horn phrase, ***mf***, bass clarinets accompany; flutes and English horn move in even rhythm; violin trill joins.
1:53	**e.**	Pizzicato cello pulsations, rhythmic activity quickens, rapid shifts between large and small wind groups; clarinet, repeated descending phrase.
2:18	**f.**	Oboe with rapid alto flute accompaniment; piercing high clarinet, ***ff***, joins; music builds to ***ff*** climax, different layers of woodwind and brass sound piled on each other.
2:52	**2. a.**	Sudden ***p***, solo high bassoon, opening fragment; clarinet trill, joined by
3:03	**b.**	Pizzicato violins, "ticking" ostinato figure.

Low held tone in bass clarinet; high chord in violins; pizzicato violins, "ticking" ostinato figure.

Omens of Spring—Dances of the Youths and Maidens

3:22   **3. a.** Sudden *f*, strings, repeated dissonant polychord with punctuations in French horns, irregular accents, moderate tempo, duple meter.

3:29   **b.** English horn, *mf*, "ticking" ostinato figure.

3:39   **c.** Strings, *f*, repeated dissonant polychord with punctuations in French horns; piccolos, trumpets, oboes join.

3:49   **d.** Pizzicato basses and cellos introduce loud, rapid interjections in high trumpet and piccolos;

3:54   **e.** Strings, *f*, repeated dissonant polychord with punctuations in French horns.

4:02   **f.** Bassoons join with melodic fragment played staccato, string pulsations; trombone joins;

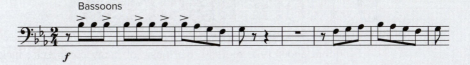

Bassoons repeat staccato melodic fragment; oboes, flute, and trombone imitate;

4:28   **g.** Sudden break in pulse, French horns, *f*, sustained tone, timpani strokes, tubas, *ff*, low sustained tone;

4:33   **h.** High "ticking" ostinato figure descends to English horn, *mf*, trills in winds and strings; loud "ticking" ostinato in violins and trumpet.

4:49   **i.** French horn, *mp*, joins with legato melody; flute answers;

descending figure in oboes and trumpet.

5:07   **j.** Legato melody in alto flute; legato melody in high flutes, pizzicato strings accompany.

5:20   **k.** Trumpets join with repeated-note melody; triangle joins.

5:34   **l.** Sudden *p*, strings and syncopated accents introduce piccolo, high legato melodic fragment; full orchestra, melodic figures repeated with long crescendo to

Ritual of Abduction

6:10   **4. a.** Sustained brass chord, violent strokes on timpani and bass drum; high trumpet, rapid-note fanfare, very fast tempo, changing meters.

6:23   **b.** Horn calls, *f*, alternate with piccolo and flutes, rapid-note fanfare; timpani, bass drum join; crescendo to

6:43   **c.** High woodwinds and brasses, *ff*, staccato passage in changing meters; horn calls; full orchestra, *ff*.

6:59   **d.** Timpani accents punctuate staccato phrases with changing meters in trumpets and high winds; timpani accents punctuate repeated rapid figure in strings.

7:18   **e.** Trill in violins, *ff*, accented chords; trill in flutes, *p*.

Part II:
Sacrificial Dance

Section A
0:00

Sacrificial Dance is the overwhelming climax of the work. It consists of sections that can be outlined as follows: A B A′ C A″ (very brief) C A‴. In the opening section (A), explosive, percussive chords fight brutal blows on the timpani. The time signature changes with almost every bar: $\frac{3}{16}\ \frac{2}{16}\ \frac{3}{16}\ \frac{2}{16}\ \frac{2}{16}\ \frac{3}{16}$. The rapid pulse and irregular, jolting accents create intense excitement.

Section B
0:27

The second section (B) begins with a sudden drop in dynamic level as a single chord is repeated obsessively. Brief silences between these repeated chords urge the listener to supply accents.

Section C
2:17

Section C features brasses and percussive sounds from five timpani, a tam-tam (gong), and a bass drum. *Sacrificial Dance* glorifies the power of rhythm, as does the entire *Rite of Spring*.

9 Neoclassicism

From about 1920 to 1950, the music of many composers, including Sergei Prokofiev, Igor Stravinsky, and Paul Hindemith (1895–1963), reflected an artistic movement known as **neoclassicism**. Neoclassicism is marked by emotional restraint, balance, and clarity; neoclassical compositions use musical forms and stylistic features of earlier periods, particularly of the eighteenth century. Stravinsky summed it up: "I attempted to build a new music on eighteenth-century classicism." Neoclassical music is not merely a revival of old forms and styles; it uses earlier techniques to organize twentieth-century harmonies and rhythms.

"Back to Bach" was the slogan of this movement, which reacted against romanticism and impressionism. (Because many neoclassical compositions were modeled after Bach's music, the term *neobaroque* might have been more appropriate.) Neoclassical composers turned away from program music and the gigantic orchestras favored at the turn of the century. They preferred absolute (nonprogrammatic) music for chamber groups. This preference for smaller performing groups partly reflected economic necessity: during the post–World War I period, economic conditions were so bad in parts of Europe that there was little money to hire large orchestras. Favoring clear polyphonic textures, composers wrote fugues, concerti grossi, and baroque dance suites. Most neoclassical music was tonal and used major and minor scales. Still, neoclassicism was more an attitude than a style. Schoenberg wrote minuets and gigues using his twelve-tone system. And though neoclassical composers referred to many past styles, their works sound completely modern. They play on the delightful tension between our expectations about old forms and styles and the novel harmonies and rhythms. In Chapter 10 we study a neoclassical work by Prokofiev, *Classical Symphony* (1917).

Neoclassicism was an important trend in other arts too. The poet T. S. Eliot often quoted and alluded to earlier writers. Picasso, who designed sets for Stravinsky's first neoclassical work, *Pulcinella* (1920), went through a phase during which he created paintings that show the influence of ancient Greek art. Picasso described the neoclassical attitude by saying that artists "must pick out what is good for us where we find it. When I am shown a portfolio of old drawings, for instance, I have no qualms about taking anything I want from them."

10 Sergei Prokofiev

The Russian composer Sergei Prokofiev wrote masterpieces in many genres including opera, symphony, concerto, and ballet.

Everett Collection/Shutterstock

The Russian Sergei Prokofiev (1891–1953), one of the leading composers of the twentieth century, was born in a Ukrainian village where his father managed an aristocrat's estate. His mother, a serious amateur pianist, was his first music teacher. Incredibly precocious, Prokofiev began composing at five and wrote an opera, *The Giant,* at age nine. At thirteen he entered the St. Petersburg Conservatory, where his dissonant compositions irritated his teachers. But at graduation, in 1914, he won highest honors as a pianist performing his Piano Concerto No. 1. Prokofiev became well-known in St. Petersburg as a pianist and modernist composer, performing and conducting his own compositions.

During 1917, Prokofiev was particularly productive, composing his *Classical* Symphony, Violin Concerto No. 1, and other works while living in a country village, where he took refuge from the violence of the Russian Revolution. The following year, he conducted the premiere of the *Classical* Symphony with the Soviet minister of culture in the audience. Prokofiev announced to the minister that he wanted to leave Russia for the United States, to which the minister replied, "You are a revolutionary in music, as we are in life. We should work together. But if you want to go to America, I will not stand in your way."

After leaving Russia in 1918, Prokofiev made his home in New York and Paris, performing as a concert pianist and composing such works as the opera *The Love for Three Oranges* (1919) and Piano Concerto No. 3; both premiered in Chicago.

Prokofiev eventually became homesick for his native land, confiding to a French music critic in 1933, "The air of foreign countries does not inspire me because I am a Russian and there is nothing more harmful to me than to live in exile." In 1936 he returned to the Soviet Union with his Spanish wife, the singer Lina Llubera, and their two sons.

The Soviet Union was an oppressive one-party regime. Starting around 1929, the dictator Joseph Stalin used forced labor camps and mass murder to promote rapid industrialization and collective agriculture. Artistic expression came increasingly under the control of the Communist Party. Composers were forced to reject modernism and write music that was accessible and melodic, without excessive dissonance and complexity.

In 1941, during World War II, Germany invaded the Soviet Union, spurring Prokofiev to compose his opera *War and Peace,* based on the novel by the Russian author Leo Tolstoy. Later in the war, Prokofiev wrote his Fifth Symphony (1944) when the Soviet army successfully counterattacked against the Nazi invaders. A week after Prokofiev conducted the Fifth Symphony's Moscow premiere in 1945, he collapsed due to high blood pressure.

After World War II, in 1948, Prokofiev, together with other leading composers, was denounced as "formalist" and criticized for "decadent influences designed to destroy the principals of classical music." Soon, performances of some of his compositions were banned, and he fell into debt. During the same year, his estranged wife Lina was arrested for "espionage"—she had tried to leave the Soviet Union—and spent eight years in a forced labor camp. Prokofiev died on March 5, 1953, the same day as Joseph Stalin, whose dictatorial regime had made his life difficult.

Prokofiev was a highly prolific composer. Along with the compositions mentioned above, his best-known works include the orchestral suite *Lieutenant Kijé* (1934), Violin Concerto No. 2 (1935), the 'symphonic fairy tale for children' *Peter and the Wolf* (1936), and the ballet *Romeo and Juliet* (1935).

Classical Symphony in D Major, Op. 25 (1917)

Prokofiev completed the *Classical* Symphony, one of his best-known works, in 1917, a year of revolutions in Russia. "I spent the summer of 1917 in the country near Petrograd [today St. Petersburg] all alone," he described later, "I deliberately did not take my piano with me . . . I was intrigued by the idea of writing an entire symphonic piece without the piano . . . So that is how the project of writing a symphony in the style of Haydn came about . . . If Haydn had lived in our era, I thought, he would have retained his compositional style while absorbing something new at the same time."

The *Classical* Symphony has four movements: Allegro, Larghetto, Gavotte (a baroque dance), Molto vivace. It lasts only about fifteen minutes and is written for a small orchestra, similar to that used in late eighteenth-century classical symphonies.

First Movement: Allegro

The brief first movement, in sonata form, conveys wit, joy, and playfulness. It departs from classical sonata form in that the exposition is *not* repeated and the recapitulation begins with the opening theme in a key other than the tonic key of D major. After a two-bar introduction, violins introduce the lighthearted opening theme. It begins with a loud orchestral chord followed by soft descending scale and a rocking two-note figure.

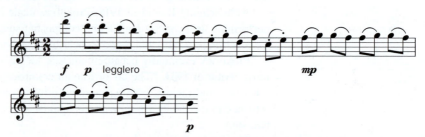

The second theme is a staccato violin melody, *pp*, with wide leaps from high to low notes. Accompanying the melody is a bassoon playing staccato.

In the development, the opening theme is presented in minor, rather than in major, and the wide-leap second theme becomes comically solemn.

Listening Outline

PROKOFIEV, *Classical* Symphony (1917)

First movement: Allegro

Sonata form, duple meter ($\frac{2}{2}$), D major

2 flutes, 2 oboes, 2 clarinets, 2 bassoons, 2 French horns, 2 trumpets, timpani, 1st violins, 2nd violins, violas, cellos, double basses

(Duration 4:12)

Listen for the contrast between the quickly descending opening theme and the second theme, with its large leaps and staccato bassoon accompaniment. Notice that in the development, the opening theme appears in minor rather than in major.

Exposition

First theme

0:00	**1. a.**	Orchestral chord, *ff*, arpeggio rises to lighthearted melody, violins, *p*.
0:13	**b.**	Orchestral chord, *ff*, lighthearted melody at lower pitch, violins, *p*.
0:23	**2. a.**	Flute, *p*, witty staccato phrase imitated in clarinets and bassoon.
0:33	**b.**	Flute, *p*, staccato phrase imitated in clarinets and bassoon at lower pitch.
0:42	**c.**	Violins, *f*, decrescendo, crescendo and climb to

Second theme

0:55	**3. a.**	High violins, *pp*, wide-leap melody, bassoon accompanies, staccato.
1:05	**b.**	High violins, *pp*, wide-leap melody, bassoon accompanies, staccato, clarinet, *p*, flute, *pp*.
1:19	**c.**	High violins, *pp*, wide-leap melody, bassoon accompanies, staccato, violin trills *pp*.
1:29	**4.**	Sudden *ff*, full orchestra, rising arpeggios, violins downward rapid scales, brief pause.

Development

1:44	**1. a.**	Loud chord, lighthearted melody in minor, violins, *p*, loud chords.
1:54	**b.**	High flute, staccato phrase, violins, *crescendo*
2:02	**c.**	Oboes and clarinets, *p*, strings, *crescendo*
2:12	**2. a.**	Low strings, *ff*, wide-leap melody, imitated by high violins, *ff*.
2:22	**b.**	Low strings, French horn *ff*, wide-leap rhythm, imitated by high strings, trumpet *ff*.
2:34	**c.**	Full orchestra fast upward arpeggios, *ff*, repeated chords lead to

Recapitulation

First theme

2:49	**1. a.**	Orchestral chord, *ff*, arpeggio rises to lighthearted melody in major, violins, *p*.
2:58	**b.**	Flute, *p*, witty staccato phrase imitated in clarinets and bassoon, *p*.
3:07	**c.**	Flute, *p*, varied staccato phrase, imitated in oboe, rising scale in oboe and flute leads to

Second theme

3:22	**2. a.**	High violins, *pp*, wide-leap melody, bassoon accompanies.
3:32	**b.**	High violins, *pp*, wide-leap melody varied
3:38	**c.**	High flute and violin trills *pp* lead to
3:48	**3.**	Sudden *ff*, full orchestra, arpeggiated chords *ff*, rapid downward and upward scales, concluding cadence.

11 Expressionism

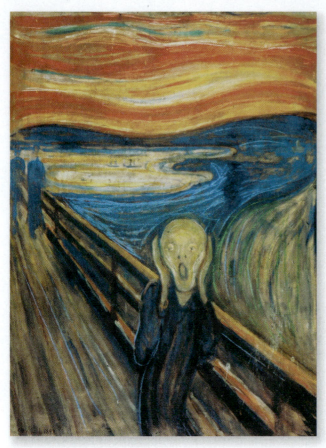

The Scream (1893), by the Norwegian expressionist Edvard Munch. Expressionist painters reacted against French impressionism; they often used jarring colors and grotesquely distorted shapes to explore the subconscious.

Dennis Hallinan/Alamy

Much music of the twentieth century reflects an artistic movement called *expressionism*, which stressed intense, subjective emotion. It was largely centered in Germany and Austria from 1905 to 1925. Expressionist painters, writers, and composers explored inner feelings rather than depicting outward appearances. They used deliberate distortion to assault and shock their audience, to communicate the tensions and anguish of the human psyche. Expressionism grew out of the same intellectual climate as Freud's studies of hysteria and the unconscious. German expressionist painting was in part a reaction against the pleasant subjects, delicate pastel colors, and shimmering surfaces of French impressionism.

The expressionists rejected conventional prettiness. Their works may seem "ugly" in their preoccupation with madness and death. Expressionist painters, such as Ernst Ludwig Kirchner, Emil Nolde, Edvard Munch, and Oskar Kokoschka, often use jarring colors and grotesquely distorted shapes. Expressionist art tends to be fragmentary; the scenes of an expressionist play may be episodic and discontinuous. Expressionism is also an art concerned with social protest. It movingly conveyed the anguish felt by the poor and oppressed. Many expressionists opposed World War I and used art to depict their horror of bloodshed.

There was close communication among expressionist writers, painters, and musicians. Many were creative in more than one art form. The painter Wassily Kandinsky wrote essays, poetry, and plays; the composer Schoenberg painted and even participated in the shows of expressionist artists.

Twentieth-century musical expressionism grows out of the emotional turbulence in the works of romantics such as Wagner and Mahler. Immediate precedents for expressionism are the operas *Salome* (1905) and *Elektra* (1908) by Richard Strauss, in which extremely chromatic and dissonant music depicts perversion and murder. In Chapters 12 and 13, we study three expressionistic compositions: *Pierrot lunaire*, Op. 21 (*Moonstruck Pierrot*, 1912), and *A Survivor from Warsaw*, Op. 46 (1947), by Schoenberg; and the opera *Wozzeck* (1917–1922), by Alban Berg. These works all stress harsh dissonance and fragmentation and exploit extreme registers and unusual instrumental effects. All three avoid tonality and traditional chord progressions. Both *A Survivor from Warsaw* and *Wozzeck* depict a nightmarish world and express a profound empathy with the poor and tormented.

12 Arnold Schoenberg

Arnold Schoenberg (1874–1951), who was born in Vienna, was an almost entirely self-taught musician. He acquired his profound knowledge of music by studying scores, playing in amateur chamber groups, and going to concerts. After he lost his job as a bank clerk at age twenty-one, he devoted himself to music, earning a poor living conducting a choir of industrial workers and orchestrating popular operettas. Performances of his own early works met with hostility from the conservative Viennese public. In 1904, Schoenberg began to teach music theory and composition in Vienna, and

Arnold Schoenberg developed the twelve-tone system, which offered the composers a new way of organizing pitch in a composition.
Omikron/Science Source

he inspired love and loyalty in his students, two of whom—Alban Berg and Anton Webern—themselves became leading composers.

Around 1908, Schoenberg took the revolutionary step of abandoning the traditional tonal system. He was a man possessed ("I have a mission," he said; "I am but the loudspeaker of an idea."). His productivity between 1908 and 1915 was incredible.

For the next eight years, however, he searched for a way to organize his musical discoveries and published nothing. Then, in 1921, he told a student, "I have made a discovery which will ensure the supremacy of German music for the next hundred years." From 1923 to 1925 Schoenberg published compositions using his new twelve-tone system. Although his music did not find a large audience, many important musicians respected it. At the age of fifty-one, he received an appointment at the Prussian Academy of Arts in Berlin.

After the Nazis seized power in Germany, Schoenberg, who was Jewish, was dismissed from his post. The same year, 1933, he and his family came to the United States, where he joined the music faculty at the University of California in Los Angeles. Schoenberg felt neglected in America: his music was rarely performed and he was financially unsuccessful. But after his death, the twelve-tone system was used increasingly by composers throughout the world. It remains an important influence to this day.

Schoenberg's Music

"I claim the distinction of having written a truly new music which, based upon tradition as it is, is destined to become tradition." This assertion by Schoenberg contains a great deal of truth: his musical language was indeed new, but it had evolved from the past and was eventually widely adopted.

His early works, such as the string sextet *Verklärte Nacht* (*Transfigured Night*, 1899), show many features of the late romantic style. Some of them—such as the immense cantata *Gurrelieder* (*Songs of Gurre*, 1901)—use very large orchestras; dissonances and angular melodies create a feeling of subjectivity; chromatic harmony is prominent; and the central tonality is weakened as the music moves through remote keys. But from 1903 to 1907, he departed further from romanticism, and in the *Chamber Symphony,* Op. 9 (1906), he uses whole-tone scales and fourth chords.

Atonality Around 1908, Schoenberg began to write atonal music. *Atonality*—the absence of key—evolved from his earlier use of chromatic harmony and the chromatic scale. But in his atonal works, all twelve tones are used without regard for their traditional relationship to major or minor scales. Dissonances are "emancipated" from the necessity of resolving to consonances. *Atonality* does not imply a single system of composition: each atonal work has its own means of achieving unity, and a piece usually grows out of a few short motives transformed in many ways.

Schoenberg's atonal compositions include Five Pieces for Orchestra, Op. 16 (1909); and *Pierrot lunaire,* Op. 21 (*Moonstruck Pierrot,* 1912). They are characterized by jagged melodies, novel instrumental effects, extreme contrasts of dynamics and register, and irregular phrases. *Pierrot lunaire* and other works by Schoenberg call for an unusual style of vocal performance—**Sprechstimme**, literally *speech-voice*—halfway between speaking and singing. Schoenberg's atonal style was soon adopted by his students Berg and Webern. Their early atonal works, like Schoenberg's, tended to be very short. Without a musical system like tonality, extended compositions were possible only when there was a long text to serve as an organizing force.

The Twelve–Tone System In the early 1920s, Schoenberg developed a more systematic method of organizing atonal music; he called it the "method of composing with twelve tones." He partly applied this new technique in Five Piano Pieces, Op. 23, and Serenade, Op. 24, and then fully elaborated it in Suite for Piano, Op. 25 (all composed from 1920 to 1923). The twelve-tone system enabled Schoenberg to write more extended compositions, such as the monumental Variations for Orchestra (1928) and the unfinished opera *Moses und Aron* (*Moses and Aaron;* 1930–1932). From 1933 to 1951, in the United States, he used the twelve-tone system in many rich and varied works.

The *twelve-tone system* is a twentieth-century alternative to tonality, a new way of organizing pitch in a composition. It is a systematized form of atonality that gives equal importance to each of the twelve chromatic tones. In a twelve-tone composition, the ordering or unifying idea is called a *tone row, set,* or *series.** The composer creates a unique tone row for each piece (the choice of rows is practically limitless because there are 479,001,600 possible arrangements of the twelve tones), and the row is the source of every melody and chord in it. No pitch occurs more than once within a row. This prevents any tone from receiving too much emphasis.

A composition is built by manipulating the tone row, which may be presented in four basic forms: forward (original form), backward (retrograde), upside down (inversion), and backward and upside down (retrograde inversion). Any of the four forms of a row may be shifted to any pitch level—that is, it may begin on any of the twelve tones while keeping the original pattern of intervals. Thus there are forty-eight (twelve times four) possible versions of a row.

Each tone of a row may also be placed in any register; this enhances the flexibility of the system and may partially explain why so many twelve-tone melodies have very wide leaps. Finally, the tones of a row may be presented one after another (as on a melodic line) or simultaneously (as chords).

We now study two works by Schoenberg: the "freely" atonal *Pierrot lunaire,* Op. 21 (*Moonstruck Pierrot;* 1912); and the twelve-tone cantata *A Survivor from Warsaw,* Op. 46 (1947), composed almost thirty-five years later.

Pierrot lunaire, Op. 21 (*Moonstruck Pierrot;* 1912)

Like Stravinsky's *The Rite of Spring,* composed around the same time, Schoenberg's *Pierrot lunaire,* or *Moonstruck Pierrot,* is a revolutionary masterpiece that profoundly influenced twentieth-century music. It is a cycle of twenty-one songs for female voice and an ensemble of five musicians who play eight instruments: piano, cello, violin-viola, flute-piccolo, clarinet–bass clarinet. The instrumental ensemble varies with each piece. For example, *The Sick Moon* (No. 7) uses only the flute; *Prayer to Pierrot* (No. 9) uses the piano and clarinet; and *O Ancient Scent* (No. 21) uses all eight instruments. A song cycle accompanied by a chamber music ensemble—rather than by piano alone—represented a departure from convention. Another novelty was the pervasive use of *Sprechstimme,* the technique of half speaking, half singing developed by Schoenberg. The rhythms and pitches of the words are precisely notated, but the voice touches the notated pitch only momentarily and then departs from it.

Pierrot lunaire is based on weird poems written in 1884 by the Belgian poet Albert Giraud and later translated into German by Schoenberg's friend Otto Erich Hartleben. Many of the poems deal with the puppet Pierrot, a tragic clown character derived from the centuries-old *commedia dell'arte* (Italian improvised theater). Pierrot, who represented the isolated modern artist, was a favorite subject for artists, writers, and musicians of the late nineteenth century and the early twentieth century.

---

*Because of its systematic use of a *series* of tones, the twelve-tone method is also referred to as *serial technique.*

The cycle divides into three groups of seven songs that evoke a surrealistic night vision. In the first group, Pierrot, a poet, drunk on moonlight, becomes increasingly deranged. The second group is a nightmare filled with images of death and martyrdom. In the third group, Pierrot seeks refuge from the nightmare through clowning, sentimentality, and nostalgia. *Pierrot lunaire* is expressionist in its weird text, eerie *Sprechstimme,* unique instrumental effects, and atonal musical language. We focus on the opening piece of the cycle, *Mondestrunken* (*Moondrunk*).

Mondestrunken (Moondrunk)

Scored for voice, piano, flute, violin, and cello, *Mondestrunken* (*Moondrunk*) begins the fantastic nocturnal journey. Its text depicts moonlight as a sacramental wine drunk with the eyes. The poet (Pierrot) becomes intoxicated as moonlight floods the still horizon with desires that are "horrible and sweet." Like the other poems in *Pierrot lunaire, Mondestrunken* is a rondeau—a verse form—of thirteen lines in which lines 1–2 reappear as lines 7–8 and line 1 repeats as line 13.

Mondestrunken is mostly soft and light in texture. It opens with a high seven-note motive that hypnotically repeats in the piano and evokes a feeling of moonlight.

The pervasive varied recurrence of this ostinato motive in different instruments unifies the piece. Schoenberg's music parallels the changing images of the text. The image of wine poured down by the moon, for example, is depicted by a descending sequence of the motive in the piano and flute.

The poet's intoxication is suggested by a sudden *forte,* thick piano chords, and the first appearance of the cello. *Mondestrunken* rounds off with a final appearance of the motive at a slower tempo in the piano and flute.

A Survivor from Warsaw, Op. 46 (1947)

A Survivor from Warsaw, a dramatic cantata for narrator, male chorus, and orchestra, deals with a single episode in the murder of 6 million Jews by the Nazis during World War II. Schoenberg wrote the text himself, basing it partly on a direct report by one of the few survivors of the Warsaw ghetto. More than 400,000 Jews from this ghetto died in extermination camps or of starvation; many others perished during a heroic revolt against the Nazis in 1943.

Jews captured by German soldiers during the Warsaw Ghetto Uprising April 19–May 16, 1943.

Everett Collection/Shutterstock

The narrator—a survivor—describes the brutal beating of Warsaw Jews by Nazi soldiers, who then determine how many of their victims will be sent to death camps. The narrator's text is spoken in English, except for some terrifying Nazi commands, which are shouted in German. The narrator's part is a kind of *Sprechstimme,* the novel speech-singing developed by Schoenberg. The rhythms of the spoken words are precisely notated, but their pitch fluctuations are indicated only approximately.

Besides English and German, the text includes Hebrew. These were the three languages of Schoenberg's life: German, his native tongue; English, his adopted language in the United States; and Hebrew, the language of the faith to which he returned. The six- minute cantata builds to an overwhelming conclusion when the male chorus sings in unison the Hebrew words of the prayer *Shema Yisroel* (*Hear, O Israel*). For centuries this has been the prayer of Jewish martyrs in their last agonized moments.

A Survivor from Warsaw is a twelve-tone composition written in 1947, when Schoenberg was seventy-two. The music vividly sets off every detail in the text.

A Survivor from Warsaw opens with a brief orchestral introduction that captures the nightmarish atmosphere that prevailed as Nazi soldiers awakened the Warsaw Jews for transport to death camps. We hear a weirdly shrill reveille in the trumpet and fragmentary sounds in the military drum and high xylophone.

During the narrator's opening lines, Schoenberg already prepares for the concluding Hebrew prayer. As the narrator speaks of the old neglected prayer, a French horn softly intones the beginning of a melody that is later proclaimed by the chorus.

An especially vivid musical description comes when the narrator tells how the Nazis counted their victims. The music itself becomes faster and louder, building to the powerful entrance of the chorus:

Shema Yisroel Adonoy elohenoo Adonoy eḥod. Veohavto es Adonoy eloheḥo beḥol levoveḥo ooveḥol nafsheḥo ooveḥol meodeḥo. Vehoyoo haddevoreem hoelleh asher onoḥee metsavveḥo hayyom al levoveḥo. Veshinnantom levoneḥo vedibbarto bom beshivteḥo beveteḥo ooveleḥteḥo baddereḥ ooveshoḥbeḥo oovekoomeḥo. ("Hear, O Israel, the Lord our God, the Lord is One! And thou shalt love the Lord thy God with all thy heart, and with all thy soul, and with all thy might. And these words, which I command thee this day, shall be in thy heart. And thou shalt teach them diligently unto thy children, and speak of them when thou sittest in thy house, and when thou goest on the way, and when thou liest down, and when thou risest up." [Deuteronomy 6:4–9])

The sung Hebrew contrasts dramatically with the spoken English and German that comes before, and it is the first extended melody in the work.

13 Alban Berg

Alban Berg (1885–1935), a student of Schoenberg, wrote music that is a unique synthesis of traditional and twentieth-century elements. Berg, who was born in Vienna, first attracted international attention in 1925, when his opera *Wozzeck* premiered in Berlin. Though its atonality baffled many critics, *Wozzeck* made such a powerful impression on the public that it was soon performed throughout Europe and in the United States. Perhaps because of chronic ill health, Berg did not perform or conduct, and he composed relatively few works. These include *Chamber Concerto,* for piano, violin, and thirteen winds (1925); *Lyric Suite,* for string quartet (1926); the opera *Lulu* (1929–1935, orchestration not completed); and the Violin Concerto (1935).

Wozzeck (1917–1922)

Wozzeck is the tragic story of a soldier who is driven to murder and madness by a hostile society. An antihero obsessed by strange visions, Wozzeck is persecuted by his

sadistic captain, used as a guinea pig by a half-demented doctor, and betrayed by the woman with whom he lives, Marie. Wozzeck stabs Marie to death and drowns while trying to wash her blood from his hands.

Berg's musical imagination was fired in 1914 when he saw *Woyzeck,* a play by the German dramatist and revolutionary Georg Büchner (1813–1837). Though written in the early 1830s, the play is amazingly modern in its starkly realistic dialogue and disconnected scenes. Berg adapted the play into an opera while in the Austrian army in World War I. His own traumatic army experiences may well have deepened his sympathy for Wozzeck.

The opera's nightmarish atmosphere makes it a musical counterpart of expressionist painting and literature. Berg conveys the tensions and torments of the unconscious through harsh dissonances and grotesque distortions. The range of emotions and styles in the music is tremendous. Though most of *Wozzeck* is freely atonal—it does not use the twelve-tone system—major and minor keys occasionally add contrast. The vocal line includes speaking, shrieking, *Sprechstimme,* distorted folk songs, and melodies with wide leaps that are difficult to sing. The gigantic orchestra closely parallels the dialogue and stage action. Descriptive effects include vivid orchestral depictions of the moon rising, frogs croaking, and water engulfing the drowning Wozzeck. Berg's music rapidly shifts between very high and very low registers, between *ffff* and *pppp*.

Wozzeck has three acts, each with five scenes. Connecting the scenes are short orchestral interludes that comment musically on the preceding action and serve as preparation for what is to come. As in Wagner's music dramas, there is a continuous musical flow within each act, and characters are associated with specific musical ideas. A novel feature of *Wozzeck* is that the music for each scene is a self-contained composition with a particular form (passacaglia, sonata form, etc.) or of a definite type (military march, lullaby). The five scenes of the last act—we study scenes 4 and 5—are organized as (1) variations on a theme, (2) variations on a single tone, (3) variations on a rhythmic pattern, (4) variations on a chord, and (5) variations on continuous running notes. But Berg did not intend for the listener to concentrate on or even be aware of these unifying techniques. He wanted the audience to be caught up in the opera's dramatic flow.

In Act II, Wozzeck has been driven to desperation by Marie's infidelity and by a savage beating from the man who has slept with her. Near the beginning of Act III, Wozzeck stabs Marie to death as they walk along a forest path near a pond.

Act III: Scenes 4 and 5

Scene 4: A path near a pond Wozzeck returns to the scene of the crime to dispose of his knife. Berg's orchestra vividly evokes the dark forest scene as a background to Wozzeck's anguished shrieks. Rising harp tones suggest the blood-red moon coming up through the clouds. Wozzeck goes mad and drowns in the pond while trying to wash the blood from his hands. Soft chromatic slides depict the engulfing water as the Captain and the Doctor, Wozzeck's tormentors, indifferently comment that someone is drowning. As Wozzeck drowns, the slides become slower and narrower in range.

The long orchestral interlude that follows is a deeply moving expression of grief for Wozzeck's tragic fate. It recalls the musical themes associated with his life. Berg described it as "a confession of the author stepping outside the dramatic events of the theater and appealing to the public as representing mankind." For this outpouring of compassion, Berg returns to tonality (the interlude is in D minor) and the musical language of late romanticism.

Scene 5: A street before Marie's door Children are playing in front of Marie's house; bright sunshine brings a glaring contrast to the darkness of the preceding scenes. One of the children cruelly tells Wozzeck's son that his mother is dead. The boy rides off on his hobby horse with the other children to see the body. The orchestra is reduced in size to produce delicate sounds that match the children's high voices, and a continuous rhythm symbolizes their utter indifference.

The opera does not end with a conclusive chord. It simply breaks off as though to suggest that the tragedy could begin again.

14 Béla Bartók

Bartók shown listening to folksongs that he had recorded in tiny villages.
Sovfoto/Getty Images

Béla Bartók (1881–1945), whose music is infused with the spirit of east European folk song, was born in Hungary. His mother gave him his first lessons on the piano, an instrument that was important to his career. For twenty-seven years (1907–1934), Bartók taught piano at his alma mater, the Budapest Academy of Music, and gave recitals throughout Europe. During the early 1900s, Bartók was influenced by the Hungarian nationalist movement, and he spent most of his free time in tiny villages, recording peasant folk songs. He became a leading authority on peasant music, and his own music was profoundly affected by it.

Though he was neglected in Hungary until the Budapest premiere of his ballet *The Wooden Prince* in 1917, Bartók was recognized early as an important composer abroad and had a successful career during the 1920s and 1930s. But he was vehemently anti-Nazi, and in 1940, he emigrated from Hungary to the United States, where he was to spend the last five years of his life. This was a bleak period for him; he had little money, he was in poor health, and he felt isolated and neglected.

In 1943, while in a hospital in New York, he received an unexpected commission for the Concerto for Orchestra, now his best-known work. The success of its first performance resulted in several other commissions. Tragically, Bartók had only a year to live and could write just two more compositions, his Sonata for Solo Violin (1944) and Third Piano Concerto (1945). Soon after his death in New York in 1945, Bartók became one of the most popular twentieth-century composers.

Bartók's Music

"I do not reject any influence," wrote Bartók, "provided this source be pure, fresh and healthy." But he emphasized that the "Hungarian influence is the strongest." He evolved a completely individual style that fused folk elements, classical forms, and twentieth-century sounds. He did arrange many folk tunes (often giving them highly dissonant accompaniments), but in most of his works he does not quote folk melodies— he uses original themes that have a folk flavor.

Bartók's genius found its most characteristic expression in instrumental music. He wrote many works for piano solo, six string quartets (which are among the finest since Beethoven's) and other chamber music, three piano concertos, two violin concertos, and several compositions for orchestra. His music embraces a wide range of emotions and is deeply expressive; and he revitalized and reinterpreted traditional forms such as the rondo, fugue, and sonata form.

Bartók always organized his works around a tonal center; but within this framework, he often used harsh dissonances, polychords, and tone clusters (though some of his late works have a more traditional and less dissonant vocabulary). Rhythmically, his music is characterized by a powerful beat, unexpected accents, and changing meters. He was imaginative in his use of tone colors, particularly of percussion instruments. In works such as Music for Strings, Percussion, and Celesta (1936), he drew unusual sounds from the xylophone and timpani. Like many twentieth-century composers, he also drew percussive, drumlike sounds from the piano.

Concerto for Orchestra (1943)

The commission that led to Bartók's Concerto for Orchestra was offered to him in 1943, while he was hospitalized in New York City. Serge Koussevitzky, the conductor of the Boston Symphony Orchestra, offered him $1,000 for a new work. While recuperating at Saranac Lake, New York, Bartók was able to work "practically day and night" on his new composition. He finished it in six weeks. Concerto for Orchestra was an enormous success at its premiere in Boston in 1944 and has since become Bartók's most popular work.

"The general mood of the work," wrote Bartók, "represents, apart from the jesting second movement, a gradual transition from the sternness of the first movement and the lugubrious death-song of the third, to the life-assertion of the last one." Bartók explained that the unusual title reflects the work's "tendency to treat the single orchestral instruments in a *concertant* or soloistic manner."

Indeed, Concerto for Orchestra is a showpiece for an orchestra of virtuosos. It is romantic in spirit because of its emotional intensity, memorable themes, and vivid contrasts of mood. Though its melodies were created by Bartók, they have a distinct folk flavor. The concerto is an example of Bartók's mellow "late" style, which is characterized by more frequent use of traditional chords. In all five movements, time-honored procedures such as A B A form, sonata form, and fugue are fused with twentieth-century rhythms and tone colors. We focus on the second movement.

Second Movement: *Game of Pairs;* Allegretto scherzando

The jesting second movement, *Game of Pairs,* which is in A B A′ form, is a "game" involving different pairs of woodwind and brass instruments. The melodic lines of each pair are in parallel motion and are separated by a distinctive pitch interval.

In the opening section (A), pairs of bassoons, oboes, clarinets, flutes, and muted trumpets play a chain of five melodies consecutively. The contrasting middle section (B) is a hymnlike melody played softly by brass instruments. When the opening section returns (A′), it has a more active accompaniment. The incisive sound of a side drum (without snares) is prominent throughout the movement. It plays syncopated solos at the beginning and the end, as well as in the hymnlike middle section.

Listening Outline

BARTÓK, Concerto for Orchestra (1943)

Second Movement: *Game of Pairs* (Allegretto scherzando)

A B A′ form, duple meter (2/4)

2 flutes, 2 oboes, 2 clarinets, 3 bassoons, 4 French horns, 2 trumpets, 2 trombones, tuba, timpani, side drum, 2 harps, 1st violins, 2d violins, violas, cellos, double basses

(Duration 6:40)

Listen for the *syncopated* side drum solos at the beginning, middle, and end of this playful movement in A B A′ *form.* Notice the pairs of woodwind instruments in A and A′ and the use of brass instruments in the hymnlike B section.

A

0:00   **1.** Solo side drum (without snares), *mf*.

0:12   **2.** Two bassoons, *p*, accompanied by pizzicato strings.

0:36   **3. a.** Two oboes, *p*, in higher register. Pizzicato strings accompany
       b. Low strings, pizzicato, while oboes sustain tones.

1:05   **4. a.** Two clarinets.
       b. Low strings, accented notes.

1:27   **5. a.** Two flutes, *mf*, in higher register.
       b. Low strings, pizzicato, while flutes sustain tones.

2:14   **6.** Two muted trumpets, *p*. Muted string tremolos, *pp*, in background.

B

3:02   **1. a.** Brasses, *mf*, hymnlike legato melody. Side drum accompanies.
       b. French horns, *p*, conclude hymnlike melody and sustain chord.

       2. Oboe, flute, and clarinet, *p*, lead to

A′

4:09   **1.** Two bassoons, *p*, opening melody. Staccato third bassoon in background.

4:33   **2. a.** Two oboes, *p*, in higher register. Clarinets and strings in background.
       b. Low strings, pizzicato, while oboes sustain tones.

4:50   **3. a.** Two clarinets. Flutes and strings in background.
       b. Low strings, accented notes.

5:19   **4. a.** Two flutes, *mf*, in higher register. Woodwinds and strings in background.
       b. Low strings, pizzicato, while flutes sustain tones.

5:44   **5.** Two muted trumpets, *mf*. Harp glissandos and muted string tremolos in background.

6:20   **6.** Woodwinds, *p*, repeated chord; solo side drum, decrescendo, ends Game of Pairs.

15 Music in America

America's musical traditions are extraordinarily rich and diverse owing to the country's multiethnic character. Our society includes Native Americans, who arrived thousands of years ago, as well as Americans whose ancestors came from Europe, Africa, Latin America, or Asia over the past four hundred years. Since the early seventeenth century, Americans have sung, played, and listened to psalms, hymns, popular songs, folk and patriotic tunes, dances, marches, and instrumental music.

This section provides a brief overview of the American musical landscape and a background for later sections of Part VI.

Colonial America

Singing psalms was a central social activity in the Protestant churches of colonial America. The very first book printed in the English-speaking colonies was the *Bay Psalm Book*. It appeared in 1640, only twenty years after the Mayflower had brought 102 Pilgrims to present-day Plymouth, Massachusetts. Translated from the original Hebrew into English verse, psalms were sung to tunes familiar to congregants who had come from England.

More than a century later came the first publication of original choral music by an American-born composer, *The New-England Psalm-Singer* (1770) by William Billings (1746–1800). This collection included "Chester," a song that became a popular patriotic anthem during the American Revolution. Billings wrote both the words and music:

Let tyrants shake their iron rod
And Slav'ry clank her galling chains,
We fear them not, we trust in God,
New England's God forever reigns.

Billings earned a meager living in Boston tanning animal hides. He also taught in the "singing schools" founded by Protestant ministers who hoped to improve the level of singing in their churches by encouraging their congregants to learn to read music.

Music in Nineteenth–Century America

The nineteenth century witnessed a population explosion in America: from 5 million people in 1800 to more than 76 million in 1900, giving rise to an expansion and diversification of musical activity.

Up to the early twentieth century, bands were the favorite instrumental organizations in America. By 1860 there were more than 3,000 bands including 60,000 musicians. Virtually every village had its band and bandstand; bands performed at picnics, parades, political rallies, dances, and carnivals. The leading American composer and conductor of band music was John Philip Sousa (1854–1932), nicknamed the "march king." His best-known marches include *The Stars and Stripes Forever, The Washington Post,* and *Semper Fidelis.* From 1892 to 1931, the famous fifty-person Sousa Band toured across America, and during the early 1900s it performed in Europe as well.

During the nineteenth century, symphony orchestras were founded in New York (1842), Cincinnati (1872), Boston (1881), and Chicago (1890). The transcontinental railroad facilitated concert tours by orchestras during the last three decades of the century. Between 1864 and 1888, the Theodore Thomas Orchestra, conducted by the

Aaron Copland drew on American folklore for his ballets *Billy the Kid, Rodeo,* and *Appalachian Spring.*
GAB Archive/Redferns/Getty images

American meant jazz. An example is his *Music for the Theater* (1925), a piece for orchestra, with elements of blues and ragtime. This "jazz period" lasted only a few years. During the early 1930s he composed serious, highly dissonant, sophisticated works (such as the highly regarded *Piano Variations,* 1930) that convey starkness, power, percussiveness, and intense concentration.

In the late 1930s, Copland modified his style again, writing more accessible works for a larger audience. These were the depression years, when many composers rejected the idea of writing for an elite audience. Copland now drew on American folklore—as in his ballets *Billy the Kid* (1938), *Rodeo* (1942), and *Appalachian Spring* (1944)—and on jazz, revival hymns, cowboy songs, and other folk tunes. His scores for films and his patriotic works (such as *A Lincoln Portrait,* 1942) also reached a mass public, and his name became synonymous with American music.

Copland accomplished the difficult feat of writing simple yet highly professional music. His textures clear; his slow-moving harmonies—often almost motionless—seem to evoke the openness of the American landscape; and though strongly tonal, his works embody twentieth-century techniques such as polychords, polyrhythm, changing meters, and percussive orchestration. He also used serial technique (that is, manipulation of a tone row or series) in such works as *Connotations* for orchestra (1962).

Aside from his numerous compositions, Copland made many other contributions to American music by directing composers' groups, organizing concerts, lecturing, writing books and articles, teaching, and conducting.

Appalachian Spring (1943–1944)

Appalachian Spring originated as a ballet score for Martha Graham, the great modern dancer and choreographer. It took Copland about a year (1943–1944) to finish the music. While composing *Appalachian Spring,* he thought, "How foolhardy it is to be

Dancer Mikhail Baryshnikov performs in the ballet *Appalachian Spring,* with music by Aaron Copland.
Robert R. McElroy/Getty Images

spending all this time writing a thirty-five-minute score for a modern-dance company, knowing how short-lived most ballets *and* their scores are." But in 1945 Copland arranged parts of the ballet as a suite for full orchestra (originally, the ballet used only thirteen instrumentalists) that won important prizes and brought his name to a large public. Today, *Appalachian Spring* is widely performed both as a ballet and as a concert piece.

The ballet concerns a "pioneer celebration in spring around a newly built farmhouse in the Pennsylvania hills" in the early 1800s. Its characters include a bride and groom, a neighbor, and a revivalist preacher with his followers. The rhythms and melodies are American-sounding and suggest barn dances, fiddle tunes, and revival hymns.

But Copland uses only one actual folk tune in the score—a Shaker melody titled *Simple Gifts.* (The Shakers were a religious sect established in America around the time of the Revolution. They expressed religious fervor through shaking, leaping, dancing, and singing.) *Appalachian Spring* is bright and transparent, has a clear tonality, and is basically tender and calm in mood. The score's rhythmic excitement comes from delightful syncopations and rapid changes of meter. As in many twentieth-century works, the orchestra includes a piano and a large percussion section.

The ballet suite has eight sections, including a duo for the bride and groom, a fast dance for the revivalist preacher and his followers with "suggestions of square dances and country fiddlers," and a finale in which the couple are left "quiet and strong in their new house." We focus on Section 7, which originally accompanied "Scenes of daily activity for the Bride and her Farmer-husband."

Hacienda (*The Cattlemen*), (4) *Danza Final* (*Final Dance*): *Malambo*. The first movement of the suite is rapid, loud, syncopated, and energetic, with violent accents on the bass drum. In contrast, the second movement is calm and lyrical, opening with a flute solo accompanied by soft pizzicato strings and harp that suggest the strumming of the gaucho's guitar. The wild, propulsive third movement features rapid shifts of meter that recall Stravinsky's *The Rite of Spring*. We focus on the climactic fourth movement, *Danza Final* (*Final Dance*): *Malambo*.

Final Dance: Malambo

The *malambo* is a dance for men performed only by the gaucho. Both the *malambo* and the gaucho are traditional symbols of Argentina. In a competitive *malambo*, one dancer tries to outshine the other through the energy and complexity of his steps.

Ginastera's comment that "always in my music there is this violent rhythm" aptly describes the fast tempo, perpetual motion, and percussive sounds of *Final Dance: Malambo*. The orchestra includes a very large percussion section, and the energetic melodies are often syncopated. The meter is $\frac{6}{8}$, and six rapid pulses per measure represent the foot tapping of the dancing gauchos. The form of this brief dance is A A' (shortened) B. Part B, which is marked *Tempo di malambo*, builds to a climax and introduces a lively *malambo* melody. In this melody, six fast pulses first subdivide into two groups of three pulses and then into three groups of two pulses. A similar rhythm appears in *America* from Leonard Bernstein's *West Side Story*, studied in Chapter 24, "Music for Stage and Screen."

Listening Outline

GINASTERA, *Estancia* Suite, Op. 8a (1941)

Final Dance: Malambo

A A' B form, Allegro, triple meter ($\frac{6}{8}$), C major

Piccolo, 2 flutes, 2 oboes, 2 clarinets, 2 bassoons, 4 French horns, 2 trombones, timpani, bass drum, snare drum, tenor drum, cymbals, triangle, tambourine, castanets, gong, xylophone, piano, 1st violins, 2d violins, violas, cellos, double basses

(Duration 3:24)

Listen, at the opening, for the high rapid ostinato in the piccolo and flute and the high *syncopated melody* in the violins. Notice the prominent use of *percussion* instruments, including xylophone and bass drum, and the lively *malambo* melody with the irregular *rhythm* 1–2–3 4–5–6, 1–2 3–4 5–6.

A

0:00	**1. a.**	Piccolo and flute, ***pp***, high rapid ostinato, pizzicato violins, three-beat pattern; low strings join, crescendo.
0:14	**b.**	Violins, ***f***, high syncopated melody, brasses join.
0:25	**c.**	Xylophone, two-note melody.
0:32	**d.**	Brasses, ***mf***, melody beginning with long note; violins, ***f***, repeat melody.
0:45	**e.**	Pizzicato violins, ***mf***, two-note ostinato, crescendo to

A'

1:00	**2. a.**	Piccolo and flute, ***f***, high rapid ostinato, pizzicato violins, three-beat pattern, French horns, downward scale, crescendo to
1:11	**b.**	Violins, ***f***, high syncopated melody.
1:22	**c.**	Xylophone, new melody, bass drum pulses, crescendo to

B Tempo di malambo

1:39	**3. a.**	Trumpets, winds, xylophone, *f*, lively *malambo* melody repeated many times; bass drum.
1:58	**b.**	Brasses, *ff*, fast repeated notes; bass drum.
2:05	**c.**	Repeated *malambo* melody, trumpets, winds, xylophone, *f*, bass drum.
2:23	**d.**	Brasses, *ff*, fast repeated notes, slides; bass drum.
2:30	**e.**	Lively *malambo* melody repeats, trumpets, winds, xylophone,
2:46	**f.**	Brasses, *ff*, syncopations; bass drum.
2:56	**g.**	Full orchestra, *malambo* melody repeats.
3:09	**h.**	High repeated notes, *ff*, full orchestra, very loud closing chord.

21 Musical Styles since 1945

Since World War II, we have lived with instant communication; television, computers, and the Internet provide access to a virtually unlimited flow of information. Not only have we been bombarded by an incredible variety of stimuli, but there has also been a constant demand for novelty. New styles in fashion and the visual arts spread rapidly and then disappear.

In music as well, the emphasis has been on novelty and change. Musical innovations since 1945 have been even more far-reaching than those of the first half of the twentieth century. There have been many new directions, and the range of musical styles and systems is wider than ever. As the American composer Milton Babbitt (1916–2011) observed in 1984, "The world of music never before has been so pluralistic, so fragmented."

Particularly since the 1970s, many composers have advocated stylistic pluralism or eclecticism. Their works include sections in a variety of styles ranging from baroque to rock. In 1999, the American composer John Adams (b. 1947) told an interviewer, "We're in a kind of post-style era. Composers of my age and younger, we are not writing in one, highly defined, overarching expression." Adams believes that the contemporary composer can follow the examples of Bach, Mahler, and Stravinsky, and be "somebody who just reached out and grabbed everything" and through musical technique and spiritual vision "turned it into something great."

Today, the Internet provides composers with instant access to a limitless variety of music. The American composer Eric Whitacre (b. 1970) has said, "Today I can go through thirty or forty genres of music just by browsing the web. As a composer I know that all sorts of sounds I hear are making their way into my brain and soul."

Characteristics of Music since 1945

Accurately describing the relatively recent past is difficult. Yet any overview of music since 1945 must include the following major developments:

1. Increased use of the *twelve-tone system*.
2. *Serialism*—use of the techniques of the twelve-tone system to organize rhythm, dynamics, and tone color.
3. *Chance music,* in which a composer chooses pitches, tone colors, and rhythms by random methods, or allows a performer to choose much of the musical material.

Untitled (1991), by the minimalist sculptor Donald Judd (1928–1994), made up of nine identical parts. Minimalist composers include Steve Reich, Philip Glass, and John Adams.

Tony Kyriacou/Shutterstock

discover that they preferred the sounds of everyday life to the ones they would presently hear in the musical program . . . . That was all right as far as I was concerned."

Cage's approach is also illustrated by his *Imaginary Landscape* No. 4 (1951), for twelve radios. The score gives precise directions to the performers—two at each radio—for manipulating the dials affecting wavelength and volume. Yet all the indications in the score were chosen by chance means. They show no regard for local station wavelengths or the time of performance. "At the actual performance of *Imaginary Landscape*," reported one member of the audience, "the hour was later than anticipated before the work's turn came on the program, so that the instruments were unable to capture programs diversified enough to present a really interesting result." This is not surprising because Cage had chosen the wavelengths and dynamics by throwing dice.

With Cage's work as an example, serial composers such as Pierre Boulez and Karlheinz Stockhausen introduced elements of chance into their compositions during the mid-1950s. Stockhausen's Piano Piece No. 11 (1956) has nineteen short segments of music printed on a large roll of paper that measures 37 by 21 inches. The segments can be played in any order, and the performer is instructed to begin with the fragment that first catches the eye. The piece is likely to be different each time it is played.

Chance music makes a complete break with traditional values in music. It asserts, in effect, that one sound or ordering of sounds is as meaningful as another. To most listeners, a piece of chance music is more often significant as an idea than as a collection of actual sounds. Some composers may be attracted by the sheer novelty of chance music, by its ability to shock and attract attention. Others are influenced by Asian philosophies such as Zen Buddhism, which stresses the harmony of beauty and nature. Finally, some composers may want to give performers a major part in the creative process.

Minimalist Music   The mid-1960s saw the development of an artistic movement called *minimalism,* which was partly a reaction against the complexity of serialism and the randomness of chance music. *Minimalist music* is characterized by steady pulse, clear tonality, and insistent repetition of short melodic patterns. Its dynamic level, texture, and harmony tend to stay constant for fairly long stretches of time, creating a trancelike or hypnotic effect. Leading minimalist composers, such as Terry Riley (b. 1935), Steve Reich (b. 1936), Philip Glass (b. 1937), and John Adams (b. 1947), have been profoundly influenced by nonwestern thought; many have studied African, Indian, or Balinese music. Minimalist music grew out of the same intellectual climate as minimalist art, which features simple forms, clarity, and understatement. Indeed, in the 1960s, minimalist musicians were appreciated more by painters and sculptors than by their fellow composers. "I gravitated towards artists because they were always more open than musicians, and I liked looking at what they did," Philip Glass has said.

Minimalist composers have generally tried to bring their music to the widest possible audience. "One mode of feedback I rely on most," writes Steve Reich, "is the popular naive reactions . . . . My work, and that of Glass and Riley, comes as a breath of fresh air to the new music world . . . . This feeling is very healthy. It's a feeling of moving back away from a recondite and isolated position, toward a more mainstream approach." Both Reich and Glass have ensembles that perform their music in

Marilyn Diptych (1962) by the pop artist Andy Warhol. Pop artists use subjects from everyday life and popular culture.

Reciprocity Images/Alamy

auditoriums and rock clubs. A turning point in public acceptance of minimalist music came in 1976, when Reich's *Music for 18 Musicians* received an ovation in Town Hall in New York and—also in New York—Glass's opera *Einstein on the Beach* sold out the Metropolitan Opera House. After the early 1970s, minimalist music became progressively richer in harmony, tone color, and texture, as is exemplified in Adams's opera *Nixon in China* (1987).

Musical Quotation Since the mid-1960s, many composers have written works in which they deliberately make extensive use of quotations from earlier music, usually fairly familiar works of the eighteenth, nineteenth, and twentieth centuries. Like minimalist music, *quotation music* often represents a conscious break with serialism, as well as an attempt to improve communication between composer and listener. The quoted material usually either conveys a symbolic meaning or is varied, transformed, and juxtaposed with other music. For example, in the outer movements of *Concerto Grosso 1985,* Ellen Taaffe Zwilich juxtaposes parts of a Handel sonata with original passages. In *Sinfonia* (1968), a composition for voices and orchestra by the Italian composer Luciano Berio (1925–2003), the third section is based on the scherzo from Mahler's Second Symphony; on this quoted material from Mahler, Berio superimposes fragments of music by Bach, Debussy, Ravel, Berlioz, Schoenberg, and other composers, creating a musical collage.

Polystylism Like Charles Ives early in the twentieth century, composers since the 1960s have often juxtaposed heterogeneous material. The use of different styles or techniques in a composition is known as *polystylism*. The American composer George Crumb (b. 1929) explained that in writing his song cycle *Ancient Voices of Children* (1970), he "was conscious of an urge to fuse various unrelated stylistic elements, . . . a suggestion of Flamenco with a Baroque quotation . . . or a reminiscence of Mahler with a breath of the orient."

Some modern composers will not only quote earlier composers but also imitate earlier styles. In String Quartet No. 3 (1972) by the American composer George Rochberg (1918–2005), there are sections of atonal music and passages in the styles of Beethoven and Mahler.

The Soviet composer Alfred Schnittke (1934–1998) described his Concerto Grosso No. 1 (1977)—written for two violins, harpsichord, prepared piano, and twenty-one strings—as "a play of three spheres: the Baroque, the Modern, and the banal." His term "Modern" refers to highly dissonant passages and "banal" to a sentimental tango theme. For Schnittke, polystylism "widens the range of expressive possibilities, it allows for the integration of 'low' and 'high' styles . . . . A composer often plans a polystylistic effect in advance, whether it is the shock effect of a clashing collage of music from different times, a flexible glide through phrases of music history, or the use of allusions so subtle that they seem accidental."

Tonal Music and a Return to Tonality As in the early twentieth century, many composers since 1945 have written tonal music, in contrast to atonal or twelve-tone music. (It may be helpful to review the discussion of alternatives to the traditional tonal system on pages 311–312.) Such tonal music spans a vast range of styles and compositional methods, and includes works by composers as diverse as Benjamin Britten, Dmitri Shostakovich, Leonard Bernstein (1918–1990), and John Adams. Tonal compositions may include central tones or chords as well as consonant sonorities. Some works are entirely tonal, and others are basically atonal but contain chord progressions that provide a fleeting sensation of tonality.

Starting in the late 1960s, some composers, such as the Americans George Rochberg (1918–2005) and David Del Tredici (b. 1937), returned to tonality after having written atonal or twelve-tone music. These composers are sometimes referred to as "new romantics," to emphasize the emotional intensity of their works.

Tonality could be a fascinating "novel" option for musicians trained in the twelve-tone system. "For me," explained Del Tredici, "tonality was actually a daring discovery. I grew up in a climate in which, for a composer, only dissonance and atonality were acceptable. Right now, tonality is exciting for me."

Electronic Music Since the development of tape studios, synthesizers, and computers in the 1950s and 1960s, composers have had potentially unlimited resources for the production and control of sound. *Electronic music* is as varied as nonelectronic music. Its spectrum includes rock, chance music, and serial compositions.

Electronic instruments let composers control tone color, duration, dynamics, and pitch with unprecedented precision. Composers are no longer limited by human performers. For the first time, they can work *directly* in their own medium—sound. There is no more need for intermediaries, that is, performers. The recording of a composition *is* the composition. Thus, a composer alone is now responsible for putting into music the subtle variations of rhythm, tone color, and dynamics that once rested with the performer.

Many composers have combined electronic sounds with live performers. Some pieces use one or more live performers in conjunction with recorded sounds. The recorded sounds may be electronic pitches or noises, or they may be previously recorded sounds of live performers. In some cases, performers may be involved in a duet with themselves, or a duet with electronically manipulated versions of their own performances. Some composers have created interactive works for performers and computer. In such compositions, the computer is programmed by the composer to respond in musically meaningful ways to the live performance.

There are also works for traditional instruments and digital synthesizers and samplers that are performed "live." In addition, traditional instruments may also be "electrified" through amplification. Composers use "electric" pianos and violins, for instance.

Electronic music is important not only in itself but also for its influence on musical thought in general. Electronic instruments have suggested new sounds and new forms of rhythmic organization. "These limitless electronic media," said Milton Babbitt, "have shown us new boundaries and new limits that are not yet understood—the very mysterious limits, for example, of the human capacity to hear, to conceptualize, and to perceive. Very often we will specify something and discover that the ear can't take in what we have specified . . . . The human organism simply cannot respond quickly enough, cannot perceive and differentiate as rapidly and precisely as the synthesizer can produce it and as the loudspeaker can reproduce it."

"Liberation of Sound" Composers today use a wider variety of sounds than ever before, including many that were once considered undesirable noises. Composers have achieved what Edgard Varèse called "the liberation of sound . . . the right to make music with any and all sounds." Electronic music may include environmental sounds, such as thunder, or electronically generated hisses and blips. But composers may also draw novel sounds from voices and nonelectronic instruments. Singers are asked to scream, whisper, laugh, groan, sneeze, cough, whistle, and click their tongues. They may sing phonetic sounds rather than words. Composers may treat their vocal text merely as a collection of sounds and not attempt to make the meaning of the words clear to the audience.

Wind and string players tap, scrape, and rub the bodies of their instruments. A brass or woodwind player may hum while playing, thus creating two pitches at once. A flutist may click the keys of the instrument without producing a tone; a pianist may reach inside the piano to pluck a string and then run a chisel along it, creating a sliding sound. To communicate their intentions to performers, composers may devise new systems of music notation because standard notation makes no provision for many noiselike sounds. Recent music scores contain graphlike diagrams, new note shapes and symbols, and novel ways of arranging notation on the page. But composers are not the only ones to invent unusual sounds. Often the players themselves discover new possibilities for their instruments. Many modern works have been inspired by the discoveries of inventive performers.

The greatest expansion and experimentation have involved percussion instruments. In many recent compositions, percussion instruments outnumber strings, woodwinds, and brasses. Traditional percussion instruments are struck with new types of beaters made of glass, metal, wood, and cloth. Unconventional instruments now widely used include tom-toms, bongos, slapstick, maracas, guiro, and vibraphone.

In the search for novel sounds, increased use has been made of *microtones*, intervals smaller than the half step. Small intervals such as quarter tones have long been used in nonwestern music, but they have only recently become an important resource for western composers. Electronic instruments have stimulated this development because they are not restricted to conventional scales and do not force players to unlearn performance habits.

Composers such as Krzysztof Penderecki (1933–2020) create sounds bordering on electronic noise through tone clusters—closely spaced tones played together. Clusters are unlike traditional chords in that one usually hears not individual tones but a mass, block, or band of sound. Composers may achieve a sense of growth or change by widening or narrowing such a band, or by making it more or less dense.

The directional aspect of sounds—how they are projected in space—has taken on new importance. Loudspeakers or groups of instruments may be placed at opposite ends of the stage, in the balcony, or at the back and sides of the auditorium. In electronic compositions such as Edgard Varèse's *Poème électronique* (1958) and nonelectronic works such as Elliott Carter's Double Concerto for harpsichord and piano with two chamber orchestras (1961), sounds are made to travel gradually in space, passing from one loudspeaker or player to another.

Mixed Media Electronic music is often presented together with visual counterparts, such as slide projections, films, light shows, gestures, and theatrical action. One such *mixed-media* presentation was Varèse's *Poème électronique,* which combined electronic sounds with images projected on walls. But multimedia works are not confined to electronic music. Chance music and other types of recent music sometimes require performers to function as both actors and sound producers, as in Crumb's *Ancient Voices of Children.* Mixed-media presentations are generally intended to break down the ritual surrounding traditional concerts and to increase communication between composer and audience.

Rhythm and Form Rhythm and form have undergone some of the most striking changes in music since 1945. Earlier in the century, composers often changed meters or used unconventional meters such as $\frac{7}{4}$ and $\frac{5}{8}$. After 1945, some composers abandoned the concepts of beat and meter altogether. This is a natural outcome of electronic music, which needs no beat to keep performers together. In non-electronic music too, the composer may specify duration in absolute units such as seconds rather than in beats, which are relative units. In some recent music, there may be several different speeds at the same time.

Grapes, 2010, by the Chinese artist, architect, and social activist Ai Weiwei, consists of twenty-six hand-made stools from the Qing Dynasty (1644–1911) assembled in a shape resembling a cluster of grapes. This sculpture focuses viewers' attention on the contrast between ancient and contemporary China. It is an example of conceptual art, in which an idea or concept is more important than traditional aesthetic concerns.In his use of "ready made" objects, Ai Weiwei was influence by the French-American artist Marcel Duchamp (1887–1968).

Nils Jorgensen/Shutterstock

More than ever, each piece of music follows its own laws, and its form grows out of its material. Some composers no longer write music in traditional forms, such as A B A, sonata form, or rondo. Indeed, form may unfold with little or no obvious repetition of material.

22 Music since 1945: Eight Representative Pieces

Sonatas and Interludes for Prepared Piano (1946–1948), by John Cage

The American composer John Cage (1912–1992) was the highly influential creator of chance music—as discussed in Chapter 21—and a major figure in the development of percussion music. He invented the ***prepared piano***, a grand piano whose sound is altered by objects such as bolts, screws, rubber bands, pieces of felt, paper, and plastic inserted between the strings of some of the keys. "In practice, the preparation

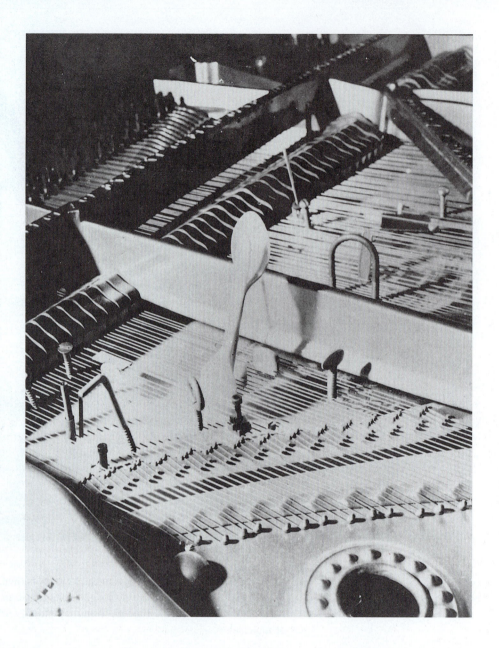

takes about three hours," Cage explained. Such preparation results in a wide variety of sounds that resemble those of drums, cymbals, xylophones, tambourines, and gongs. When the pianist's finger strikes a key, sometimes more than one sound is produced.

Cage invented the prepared piano around 1940, when he was asked to write music for a modern dance on an African theme. The dance was to be performed in a small auditorium with enough space for a small grand piano, but not for a group of percussionists. "In effect," Cage wrote, "the prepared piano is a percussion ensemble under the control of a single player."

The large-scale *Sonatas and Interludes* (1946–1948), lasting around sixty-six minutes, is Cage's best-known work for prepared piano and one of his most widely performed and recorded compositions. It includes twenty short pieces—sixteen one-movement sonatas and four interludes—ranging in length from one and a half minutes to five minutes. *Sonatas and Interludes* reflects the composer's study of eastern philosophy. Cage explained that the cycle aims to express the range of stylized emotional states described in Indian aesthetic theory: "the heroic, erotic, wondrous, mirthful, odious, sorrowful, fearful, angry, and their common tendency toward tranquility." We focus on the second sonata of the cycle.

Sonata II

The two-minute Sonata II, in A A B B form, is characterized by a gradual thickening of texture and increase in rhythmic momentum. Part A moves from a single melodic line—sometimes accompanied by percussive sounds—to a two-voice texture. This part is predominantly soft, in a fairly high register. Short phrases, arranged in question-and-answer pairs, are framed by silences. In two phrases, a melodic fragment immediately repeats.

Part B is almost twice as long as A and has more extended phrases and a richer texture. It begins abruptly with a loud, dense sonority that contrasts with the gentle, lingering sounds and pause ending part A. The concluding phrase of part B is the most climactic and rhythmically active. It begins with a torrent of high running notes and ends with a high trill-like figure and a single accented tone.

Part A
0:00
Part A repeated
0:24

Part B
0:49
Part B repeated
1:27

Poème électronique (*Electronic Poem;* 1958), by Edgard Varèse

Edgard Varèse (1883–1965), one of the great innovators of twentieth-century music, was born in France but spent most of his life in the United States. As early as 1916, he dreamed of freeing music from the limitations of traditional instruments and expanding the vocabulary of sounds. During the 1920s and 1930s, Varèse pioneered in the exploration of percussive and noiselike sounds, and he wrote the first important work for percussion ensemble (*Ionisation,* 1931).

But it was the new electronic developments of the 1950s that enabled Varèse to realize his vision of a "liberation of sound." In 1958, at the age of seventy-five, he composed *Poème électronique,* one of the earliest masterpieces of electronic music created in a tape studio. The eight-minute work was designed to be heard within the pavilion of the Philips Radio Corporation at the 1958 Brussels World's Fair. Varèse obtained unique spatial effects by projecting sound from 425 loudspeakers placed all over the interior surfaces of the pavilion. The composer worked in collaboration with the architect Le Corbusier, who selected a series of images—photographs, paintings, and writing—that were projected on the walls as the music was heard. However, Varèse did not make any attempt to synchronize the sounds with the images chosen by Le Corbusier, which included "birds and beasts, fish and reptiles, . . . masks and skeletons, idols, girls clad and unclad, cities in normal appearance and then suddenly askew," as well as atomic mushroom clouds.

Because it was created in a tape studio, *Poème électronique* exists in only a single "performance" whose duration (eight minutes) is fixed on audiotape. Varèse's raw sound material—tones and noises—came from a wide variety of sources, including electronic generators, church bells, sirens, organs, human voices, and machines. The sounds are often electronically processed in such a way that they cannot be precisely identified. In the Listening Outline, the effect of such sounds is conveyed by words placed in quotation marks; for example, "wood blocks" or "chirps." Varèse organized his sounds into an electronic poem that seems weird yet is amazingly logical and compelling.

Poème électronique divides into two main sections, the first lasting two minutes thirty-six seconds and the second five minutes twenty-nine seconds. Each section begins with low bell tolls and ends with sirens. Heard several times during *Poème* is a distinctive group of three rising tones. Human voices and recognizable organ tones appear only during the second section. Varèse once remarked about the female voice heard toward the end: "I wanted it to express tragedy—and inquisition."

Listening Outline

VARÈSE, *Poème électronique* (*Electronic Poem*; 1958)

Tape studio
(Duration 8:00)

Listen for the repeated low bell tolls that begin each of the two main sections and the siren that ends each main section. Notice the group of three rising *tones* heard in both sections, and in the second section the human voice on "Oh-gah," organlike tones, and a high female voice.

0:00	**1. a.**	Low bell tolls. "Wood blocks." Sirens. Fast taps lead into high, piercing sounds. Two-second pause.
0:43	**b.**	"Bongo" tones and higher grating noises. Short "squawks." Three-tone group stated three times.
1:11	**c.**	Low sustained tones with grating noises. Sirens. Short "squawks." Three-tone group. Two-second pause.
1:40	**d.**	Short "squawks." High "chirps." Variety of "shots," "honks," "machine noises." Sirens. Taps lead to

2:36	**2. a.** Low bell tolls. Sustained electronic tones. Repeated "bongo" tones. High and sustained electronic tones. Low tone, crescendo. Rhythmic noises lead to
3:41	**b.** Voice, "Oh-gah." Four-second pause. Voice continues softly.
4:17	**c.** Suddenly loud. Rhythmic percussive sounds joined by voice. Low "animal noises," scraping, shuffling, hollow vocal sounds. Decrescendo into seven-second pause.
5:47	**d.** Sustained electronic tones, crescendo and decrescendo. Rhythmic percussive sounds. Higher sustained electronic tones, crescendo. "Airplane rumble," "chimes," jangling.
6:47	**e.** Female voice. Male chorus. Electronic noises, organ. High taps. Swooping organ sound. Three-note group stated twice. Rumble, sirens, crescendo.

Libertango (1974), by Astor Piazzolla

Astor Piazzolla in 1984.
picture-alliance/Newscom

The ***tango*** is a dance of Argentinian origin in quadruple meter for couples in close embrace. It became popular around 1890 in the slums of Buenos Aires. Performances by Argentinian dancers and musicians in Paris inspired a tango craze in Europe and America in the early 1900s (1912–1913).

Argentinian composer Astor Piazzolla (1921–1992) created a unique style of tango music intended for concerts as well as dancing that fused traditional dance with elements from classical music and jazz. In the 1950s, the dissonant harmonies, complex textures, and electric guitar of Piazzolla's "new tango" (*Tango Nuevo*) angered fans of traditional tango music, but within a decade his avant-garde style gained favor. Since the 1980s his compositions have been performed worldwide by leading musicians and ensembles, including the cellist Yo-Yo Ma and the Kronos Quartet. Today, Piazzolla's music is appreciated around the world by listeners of jazz, classical, and world music.

Born in Argentina, Piazzolla grew up in New York City, after emigrating there with his parents when he was four years old. At eight he began to play the ***bandoneon***, an instrument of the concertina family—similar to an accordion but operated only with buttons rather than a keyboard—that is used in tango bands. Piazzolla soon became a virtuoso on his instrument, playing Bach and Chopin as well as tangos, jazz, and folk music. At thirteen, he accompanied Carlos Gardel during the year (1934) that the Argentine superstar tango singer and composer spent in New York.

In 1937 Piazzolla and his parents returned to Argentina, where he studied musical composition from age twenty to twenty-five with Alberto Ginastera, an important Argentinian composer (discussed in Chapter 20). While studying, he supported himself by playing in night club tango bands. "I did my composition homework in dressing rooms," Piazzolla later recalled. His assignments included analysis of musical scores by Stravinsky and Bartok, composers who influenced his own style.

When Piazzolla was thirty-two, his *Buenos Aires* Symphony won a prize that subsidized a year (1954–1955) of study in Paris with Nadia Boulanger, the teacher of Aaron Copland and Philip Glass. After examining his "classical" musical scores, she asked Piazzolla to play his tangos. She immediately exclaimed, "Astor, this is beautiful. I like it a lot. This is the true Piazzolla—do not ever leave him." For Piazzolla, his teacher's comment "was the great revelation of my musical life."

In 1955 Piazzolla returned to Argentina. During the 1960s he became one of the leaders of the avant-garde, admired by intellectuals and university students. He formed his New Tango Quintet (*Quinteto Nuevo Tango*), made recordings, performed in nightclubs, on television, in concerts, and composed the hit song *Ballad for a Madman* (*Ballada para un loco*).

In 1973, urban guerrilla violence and a political crisis in Argentina resulted in an economic downturn that directly influenced Piazzolla's income. Encouraged by European impressarios, Piazzolla left Argentina the next year at age fifty-three, first settling in Rome and then in Paris. Up to his late sixties, Piazzolla toured the world and composed many works, including *Le Grand Tango* (1981) for the Russian cellist Mstislav Rostropovich and *Five Tango Sensations* for the Kronos Quartet. In Paris on August 4, 1990, he suffered a major stroke and was subsequently taken to Buenos Aires, where he died on July 4, 1992. The *New York Times* obituary hailed him as the "modern master of tango music."

Piazzolla composed *Libertango* in 1974 while living in Rome, describing it as a "song to liberty." One of Piazzolla's best-known compositions, *Libertango,* has appeared in many musical arrangements, such as "I've Seen That Face Before" (1981), by the Jamaican singer Grace Jones. It was used in the soundtrack of Roman Polanski's film *Frantic* (1988) and Sally Potter's *The Tango Lesson* (1997). In our recording, *Libertango* is performed by a sextet, including cello—played by Yo-Yo Ma—piano, bandoneon, violin, electric guitar, and double bass.

Libertango is in A B A form. The opening A section creates tremendous drive, excitement, and anticipation. Two simultaneous heavily accented rhythmic patterns compete with each other: a bass line with a strong downbeat and a higher seven-note figure in rapid notes. These rhythmic patterns persist throughout *Libertango*.

The accents in the seven-note figure are mostly out of phase with the accents of the bass line, heightening the rhythmic tension. Only on the fourth beat of the measure do the accents meet, giving the listener a rhythmic jolt.

In the B section, the cello introduces the lyrical legato main melody that includes long notes and moves downward. Following the main melody, the bandoneon presents a higher contrasting melody in faster notes. Each melody in the B section is accompanied by the two competing rhythmic patterns. The close of the B section leads without pause into a repetition of the opening A section.

Listening Outline

PIAZZOLLA, *Libertango* (1974)

Quadruple meter ($\frac{4}{4}$)
Cello, piano, bandoneon, violin, electric guitar, double bass
(Duration 3:10)

Listen for the two simultaneous and competing *rhythms* that pervade *Libertango:* a *syncopated* seven-note melodic figure and a three-note bass line with a strong *downbeat*. Notice the main melody played by the cello and the contrasting melody at a higher pitch played by the bandoneon.

A

0:00	**1.**	Syncopated seven-note figure above bass line with strong downbeat, piano, bandoneon, double bass, guitar, introduce

B

0:27	**2. a.**	Cello, main melody, accompanied by syncopated seven-note figure.
0:56	**b.**	Cello and violin, octave higher, repeat main melody.

1:23   **3. a.** Bandoneon, contrasting melody at higher pitch, with faster notes, seven-note figure
        accompanies.

1:38   **b.** Bandoneon, decorated main melody with faster notes, seven-note figure accompanies.

A

1:53   **4. a.** Full ensemble, seven-note figure.

2:18   **b.** Fade out ends *Libertango*.

Short Ride in a Fast Machine (1986), by John Adams

John Adams conducting the Los Angeles Philharmonic in 2012.

Lawrence K. Ho/*Los Angeles Times* via Getty Images

John Adams (b. 1947) is a leading American composer who has been aptly described as a postminimalist. His music combines the driving pulse, constant repetition, and clear tonality of minimalism with lyrical, expressive melodies and varied orchestral colors. "I grew up in a household where Benny Goodman and Mozart were not separated," Adams once recalled. Indeed, his works reflect the influence of American popular music as well as composers such as Stravinsky and Reich.

A conductor as well as a composer, Adams taught and directed the New Music Ensemble at the San Francisco Conservatory of Music from 1972 to 1982 and was composer in residence with the San Francisco Symphony Orchestra from 1982 to 1985. In 2009, he was appointed creative chair of the Los Angeles Philharmonic to compose works for the orchestra while serving as a member of its planning team. His compositions include *Harmonium* (1980), for chorus and orchestra; the orchestral works *Harmonielehre* (1985), *Short Ride in a Fast Machine* (1986) and *City Noir* (2009); and the operas *Nixon in China* (1987), *The Death of Klinghoffer* (1991), *Dr. Atomic* (2005), dealing with J. Robert Oppenheimer, the physicist known as the father of the atomic bomb, and *A Flowering Tree* (2006), based on a folktale from southern India. In 2003, Adams won the Pulitzer Prize in Music for *On the Transmigration of Souls* (2002), a work for chorus and orchestra commissioned by the New York Philharmonic in commemoration of those who died in the terrorist attacks on the Pentagon and the World Trade Center on September 11, 2001. In 2015, Adams's *Scheherazade.2,* a dramatic symphony for violin and orchestra, was premiered at Lincoln Center, New York City. His third piano concerto, *Must the Devil Have the Best Tunes* (2018), was commissioned by the Los Angeles Philharmonic Orchestra, premiered by the pianist Yuja Wang.

Short Ride in a Fast Machine, a four-minute fanfare, is one of the most widely performed orchestral works by a living American composer. The work was commissioned by the Great Woods Festival to celebrate its inaugural concert at Great Woods, Mansfield, Massachusetts. *Short Ride in a Fast Machine* generates enormous excitement because of its rapid tempo, rhythmic drive, and powerful, colorful sonorities. The large orchestra includes two synthesizers and a variety of percussion instruments played by four musicians. These percussion instruments include a sizzle cymbal (a large cymbal with loose rivets placed in a ring of holes) and crotales (small cymbals of definite pitch). *Short Ride in a Fast Machine* is pervaded by steady beats in the wood block, rapid-note ostinatos in synthesizers and clarinets, and repeated orchestral chords that alternate between regular pulsations and irregular rhythms. The climax comes toward the end, when Adams introduces a stirring, fanfare-like melody in the trumpets.

Listening Outline

ADAMS, *Short Ride in a Fast Machine* (1986)

Delirando (deliriously)

2 piccolos, 2 flutes, 2 oboes, English horn, 4 clarinets, 3 bassoons, contrabassoon, 4 French horns, 4 trumpets, 3 trombones, tuba, timpani, wood blocks, pedal bass drum, large bass drum, suspended cymbal, sizzle cymbal, large gong (tam-tam), tambourine, triangle, glockenspiel, xylophone, crotales, 2 synthesizers, 1st violins, 2d violins, violas, cellos, double basses

(Duration 4:11)

Listen for steady wood block pulsations, rapid-note ostinatos in synthesizers, and repeated *chords* alternating between regular and irregular *rhythms*. Notice the prominence of *percussion* instruments and the climactic effect of the fanfare-like trumpet *melody* near the end of the *Short Ride*.

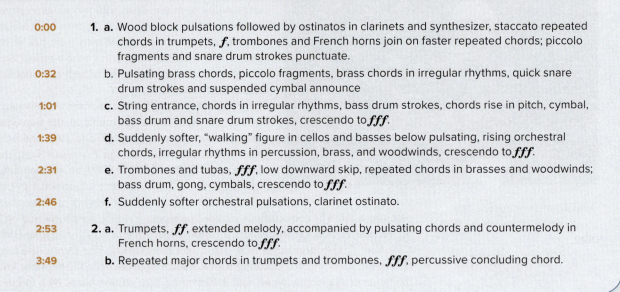

0:00	**1. a.**	Wood block pulsations followed by ostinatos in clarinets and synthesizer, staccato repeated chords in trumpets, *f*, trombones and French horns join on faster repeated chords; piccolo fragments and snare drum strokes punctuate.
0:32	**b.**	Pulsating brass chords, piccolo fragments, brass chords in irregular rhythms, quick snare drum strokes and suspended cymbal announce
1:01	**c.**	String entrance, chords in irregular rhythms, bass drum strokes, chords rise in pitch, cymbal, bass drum and snare drum strokes, crescendo to *fff*.
1:39	**d.**	Suddenly softer, "walking" figure in cellos and basses below pulsating, rising orchestral chords, irregular rhythms in percussion, brass, and woodwinds, crescendo to *fff*.
2:31	**e.**	Trombones and tubas, *fff*, low downward skip, repeated chords in brasses and woodwinds; bass drum, gong, cymbals, crescendo to *fff*.
2:46	**f.**	Suddenly softer orchestral pulsations, clarinet ostinato.
2:53	**2. a.**	Trumpets, *ff*, extended melody, accompanied by pulsating chords and countermelody in French horns, crescendo to *fff*.
3:49	**b.**	Repeated major chords in trumpets and trombones, *fff*, percussive concluding chord.

Lux Aurumque (Light and Gold; 2000, for a cappella chorus), by Eric Whitacre

Much music conveying a feeling of spirituality has been composed during the late twentieth and early twenty-first centuries. Often written for chorus, this music is set to a wide range of sacred and secular texts originally written in Greek, Hebrew, Latin, Arabic, English, Spanish, Persian, and Sanskrit, among other languages. Though varied in style and technique, such choral works usually include consonant chords and major and minor scales, and are immediately accessible to the listener. Leading representatives of this approach are the Polish composer Henryk Gorecki (1933–2010), the Estonian Arvo Pärt (b. 1935), the Englishman John Tavener (1944–2013), and the American Eric Whitacre (b. 1970), whose *Lux Aurumque* exemplifies this genre. (Whitacre's career and Internet Virtual Choir are discussed in the Performance Perspectives box on page 377.)

At the beginning of the twenty-first century, Eric Whitacre (b. 1970) emerged as an important composer and conductor of choral music. Born in a small farming town in northern Nevada, he played synthesizers in a rock band in his teens, and dreamed of becoming a pop star. But Whitacre changed direction at age eighteen, when he sang in the University of Nevada chorus and was overwhelmed by the beauty of Mozart's *Requiem*. "In my entire life," Whitacre recalled, "I had seen in black and white and suddenly everything was in shocking Technicolor. The most transformative experience I've ever had." Whitacre began to compose when he was twenty-one, and four years later he enrolled at the Juilliard School, where he earned an MA in music composition.

In 2009 his music became known to millions of listeners though his Internet Virtual Choir project. In 2012 he won a Grammy for *Light and Gold* (2010), his first album as both composer and conductor, which became the number one classical album in the United States. Whitacre's music is frequently performed by choirs in many countries, including the United States, France, England, Switzerland, and Germany. His choral music often alternates consonant chords with sweetly dissonant chords including tone clusters, tones only a half step or a whole step apart. Text and music are sensitively fused in his works. Whitacre says that a choral composer's "first and greatest responsibility is to the poem. I work very hard to understand the meaning of each poem I am setting, and when it comes time to compose the music I simply try to quiet myself enough to hear the notes already hidden below the poet's words."

Lux Aurumque is a brief piece for unaccompanied mixed chorus with a Latin text about light and the soft singing of angels. Whitacre originally wrote the poem in English, using the pen name Edward Esch, but he had it translated into Latin by the American poet Charles Anthony Silvestri. "I love setting Latin," Whitacre has explained, "because of the pure, perfect vowels, and the stoicism and formality it instantly creates. It also allows me to meditate on words, setting them over and over." In *Lux Aurumque*, words of the text usually repeat several times in succession.

Lux,	Light,
calida gravisque pura velut auram	warm and heavy as pure gold
et canunt angeli molliter	and the angels sing softly
modo natum	to the newborn baby

Lux Aurumque by Eric Whitacre. Reprinted with permission of Walton Music Corp./GIA Publications.

A slow tempo, legato performance, and very soft dynamics contribute to the dreamlike mood of *Lux Aurumque*. Its highly varied sounds include a solo soprano voice joining with the chorus, and the chorus singing consonant dyads—two tones sounded simultaneously—as well as mildly dissonant eight-note chords. These eight-note chords, which include tone clusters, result when the individual choral parts—soprano, alto, tenor, and bass—are divided into two. Often a single word begins with a consonance and ends with a dissonance. (See *Lux, calida, pura, canunt,* and *natum* in the Vocal Music Guide.) In his score, Whitacre points out that "if the tight harmonies are carefully tuned and balanced they will shimmer and glow."

Lux Aurumque consists of a main section and a shorter concluding section. The main section is in minor and includes a very brief soprano solo. The concluding section begins in minor with the same music as the main section, an octave lower. *Lux Aurumque* ends with a feeling of peace and resolution as minor gives way to major, and the 1st sopranos softly sustain a single tone while the other voices sing very low eight-note chords.

Vocal Music Guide

WHITACRE, *Lux Aurumque (Light and Gold; 2000)*

(Duration 4:15)

Listen for the slow *tempo, legato* singing, and very soft *dynamics* of this piece for unaccompanied (a cappella) mixed *chorus.* Notice the shifts between *minor* and *major,* and the difference in choral sound between *consonant chords* and mildly *dissonant chords* including tone clusters.

Consonance-dissonance, brief pause, minor key.	*Lux*	Light
	Lux	
Soprano solo joins.	*Lux*	
	Lux	
	calida	warm
	calida	
Sopranos/tenors descending chromatic scale	*gravisque*	and heavy
	gravisque	
	pura	as pure
High note on *pu.*	*pura*	
	velut aurem	as gold
	et canunt	and sing
Basses descend on *ca.*	*et canunt*	
Major chord on *li.*	*angeli*	angels
Opening music returns one octave lower, minor key.	*canunt*	sing
	canunt	
	canunt	
	molliter	softly
1st sopranos sustain tone on tum above low chords, major key.	*natum*	baby
	natum	
	natum	
	modo natum.	newborn baby.

Lux Aurumque by Eric Whitacre. Reprinted with permission of Walton Music Corp./GIA Publications.

Performance Perspectives

Eric Whitacre Conducting his *Lux Aurumque,* performed by the Virtual Choir

Inspired by the sweet voice of a fan who uploaded a video of herself singing one of his choral works, the American composer Eric Whitacre invited singers to submit videos of themselves performing individual vocal parts of his choral piece *Lux Aurumque* (Light and Gold). He uploaded the sheet music of *Lux Aurumque,* along with a video of himself conducting an imaginary silent choir, and a rehearsal piano track to help singers perform their parts. YouTube videos sent by 185 singers from twelve countries were combined and coordinated to form a Virtual Choir performance of *Lux Aurumque* that has been viewed more than 5 million times.

"I was moved to tears when I first saw it," Whitacre has said. "Singing

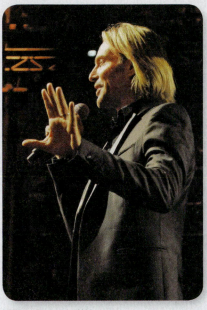

WENN Rights Ltd/Alamy

together, and making music together, is a fun-damental human experience. And I love the idea that technology can bring people together from all over the world. People seem to be experiencing an actual connection. I feel a closeness to this choir, almost like a family."

Since its debut in 2009, the Virtual Choir has performed two other compositions by Whitacre, with an increasing number of participating singers: *Sleep* in 2011 with over 2,051 voices from fifty-eight countries and *Water Night* in 2012 with 3,746 voices from seventy-six countries. The success of Whitacre's Virtual Choir project illustrates the Internet's enormous influence on the musical culture of the early twenty-first century.

L'amour de loin (Love from Afar; 2000), by Kaija Saariaho

Kaija Saariaho in 2004.
Raphael GAILLARDE/Gamma-Rapho via Getty Images

Born in Helsinki, Finland, Kaija Saariaho (b. 1952) is one of the leading composers of the twenty-first century. She studied music at the Sibelius Academy in Helsinki, where in the early 1970s she was the only woman in the class. "There were some old teachers who didn't want to teach me. They thought it was a stupid waste of time. They thought I would stay for a couple of years and then get married." In 1982, she moved to Paris, where she developed techniques of live electronics and computer-assisted composition at IRCAM, the contemporary music institute.

In the 1980s and 1990s, Saariaho composed works in a variety of genres, including multimedia pieces combining music, text, tape, electronics, video, and dance. "My music is about color and light," she has said. For Saariaho, sounds evoke all the senses. "The visual and the musical world are one to me . . . . Different senses, shades of color, or textures and tones of light, even fragrances and sounds blend in my mind. They form a complete world in itself."

The premiere of Saariaho's first opera, *L'amour de loin* (*Love from Afar*), in 2000 came relatively late in her career. The great success of this work spurred the composition of other operas: *Adriana Mater* (2005), *Emilie* (2010), and *Only the Sound*

Remains (2015). "It is a huge thing for me when I compose an opera," Saariaho has observed. "I become each character in a way." In 2016, the Metropolitan Opera in New York staged *L'amour de loin*. The only other opera by a female composer ever presented by the Metropolitan Opera before this was Ethel Smyth's *Der Wald* (*The Forest*) in 1903.

L'amour de loin deals with the twelfth-century troubadour, Prince Jaufré Rudel of Blaye—in present-day southwestern France—and his idealized love for the beautiful Countess Clémence who lives in far-away Tripoli, in Lebanon. Jaufré hears about Clémence from the Pilgrim, who has traveled to the Holy Land. She immediately becomes an obsession, and he dreams about her day and night. Jaufré sails to Tripoli, accompanied by his companions, but during the voyage he becomes ill. When Jaufré and Clémence finally meet, they declare their love and he dies in her arms.

L'amour de loin is set to a French text written by Amin Maalouf, a Lebanese novelist who, like Saariaho, lives in Paris. The opera features the blending of instrumental and electronic sounds. Vocal lines are often conversational and sometimes accompanied by low sustained tones. Though a male role, the Pilgrim is written for a mezzo-soprano. There is a tradition in opera of "trouser roles," women playing boys or men on stage.

Act IV, Scene 3: Tempest

Act IV, scene 3 takes place on board a ship sailing to Tripoli, as the sea becomes increasingly turbulent. Jaufré, a baritone, becomes severely ill due to his anguish at having impulsively set out to meet his "love from afar." His companions, a chorus of tenors and basses, mock him as a brave warrior who fears a rough sea. This male chorus often sings "ah" as an accompaniment to Jaufré's vocal lines. The Pilgrim tells Jaufré that Countess Clémence knows that he is coming to meet her. Near the end of this scene, Jaufré regrets that he has set out on this voyage. Act IV ends with stormy orchestral and electronic sounds.

City Scape (2002), by Jennifer Higdon

Jennifer Higdon in 2005.
APRIL SAUL/KRT/Newscom

Jennifer Higdon (b. 1962) is one of the most widely performed American composers of the twenty-first century; in 2010 she won the Pulitzer Prize for Music for her Violin Concerto and a Grammy Award for Best Contemporary Classical Composition for her Percussion Concerto (2005).

Born in Brooklyn, New York, she grew up in Atlanta, Georgia, and then moved with her family to Seymour, Tennessee, where she lived on a forty-acre farm. In her teens, she taught herself the flute and played in her high school band. She listened to the Beatles, reggae, bluegrass, and country music, discovering classical music at age eighteen while studying flute at Bowling Green State University in Ohio. Only at twenty-one did she focus on music composition, which she studied at the Curtis Institute of Music and the University of Pennsylvania, where she was awarded a doctorate. In 1994, she returned to the Curtis Institute as a teacher and has influenced many young composers and performers.

Higdon was propelled to fame by the success of her orchestral tone poem *Blue Cathedral,* which has been performed more than six hundred times worldwide since its premiere in Philadelphia in 2000. Since then she has written an impressive series of instrumental and vocal works, including the Concerto for Orchestra (2002), Percussion Concerto (2005), the opera *Cold Mountain* (2015). In 2020, she won her third Grammy Award for her Harp Concerto (2018). Higdon's music is attractive to listeners because of its expressiveness, rhythmic vitality, imaginative tone colors, and personal synthesis of past and contemporary musical idioms.

City Scape was commissioned and premiered in 2002 by the Atlanta Symphony Orchestra, under the direction of conductor Robert Spano. According to Higdon, *City Scape* is "a metropolitan sound picture written in orchestral tones . . . I have so many memories of Atlanta—playing around Lenox Square, running around the Woodruff Arts Center as a kid . . . I knew I had a lot of inspiration there, in the city itself . . . I have such a strong association with that city, having lived there for ten years when I was growing up. In fact, the Atlanta Symphony was the first orchestra that I ever heard live. It came very naturally . . . I had concrete images in my head of different aspects of Atlanta." City Scape consists of three movements: *SkyLine, river sings a song to trees,* and *Peachtree Street.* We focus on the third movement.

Third Movement: *Peachtree Street*

Higdon writes that "*Peachtree Street* is a representation of all those roadways and main arteries that flow through cities (Peachtree Street is the main street that runs through downtown Atlanta). . . . Every main street that runs through a city is loaded with the energy and bustle of commerce, reflecting the needs and wants of its citizens. . . . Because there is so much diversity in city streets, I've created a movement that explores the diverse sections of the orchestra, their relationships, and their combination in creating a larger voice."

Peachtree Street is in rondo form. A rondo features a main theme that recurs several times in alternation with other themes or sections, as we have seen in Part IV, Chapter 6. The energetic main theme (A) of *Peachtree Street* is played loudly by the orchestra and appears six times, separated by other sections: A B A C A D A E A E A. This energetic theme is syncopated and features repeated notes in the trumpets. Starting with its third appearance, the main theme is shortened. The other sections, B, C, D, and E, feature individual instrumental groups—strings, woodwinds, percussion—and tend to be softer and more polyphonic in texture than the main theme.

Listening Outline

HIGDON, *City Scape* (2002)

Third Movement: *Peachtree Street*
2 flutes, 2 oboes, 2 clarinets, 2 bassoons, 4 French horns, 2 trombones, tuba, timpani, snare drum, crash cymbal, bass drum, brake drum, tom tom, xylophone, glockenspiel, suspended cymbal, Chinese cymbal, 1st violins, 2d violins, violas, cellos, double basses
Rondo form: A B A C A D A E A E A
(Duration 6:06)

Listen for the contrast between the *syncopated* main theme, played by the full orchestra, and sections, B, C, D, and E, played by individual instrumental groups (*strings, woodwinds,* and *percussion*).

A

| | 0:00 | **1.** | Energetic main theme, orchestra *ff*, syncopations, trumpets, quick repeated notes, cymbal crashes. |

B

| | 0:49 | **2.** | New motive in cellos, imitated by violins, polyphonic texture, crescendo to |

A		
	1:20	**3.** Main theme, orchestra, ***ff***, trumpets, quick repeated notes, crescendo
C		
	1:40	**4.** Woodwinds, flute solo, oboe melody leads to
A		
	2:24	**5.** Shortened main theme, orchestra, ***f***, trumpets, quick repeated notes, *crescendo to* quickly leads to
D		
	2:31	**6.** Timpani, glockenspiel, xylophone, decrescendo, strings, woodwinds join, crescendo to
A		
	3:14	**7.** Shortened main theme, orchestra, ***ff***, brasses, ***ff***, syncopations
E		
	3:30	**8.** High woodwinds descend, decrescendo, tempo slows, French horns. ***p***, repeated tones, crescendo to
A		
	4:12	**9.** Shortened main theme, orchestra, ***ff***.
E		
	4:30	**10.** Woodwinds descend, decrescendo, tempo slows; low strings, ***f***, joined in turn by woodwinds, percussion, brasses.
A		
	5:29	**11.** Shortened main theme, orchestra, ***ff***, trumpets, quick repeated notes, crescendo, bass drum, cymbal crashes end *Peachtree Street*.

Inura (2009), by Tania León

Tania León in 2013.

Jeff Vespa/WireImage/Getty Images

Tania León (b. 1943), composer and conductor, is Distinguished Professor of the City University of New York and a member of the American Academy of Arts and Letters. Born in Havana, Cuba, she began to play piano at age four and later attended music schools. "Growing up in Cuba was a kaleidoscopic experience with sound," León recalled. "You might be walking in the streets and there is a drummer, or turn around the corner and all of a sudden there is somebody playing the guitar with the background of somebody playing the trumpet. You have all these revelers in the back of my house preparing themselves for the carnival even when I was actually trying to play Chopin or Tchaikovsky . . . . They would parade in front of the house. I would stop playing the piano, go see the revelers pass by, and we'd dance."

León came to the United States in 1967 to continue her education at New York University. Two years later, she became conductor of the Dance Theater of Harlem, where she established an orchestra and a music school. Since then, León has made guest appearances as a conductor of major orchestras throughout the world. León has composed prolifically in almost every musical genre. Her opera, *Scourge of Hyacinths* (1994), was commissioned by the Munich Biennale, where it was awarded the BMW Prize. Its libretto—which deals with an innocent man who was falsely accused—is based on a radio play by Wole Soyinka, the Nobel Prize-laureate Nigerian writer. In 2020, the New York Philharmonic gave the world premiere of León's orchestral piece *Stride*, which was inspired by the career of Susan B. Anthony, the nineteenth-century women's rights activist.

León composed *Inura* in 2009 for DanceBrazil, an American dance company that performs works based on Brazilian music and dance. *Inura* is written for mixed chorus, strings, and percussion. The vocal text, in the language of Yoruba/Brazilian Portuguese, is drawn from prayers of the Yoruban Candomle religion passed down through generations.

According to León, *inura* (pronounced 'ee-noorah') refers to the "*Exu* energy that exists in each one of us." *Exu* (pronounced 'ee-shoo') is one of the most important deities of the Afro-Brazilian Yoruba tradition. He is the messenger between the world of the people and the world of gods . . . . *Exu* thrives on the diversity of life, engenders contradiction and paradox, loves every color that exists, commands sexuality in all its forms, and does not distinguish between good and evil."

León observes that "each section of the ballet shows a different manifestation of *inura*—from our first contact with it as children to our more complex experiences with it later in life." In composing *Inura*, León "wanted to make a sonic commentary between what we perceive as African influences versus European influences." *Inura* comprises eight uninterrupted sections with engaging titles such as *The Power, The Sharing, Teaching, Understanding,* and *Respect.* We study Section 2: *The Sharing.*

Section 2: *The Sharing*

The Sharing is propulsive, energetic, and exuberant, scored for twelve singers, nine string players, and five percussionists. Four of the drummers are Brazilians who play polyrhythms—several different rhythms simultaneously—a characteristic of music from sub-Saharan Africa. The Brazilian percussionists perform on traditional Brazilian instruments similar to those used by musicians from the Benin region of West Africa. In *The Sharing,* the Brazilian percussionists play rapidly and without interruption throughout. León relates that these drummers flew from Brazil to New York for the premiere performances and recording sessions and "memorized the different percussion parts they played . . . . They simply are incredible musicians." Another African element in *The Sharing* is the use of *call and response,* a vocal style in which chantlike phrases of a soloist are repeatedly answered by those of a chorus. León creates variety by alternating between passages with instruments alone and those with instruments and voices.

Listening Outline

LEÓN, *Inura* (2009)

Section 2: The Sharing

Sopranos, altos, tenors, basses, 1st violins, 2d violins, cellos, double bass, percussion
(Duration 3:49)

Listen for the polyrhythm of the *percussion* group and the contrast in *tone color* between instrumental sections and those with voices and instruments.

0:00	**1. a.**	Tenor solo, polyrhythmic percussion; soprano, alto exclamation.
0:17	**b.**	Shrill strings, chorus answers, percussion briefly alone.
0:31	**2. a.**	Tenors, chantlike melody, percussion.
0:50	**b.**	Sopranos, altos legato, answered by strings, tenors.
1:01	**c.**	Strings and percussion alone.

1:16	**3. a.** Chorus joins instruments.
1:30	**b.** Tenor solos answered by sopranos, altos.
2:00	**c.** Strings and percussion alone.
2:13	**4. a.** Chorus joins strings and percussion
2:18	**b.** Strings and percussion alone.
2:31	**c.** High voices join instruments, tenors, legato phrases.
2:50	**d.** Strings and percussion alone.
2:59	**5. a.** Chorus alternates with tenors; strings and percussion accompany.
3:09	**b.** Percussion, strings briefly alone.
3:14	**c.** Chorus alternates with tenor solos.
3:34	**d.** Decrescendo, percussion, tenors; solo tenor and violin held tone.

23 Jazz

About the time Schoenberg and Stravinsky were changing the language of music in Europe, a new musical style called *jazz* was being developed in the United States.* It was created by musicians—predominantly Black Americans—performing in the streets, bars, brothels, and dance halls of New Orleans and other southern cities.

Jazz can be described generally as music rooted in improvisation and characterized by syncopated rhythm, a steady beat, and unique tone colors and performance techniques. Although the term *jazz* became current in 1917, the music itself was probably heard as early as 1900. We do not know exactly when jazz started, or how it sounded at first, because this new music existed only in performance, not musical notation. Moreover, very little jazz was captured on recordings before 1923, and none at all before the Original Dixieland Jazz Band recorded in 1917.

Since its beginnings, jazz has developed a rich variety of substyles, such as New Orleans style (including Dixieland), swing, bebop, cool, free jazz, and jazz rock. It has produced such outstanding figures as Louis Armstrong, Duke Ellington, Benny Goodman, Charlie Parker, and Miles Davis. Its impact has been enormous and worldwide, affecting not only many kinds of popular music, but the music of such composers as Maurice Ravel, Darius Milhaud, George Gershwin, and Aaron Copland.

Jazz in Society

The world of jazz has witnessed many changes since its beginnings at the turn of the century. Geographically, its center has shifted from New Orleans to Chicago, Kansas City, and New York. Today, it is hard to speak of *a* jazz center because jazz, in its many substyles, is heard worldwide, from Los Angeles to Tokyo. Jazz has changed in function too. For a long time, it was basically music for dancing; but since the 1940s, many newer jazz styles have been intended for listening. Now we are as likely to hear jazz in a concert hall or college classroom as in a bar or nightclub. The image of jazz has also changed. Like the blues and rock music, it was originally condemned for its emphasis on sexuality, but it has long since become respected as an American art form.

---

*Two excellent recorded anthologies of jazz are the *Smithsonian Collection of Classic Jazz* and Ken Burns's *Jazz: The Story of American Music.*

Duke Ellington was probably the most important swing-band composer, arranger, and conductor.
Herve GLOAGUEN/Gamma-Rapho via Getty Images

As both a trumpeter and a singer, Louis "Satchmo" Armstrong had a worldwide impact on jazz.
Bettman/Getty Images

The Superior Band of New Orleans, c. 1910. One major source of jazz was the American band tradition.
JP Jazz Archive/Redferns/Getty Images

In recent years, jazz has been sponsored by a number of major American cultural institutions. Lincoln Center in New York City has sponsored the Jazz at Lincoln Center Orchestra, and the Smithsonian National Museum of American History in Washington, D.C. has founded the Smithsonian Jazz Masterpieces Orchestra. Many colleges and universities now offer courses in jazz as part of the music curriculum.

Roots of Jazz

Early jazz blended elements from many musical cultures, including west African, American, and European. West African influences included an emphasis on improvisation, drumming, percussive sounds, and complex rhythms, as well as a feature known as *call and response*. In much west African vocal music, a soloist's phrases are repeatedly answered by a chorus. Similarly, in jazz, **call and response** occurs when a voice is answered by an instrument, or when one instrument (or group of instruments) is answered by another instrument (or group).

Actually, the call-and-response pattern of jazz was derived more directly from Black American church services in which the congregation vocally responds to the preacher's "call." Other American influences on jazz were the rich body of music that Blacks developed here—including work songs, spirituals, gospel hymns, and dances like the cakewalk—and the music of white America. Nineteenth-century American and European musical traditions became elements in the background of jazz. In addition to hymns, popular songs, folk tunes, and piano pieces, the American band tradition was a major influence. Many marching band instruments were used in early jazz bands, and band music helped shaped the forms and rhythms of early jazz. Along with band music, the immediate sources of jazz were ragtime and blues.

Scott Joplin was the best-known ragtime composer.
LOC/Notated Music/Science Source

Ragtime

Ragtime (1890s to about 1915) is a style of composed piano music developed primarily by Black pianists who played in southern and midwestern saloons and dance halls. It is generally in duple meter ($\frac{2}{4}$) and performed at a moderate march tempo. The pianist's right hand plays a highly syncopated melody, while the left hand steadily maintains the beat with an "oom-pah" accompaniment. The "king of ragtime" was Scott Joplin (1868–1917), whose most famous pieces include *Maple Leaf Rag* and *The Entertainer*.

Blues

Blues refers to a form of vocal and instrumental music and to a style of performance. Blues grew out of Black American folk music, such as work songs, spirituals, and the field hollers of slaves. Exactly when blues originated is uncertain, but by around the 1890s it was sung in rural areas of the south. The original "country blues," usually performed with guitar accompaniment, was not standardized in form or style.

The poetic and musical form of blues crystallized around 1910 and gained popularity through the publication of *Memphis Blues* (1912) and *St. Louis Blues* (1914), by W. C. Handy (1873–1958). During the

1920s, blues became a national craze among Black Americans. Records by such blues singers as Bessie Smith sold in the millions. The 1920s also saw the twelve-bar blues (more on this below) become a musical form widely used by jazz instrumentalists as well as blues singers. Since then, jazz and blues have been intertwined. In the 1930s, the singer-guitarist Robert Johnson (1898–1937) combined the sound of country blues—vocal melody accompanied by acoustic guitar—with the formal structure of blues to create music that has influenced many jazz and rock guitarists up to the present day.

From the 1920s to the 1950s, Chicago became a blues center because many Black American blues singers and instrumentalists had migrated there from the south in the decades after World War I. The 1940s saw the emergence in Chicago of a new, highly energetic blues style—sometimes called *urban blues*—that derived from earlier blues but used electric guitar and amplification. One of the best-known performers of urban blues was Muddy Waters (1915–1983), who had a distinctive style of moaning and shouting. The continuing impact of the blues is apparent in such popular contemporary styles as rhythm and blues, rock and roll, and soul.

Vocal blues is intensely personal, often containing sexual references and dealing with the pain of betrayal, desertion, and unrequited love. The lyrics consist of several three-line stanzas, each in the same poetic and musical form. The first line is sung and then repeated to roughly the same melodic phrase (a a'); the third line has a different melodic phrase and text (b). Here is stanza 4 of Bessie Smith's *Lost Your Head Blues*, which we study:

> a : I'm . . . . goodbye.
> a': I'm . . . . goodbye.
> b : But . . . . why.

A blues stanza is set to a harmonic framework that is usually twelve bars in length. This harmonic pattern, known as **twelve-bar blues**, involves only three basic chords: tonic (I), subdominant (IV), and dominant (V). The specific ordering of these chords can be outlined as follows: tonic (4 bars)—subdominant (2 bars)—tonic (2 bars)—dominant (2 bars)—tonic (2 bars). Here is how the three-line stanza is set to this chord progression:

	Line 1 (a)				Line 2 (a')				Line 3 (b)			
Bars	1	2	3	4	5	6	7	8	9	10	11	12
Chords	I				IV		I		V		I	

Each stanza of the text is sung to the same series of chords, although other chords may be inserted between the primary chords of the twelve-bar blues form outlined previously. Singers either repeat the same basic melody for each stanza or improvise new melodies to reflect the changing moods of the lyrics. The music is almost always in quadruple meter ($\frac{4}{4}$), and so each bar contains four beats.

Blues singers and instrumentalists have a special style of performance involving "bent" notes, and vocal scoops and slides. Their melodies—both composed and improvised—contain many "blue" notes, which are produced by slightly lowering or flatting the third, fifth, and seventh tones of a major scale. Blues rhythm is also very flexible. Performers often sing or play "around" the beat, accenting notes either just before or after it.

Jazz instrumentalists imitate the performing style of blues singers and use the harmonic pattern of twelve-bar blues as a basis for improvisation. This twelve-bar pattern is repeated over and over while new melodies are improvised above it. As with the baroque ground bass, the repeated chord progression provides unity while the free flow of improvised melodic lines contributes variety. Music in this twelve-bar form can be

Bessie Smith was one of the most influential blues singers.
Edward Elcha/Michael Ochs Archives/Getty Images

happy or sad, fast or slow, and in a wide range of styles. *Lost Your Head Blues* (1926), a vocal blues by Bessie Smith, illustrates twelve-bar blues.

Lost Your Head Blues (1926), by Bessie Smith

Bessie Smith (1894–1937), known as the "empress of the blues," was the most famous blues singer of the 1920s. Her *Lost Your Head Blues* is a well-known example of blues form and performance style. The lyrics express the feelings of a woman who plans to leave her man because she's "been treated wrong." Each of the poem's five stanzas is set to the twelve-bar blues pattern. Typically, a cornet response follows each line that is sung.

Lost Your Head Blues begins with a four-bar introduction by the accompanying cornet (Joe Smith) and piano (Fletcher Henderson). Bessie Smith then sings a melody that she'll repeat—with extensive variations of pitch and rhythm—in each stanza. Her "blue" notes, microtonal shadings, and slides between pitches are essential to the effect of the song. Notice the eloquent slides up to *I* in her singing of *I was with you baby,* as well as the ornamental quiver on *down* when she sings the words *throw'd your good gal down.* There are many syncopated rhythms because words are often sung just before or after the beat. Bessie Smith's vocal melody is highly sensitive to the words. For example, the long high notes at the beginning of the last stanza ("*Days* are lonesome, *nights* are long") produce a wonderful climax. Throughout the song, Bessie Smith's vocal inflections are perfectly matched by the cornet's improvised responses and echoes.

(Due to copyright restrictions, each line of the lyrics in the following Vocal Music Guide is abridged.)

Vocal Music Guide

SMITH, *Lost Your Head Blues* (1926)

(Duration 2:52)

Listen for the "blue" notes, microtonal shading, *syncopated rhythms,* and slides between *pitches* in the vocal melody. Notice the repeated twelve-bar blues pattern: tonic (4 bars); subdominant-tonic; (4-bars); dominant-tonic (4 bars).

Cornet and
piano introduction.

Tonic	I . . . . dime.
Subdominant-Tonic	I . . . . dime.
Dominant-Tonic	Now . . . . down.
	Once . . . . twice.
	Once . . . . twice.
	When . . . . nice.

	When . . . . kind.
	When . . . . kind.
	But . . . . mind.
	I'm . . . . goodbye.
	I'm . . . . goodbye.
	But . . . . why.
Long high notes	Days . . . . long.
on Days and *nights*	Days . . . . long.
	I'm . . . . wrong.

Performance Perspectives

Bessie Smith Singing *Lost Your Head Blues*

Since Bessie Smith's death in 1937, her recordings not only have delighted listeners worldwide but have had a powerful impact on several generations of singers. The rock star Janis Joplin (1943–1970) said of her: "No one ever hit me so hard. Bessie made me want to sing."

Bessie Smith was born in 1894 to poor Black American parents in a one-room shack in Chattanooga, Tennessee. She began her professional career at eighteen, when she joined an entertainment troupe that included Gertrude "Ma" Rainey, a leading blues singer. Over the next decade Smith gradually achieved stardom as she performed in theaters, tents, dance halls, and cabarets, primarily before Black audiences in the south and northeast.

A turning point in Bessie Smith's career came in 1923, when her first commercial 78-rpm record—*Down Hearted Blues*—sold 780,000 copies in less than six months. Her powerful voice, emotional intensity, clear diction, and expressive "bent" notes won for her the uncontested title "empress of the blues." She became the highest-paid Black American performer and in 1925 was able to buy her own bright yellow railroad car to transport her troupe of about

Edward Elcha/Michael Ochs Archives/Getty Images

forty, along with equipment and a large tent. She continued to record blues—including about two dozen of her own compositions—with leading jazz musicians such as Louis Armstrong.

The story of Bessie Smith illustrates how the advent of recording technology changed the position of the performer in musical life. Up until the twentieth century, performers had an impact only on those who heard them in person. Unlike composers, whose notated compositions could be enjoyed by later generations, performers created for the moment, their work surviving only in written descriptions or visual representations. This situation changed dramatically with the invention of recording. Beginning with phonograph records, and later through radio, film, television, compact discs, and digital media, artists like Bessie Smith found a much wider audience and exerted lasting influence.

Many singers have described the impact of Bessie Smith's recordings. The gospel singer Mahalia Jackson (1911–1972), for example, recalled how, as a youngster in New Orleans, she would imitate Bessie Smith: "I'd play that record over and over again, and Bessie's voice would come out so full and round. . . . I'd make my mouth do the same thing."

In 1989 Bessie Smith was inducted into the Rock and Roll Hall of Fame in Cleveland; and in 2001 a play featuring the songs she made famous, *The Devil's Music: The Life and Blues of Bessie Smith,* was performed in New York City. Thanks to her recordings, the epitaph on her tombstone has proved prophetic. "The greatest blues singer in the world will never stop singing."

Bessie Smith's performance of *Lost Your Head Blues* is included in the recordings.

New Orleans style (or Dixieland) was typically played by five to eight performers. King Oliver (standing, at left rear) is shown here with his Creole Jazz Band in 1923. The band included Louis Armstrong (seated, center) and Lil Hardin (at the piano).
Michael Ochs Archives/Getty Images

piece. In between, individual players were featured in improvised solos, accompanied by the rhythm section or by the whole band. Sometimes there were brief unaccompanied solos, called **breaks**. The band's performance might begin with an introduction and end with a brief coda.

Notable figures of New Orleans jazz include Ferdinand "Jelly Roll" Morton and Joseph "King" Oliver. Oliver's *Dippermouth Blues* (1923) is a fine example of instrumental blues and New Orleans style. Especially important is the trumpeter and singer Louis "Satchmo" Armstrong (1901–1971), who was one of the greatest jazz improvisers. He revealed new dimensions of the trumpet, showing that it could be played in a higher register than had been thought possible.

Armstrong also popularized *scat singing*, vocalization of a melodic line with nonsense syllables. Starting in 1925, he made a series of recordings with bands known as Louis Armstrong's Hot Five and Louis Armstrong's Hot Seven. These recordings established his reputation as a leading jazz trumpeter.

Hotter Than That (1927), by Louis Armstrong and His Hot Five

Hotter Than That, an outstanding performance by Louis Armstrong and His Hot Five, is based on a tune written by Lillian Hardin Armstrong (1898–1971), who was Armstrong's wife and the pianist of the band. This performance shows how New Orleans style developed in Chicago during the 1920s. The emphasis is on improvisatory solos, based on the harmonic structure of the thirty-two-bar tune *Hotter Than That.* Collective improvisation—so important in earlier New Orleans style—is restricted to the introduction and the last of four choruses. Louis Armstrong performs as both trumpeter and vocalist. His vocal solo, an example of scat singing, is like his trumpet playing in sound and style. Other solos are by the clarinetist Johnny Dodds and the trombonist Kid Ory. At the middle and end of each chorus is a brief unaccompanied solo, a break. Listen for the syncopations of Armstrong's vocal melody (chorus 3), the call and response between voice and guitar in the interlude following chorus 3, and the dissonant guitar chord that gives *Hotter Than That* an unusual, inconclusive ending.

Listening Outline

LOUIS ARMSTRONG AND HIS HOT FIVE, *Hotter Than That* (1927)

Cornet, voice (Louis Armstrong), piano (Lillian Hardin Armstrong), clarinet (Johnny Dodds), trombone (Kid Ory), guitar (Lonnie Johnson)

Rapid tempo, quadruple meter ($\frac{4}{4}$)

Introduction—four choruses of thirty-two bars—coda

(Duration 2:59)

Listen for the collective improvisation in the introduction and last chorus in contrast to the improvised solos in choruses 1–3. Notice Louis Armstrong's scat singing in chorus 3 and the inconclusive ending on a *dissonant guitar chord.*

Introduction (8 bars)

       0:00   **1.** All instruments, trumpet predominates, collective improvisation.

Chorus 1 (32 bars)

       0:09   **2.** Trumpet solo, accompanied by piano and guitar. Trumpet briefly alone, piano and guitar rejoin.

Chorus 2 (32 bars)

       0:43   **3.** Clarinet solo, piano and guitar accompany.

Chorus 3 (32 bars)

       1:19   **4.** Vocal solo, scat singing, guitar accompanies.

Interlude (20 bars)

       1:54   **5.** Voice imitated by guitar. Piano leads into

Chorus 4 (32 bars)

       2:17   **6. a.** Muted trombone solo, piano and guitar accompany.

       2:33   **b.** Trumpet, other instruments join, collective improvisation.

Tag (4 bars)

                 c. Trumpet, guitar, dissonant chord at end.

Swing A new jazz style called *swing* developed in the 1920s and flourished from 1935 to 1945 (the "swing era"). It was played mainly by *big bands*; the typical *swing band* had about fourteen or fifteen musicians grouped into three sections: saxophones (three to five players, some doubling on clarinet), brass instruments (three or four each of trumpet and trombone), and rhythm (piano, percussion, guitar, and bass). A band of this size needed music that was more composed than improvised and was also *arranged,* or notated in written-out parts for each musician to read. With swing, the arranger became an important figure in jazz.

Melodies were often performed by entire sections of a swing band, either in unison or in harmony. The main melody was frequently accompanied by saxophones and brasses playing short, repeated phrases called *riffs*. The saxophone became one of the most important solo instruments, and percussionists also had a more prominent and spectacular role.

The swing era produced hundreds of "name" bands—both Black and white—for example, those of Count Basie, Glen Miller, Tommy Dorsey, and Benny Goodman (the "King of Swing"). Some of the swing bands included leading musicians, such as the saxophonists Coleman Hawkins and Lester Young, and featured singers like Billie Holiday, Ella Fitzgerald, and Frank Sinatra. Duke Ellington (1899–1974) was perhaps the most important composer, arranger, and conductor of the swing era. Ellington's works are richer in harmony and more varied in form than those of his contemporaries.

improvise some chord changes . . . The melody had a Latin, even oriental feeling to it . . . a special kind of syncopation in the bass line." Initially, Gillespie named the tune *Interlude*, but later the song was renamed *A Night in Tunisia*, because it sounded "exotic," and Tunisia was in the news during World War II.

A Night in Tunisia consists of an introduction and three choruses in A A B A form, each 32 bars in length, with a 14-bar interlude connecting chorus 1 and 2. The tempo is extremely fast and the beat is usually marked by the pizzicato bass and by the "ride" cymbal played with brushes.

The introduction presents a syncopated bass motive in Afro-Cuban rhythm. In chorus 1, Gillespie plays a muted trumpet to introduce the Afro-Cuban style melody, which is accompanied by the other instruments. Following the melody is a swing-based interlude in which the saxophone and vibraphone play a jazzy repeated figure in unison. (A *vibraphone* is a percussion instrument with tuned metal bars and tubular metal resonators that produce a vibrato by means of motor-driven metal vanes.) In chorus 2, Gillespie uses an open (nonmuted) trumpet to create a spectacular solo, accompanied by bass, piano, and percussion. Gillespie improvises a jagged melodic line, with unexpected accents and rests, extremely high tones, and a torrential flow of rapid notes. In chorus 3, the saxophone and vibraphone each have improvised solos.

Cool Jazz

Cool jazz (which emerged in the late 1940s and early 1950s) was related to bop but far calmer and more relaxed. Cool jazz pieces also tended to be longer than bebop works and relied more heavily on arrangements. They sometimes used instruments that were new to jazz, including the French horn, flute, and cello. The tenor saxophonists Lester Young (1909–1959) and Stan Getz (b. 1927), the pianist Lennie Trístano (1919–1978), and the trumpeter and bandleader Miles Davis (1926–1991) were important figures.

Free Jazz

Until about 1960, jazz improvisations tended to keep the length and chord structure of the original theme, if not its melody. But during the 1960s, some musicians created *free jazz*, a style that was not based on regular forms or established chord patterns. *Free Jazz*, recorded in 1960 by Ornette Coleman (b. 1930) with several other musicians improvising individually and collectively, is an example; it can be compared to the chance music created by John Cage and his followers. Another musician who played an important role in the development of free jazz was John Coltrane (1926–1967), who was influential as an improviser, tenor and soprano saxophonist, and composer.

Jazz Rock (Fusion)

Rock became a potent influence on jazz starting in the late 1960s. This influence led to *jazz rock*, or *fusion*, a new style combining the jazz musician's improvisatory approach into a style employing rock musical forms, rhythms, and tone colors. Instruments used by a jazz rock group were either electronic or acoustic and often included synthesizers and electric piano, guitar, and bass. In jazz rock and fusion, the bass player assumes a more melodic role in addition to the more traditional functions of providing the beat and emphasizing the harmonic foundation. The percussion section was sometimes larger than that in earlier jazz groups and often included a percussionist— or sometimes multiple percussionists—performing on instruments from Africa, Latin America, or India.

Miles Davis, a leading musician in cool jazz, was also important in jazz rock. Herbie Hancock, Chick Corea, Joe Zawinul, and Wayne Shorter—who made recordings with both Zawinul and Davis—became pacesetters of jazz rock in the 1970s, 1980s, and 1990s.

In addition to these jazz musicians who began to incorporate rock elements, a number of rock musicians began to incorporate jazz improvisation and other elements of the style into their recordings and performances. Two of the most successful of these jazz rock groups during the late 1960s and early 1970s were Chicago and Blood, Sweat & Tears.

Miles Runs the Voodoo Down (1969), by Miles Davis

Miles Runs the Voodoo Down is from the Miles Davis album *Bitches Brew,* one of the early milestones of jazz rock (fusion). It is performed by a large ensemble of twelve musicians including only three brass and woodwind instruments—trumpet (Miles Davis), soprano saxophone (Wayne Shorter), bass clarinet (Bennie Maupin)—but a very large rhythm section: drums (Lenny White, Jack De Johnette, Charles Alias), percussion (Jim Riley), electric pianos (Chick Corea, Larry Young), electric bass (Harvey Brooks), string bass (Dave Holland), and electric guitar (John McLaughlin). *Miles Runs the Voodoo Down* evokes the feeling of a ritual dance through its slow beat, unchanging harmony, and constant background of rock ostinatos in the electric bass and repeated rhythmic figures in African and South American percussion instruments. We focus on the opening four minutes of this extended piece (lasting fourteen minutes), which features a spectacular improvised solo by Miles Davis.

Miles Runs the Voodoo Down opens softly and ominously with repeated rhythmic and melodic figures in the percussion and electric bass. Other instruments gradually join, creating a hypnotic rhythmic background that becomes increasingly prominent during Miles Davis's solo, which begins half a minute into the piece. The solo conveys a blues feeling because Davis often slides from one pitch to another. It is a free and imaginative flow of musical ideas, not based on a regular form or an established chord pattern. The trumpet opens in a middle to low register. Later, Davis's improvisation moves through a very wide range and includes a variety of brief and extended phrases, screaming high held tones, rapid passages in bebop style, and many inflections that sound vocal. *Miles Runs the Voodoo Down* beautifully integrates jazz improvisation with the rhythms and electronic resources of rock.

Miles Davis.
David Redfern/Redferns/Getty Images

Jazz rock is only one of the substyles that could be heard since the 1970s. Every kind of jazz we've studied—New Orleans, swing, bebop, cool jazz, and free jazz—has its fans and devoted performers. As they have done since the early days, jazz musicians continue to explore new resources to further the development of their art.

24 Music for Stage and Screen

Musical Theater

Along with jazz and rock, the *musical* was one of the most important American contributions to twentieth-century popular culture. Shows such as *Oklahoma! South Pacific, West Side Story,* and *My Fair Lady* are performed and enjoyed all over the world.

Elements of the Musical

A *musical,* or *musical comedy,* is a type of theater that fuses script, acting, and spoken dialogue with music, singing, and dancing and with scenery, costumes, and spectacle. Most musicals are in fact comedies, though some are serious. Many have been produced in theaters around Broadway in New York (hence the term *Broadway musical*), but successful musicals reach nationwide and even worldwide audiences, and some are made into movies (such as *The Sound of Music, Hair, Evita, Chicago, Rent,* and *The Producers*).

Generally, a musical is in two acts, of which the second is shorter and brings back some of the melodies heard earlier. Traditionally, the songs consisted of an introductory section (called the *verse*) and a main section (called the *chorus*) in A A B A form (thirty-two bars). Hit tunes from musicals, such as *Ol' Man River* (from *Show Boat*) or *Some Enchanted Evening* (from *South Pacific*), have often had lasting appeal, detached from their original theatrical context.

The American musical embraces a variety of styles, yet it is a distinct type of musical theater, separate from opera. In contrast to opera, it tends to use simpler harmonies, melodies, and forms; it contains more spoken dialogue, and its songs have a narrower pitch range. Also, the musical is even more of a collaborative effort: one composer may create the songs, but other musicians are responsible for the orchestration, the overture, connective musical passages, and music accompanying dances. The spoken dialogue and lyrics are usually written by several people. Still, certain works, such as Stephen Sondheim's *Sweeney Todd* (1979), fall somewhere between musicals and operas; and some, such as Sondheim's *A Little Night Music* (1973), are eventually performed by opera companies.

Development of the Musical

Sources of the American musical include a variety of musical and dramatic forms of the late nineteenth century and the early twentieth century, including operetta, vaudeville, and the revue. *Operetta,* or *comic opera,* combines song, spoken dialogue, and dance with sophisticated musical techniques. Examples are the operettas of the Englishmen W. S. Gilbert and Arthur Sullivan, such as *The Mikado* (1885); and those of the American Victor Herbert, such as *Babes in Toyland* (1903) and *Naughty Marietta* (1910). A more popular antecedent was *vaudeville,* a variety show with songs, comedy, juggling, acrobats, and animal acts, but no plot. The *revue,* a variety show without a plot but with a unifying idea, was often satirical and featured chorus girls and comedians.

The years from about 1920 to 1960 saw a golden era of the American musical, created by songwriters and composers such as Irving Berlin (1888–1989), Jerome Kern (1885–1945), George Gershwin (1898–1937), Cole Porter (1893–1964), Richard Rodgers (1902–1979), Frank Loesser (1910–1969), and Leonard Bernstein (1918–1990). Plots became more believable and wider in range; song and dance were better integrated with the story, and musical techniques became more sophisticated.

A pathbreaking musical with a serious plot was *Show Boat* (1927, music by Jerome Kern and lyrics by Oscar Hammerstein II), which treated interracial romance. Its songs—including *Ol' Man River* and *Why Do I Love You?*—revealed character and were smoothly woven into the action. In the 1930s, some musicals satirized social and political institutions. A prominent instance was George and Ira Gershwin's *Of Thee I Sing* (1931), which poked fun at American presidential elections. In the late 1930s, ballet became more significant and was used to carry the action forward. For example, the climax of the musical *On Your Toes* (1936) was a ballet by George Balanchine (1904–1989) called *Slaughter on Tenth Avenue*. *Oklahoma!*—by Richard Rodgers and the lyricist Oscar Hammerstein II—was a landmark in the integration of dance, songs, and plot; its ballets, created by Agnes de Mille and inspired by square dances, were important for the progress of the story. After World War II, however, an increasing number of shows were set in foreign lands, such as Siam (*The King and I;* 1951), France (*Fanny;* 1954), England (*My Fair Lady;* 1956), and Russia (*Fiddler on the Roof;* 1964). Postwar musicals also began to explore new kinds of serious subjects, such as teenage gang warfare in *West Side Story* (1957).

After 1960, some composers of Broadway shows continued to write traditional songs—a conservative trend also reflected in the many revivals of classic musicals. However, other composers departed from traditional A A B A form; and often their songs were so much a part of the context that they were unlikely to become hits on

The musical has been one of the most important American contributions to popular culture. Shown here is a scene from *Hamilton: An American Musical* (2015), with music, lyrics, and book by Lin-Manuel Miranda (b. 1980), who also starred in the show.
SARA KRULWICH/The New York Times/Redux Pictures

their own. Like jazz, the musical was affected by the "rock revolution" of the 1960s. One of the rock musicals was *Hair* (1967), which reflected the hippie movement and had a scene of total nudity. Rock elements were also incorporated into *Jesus Christ Superstar* (1971), by the British musician Andrew Lloyd Webber (b. 1948), who also created *Cats* (1982) and *Phantom of the Opera* (1987), the longest-running Broadway musical ever. The unusual prominence of European composers on the American musical scene was also reflected in *Les Misérables* (1986) and *Miss Saigon* (1989), written by the Frenchmen Claude-Michel Schönberg and Alain Boublil. Highly successful musicals of recent years include *Rent* (1996), *The Lion King* (1997), *Wicked* (2003), *The Book of Mormon* (2011), and *Hamilton* (2015).

Perhaps the most original contributions to American musical theater since the 1960s have been made by the composer-lyricist Stephen Sondheim (b. 1930), who first became known as the lyricist for *West Side Story*. Many of his works are "concept musicals," based more on an idea than on a traditional plot. They include *Company* (1970); *Sunday in the Park with George* (1984); and his most ambitious work, *Sweeney Todd, the Demon Barber of Fleet Street* (1979), which blurs the boundary between the musical and opera. His musical style fuses elements of the traditional Broadway song with elements of Stravinsky, Copland, and Bernstein.

Leonard Bernstein

The versatile American musician Leonard Bernstein was a composer of musicals and symphonic works, as well as an outstanding conductor, concert pianist, and author-lecturer.

Art Reserve/Alamy Stock Photo

The extraordinarily versatile Leonard Bernstein (1918–1990) was a twentieth-century culture hero—conductor, pianist, author, lecturer, and composer of orchestral and vocal works, including *West Side Story*. Bernstein was born in Lawrence, Massachusetts, graduated from Harvard University, and studied piano and conducting at the Curtis Institute in Philadelphia. His spectacular career was launched when a guest conductor became ill; Bernstein took the podium with no rehearsal and on a few hours' notice. The concert, which was broadcast on nationwide radio, was hailed as a "dramatic musical event" on the front page of the *New York Times*.

"I have a deep suspicion that every work I write, for whatever medium, is really theater music in some way." Bernstein's words apply not only to his musicals, operas, and ballets and his theater piece *Mass* (1971), but also to his choral work *Chichester Psalms* (1965) and his three programmatic symphonies—*Jeremiah* (1942), *The Age of Anxiety* (1949), and *Kaddish* (1963). His music is clearly tonal, enlivened by syncopations and irregular meters, and infused with jazz and dance rhythms. Like Stravinsky and Copland, who both influenced him, Bernstein wrote very successful ballets, including *Fancy Free* (1944) and *Facsimile* (1946). Dance numbers play an important and dramatic role in his musicals *On the Town* (1944), *Wonderful Town,* (1953) and *West Side Story* (1957). Bernstein accomplished the difficult feat of bridging the worlds of "serious" and popular music. He died in 1990, mourned by people all over the world.

West Side Story (1957)

On January 6, 1949, the choreographer Jerome Robbins first suggested to Leonard Bernstein that they collaborate on a modern version of Shakespeare's *Romeo and Juliet* set in the slums of New York. Bernstein was very enthusiastic about the "idea of making a musical that tells a tragic story in musical-comedy terms, using only musical-comedy techniques, never falling into the 'operatic' trap. Can it succeed? . . . I'm excited. If it can work—it's the first." *West Side Story*—with music by Bernstein, spoken

Tonight scene from *West Side Story.*

Brill/ullstein bild via Getty Imagess

dialogue by Arthur Laurents, and lyrics by Stephen Sondheim—was completed seven years later.

West Side Story deals with a conflict between gang rivalry and youthful love. The feud between the lovers' families in Shakespeare's *Romeo and Juliet* is transformed into warfare between two teenage street gangs: the Jets, native-born Americans led by Riff; and the Sharks, Puerto Ricans led by Bernardo. The plot revolves around a fight ("rumble") between the gangs and the doomed love of Tony (the Romeo character), a former member of the Jets; and Maria (the Juliet character), Bernardo's sister. Tony kills Bernardo after a vain attempt to break up a fight between the leader of the Sharks and Riff. Later he is shot by one of the Sharks and dies in Maria's arms.

Though it included rough street language and ended unhappily, *West Side Story* was a tremendous popular success and became an Oscar-winning musical film (1961). It was an unprecedented fusion of song and drama with electrifyingly violent choreography (by Jerome Robbins and Peter Gennaro). Compared with the average Broadway show, *West Side Story* had more music; more complex and unconventional music; and a wider range of styles, from vaudeville (*Gee, Officer Krupke*) and Latin rhythms (*America*) to bebop fugue (*Cool*) and quasi-operatic ensemble (*Tonight*). We focus on *America* and the *Tonight* Ensemble.

America

The energetic ensemble *America* brilliantly combines Latin-flavored song and dance. Two young women of the Sharks gang, Rosalia and Anita—Bernardo's girlfriend—express opposing feelings about their homeland, Puerto Rico, and their adopted country, America. The ensemble creates a lighter mood after the emotional intensity of previous scenes and helps develop the character of the witty and high-spirited Anita.

America begins with an atmospheric introduction in a moderate tempo. The introduction is marked *Tempo di Seis* and is performed by the two soloists. (*Seis* is a type of Puerto Rican song and dance music.) The homesick Rosalia first sings the words *Puerto Rico, You lovely island, Island of tropical breezes,* eliciting Anita's mocking response—to the same melody—*Puerto Rico, You ugly island, Island of tropic diseases.*

The debate continues in the joyful main part of the song, in a faster tempo marked *Tempo de Huapango.* (*Huapango* refers to a type of Mexican dance.) An outline on the next page shows the form of this fast main part. In the outline, A indicates the refrain, or recurring main melody, first sung to the words, *I like to be in America* by Anita. B consists of brief solos by Rosalia, each followed by Anita's sarcastic responses. Instrumental interludes meant for dancing are referred to as C. These interludes illustrate the dramatic importance of dance throughout *West Side Story.*

The music of *America* has a Hispanic flavor with alternations between $^6_8$ and $^3_4$ meter, similar to those in *Final Dance: Malambo* by the Argentinean Alberto Ginastera (studied in *Chapter 20*). As in *Final Dance: Malambo,* six fast pulses are divided into two groups of three pulses and three groups of two pulses: 1-2-3 4-5-6 1-2 3-4 5-6.

Also contributing to the Latin atmosphere in *America* are the sounds of the claves and guiro—both percussion—and guitar, instruments typical of South America.

(In the film version of *West Side Story,* the music of *America* remains the same, but some words are changed, and Bernardo and the Shark men sing and dance together with the young women.)

The following outline is meant to clarify the form of *America.*

Introduction, Moderato, Temo di Seis
Rosalia sings.
Then Anita sings to the same melody.
Introduction ends with Anita's solo.

Tempo di Huapango, Fast tempo

A	*I like . . .*	Anita
B	*I like . . .*	Rosalia and Anita
A	*Automobile . . .*	Anita and young women
B	*I'll drive . . .*	Rosalia and Anita
A	*Immigrant . . .*	Anita and young women
C	Instrumental, dance around Rosalia	
B	*I'll bring . . .*	Rosalia and Anita
A	*I like . . .*	Anita and young women
C	Instrumental, dance around Rosalia with whistling	
B	*When . . .*	Rosalia and Anita
C′	Varied and shortened instrumental dance	

Tonight Ensemble

In the *Tonight* ensemble, Bernstein projects several emotions at the same time: Riff, Bernardo, and their gangs excitedly planning for the upcoming fight; Anita looking forward to the "kicks" she's "gonna get"; and Tony and Maria anticipating the joy of being together. Riff, Bernardo, and Anita sing quick, staccato tones in a narrow range, whereas Tony and Maria sing the legato, soaringly lyrical *Tonight* melody, heard in an earlier "balcony scene" on Maria's fire escape. As Verdi did in the Quartet from *Rigoletto,* Bernstein lets us hear the voices separately before combining them in an ensemble. Such dramatic ensembles were uncommon in musicals, which tended to feature solo songs with "hit" potential.

Listening Outline

BERNSTEIN, *Tonight* Ensemble from *West Side Story* (1957)

Riff, Bernardo, Anita, Tony, Maria, gang members, orchestra
Fast and rhythmic.
(Duration 3:38)

Listen for the quick *staccato tones* in a narrow *range* sung by Riff, Bernardo, and Anita in contrast to the *legato Tonight* melody sung by Tony and Maria. Notice that the voices are heard separately before they are combined in an ensemble.

0:00	**1. a.**	Orchestra, menacing staccato melody with syncopations introduces
0:07	**b.**	Riff, Bernardo, and their gangs alternate and then sing together quick, staccato phrases with syncopations.
1:08	**c.**	Anita repeats previous phrases.
1:25	**d.**	Tony, lyrical *Tonight* melody.
2:15	**2. a.**	Orchestra, *ff*.
2:23	**b.**	Riff, quick staccato phrases.
2:40	**c.**	Maria, lyrical *Tonight* melody, with Riff's staccato phrases, and brief interjections (*All right, Tonight*) by Tony and Anita. Tony joins Maria on *Tonight* melody.
3:29	**d.**	Voices join on sustained high tones (*Tonight*), *ff*.

Lin–Manuel Miranda

Lin-Manuel Miranda (b. 1980), composer, playwright, lyricist, actor, and singer, is best known for his landmark hip hop musical *Hamilton*. Born in New York City, the son of immigrants from Puerto Rico, he grew up listening with them to recordings of musicals. Miranda composed music from the age of nine and majored in theater studies at Wesleyan University in Connecticut. In his sophomore year he wrote an early version of his musical *In the Heights*, first performed by the university's student theater company and eventually premiered on Broadway in 2008, winning Tony Awards for best musical and best musical score. While rehearsing *In the Heights*, Miranda worked as a substitute teacher of English at Manhattan's Hunter College High School, which he had attended as a student.

In 2008, on vacation in Mexico, Miranda read Ron Chernow's biography of Alexander Hamilton, one of America's founding fathers. Even before finishing the book, Miranda realized that Hamilton's action-filled life would make a good subject for a musical. He worked on the rap song *My Shot* for a whole year and in 2009 performed it during the White House Evening of Poetry, Music, and the Spoken Word. *Hamilton* premiered on Broadway in 2015 with Miranda in the title role, and the next year he won the Pulitzer Prize for Drama.

Since *Hamilton*, Miranda has turned his attention to film. He wrote songs for *Moana* (2016), a computer-animated musical adventure film released by Walt Disney Pictures, appeared in *Mary Poppins Returns* (2018), and acted and co-produced the film adaption of his musical *In the Heights* (2020).

Hamilton: An American Musical (2015), by Lin–Manuel Miranda

Few Broadway shows have had as wide an impact as the hip-hop musical *Hamilton: An American Musical,* by Lin-Manuel Miranda. People have *Hamilton*-themed birthday parties and lines from the show appear in wedding vows. Miranda, who wrote the music, book, lyrics, and originated the title role, was inspired to create the musical from reading the biography of Hamilton by Ron Chernow.

The musical, in two acts, depicts America's founding fathers and mothers and celebrates the contributions of immigrants to our society. Before this show, Alexander Hamilton, pictured on the ten-dollar bill, was known for getting killed in a duel with Aaron Burr. Now he is also known as the ambitious young immigrant from the Caribbean who became Washington's right-hand man in the Revolutionary War and America's first Secretary of the Treasury.

The show traces Hamilton's life from age nineteen to his death at forty-seven. It ends with an epilogue in which Hamilton's widow Eliza preserves his legacy.

To reflect America's diversity, Miranda casts most of the characters in *Hamilton as* Black Americans, Latinos or Asians. His rapid-fire rapped lyrics are packed with internal rhymes that sound conversational. The musical genres in *Hamilton* range from hiphop, rhythm and blues, soul and pop to Beatles-style songs sung by King George III.

We study the popular *My Shot,* the third number in Act I.

My Shot

My Shot is dominated by Hamilton's recurring verbal and musical statement that he will not miss any opportunity (section A). Section A appears four times, the last two strengthened by the whole ensemble. Ironically, in the fatal duel with Burr, Hamilton *does* throw away his shot by firing in the air. The word "shot" is highlighted by syncopation, it accents the offbeat. Apart from the opening section A, we hear solos by friends Lafayette, Laurens, Mulligan, and Burr and by Hamilton. Rapping in *My Shot* is accompanied by syncopated percussion and a repeated instrumental melody and set of chords.

Music in Film

Early Film Music

Music for film began in the 1890s and emerged as an important musical genre during the twentieth century. During the silent-film era (c. 1890–1926), live pianists, organists, and orchestras accompanied films, both to heighten the emotional effect and to drown out the noise of the movie projector. In the first "talking movie," *The Jazz Singer* (1927), starring Al Jolson, the sound was recorded on vinyl discs. By 1929, new technology enabled sound to be recorded directly on the celluloid filmstrip.

Functions and Styles of Film Music

Synchronized with images on a screen, *film music* provides momentum and continuity, and suggests mood, atmosphere, character, and dramatic action. As in opera and ballet, music in film can convey unspoken thoughts and the emotional implications of a setting. It can clarify the meaning of a scene and enhance the excitement of the action. Movies range widely in the amount and function of the music they contain. At one extreme are musicals and films about musicians, in which musical performer-actors appear on screen and music captures the viewers' attention. At the other extreme are films in which music discreetly accompanies the drama, without diverting viewers from the onscreen action and dialogue.

Most movie music is commissioned for specific films, but some sound tracks include segments of previously existing compositions. Film music is extraordinarily diverse in style, ranging from the rock and roll of *Pulp Fiction* (1994) to the minimalism, electronic sounds, and eerie string effects of *The Matrix* (1999). Many people have come to appreciate classical music by hearing it in such films as *Fantasia* of 1940 (Bach, Beethoven, Stravinsky); *2001: A Space Odyssey* of 1968 (Richard Strauss, Johann Strauss, Ligeti); *Amadeus* of 1984 (Mozart); *Shine* of 1996 (Rachmaninoff); and *The Pianist* of 2002 (Chopin). Important composers of American film music include Franz Waxman (*The Bride of Frankenstein,* 1935), Aaron Copland (*The Heiress,* 1948), Dimitri Tiomkin (*The Old Man and the Sea,* 1958), Bernard Herrmann (*Vertigo,* 1958), and John Williams (*Star Wars,* 1977; *Harry Potter and the Sorcerer's Stone,* 2001). Recent composers who are well regarded include James Horner (*Titanic,* 1997), Tan Dun (*Crouching Tiger, Hidden Dragon,* 2000; *Hero,* 2002), and Danny Elfman (*Spider-Man,* 2002 and 2004). Sometimes, a composer will collaborate with a particular director on many films, as John Williams did with Steven Spielberg (*Jaws,* 1975; *E.T. The Extra-Terrestrial,* 1982; *Schindler's List,* 1993).

Creating Film Music

Up to the 1950s, a major Hollywood film studio such as MGM or Paramount would have a resident orchestra and staff composers, conductors, and arrangers. Since the 1960s, most film music is composed, arranged, and performed by freelance musicians. Typically, the composer views the movie and—in collaboration with the director, producer, editor, and music editor—decides exactly where music will appear in the film, and how long the musical passage, known as a *cue,* will last. Composition, orchestration—usually by one or more orchestrators—and recording are often completed within a few months or less. John Williams has vividly described his preferred method of composing for film: "I'll get a sense of the film's kinetic ebb and flow . . . a sense of where the film may be slowing down, or where it's accelerating, and where I can pick up on the rhythms of the film." For Williams, the "most important issue in scoring films is tempo. Anyone who takes a home movie and puts records to it knows this: if you put one piece of music to it, the film will be one kind of musical experience, and another piece of music will change the experience totally." While composing, Williams will view the scene "many times and have a timing cue sheet that's been prepared for the scene and then I'll write three or four bars and go back and look at it and then write four bars more and look at it again. And it's a constant process of writing, looking, checking, running it in my mind's ear against the film, even conducting with a stopwatch against the action of the film."

Music and Image

In movie scores, musical themes—or leitmotifs—often become associated with specific characters, objects, emotions, or ideas in the film, a technique derived from the music dramas of Richard Wagner. The "shark theme" in *Jaws* (1975), the "007 theme" in the James Bond movies, and the "imperial march" (Darth Vader) theme in the *Star Wars* movies are well-known examples. As in Wagner's music dramas, these musical themes are varied and transformed to convey evolving dramatic situations and changes of character. They can remind the audience of the associated character, whether or not he or she appears onscreen.

The mood of movie music does not always match that of the synchronized visual image. In such instances, the music is meant to produce a distancing or ironic effect. Well-known instances are *Goodfellas* (1990) and *Kill Bill* (2003), in which scenes of horrific violence are accompanied by gentle or happy music, making the action seem almost unreal.

During the past few decades, the importance of music in film has become widely recognized. Interest in film music continues to grow, as many moviegoers have come to appreciate the significant contributions of this musical genre. Today, sound track albums and concert performances bring film music to millions of people outside the movie theater.

Raiders of the Lost Ark (1981), Directed by Steven Spielberg, Music by John Williams

John Williams in 1997.
Bachrach/Getty Images

Raiders of the Lost Ark (1981; later titled *Indiana Jones and the Raiders of the Lost Ark*) was one of the most successful collaborations between director Steven Spielberg and John Williams. It was followed by three sequels, *Indiana Jones and the Temple of Doom* (1984), *Indiana Jones and the Last Crusade* (1989), *Indiana Jones and the Kingdom of the Crystal Skull* (2008), as well as a TV series, *The Young Indiana Jones Chronicle* (1992–96).

Raiders of the Lost Ark is set in the late 1930s, when Nazi Germany prepared to initiate World War II. Two American government officials ask Dr. Indiana Jones ("Indy"), an adventurous archaeologist, to prevent the Nazis from finding an ancient object—reportedly hidden near Cairo in Egypt—whose supernatural power might help them win a future war. Indy identifies the object as the Ark of the Covenant, a gold-covered chest described in the Biblical Book of Exodus as containing the tablets of the ten commandments.

In his search for the Ark near Cairo, Indy is helped by Marion Ravenwood, his former lover and the daughter of his archeological mentor. He is also assisted by his friend Sallah, a skilled excavator. His competitor in this search is the French archeologist Dr. Belloq, who supervises excavations for the Nazis. We study the gripping Desert Chase Scene, in which Williams' background music plays an essential role in heightening the tension on screen.

Desert Chase Scene

Riding on horseback, Indy pursues a Nazi truck containing the Ark. Williams' music, heard continuously throughout the scene, provides a musical counterpart to the excitement and danger of the chase. The scene contains very little dialogue.

The popularity of songs is measured in charts issued by *Billboard Magazine*. Since 1958, Billboard Hot 100 ranks songs based on sales of physical and digital recordings, online streaming, and amount of time played on American radio stations. In 2019, rapper Lil Nas X's *Old Town Road* set a record when it topped the Hot 100 for nineteen consecutive weeks.

Recent popular music continues a centuries-long tradition of secular song. In this book we have studied songs ranging from the courtly love song *A Chantar* (*I Must Sing*) in the twelfth century to *My Shot* from the hit musical *Hamilton,* premiered on Broadway in 2015.

Popular songs tend to be constructed of short sections. The earliest rock music is often in twelve-bar blues form, such as Bessie Smith's *Lost Your Head Blues*, discussed in Chapter 23. Even more widely used is thirty-two bar A A B A form. The main melody, refrain, or chorus of the song is 32 bars in length in four 8-bar sections. Recall that *Over the Rainbow*, studied in Part I, Chapter 5, has this form. The first A presents the main melody and lyrics. The second A repeats the melody with new lyrics. Section B, called the bridge, introduces a contrasting melody and different lyrics. The final A repeats the initial melody with new lyrics. In both A A B A form and ternary form (A B A), studied in Part I, Chapter 9, the contrast of the B section is an essential element. Songs in which the music remains the same for each stanza of the lyrics are in strophic form, discussed in Part V, Chapter 3.

Verse-chorus form is another important structure in popular music. In this form, each verse, or stanza, is followed by a refrain (repeated section, also called a "chorus"). In the verse sections, the different stanzas of text are set to the same music. In the refrain or chorus, however, both text and music are repeated. The chorus typically includes a "hook line," a repeated lyric and melody that becomes the most memorable part of the song. (Bob Dylan's *Blowin' in the Wind,* studied later, is in verse-chorus form.)

Music Genres and Star Performers from the 1950s to the Present

1950s As a result of the "baby boom" after World War II, there were more young Americans in the 1950s and 1960s who spent more on recordings and concert tickets because of a generally rising economy. In the 1930s and 1940s, teenagers listened to the same music as their parents, but in the 1950s, they developed their own taste in music.

Popular singers such as Frank Sinatra, Doris Day, Nat "King" Cole, Perry Como, Peggy Lee, and Patti Page dominated the early 1950s. Sinatra was a master of the microphone and explained that"it was my idea to make my voice work in the same way as a trombone or violin—not sounding like them, but 'playing' the voice like an instrument." One of his biggest hits was the romantic song *Three Coins in a Fountain*, written for a film of the same name.

The 1950s saw a folk music revival led by the singer and banjo player Pete Seeger. ***Folk music*** consists of songs of unknown authorship passed down through oral tradition, usually accompanied by acoustic guitar and harmonica. Performers of folk music sympathized with the underprivileged and celebrated the diversity of American culture. Folk music inspired a genre called *urban folk music*, which was written by composers who usually lived in cities. Prominent urban folk groups were the Kingston Trio and the Weavers, a quartet led by Seeger.

During World War II many Southerners migrated to major American cities, such as New York, Detroit, and Los Angeles. They became part of the mass audience for ***country music*** (also known as country and western), a folk-like guitar-based style associated with rural Americans. A country music hit of 1950 was Patti Page's recording of

Chuck Berry on stage playing
the guitar in 1965.
Everett Collection/Shutterstock

The Tennessee Waltz, by Redd Stewart and Pee Wee King, about a friend who stole a sweetheart.

Country music was spread through 650 radio stations specializing in this genre. A center of country music was the *Grand Ole Opry*, a weekly country music stage concert broadcast from Nashville Tennessee. By 1950 the show had a cast of about 150, including singers, instrumentalists, and comedians. Hank Williams was a major country star known for the song *My Son Calls Another Man Daddy*, by Jewell House, which expresses the pain of a man in jail, a well-known theme in country music.

During the 1950s, *rhythm and blues (R&B)* was Black American dance music that fused blues, jazz, and gospel styles. It differed from earlier blues in its more highly emphasized beat and its use of saxophones and electric guitars. Among the most popular R&B performers were B.B. King, Ray Charles, Ruth Brown, and Little Richard, as well as gospel-tinged vocal groups, such as the Drifters. Versions, or covers, of songs became common practice. For example, many rhythm and blues hits were issued with less sexually explicit lyrics, such as Little Richard's *Tutti Frutti* and *Long Tall Sally* by Pat Boone, a month after the release of the originals.

Rhythm and blues strongly influenced a new kind of popular music that was first called *rock 'n' roll* and then simply *rock*. It was the first music genre that specifically targeted teenagers, who saw rock 'n' roll as an expression of rebellion. The term *rock 'n' roll* was first used by the Cleveland disc jockey Alan Freed on his nighttime Moondog show.

Elvis Presley was the "king"
of rock and roll.
Fotos International/Getty Images

Though rock includes diverse styles, it tends to be vocal music with a hard-driving beat, featuring electric guitar accompaniment and heavily amplified sound. Chuck Berry, one of the pioneers of rock and roll, helped make the electric guitar its main instrument. The singing styles of rock are drawn largely from Black American, folk, and country music. Unlike the crooning sound cultivated by earlier vocalists, rock singers may shout, cry, wail, or growl. Bill Haley and his Comets' *Rock Around the Clock* is often identified as the first big hit of the new genre. The song was recorded in 1954, but did not become number one until a year later when it was prominently featured in *The Blackboard Jungle*, a provocative movie about youthful rebellion in a New York City high school. To many adults, the new music—with its loudness, pounding beat, and sexual directness—embodied rebellion, projected by Elvis Presley, who reigned as the "king" of rock and roll.

1960s America in the 1960s saw much social unrest, including opposition to military intervention in Vietnam and the struggle of Black Americans to achieve civil rights. The assassinations of President John F. Kennedy (1963) and the civil rights leader Martin Luther King Jr. (1968) shocked the nation. Many young people were part of a counterculture that involved a freer attitude toward sexuality, dress, lifestyle, and psychedelic drugs.

A showcase for the counterculture movement was the Woodstock Music Festival in August 1969, where more than 400,000 people listened in the open fields in Bethel, New York, to the music of Joan Baez, Janis Joplin, Jimi Hendrix, Jefferson Airplane, Santana, and many others.

Jimi Hendrix in Woodstock. His brilliant guitar playing during the 1960s influenced later rock performers.
Warner Bros/Kobal/Shutterstock

During the 1960s, much of the rock music performed by Black American performers was called *soul,* a term that emphasized its emotionality, its gospel roots, and its relationship to the Black community. Soul musicians included James Brown, Ray Charles, and Aretha Franklin, whose death in 2018 was mourned by an entire nation.

Motown—derived from Motor Town U.S.A., a nickname for Detroit, the city from which the style emerged—was a genre that blended soul music with pop. The Black American song writer and music promoter Berry Gordy Jr. founded and owned Motown records, which became an international success with many hit songs in the 1960s and 70s. He signed groups such as the Supremes (initially featuring Diana Ross) and the Jackson Five, carefully controlling their public image. Motown records aimed at youth; its recording labels read "the sound of young America."

An era of British influence, often referred to as the first British invasion, began in 1964 with the American tour of the Beatles, an English rock group whose members probably are the most influential performers in the history of rock. The Beatles— singer-guitarists-song writers Paul McCartney, John Lennon, and George Harrison, and drummer Ringo Starr—dominated the popular music scene in the United States, along with the Rolling Stones and other British groups. The Beatles' first appearance on the popular Ed Sullivan Show drew an estimated seventy-three million viewers, a record for the time.

Influenced by the Beatles, rock musicians of the middle and late 1960s explored a wider range of sources for sounds and musical ideas. They experimented with electronic effects, with "classical" and nonwestern instruments, and with unconventional scales, chord progressions, and rhythms. Rock also absorbed elements of folk music and often had lyrics dealing with such contemporary issues as war and social injustice. The diversity of rock styles in the late 1960s is reflected in the terms *folk rock*, *jazzrock*, *psychedelic rock*, *acid rock*, and *art rock*. Many rock performers assembled *concept albums*, such as *Sgt. Pepper's Lonely Hearts Club Band* (1967) by The Beatles and *Bookends* (1968) by Simon and Garfunkel, in which the songs are linked by a basic idea.

Popular urban folk music performers of the sixties included Joan Baez and the group Peter, Paul and Mary, whose debut album of the same name has so far sold more than two million copies.

The most influential urban folk musician was the singer-songwriter-poet Bob Dylan, who was awarded the Nobel Prize for Literature in 2016. His songs *Blowin' in the Wind* (1963)—a song against war and bigotry—and *The Times They Are a-Changin'* (1964)—a song celebrating change—gave voice to the younger generation. Born in Duluth, Minnesota, Dylan settled in New York City at age twenty in 1961 and performed traditional folk songs in Greenwich Village cafes. "Folk music was all I needed to exist," he later wrote. Dylan described his songs as noncommercial because they dealt with "Cadillacs that only got five miles to the gallon, floods, union hall fires, darkness and cadavers at the bottom of rivers." In 1965, his album *Bringing It All Back Home* included a rock group playing electronic instruments, arousing criticism from folk music fans. Previous performers had always played acoustic guitars. Dylan's *Never Ending Tour* began in 1988, and by 2019 he and his band had played 3,000 concerts.

Bob Dylan performing in Nice, France.

THIERRY ORBAN/Sygma via Getty Images

Blowin' in the Wind (1962), by Bob Dylan

Bob Dylan's *Blowin' in the Wind* was released in his second album, *The Freewheelin' Bob Dylan,* in May 1963 and three weeks later was included in a recorded performance by Peter, Paul and Mary that became an international sensation. Soon the song became associated with the 1960s civil rights and antiwar movement.

Dylan acknowledged that its melody derives from the Black-American *No More Auction Block* and said that *"Blowin' in the Wind* has always been a spiritual." The song touches upon freedom, peace, and war—ideas that resonated in 1962 with the cold war between Russia and America. For Dylan the song speaks of those "that turn their heads away when they see wrong and know it's wrong."

The lyrics consist of three stanzas, with four pairs of lines in each stanza. The first three pairs of lines pose rhetorical questions ending with a rhyming word. The fourth pair provides the answer "blowin' in the wind." This ambiguous phrase has been understood as implying eventual change, the renewal of life, or the power of creation.

Here is an outline of the first stanza.

Lines 1 and 2	"How many roads . . .man?"	Question
Lines 3 and 4	"How many seas . . .sand?"	Question
Lines 5 and 6	"How many times . . .banned?"	Question
Lines 7 and 8	"blowin' in the wind."	Answer

The next two stanzas have the same structure: the questions are different, but the elusive "answer" is always the same.

The song is in strophic form, repeating the same music for each of its three stanzas. The first three pairs of lines are sung to similar questioning musical phrases, each ending inconclusively on a tone other than the tonic note. The "answering" final pair of lines is sung to a contrasting phrase that ends with a complete cadence on the tonic note.

In his original recorded performance, Dylan accompanies himself on an acoustic guitar and adds a phrase on the harmonica after every stanza. Playing the harmonica is essential to his image as a folk musician.

The Beatles on the Ed Sullivan Show, 1964.
Tracksimages.com/Alamy

Lucy in the Sky with Diamonds (1967), by The Beatles

Lucy in the Sky with Diamonds is the third song in the album *Sgt. Pepper's Lonely Hearts Club Band.* A landmark of rock, the album was one of the first rock recordings to be presented as a "concept" album analogous to the song cycle of the romantic period. Its thirteen songs are linked by the ruling idea of a music hall show with a dazzling succession of acts and by the reprise of the opening song as the next-to-last song on the recording.

The impact of this recording comes largely from its great variety of sounds and electronic effects, including audience noises, barnyard sounds, and weird orchestral tone clusters. There is also a wide range of styles, including rock and roll, music hall, blues, and classical Indian music.

Lucy in the Sky with Diamonds, written by John Lennon and Paul McCartney, evokes a world of daydream and fantasy, with imagery such as "tangerine trees," "rocking horse people," and "newspaper taxis." Lennon has said that the song's title was inspired by a picture his son Julian brought home from nursery school depicting his classmate Lucy in the sky with diamonds. Others have interpreted these images as psychedelic and believe the lyrics relate to the drug LSD because of the first letters of Lucy, Sky, and Diamonds. LSD was believed to open the mind to unexplored realms.

In verse-chorus form, the song features a sharp contrast between the verse, which is soft and gently pulsating in triple meter, and the chorus, which is loud and heavily accented in quadruple meter. Often the vocal parts are electronically modified to sound slightly "unreal." In the choruses, the vocal melody is often doubled at a higher pitch.

1. Introduction	Unaccompanied melody, electric organ (sounding like a harpsichord).
2. Verse 1	a. "Picture yourself:" Soft, triple meter, stepwise vocal melody in narrow range, accompanied by electric organ melody and electric bass.
	b. "Cellophane flowers:" Soft, triple meter, repeated-note vocal melody, doubled by guitar and electronically manipulated to sound slightly "unreal;" electric bass marks beat.
3. Chorus	"Lucy in the sky:" Loud, quadruple meter, descending phrase sung three times in higher register than verse melodies; drummer accents second and fourth beat of each bar.

4. Verse 2	a. "Follow her down:" Soft, triple meter, stepwise vocal melody.
	b. "Newspaper taxis:" Soft, triple meter, repeated-note vocal melody.
5. Chorus	"Lucy in the sky:" Loud, quadruple meter, repeated descending vocal phrase.
6. Verse 3	"Picture yourself:" Soft, triple meter, stepwise vocal melody.
7. Chorus	"Lucy in the sky:" Loud, quadruple meter, repeated descending vocal phrase; fade out at end.

Performance Perspectives

Carlos Santana

The guitarist and songwriter Carlos Santana fuses rock with Latin and African rhythms as well as elements of jazz and the blues. A major figure in Spanish-language rock, and leader of the band Santana, he was inducted into the Rock and Roll Hall of Fame in 1998.

Santana, a fourth-generation musician, was born in 1947 in the town of Autlán de Novarra in Mexico. When he was five, his father—a violinist and bandleader—began teaching him the violin, and at eight he switched to the guitar. In 1955, Santana moved with his family to Tijuana, Mexico, where he sang and played guitar on the streets for tourists. At age fourteen, he moved to San Francisco, and five years later he formed the Santana Blues Band. A turning point in Santana's career came in 1969, when his band created a sensation at the Woodstock rock festival, and its first album, *Santana,* was hailed by *Rolling Stone* magazine as "an explosive fusion of Hispanic-edged rock, Afro-Cuban rhythms, and interstellar improvisation."

During the 1970s, Santana's band became one of the most famous in the world as a result of its best-selling recordings and concert tours in the United States, Europe, and Africa. Some of his band's albums of the early 1970s, including *Caravanserai* (1972), were close in style to jazz-rock fusion. Besides recording with his band, Santana has also made solo albums that have had a powerful impact on the rock scene. He often records with star performers in other fields, such as Bob Dylan (folk rock), Herbie Hancock (jazz), Wayne Shorter (jazz), and John McLaughlin (jazz-rock fusion). Remarkably for a rock performer, at age fifty-two Santana created his biggest hit

Tim Mosenfelder/Getty Images

so far, the album *Supernatural* (1999), which was voted Best Rock Album of the Year and has sold more than 21 million copies worldwide.

Santana usually begins to create a song by recording his guitar improvisation for two or three hours. Then he selects the best segments, and works on them with a collaborator. Santana has vividly described the way he created the song *Love of My Life,* together with the singer and guitarist Dave Matthews. "I was picking up my son from school and I thought, OK, time to listen to some radio. I turned on a classical station and the first thing I heard was this melody . . . . They didn't say who the composer was." Santana went into a record store and sang the melody for a salesperson, who told him that it came from Brahms's Third Symphony (studied in Part V, Chapter 16). He bought the recording and later played Brahms's melody—with slightly changed rhythm—for Dave Matthews and recited the beginning of the lyrics. "Dave sat down and—bam—wrote the song lyrics right there on the spot, and we recorded it."

"Playing the guitar is both a physical and a meta-physical experience," Santana once wrote. "When you can play from your heart, you are being open and honest . . . . The instrument becomes the vehicle by which you can reach others with the music." Santana's guitar sound has a vocal quality. "When you listen to vocalists like Aretha Franklin and Dionne Warwick, you learn to phrase differently," Santana has said. "I love musicians who make you want to cry and laugh at the same time . . . . You want to bend notes, you want to be able to express joy . . . anger, and a cry."

1970s The 1970s saw the continuation of many styles from the 1960s, the revival of early rock and roll, and the rise of a dance music called *disco*, played at nightclubs called discotheques. Emerging new stars included singer-songwriters Billy Joel and Bruce Springsteen, as well as the "disco queen" Donna Summer. A blend of country music and rock called *country rock* became popular in the early 1970s. Country music itself moved into the mainstream as its stars, including Johnny Cash, Willie Nelson, and Dolly Parton, whose *Coat of Many Colors* (1971), telling how her mother made her a coat out of rags, won national acclaim.

Other musical styles of the seventies included *reggae*, from Jamaica; *funk*, a syncopated development of soul music; *punk rock* with lyrics expressing the dark aspects of life; and *new wave*, a technically refined and stylistically eclectic derivative of rock.

During the 1970s and early 80s, there was a second British invasion of America. The British rock group Queen gave theatrical shows in American stadiums using large sound systems, lighting rigs, and costumes. Its lead singer, Freddy Mercury, is the subject of *Bohemian Rhapsody*, a highly successful, Academy-award winning film released in 2018, almost forty years after Mercury's death.

The British rock singer, songwriter, and actor David Bowie was also highly innovative and influential during the 1970s. In one of his many stage personae (Aladdin Sane), he wore women's clothing and dyed his hair bright orange. He developed his Ziggy Stardust persona and developed *glam* (short for glamour) *rock*, which stressed spectacular costumes.

The mid-1970s saw the development of rap music. Derived from Black American oral poetry, **rap music** is made up of rhythmic and rhymed chanting with a percussive background of steady beats and complex rhythms. Lyrics highlighted the skill of the rapper. Part of a cultural movement called **hip hop**, rap was created by Black Americans and immigrant Caribbean-Americans in the Bronx, a borough of New York City. One of the pioneers, Caribbean immigrant DJ Kool Herc, was a disc jockey who entertained at dance parties by spinning and mixing vinyl recordings on two turntables to produce rhythmic, percussive sounds. His rhymed calls to the dancers helped develop rapping. In 1979, the song *Rappers Delight* by the trio The Sugarhill Gang introduced rap music internationally.

1980s and 1990s During the 1980s and 90s, technology continued to impact the music industry on all levels, and turntables were soon abandoned favor of electronic equipment, including drum machines and digital samplers. With an expanded audience, rap lyrics started to deal with social issues, as in *The Message,* by Grandmaster Flash and the Furious Five, which depicted the desperation generated by inner-city life. Hip hop culture can be seen on the big screen with the 1982 documentary film *Wild Style,* which follows a group of graffiti artists and features rappers (including Grandmaster Flash), DJs, and break dancers. In 1986, the trio Beastie Boys released *Licensed to Ill,* which became the first rap album to top the Billboard 200. Run-DMC, whose cover of Aerosmith's 1975 track *Walk This Way* (1975), pioneered the fusion of rap with rock.

The late 1980s saw the emergence of West Coast *gangsta rap* with *Straight Outta Compton,* a song by NWA. The group provoked controversy with its violent, profane, and sexually explicit lyrics that aimed to show the hardships of life in a crime-ridden south Los Angeles neighborhood. The rappers of NWA—Ice Cube, MC Ren and Eazy-E—aimed to promote their hometown as a hip hop center. By 1999, rap music was the best-selling music genre, with sales of 81 million CDs.

MTV, a cable television network broadcasting music videos, was launched in 1981 and contributed to the popularity of performers such as Madonna and Prince. MTV helped inaugurate the era of the music video. An early and important innovator in music video production was Michael Jackson. His *Thriller* video (1983) doubled the sales of his *Thriller* album, released in 1982, and Jackson's dance routines helped shape the look of music videos for years to come.

As part of the second British invasion started in the seventies, new wave bands from Britain, such as the Police and Clash made extensive use of electronic technology—synthesizers and computers—and often featured outlandish costumes. The 1980s saw a renewed interest in *heavy metal*, a type of rock characterized by pounding drums, heavily amplified bass, guitars played at peak volume, and lyrics with overt references to sex and violence. Popular heavy metal bands of the period include Metallica, Iron Maiden, and Guns N' Roses.

In the 1990s, many young people became disenchanted with the polished sounds of mainstream rock and embraced grunge, an alternative rock style that originated in Seattle. *Grunge* featured raucous electric guitar sounds and angry lyrics of despair. Bands such as Nirvana, Pearl Jam, and Alice in Chains were all influenced by punk rock and heavy metal.

Purple Rain (1984), by Prince and members of The Revolution

Prince designed the partially autobiographical film *Purple Rain* (1984) to showcase his many talents. The film and its soundtrack had commercial and critical success, and he won an Academy Award for best original song score. Building on the success of the film and album, Prince and his band went on an international tour of 98 concerts in 1984-85.

In the film, Prince stars as "The Kid," the front man of The Revolution, a Minneapolis-based rock band. In the film, The Kid sings the song *Purple Rain* as an apology to his girlfriend and two members of his band for offending them. He dedicates the song to his father.

Prince performing on stage, Purple Rain Tour.

Richard E. Aaron/Redferns/Getty Images

Purple Rain has a slow tempo and fuses elements of rock and roll, rhythm and blues, and gospel. In verse-chorus form, *Purple Rain* is made up of three stanzas and a long concluding section. The vocal lines of the verses are often speech-like, with many repeated tones. At the beginning of the chorus, on the words "purple rain, purple rain," Prince's melody is narrow in range and moves stepwise. In the second and third choruses, he is joined by backup singers. Prince sings in a very high register in the long concluding section, which begins with his dazzling guitar solo.

Prince explained that "purple rain" refers to "when there's blood in the sky—red and blue = purple . . . purple rain pertains to the end of the world and being with the one you love and letting your faith/god guide you through the purple rain."

Here is an outline:

1. Introduction	Electric guitar solo, joined by percussion, electric piano
2. Verse	"I never meant . . ."
3. Chorus	"Purple rain" sung six times.
4. Verse	"I never wanted . . ."
5. Chorus	"Purple rain" sung six times. Backup singers join.
6. Verse	"Honey I know . . ."
7. Chorus	"Purple Rain . . ." Backup singers join.
8. Conclusion	a. Prince's long electric guitar solo, accompanied by instruments
	b. Prince repeats descending phrases in very high register.
	c. Loud instrumental ending

2000s The end of the twentieth century saw the rise of digitalization, which allowed files to be compressed to 1/12th their original size for easy storage and distribution over the Internet. At the turn of the century, Napster and other peer-to-peer websites allowed users to directly share digital files, bypassing record companies completely. The drop in sales of physical recordings was made more acute by the popularization of streaming, which makes all recorded music instantly available on any device. These new technologies caused a radical transformation in the music industry and changed the relationship among artists, audiences, and entertainment companies.

Artists today generate most of their income through touring, and the price of concert tickets rose by nearly 400% between 1981 and 2012. Music has increasingly become a springboard for other business ventures. In 2013, Beyoncé and Jay-Z were named by *International Business Times* as pop music's first billionaire couple.

The story of popular music in the twentieth and twenty-first centuries is one of ever-increasing variety, a trend accelerated by the Internet, which allows new music to spread quickly by virtue of easy access. This variety means that it is sometimes difficult to classify artists as they fuse genres in individual works or move between genres during the course of their careers. Collaborations across genres and sampling (reusing one recording in another) are also common. *I Can* (2003), by Nas, for example, samples *Für Elise*, by Beethoven, and *Impeach the President*, by the Honey Drippers.

As the early 2000s dawned, the variety of popular music genres in wide circulation included hip hop, rock, pop, country, and electronic dance music (EDM). Hip hop became dominant, and Jay-Z, best known for *The Black Album* (2003), was the genre's most influential performer. Other prominent rappers included Eminem, Kanye West, Nas, Drake, and Kendrick Lamar.

Female singer-songwriters are assuming an increasingly prominent role in the music industry, each with a unique approach, reflecting the diversity of style and genre in the early 2000s. Beyoncé's songs blend R&B, pop, hip hop, and dance. Taylor Swift, whose first recording appeared when she was only sixteen, saw herself as a county music performer until her fifth studio recording *1989* (2014), which she described as pop. Maria Carey's hit *We Belong Together* of 2005, is a R&B ballad reminiscent music of the 1970s. The following songs are intended to give an overview of popular music since 2000 and represent the current diversity of styles, genres, and artists.

Irreplaceable (2006), by Beyoncé, Shaffer "Ne Yo" Smith, Tor Erik Hermansen, Mikkel Eriksen, Espen Lind, and Amund Bjorklund

Irreplaceable is from Beyoncé's second solo album *B'Day*, released on September 4, 2006, to coincide with her twenty-fifth birthday. The song remained at the top of the U.S. singles chart for ten weeks. Shaffer "Ne Yo" Smith originally wrote *Irreplaceable* as a country song, but changes of instrumentation and vocal arrangements transformed it into a version that fuses pop and rhythm and blues.

In *Irreplaceable*, a woman tells her unfaithful ex-boyfriend to leave her house, together with his belongings, indicating that he is replaceable. Beyoncé has said about *Irreplaceable* that "basically we can't forget our power and our worth. And sometimes you're so in love, you forget that. And sometimes you feel that you're not being appreciated. And sometimes they forget that they can be replaced."

Beyoncé is accompanied by a backup female singing group, acoustic guitar, cello, and percussion. The song is in a moderate tempo and in verse-chorus form, which is outlined as follows:

Introduction	Strummed guitar, "To the left . . ."
Verse 1	"You got me twisted . . ."
Chorus	"You must not know . . ."
Verse 2	"So go ahead . . ."
Chorus	"You must not know . . ."
Bridge	"So since I'm not . . ."
Interlude	"To the left . . ."
Chorus	"You must not know . . ."

Beyoncé and Jay-Z in concert, Detroit, 2018.

PictureGroup/Shutterstock

In verse 1, the melodic line is conversational, with many repeated tones, as in the repeated phrase "To the left." Changes of register reinforce a change of thought. The phrase "in the closet etc.", for example, is in a low register of Beyoncé's voice, but she moves to a higher register for "And keep talking . . ."

The chorus opens with the vocal group singing a downward broken chord on the words "You must not." Beyoncé takes over on the words "I could have." The words "I could have another you" bring a wide upward leap on the first two syllables (*a-noth*) of "another." A minor harmony stresses the line beginning "so don't you"—in which Beyoncé tells her ex-boyfriend that he shouldn't think that he is irreplaceable. The vocal group plays an important role in the bridge and interlude as well as in the choruses. In the video of *Irreplaceable,* Beyoncé is shown singing into a microphone accompanied by her vocal group, reinforcing the song's message of female empowerment.

Shake It Off (2014), by Taylor Swift, Max Martin, and Shellback

Shake It Off is a mega-hit dance pop song in a very fast tempo written by Taylor Swift, Max Martin, and Shellback. The lead single in her fifth album, *1989*, it marks her shift from country music to pop superstardom.

Like many of Swift's songs, *Shake It Off* relates to her personal life. She has said that "I've had every part of my life dissected—my choices, my actions, my words, my body, my style, my music. When you live your life under that kind of scrutiny, you can either let it break you . . . . I guess the way that I deal with it is to shake it off."

Shake It Off is in verse-chorus form with a distinctive transition from verse to chorus. The lyrics, in three stanzas, alternate between critics' negative views of her ("got nothing in my brain") and her positive outlook ("it's gonna be alright"). The verse opens with varied repetitions of a short musical idea in rapid notes, sung assertively. It ends with a contrasting melodic idea in slower notes, sung more softly.

Taylor Swift.
Chelsea Lauren/Shutterstock

The chorus ("Cause the players gonna play") brings long descending melodic lines on the repeated words "play," "hate," and "shake." Swift's solo is accompanied by saxophone, trumpet, trombone, electric bass, synthesized strings, and vocal *"oohs."* Swift's vocal range in *Shake It Off* is wide, spanning two octaves.

After the second chorus, Swift speaks and then raps. The song has an unusual ending with all instruments in unison on a single tone. Here is an outline of the first verse-chorus section.

Brief introduction: Syncopated percussion, rapid beat.	
Verse	a. " I stay up too late;" assertive rapid notes.
	b. "But I keep cruising;" softer, slower notes.
Chorus	"Cause the players gonna play;" long descending melodic lines, brasses, electric bass, vocal "oohs."

GOD (2017), by Kendrick Lamar

GOD is from Lamar's fourth studio album *DAMN*, which was awarded the Pulitzer Prize in music in 2018, marking the first time this prestigious award was given to a rapper. The Pulitzer board described DAMN as "a virtuosic song collection, unified by its vernacular authenticity and rhythmic dynamism that offers affecting vignettes capturing the complexity of modern Black-American life." Stylistically the album spans many styles, including seventies soul, psychedelia, old school hip hop, and modern pop.

GOD can be outlined as follows:

Introduction	Instrumental
Chorus	"This is what God feel like . . ."
Verse 1	"Ever since a young man . . ."
Chorus	"This is what God feel like . . ."
Verse 2	" . . . is you talking to?"
Interlude	Instrumental
Chorus	"This is what God feel like . . ."
Postlude	Instrumental

The chorus dwells on Lamar's success as a rapper and his god-like status compared to "what God feel like." In Verse 1, he boasts of his success ("Y'all gotta see that I won"), asks not to be judged, and recalls the disciplining his mother gave him when he was young. In Verse 2, he says that life is a gamble, but he can handle it and has felt pain more than others.

Long-held digitally generated chord progressions serve as an introduction, accompany the voices, and serve as an interlude after Verse 2, and a postlude after the final chorus. Hip hop percussion begins after the introduction and continues until the postlude.

Lamar sings the lyrics of the chorus and is joined by other voices on "you feel." In Verse 1 he begins by rapping, but begins to sing starting with "Slick as El DeBarge." Verse 2 is rapped by Lamar until the last lines, which bring new low voices.

Kendrick Lamar at the Pulitzer Awards Luncheon at Columbia University in 2018.
Bebeto Matthews/AP Images

The Twentieth Century and Beyond: Summary

Music in Society

- The early twentieth century was a time of revolt, with more fundamental changes in the language of music than any time since the baroque era.
- The variety of musical styles of the early twentieth century reflects the vast diversity of life during this time.
- The United States became a potent force in music.
- Recordings, radio, and television became new modes for hearing music, bringing music to larger audiences and increasing the range of music available to everyone.
- Women and people of color began to play major roles in professional music making.
- American colleges and universities have indirectly become important patrons of music.

Characteristics of Twentieth-Century Music

- Tone color became a more important element of music than it ever was before.
- Noiselike and percussive sounds are used often.
- There is less emphasis on blended sound; individual tone colors are heard clearly.
- Melodies often are no longer tied to traditional chords, major or minor keys, or a tonal center.
- Traditional distinctions between consonance and dissonance were often abandoned.
- New chord structures and alternatives to the traditional tonal system were explored.
- Rhythm is one of the most striking elements of twentieth-century music, used to generate power, drive, and excitement.

Characteristics of Music since 1945

- The twelve-tone system was expanded to include elements other than pitch, such as rhythm, timbre, and dynamics.
- The element of chance was introduced to music composition and performance.
- The mid-1960s saw the development of minimalist music, characterized by a steady pulse, clear tonality, and insistent repetition of short melodic patterns.
- In quotation music, composers deliberately make extensive use of quotations from earlier music.
- An important trend is polystylism, the use of different styles or techniques in a composition.
- Some composers have embraced tonal music and a return to tonality.
- The introduction of tape studios, synthesizers, computers, and mixed media are notable developments.
- The greatest expansion and experimentation have involved percussion instruments.
- Rhythm and form have undergone some of the most striking changes in music since 1945.

Jazz

- Jazz developed in New Orleans around the turn of the century.
- Jazz features a small combo of three to eight players, or a big band of ten to fifteen.
- Improvisation lies at the heart of jazz and adds freshness and spontaneity.
- Syncopation and rhythmic swing are distinctive features of jazz.

Music for Stage and Screen

- Along with jazz and rock, the musical was one of the most important American contributions to twentieth-century popular culture.
- The golden era in American musical theater was created from about 1920 to 1960. After 1960, some composers departed from traditional forms.

Popular Music Genres

- The term "popular music" refers to music enjoyed by a large segment of the population and marketed by the music industry. This chapter surveys popular music genres and star performers from the 1950s to the present.

FEATURED COMPOSERS OR PERFORMERS

Claude Debussy (1862–1918)
Maurice Ravel (1875–1937)
Lili Boulanger (1893–1918)
Igor Stravinsky (1882–1971)
Sergei Prokofiev (1891–1953)
Arnold Schoenberg (1874–1951)
Alban Berg (1885–1935)
Béla Bartók (1881–1945)
Charles Ives (1874–1954)
George Gershwin (1898–1937)
William Grant Still (1895–1978)
Aaron Copland (1900–1990)
Alberto Ginastera (1916–1983)
John Cage (1912–1992)
Edgard Varèse (1883–1965)
Astor Piazzolla (1921–1992)
John Adams (b. 1947)
Eric Whitacre (b. 1970)
Kaija Saariaho (b. 1952)
Jennifer Higdon (b. 1962)
Tania León (b. 1943)
Bessie Smith (1894–1937)
Louis Armstrong (1901–1971) and His Hot Five
Dizzy Gillespie (1917–1993)
Miles Davis (1926–1991)
Leonard Bernstein (1918–1990)
Lin-Manuel Miranda (b. 1980)
John Williams (b. 1932)
Bob Dylan (b. 1941)
The Beatles
Prince (1958–2016)
Beyoncé (b. 1981)
Taylor Swift (b. 1989)
Kendrick Lamar (b. 1987)

All over the world, music is closely linked with religion, dance, and drama. Shown here is a gamelan, an Indonesian orchestra.

PART VII

Nonwestern Music

The highest aim of our music is to reveal the essence of the universe it reflects … through music one can reach God.

—Ravi Shankar

LEARNING OBJECTIVES

- Identify the characteristics of music in the nonwestern world.

- Analyze the various functions of music in sub-Saharan Africa.

- Describe the elements of music in sub-Saharan Africa.

- Discuss the elements of Indian classical music.

- Examine the life and career of Ravi Shankar.

The Diversity of Nonwestern Music

Nonwestern music reflects and expresses the diversity of the world's languages, religions, geographical conditions, social and economic systems, values, beliefs, and ways of life. Each culture has its own characteristic instruments, performance practices, tonal systems, and melodic and rhythmic patterns. Nonwestern societies also differ in their range of musical styles: some have only folk music, some have both folk and popular music, and some have complex classical music as well. Thus nonwestern music can offer a wide range of listening experiences and cultural insights. Moreover, nonwestern traditions were an important source of inspiration for western music of the twentieth and twenty-first centuries. For example, they influenced the French composer Claude Debussy, the British rock star George Harrison, the Black American jazz artist John Coltrane, and the American composer Elliott Carter.

African music is closely associated with dancing. While moving, a dancer often sings or plays an instrument.
CARL DE SOUZA/AFP/Getty Images

The koto, a plucked string instrument, is important in traditional Japanese music.
Brent Winebrenner/Getty Images

1 Music in Nonwestern Cultures

Characteristics of Nonwestern Music

Music of the nonwestern world is too varied to allow easy generalizations. Yet some features are common to most traditions: All music is closely linked with religion, dance, and drama; it can be both entertainment and an accompaniment to everyday activities, magic rites, and ceremonies; and it is often used to send messages and to relate traditions.

Oral Tradition Nonwestern music is most often transmitted orally from parent to child or from teacher to student. Compositions and performance techniques are learned by rote and imitation. Music notation is far less important in nonwestern than in western culture. Many musical cultures do not have notation; and when notation exists, it traditionally serves only as a record, not for teaching or performance.

Improvisation Improvisation is important in many nonwestern musical cultures. Performers usually base their improvisations on traditional melodic phrases and rhythmic patterns. Often it is a highly disciplined art that requires years of training. Indian and Islamic musicians, for instance, create music within a framework of melody types, each associated with a specific mood, a specific set of tones, and characteristic phrases. Although in some cultures the traditional songs and instrumental pieces are performed similarly from generation to generation (as in Japan, where improvisation in classical music is practically nonexistent), in other traditions, pieces are treated with great flexibility. In Iran (Persia) and sub-Saharan Africa, for example, performers freely vary melodies and add sections.

Voices Singing is the most important way of making music in the vast majority of nonwestern cultures. Each tradition has its own preferred vocal timbres: for example, middle eastern and north African singers cultivate a nasal, intense, strained tone, whereas singers in sub-Saharan Africa prefer a more relaxed, open-throated sound. Vocal techniques include shouting, crying, whispering, sighing, humming, yodeling, and singing through the teeth.

Instruments Nonwestern instruments produce a wealth of sounds and come in a wide variety of sizes, shapes, and materials. Scholars usually group these instruments into four categories, based on what generates the sound.

1. *Chordophones* are instruments—such as harps and lutes—whose sound generator is a stretched string.
2. *Aerophones* are instruments—such as flutes and trumpets—whose sound generator is a column of air.
3. *Membranophones* are instruments—basically, drums—whose sound generator is a stretched skin or another membrane.
4. *Idiophones* are instruments—such as bells, gongs, scrapers, rattles, and xylophones—whose own material is the sound generator (no tension is applied).

The musical style of a culture is an important factor in its choice of instruments. For example, chordophones (strings) are prominent in Islamic and Indian classical music, whose highly ornamented melodies require instruments with great flexibility of pitch.

The Indonesian gamelan ensemble consists mainly of metal percussion instruments but also includes bamboo flutes and string instruments. In Indonesia, the gamelan plays an important role in dances, rituals, and shadow puppet shows.

John S Lander/LightRocket via Getty Images

Idiophones and membranophones (such as bells, rattles, and drums) are featured in sub-Saharan Africa, where rhythm is strongly emphasized and music is closely linked with dancing.

A second factor is geography, which determines the availability of raw materials. Bronze idiophones are prominent in southeast Asia; Indonesian orchestras (gamelans) include bronze gongs, chimes, and xylophones. Instruments made of animal skins and horns are common in parts of sub-Saharan Africa, where these materials are easily found. Among the Aniocha Ibo of Nigeria, for example, drums are made of animal skins, and some aerophones (winds) are made from elephant tusks. Where raw materials are scarce, as in the deserts of Australia, instruments may be few.

Along with musical style and geography, religious beliefs may influence the choice of materials. In Tibet, for example, trumpets and drums are made from the bones and skulls of criminals in order to appease demons. Instruments often have symbolic associations and are linked with specific gods and goddesses. They may be shaped like birds, animals, or fish.

Melody, Texture, and Rhythm In Asia, the near east, and north Africa, most music emphasizes melody and rhythm, rather than harmony or polyphony. Texture is often monophonic, consisting of an unaccompanied melody or a melody supported by percussion. In India and the near east, the melodic line is frequently supported by a drone, one or more sustained tones. In many parts of the world—such as north Africa, the middle east, southeast Asia, and the far east—all parts may perform the same basic melody, with differing ornamentation or rhythm, a procedure called *heterophonic texture*. Homophonic and polyphonic textures tend to be more common in sub-Saharan Africa than in Asia.

Nonwestern music uses a wide variety of scales. Most often, scales have five, six, or seven tones. Nonwestern melodies commonly use intervals smaller or larger than those standard in the west. Microtones—intervals smaller than the western half step—are frequent in the music of India and the near east. And much nonwestern music has very complex rhythms; drummers in India and sub-Saharan Africa spend many years learning their sophisticated art.

Interaction between Nonwestern and Western Music

After 1900, nonwestern music felt the impact of American and European music. This influence resulted from increased urbanization, adoption of western technology, and access to radios, films, recordings, and western instruments. Western elements are often found in the popular music heard in the large cities of Africa, Asia, and the near east. One example of such popular music is the *high life* of west Africa, which combines European instruments with the steady rhythm characteristic of Africa. Some composers in the nonwestern world combine traditional elements with western forms and styles. And in many areas, western and traditional music exist side by side. Yet there are vast areas of the world where traditional music is dominant. Many governments subsidize traditional performing groups to preserve their rich national heritage.

In the sections that follow, the traditional music of sub-Saharan Africa and India is studied as a sample of the wealth of nonwestern music.

2 Music in Sub–Saharan Africa

The African continent can be subdivided into north Africa, which includes Morocco, Algeria, Tunisia, and Egypt; and sub-Saharan Africa, the area south of the Sahara Desert, which includes Ghana, Nigeria, Mozambique, and Angola, among many other countries. North Africa is predominantly Muslim and Arabic-speaking, and its music is closely related to that of the middle east. This section focuses on the music of sub-Saharan Africa, sometimes called "black Africa," and generally, throughout the section, the word *Africa* pertains to sub-Saharan Africa.

Sub-Saharan Africa, which is environmentally and culturally diverse, has several thousand peoples with different religions, social customs, and more than 700 languages. Though urban growth and industrialization are transforming sub-Saharan Africa today, many Africans still hold to traditional ways of life. Most groups have polytheistic religions, live in villages, and devote themselves to traditional occupations such as agriculture and raising cattle.

The music of sub-Saharan Africa is as diverse as its people. Even so, most of it features complex rhythms and polyrhythms, percussive sounds, and a wide variety of instrumental ensembles. Vocal music is often performed by a soloist and a responding chorus. Of course, the different cultures of Africa have influenced each other. For example, in parts of sub-Saharan Africa, such as Ghana and northern Nigeria, musical styles have been influenced by Arabic culture.

Music in Society

Music permeates virtually every aspect of African life. It is used to entertain; to accompany dances, plays, religious ceremonies, and magic rites; and to mark such events as birth, puberty, marriage, and death. There are work songs; specific songs or dances to treat the ill; litigation songs; songs praising leaders, criticizing

Singing and playing instruments are interwoven into the fabric of African life.

TheGift777/Getty Images

authority, and recounting history; and many songs for particular occasions (for example, among the Fon—a people in Dahomey in west Africa—children sing a special song when they lose their first tooth). Singing and playing instruments are so interwoven into life that the abstract word *music*—as understood in the west—is not used by most African peoples, though there are words for *song, dance,* and *poetry.*

African music is closely associated with dancing; both arts are basic to many ceremonies, rituals, and celebrations. While moving, a dancer often sings or plays rattles or other idiophones that are held or tied to the body.

African music is also intimately linked with language. Many languages are *tone languages,* in which a word can have several meanings, depending on its relative pitch. Tone languages permit the use of music for communication: drummers, trumpeters, and other musicians convey messages and tell stories by imitating the rhythms and pitch fluctuations of words. *Talking drums*—capable of two or more different pitches—are often used to send musical messages.

In Africa, music making is a social activity in which almost everyone participates. Music is usually performed outdoors, and there is spontaneous music making as well as performances by social and music groups at ceremonies and feasts. There is no musical notation; musical tradition, like folklore and history, is transmitted orally.

Elements of African Music

Rhythm and Percussion Rhythm and percussive sounds are highly emphasized in African music, reflecting the close link between music and dance. African music tends to feature complex polyrhythms; usually, several different rhythmic patterns are played simultaneously and repeated over and over, and each instrument goes its own rhythmic way. Dancers may choose to follow any of several rhythmic patterns—one dancer may follow a pattern played with a bell while a second follows a rattle and a third a drum.

Percussion ensembles consist mainly of drums, xylophones, or rattles carefully chosen to provide contrasts of tone color and pitch. The human body itself is often used as a percussion instrument. Hand claps, foot stamps, and thigh or chest slaps are common sounds in African music.

Vocal Music African singers use a wide variety of vocal sounds. Even within a single performance a singer may shift from an open, relaxed tone to one that is tighter and more constricted. Singers sometimes whisper, hum, grunt, shout, imitate animal noises, and yodel (move quickly from a chest voice to a falsetto).

Much African vocal music is characterized by a performance style known as *call and response,* in which the phrases of a soloist are repeatedly answered by those of a chorus. An exciting overlap often results when the leader resumes singing before the chorus has completed its response. Singers are often accompanied by percussion ostinatos (repeated rhythmic patterns). Typically, short musical phrases are repeated over and over to different words.

Texture Unlike many other nonwestern cultures, African societies often have music that is homophonic or polyphonic in texture. Several voice parts may sing the same melody at different pitch levels, occasionally producing a series of parallel chords. Some African peoples also perform polyphonic music in which the different melodic lines are quite independent.

African Instruments

A great variety of instruments and instrumental ensembles is found in Africa. Ensembles have from two to twenty or more players and may consist of instruments of indefinite pitch (bells, rattles, log drums), definite pitch (flutes, trumpets, xylophones, plucked lutes), or a combination of both (flutes, drums, bells).

Idiophones The most common instruments in Africa are idiophones, such as bells, rattles, scrapers, xylophones, and log drums. Most are struck or shaken, but others are scraped, rubbed, plucked, or stamped against the ground. Many—such as rattles, bells, and stone clappers—are instruments of indefinite pitch. A few—such as the xylophone and *mbira,* or *thumb piano*—are tuned instruments.

Xylophones are particularly important in Africa; they are played solo, in small groups, and in larger orchestras and exist in different sizes ranging from soprano to double bass. In some parts of Africa, a single large xylophone is played by several performers simultaneously. Xylophones have ten to twenty or more slats, sometimes with gourd resonators. Spiderwebs are often placed over small holes in the resonators to create a buzzing sound.

The *mbira* (*sansa, kalimba,* or *thumb piano*) is a melodic idiophone capable of producing elaborate melodies. From eight to more than thirty tongues made of metal or bamboo are attached to a sounding board or box. The tongues are plucked with the thumbs and forefingers. Vocalists often use the mbira to accompany themselves.

Another important idiophone is the *slit drum,* a hollowed-out log with a long slit on top. Some slit drums are small enough to be held in the hand, whereas others are tree trunks more than twenty feet long. Variations in the width of the slit allow two and sometimes four different tones to be produced when the slit is struck. The slit drum is used both as a "talking drum" for signaling and as a musical instrument.

Membranophones Drums with stretched skins or other membranes are also important in African culture. They are essential to many religious and political ceremonies, and they are used for dancing and regulating the pace of work. Talking drums are used to send messages over long distances, and drums are often considered sacred or magical. The manufacture of drums is usually accompanied by special rites, and drums are sometimes housed in special shrines and given food and offered sacrifices. Drums are often regarded as the property of the group, rather than that of an individual, and they symbolize power and royalty.

Drums are usually played in groups of two to four, though some ensembles are made up of as many as fifteen drums, played by four to six performers. The drums are often tuned to different pitches and create melodic music similar to that of xylophone ensembles. The chief drummer is typically free to improvise within a traditional framework; the other drummers repeat certain rhythmic patterns. African drummers are among the most sophisticated in the world, producing complicated rhythms and a wide range of tone colors and pitches.

Drums come in many sizes, shapes, and forms. There are drums shaped like cones, cylinders, kettles, barrels, goblets, and hourglasses. They are made from logs, gourds, and clay. They may have one or two drumheads made from animal skins. Some drums produce a single sound; others—such as the hourglass-shaped *pressure drum* (which often imitates the spoken "tone language")—can produce a variety of pitches. Devices used for special effects include seeds or beads inside a closed drum or pieces of metal or small bells attached to a drum's rim.

Aerophones and Chordophones The most common aerophones (winds) are flutes, whistles, horns, and trumpets. Reed instruments are less widespread. Flutes are usually made of bamboo, cane, or wood; horns and trumpets are made from animal horns, elephant tusks, wood, bamboo, and gourds.

Chordophones (strings) are plucked or struck, perhaps reflecting the African musician's preference for percussive sounds. One of the most widely used chordophones is the musical bow, whose string is plucked or struck with a stick. Some musical bows have a gourd resonator; with others, the player's mouth is used as the resonator.

Ompeh

Percussive sounds, complex polyrhythms, and a call-and-response pattern are featured in *Ompeh*, a song from the central region of Ghana, recorded by the ethnomusicologist Roger Vetter in the coastal town Winneba in 1992–1993. "Within this area," Vetter observes, "are to be found several ethnic/linguistic identities and a colorful palette of musical instruments, ensembles, and repertoires that fulfill the musical needs of small and large communities alike." *Ompeh* is performed by a recreational amateur ensemble of singers and percussionists who specialize in *ompeh*, a type of music of the Akan-speaking peoples in Ghana.

In the performance, brief solo melodies for male voice are each followed by longer responses from a chorus singing mostly in thirds. (From *do* to *mi* in the scale is an interval of a third.) Each choral response is introduced by a single held tone sung by a higher solo male voice. We also hear a percussion ensemble—consisting of a bamboo slit drum, pan rattles (made from aluminum pie plates), a two-headed cylindrical drum (*ogyamba*), a large barrel-shaped hand drum (*ompehkyen*), and a metal bell (*afirikyiwa*)—producing a variety of rhythms, pitches, and tone colors. The metal bell serves as the timekeeper of the group. Its repeated rhythm reflects the influence of *high life*, a type of popular music from Ghana.

The text of *Ompeh* relates to the group's performances, for which chairs are set up on the earth and the singers dance to the music. There are three references to death in the song. The first, *I'm dying*, has to do with pairing contradictions in Akan poetry, as in "I'm dying of laughter." The second and third references are more threatening. The singers become combative when they realize that the *Tokoraba* people have arrived and warn them that they will be sent to a distant place, *The land of the dead.* In this song, the performers combine two of the many languages spoken in Ghana: Ga and Fante.

Soloist

A woyaa woyaa	We go, we go,
E wo asi wo agwa e	They've set the chairs,
Asaase e	Earth,
Eba anadwo kakra	When night falls,
Wo asi wo agwa e	They've set the chairs,
Mere wuo o	I'm dying.

Chorus

E a woyaa woyaa	We go, we go,
Daa wo asi wo agwa e	They've set up chairs daily,
Asaase e	Earth,
Eba anadwo kakra	When night falls,
Wo asi wo agwa e	They've set the chairs,
Mere wuo o	I'm dying,
A woyaa woyaa	We go, we go,
Krohinko sane e	We swing back and forth,
Kowa e	Kowa e [perhaps a name]
Owuo e, sane e, Kowa e	Death, problem, Kowa e,
A woyaa Tokoraba wose wo ba	We are going, Tokoraba people say they are here,
Saman wa	The land of the dead is far.

Reprinted with permission of Dr. Kwasi Ampene.

Listening Outline

Ompeh (date unknown)

2 solo male voices, chorus, bamboo slit drum, metal bell, pan rattle, cylindrical drum, large barrel-shaped hand drum
(Duration 2:08)

Listen for the *percussive sounds,* complex polyrhythms, and call-and-response pattern in this song from the Republic of Ghana, in west Africa. Notice that brief *solo melodies* for male voice are each followed by longer responses from a *chorus.*

0:00	**1. a.**	Bamboo slit drum, followed by metal bell, pan rattles, cylindrical drum.
0:14	**b.**	Solo vocal melody joins.
0:23	**c.**	Higher solo voice introduces choral response in thirds.
0:34	**d.**	Barrel-shaped bass drum joins accompaniment to chorus, percussion continues throughout.
0:51	**2. a.**	Solo vocal melody.
1:00	**b.**	Higher solo voice introduces choral response in thirds.
1:25	**c.**	Percussion alone.
1:31	**3. a.**	Solo vocal melody.
1:40	**b.**	Higher solo voice introduces choral response in thirds.
2:04	**c.**	Percussion alone closes segment.

3 Classical Music of India

The musical traditions of India, which include folk and popular music, date back more than 3,000 years and are thus among the oldest in the world. Between the twelfth and sixteenth centuries, Indian classical music developed two distinct traditions: *Karnatak music,* of south India; and *Hindustani music,* of north India (an area that now includes Pakistan). The centers of north Indian music were the princely courts, whereas south Indian music was performed in temples. The music of north India absorbed many Persian elements because many of its rulers came from Persia and were Muslims. The music of south India developed more along its own lines.

When India came under British rule during the nineteenth century, north Indian classical music was still performed mainly for small, elite audiences at princely courts. But aristocratic patronage declined during the twentieth century as India made the transition from British rule to independence. Many musicians lost their jobs around 1947—the date of India's independence—when almost 600 princely states of India were abolished as political units and merged with neighboring territories. Indian performers turned to the general public for support, just as European musicians did during the eighteenth and nineteenth centuries.

Today, Indian musicians broadcast on radio and television, make recordings, and compose music for films. Some teach in colleges or give concerts for large audiences. Many Indian artists now travel and give concerts throughout the world.

Performers

Indian performers consider their music spiritual in character. "We view music as a kind of spiritual discipline that raises one's inner being to divine peacefulness and bliss," writes Ravi Shankar (1920–2012), one of the most important Indian musicians. "The highest aim of our music is to reveal the essence of the universe it reflects; … through music, one can reach God." This spiritual emphasis is reflected in the texts of south Indian songs, which have religious associations. Indian musicians venerate their *guru* (*master* or *teacher*) as representative of the divine. A special initiation ceremony usually occurs when a guru accepts a disciple. The student is then expected to surrender his or her personality to the guru.

Musical traditions are transmitted orally from master to disciple, who learns by imitation, not by studying textbooks or written music. For example, Indian music students imitate their teacher phrase by phrase at lessons and sing or play along at concerts. Although India has various systems of musical notation, they give only the basic melodic and rhythmic elements. The development of these elements—the essential ornaments and musical elaborations—cannot be notated and must be learned from a teacher.

Improvisation

Improvisation has an important role in Indian music. In few other cultures is improvisation as highly developed and sophisticated. The improviser is guided by complex melodic and rhythmic systems that govern the choice of tones, ornaments, and rhythms. Before being allowed to improvise, young musicians must study for years and practice many hours a day, mastering basic rules and techniques. Improvisations are generally performed by a soloist and a drummer. They last anywhere from a few minutes to several hours, depending on the occasion and the mood of the performers and audience. Both vocalists and instrumentalists improvise.

Elements of Indian Classical Music

Indian music is based on the human voice—so much so that the pitch range of all Indian music is restricted to less than four octaves. Instrumentalists often imitate a vocal style of performance. Composed pieces are songs performed by a singer or an instrumentalist, with the instrumentalist imitating vocal styles. And songs are used as a springboard for improvisation.

There have been many composers in south India, producing thousands of songs. The greatest composers were Tyagaraja (1767–1847), Muthuswamy Dikshitar (1775–1835), and Shyama Sastri (1762–1827). These three musicians were born in the same village and were contemporaries of Haydn, Mozart, and Beethoven; they are called the "musical trinity."

Highly embellished melody—both vocal and instrumental—is characteristic of Indian music. Melodies often move by microtones (intervals smaller than a half step). Melodic lines are subtly embellished by microtonal ornaments, tiny pitch fluctuations around notes. Slides of pitch provide graceful transitions from one note to another.

Indian melodies are almost always accompanied by a drone instrument that plays the tonic and dominant (or subdominant) notes throughout the performance. The basic texture of Indian music, therefore, consists of a single melody performed over an unchanging background. Rather than the harmonic progression and polyphonic texture of western music, Indian music has melodic and rhythmic tension and relaxation. The main drone instrument is the **tambura,** a long-necked lute with four metal strings that are plucked continually in succession. The constant sound of the drone contributes vitally to the atmosphere of the music. In addition to the soloist and the tambura players, a drummer maintains the rhythmic structure and may also perform rhythmic improvisations.

The sitarist Ravi Shankar is accompanied here by a tabla (a pair of single-headed drums) and a tambura (a drone instrument).
John Reader/Getty Images

Melodic Structure: Raga In Indian classical music, melody is created within a melodic framework called *raga*. A *raga* is a pattern of notes. A particular raga is defined partly by the number of its tones and the pattern of its intervals. Each raga has an ascending and descending form with characteristic melodic phrases and tonal emphases. Particular ornaments and slides from one note to another give each raga its individuality.

The term *raga* comes from a word meaning *color* or *atmosphere,* and an ancient saying describes raga as "that which colors the mind." Ragas have many extramusical associations. Each raga is linked with a particular mood, such as tranquility, love, or heroism. Ragas are also associated with specific gods, seasons, festivals, and times of day or night. They involve so many dimensions that Indian musicians spend a long time learning each one. Some distinguished musicians restrict themselves to performing only about a dozen ragas. Within the framework of a raga, great artists can create and improvise a limitless variety of music.

Rhythmic Structure: Tala Rhythm is organized into cycles called *talas*. A **tala** consists of a repeated cycle of beats. Although beat cycles range from 3 to more than

100 beats in length, the most common cycles have 6 to 16 beats. A cycle is divided into groups of beats. For example, the 10-beat tala called *jhaptal* is divided 2-3-2-3, and the 10-beat tala called *shultal* is divided 4-2-4:

Jhaptal

| |1 | 2 | |3 | 4 | 5 | |6 | 7 | |8 | 9 | 10| |

Shultal

| |1 | 2 | 3 | 4 | |5 | 6 | |7 | 8 | 9 | 10| |

    Each beat in a tala may be divided into smaller time values, just as a quarter note in western music may be divided into eighth or sixteenth notes. The most important beat of the tala cycle is the first. The soloist usually plays an important note of the raga on the first beat. Apart from the main beat, other beats receive secondary accents at the beginning of each group division. Singers and members of the audience often keep time with hand and finger movements on accented beats and hand waving on less important ones. Talas are performed in a variety of tempos ranging from slow to very fast.

    The rhythm of Indian music is remarkably complex and sophisticated. Young drummers spend years with a master drummer memorizing hundreds of talas and their variations. Drummers and instrumental soloists sometimes have exciting dialogues in which rhythmically intricate phrases are rapidly tossed back and forth.

Instruments

Although the most important performing medium in India is the voice, there are a dazzling variety of instruments of all kinds. In north Indian classical music, instruments have become about as popular as the voice. Many instruments are associated with specific gods and goddesses. For example, the flute is associated with the Hindu god Krishna, and the *vina*—a plucked string instrument—is linked with Sarasvati, the Hindu goddess of wisdom. We describe only a few of the best-known instruments.

    The **sitar** is the most popular chordophone of north India. It is a long-necked lute with nineteen to twenty-three movable frets. There are seven strings, which are plucked: five are used for melodies, and two supply drone and rhythmic effects. The sitar also has nine to thirteen sympathetically vibrating strings that give the instrument its characteristic sound. These strings lie under the frets, almost parallel to the plucked strings. The most famous sitarist is Ravi Shankar.

    The *vina* is the most ancient plucked string instrument of south India. It has four strings for playing melodies, and three strings at the side of the fingerboard can be used for drone and rhythmic effects.

    The *sarod* is a north Indian string instrument plucked with a plectrum of ivory or coconut shell. It has six main strings: four for melodies and two for drones and rhythm. Eleven to sixteen other strings vibrate sympathetically.

    The *mridangam* is a two-headed barrel drum popular in south India. It is played with the open hands and fingers. The right drumhead is tuned to the tonic, and the left head functions as a bass.

    The north Indian counterpart of the mridangam is the **tabla,** a pair of single-headed drums played by one performer. The right-hand drum is generally tuned to the tonic note, and the left-hand drum functions as a bass drum. These drums, which are played with the hands and fingers, can produce a wide variety of pitches and tone colors. The tabla is vital to north Indian concerts and is used for solos as well as accompaniments.

Maru–Bihag, by Ravi Shankar

The performance here is an improvisation by the sitarist Ravi Shankar on the evening raga *Maru-Bihag.* As usual, the sitar is accompanied by a pair of drums (tabla) with

Performance Perspectives

Ravi Shankar, Sitarist, Performing *Maru-Bihag*

The sitarist and composer Ravi Shankar (1920–2012) exerted a greater influence on western culture than any other performer of Asian music in the twentieth century. Starting in the 1950s, he introduced audiences around the world to a new sonic universe in the art music of his homeland, India. At the same time, his collaborations with composers and performers from Philip Glass to the Beatles brought profound new ideas into our musical culture.

Shankar was born in the ancient holy city of Benares (Varanasi), where he was surrounded by traditional music. At age ten, he left his country for Paris to participate in a dance troupe led by his oldest brother Uday, a famous dancer and choreographer. When he was eighteen, Shankar returned to India, where he spent seven and a half years studying the sitar with a master musician who became his guru, or teacher. "Taking a guru was the most important decision of my life," Shankar later recalled. "It demanded absolute surrender, years of fanatical dedication and discipline." He learned from his guru "how sacred music is, and how it should be kept that way when you perform."

Around 1956, after becoming prominent in India as a performer and composer, Shankar began to give concert tours around the world. He collaborated with distinguished western musicians, such as the violinist Yehudi Menuhin and the composer Philip Glass, and composed concertos for sitar and orchestra, as well as works combining the sitar with the western flute and the Japanese koto (a plucked stringed instrument). It was through these creative encounters that ideas and concepts from Indian musical traditions spread into western musical practice. He showed that in Indian

ITV/Shutterstock

music, for example, improvisations "are not just letting yourself go, as in jazz—you have to adhere to the discipline of the ragas and the talas without any notation in front of you." This idea of "structured freedom" found its way into the music of Philip Glass and other composers. Shankar's performances also exemplified the idea that music has a spiritual role: "My goal has always been to take the audience along with me deep inside, as in meditation, to feel the sweet pain of trying to reach out for the supreme, to bring tears to the eyes, and to feel totally peaceful and cleansed."

It was this emphasis on the spiritual that made Shankar a superstar in the 1960s through his connection with the Beatles. In 1966, the Beatles went to India, where Shankar taught the sitar to their guitarist George Harrison. Subsequently, Harrison wrote songs permeated by the sounds of Indian music, including *Love You To,* from the album *Revolver.* George Harrison has aptly said that Shankar merits the title "godfather of world music" because "he has shown it is possible to introduce an apparently alien art form successfully into another culture." In the late 1960s, Shankar performed before hundreds of thousands at rock festivals, including Monterey and Woodstock.

Shankar performed widely until his mid-eighties, and his musical legacy is continued by his two daughters: the sitar virtuoso Anoushka Shankar, who has made several solo albums and toured the world with her father's ensemble; and the pop singer Norah Jones, who has sold more than 50 million albums worldwide.

Ravi Shankar's performance of *Maru-Bihag* is included in the recordings.

a *tambura* (a drone instrument) in the background. In his spoken introduction to the recorded performance, Shankar illustrates the raga pattern and the tala (beat cycle) used as a basis for this performance.

The tala, played by the tabla, consists of 10 beats divided to give 2-3-2-3. In the illustration as well as the performance, it is not easy to perceive the beats. Each one is often subdivided into shorter drum strokes, and accents often come off the beat.

The performance opens with an *alap,* a rhapsodic introductory section in which the sitar is accompanied only by the tambura playing the tonic and dominant notes of the raga pattern. The sitarist plays in free rhythm, without regular beat or meter. Shankar conveys the basic mood and character of the raga by gradually unfolding its melodic pattern, characteristic phrases, and important tones. There are many long notes, microtonal ornaments, and slides from tone to tone. After opening with a downward glissando (glide) across the sympathetic strings, Shankar first explores the lowest notes of the melody and then plays slightly higher ones. In this performance the introductory section (alap) is two minutes in length. (In other performances, however, the alap can last as long as an hour.)

The entrance of the tabla playing the tala (beat cycle) marks the second phase of the performance. Shankar presents the *gat,* a short composed phrase that recurs many times. Between these recurrences, there are longer sections of improvisation. As the improvisation progresses, Shankar generates excitement by using increasingly rapid notes and by moving through the low and high registers of the sitar. This performance is a spectacular display of virtuosity and musical imagination.

Nonwestern Music: Summary

Characteristics of Nonwestern Music

Oral Tradition

- Nonwestern music is often transmitted orally.
- Music notation is either nonexistent or far less important in nonwestern cultures than in western cultures.

Improvisation

- Improvisation is an important feature of many nonwestern musics, and in some cultures it is a highly sophisticated art requiring years of training.

Voices

- Singing is the most important way of making music in the vast majority of nonwestern cultures, but vocal timbres vary widely from one culture to another.
- Vocal techniques may include shouting, crying, whispering, sighing, humming, yodeling, and singing through the teeth.

Instruments

- Nonwestern instruments produce a wealth of sounds and come in a wide variety of shapes, sizes, and materials.
- A culture's use of instruments is influenced by its geography, raw materials available, and religious beliefs.

Melody, Texture, and Rhythm

- In many parts of the world, music often has a heterophonic texture.
- Nonwestern music uses a wide variety of scales.
- Nonwestern melodies commonly use intervals smaller or larger than those used in the western world, or they use microtones, particularly in India and the near east.
- Much nonwestern music has very complex rhythms.

Interaction between Nonwestern and Western Music

- After 1900, nonwestern music felt the impact of American and European music.
- In many areas, western and traditional music exist side by side.

Music in Sub-Saharan Africa

- The African continent is more than three times the size of the United States.
- Sub-Saharan Africa has several thousand peoples, more than 700 different languages, and music that is as diverse as its people.
- Music permeates virtually every aspect of African life.
- Music is essential to many African ceremonies, and a large number of songs are meant for particular occasions.
- Music is closely associated with dancing and closely linked with language.
- One word can have four meanings, depending on its pitch.
- Music making is a social activity in which almost everyone participates.
- African music emphasizes rhythm and percussive sounds. Singers use a wide variety of vocal sounds.
- Much African music uses call and response, which also is a major feature of early jazz.

IMPORTANT TERMS

Chordophone, p. 423
Aerophone, p. 423
Membranophone, p. 423
Idiophone, p. 423
Heterophonic texture, p. 424
Call and response, p. 426
Tambura, p. 431
Raga, p. 431
Tala, p. 431
Sitar, p. 432
Tabla, p. 432

FEATURED GEOGRAPHICAL REGIONS

Music in sub-Saharan Africa, p. 425
Classical music of India, p. 430

FEATURED PERFORMER

Ravi Shankar (1920–2012)

- Unlike many other nonwestern cultures, African societies often have music that is homophonic or polyphonic in texture.
- The most common instruments in Africa are idiophones. Membranophones are also important in African culture.

Classical Music of India

- The musical traditions of India are among the oldest in the world. All Indian music is based on the human voice, yet there is a dazzling variety of instruments too.
- Two distinct traditions developed by the sixteenth century: Karnatak music of south India, and Hindustani music of north India.
- Indian performers consider their music spiritual in character, as reflected in the texts of south Indian songs, which have religious associations.
- Vocal and instrumental improvisation have an important role in Indian music, where it is highly developed and sophisticated, and takes years to master. Improvisations can last anywhere from a few minutes to several hours.
- Vocal and instrumental melodies are highly embellished, often move by microtones, and are almost always accompanied by a drone instrument.
- The rhythm of Indian classical music is remarkably complex and sophisticated.
- In Indian classical music, melody is created within a melodic framework called *raga,* a pattern of notes with extramusical associations. Rhythm is organized into cycles called *tala,* a repeated cycle of beats.

Design Elements: (Listening Icon): McGraw Hill Education; (Baroque violin): McGraw Hill Education

Glossary

A cappella Choral music without instrumental accompaniment.

Absolute music Instrumental music having *no* intended association with a story, poem, idea, or scene; nonprogram music.

Accelerando Becoming faster.

Accent Emphasis of a note, which may result from its being louder, longer, or higher in pitch than the notes near it.

Accordion Instrument consisting of a bellows between two keyboards (piano-like keys played by the right hand, and buttons played by the left hand) whose sound is produced by air pressure that causes strips of brass or steel to vibrate.

Adagio Slow.

Aerophone Any instrument—such as a flute or trumpet—whose sound is generated by a vibrating column of air.

Affections Emotional states such as joy, grief, and agitation represented in baroque music through specific musical languages.

Aleatory music See *chance music.*

Allegretto Moderately fast.

Allegro Fast.

Alto (contralto) Female voice of low range.

Andante Moderately slow, a walking pace.

Answer Second presentation of the subject in a fugue, usually in the dominant scale.

Aria Song for solo voice with orchestral accompaniment, usually expressing an emotional state through its outpouring of melody; found in operas, oratorios, and cantatas.

Arpeggio See *broken chord.*

Ars nova *See* new art.

Art song Setting of a poem for solo voice and piano, translating the poem's mood and imagery into music, common in the romantic period.

Atonality Absence of tonality, or key, characteristic of much music of the twentieth and early twenty-first centuries.

Bandoneon An instrument of the concertina family, similar to an accordion but operated only with buttons rather than a keyboard, that is used in tango.

Bar Another term for *measure,* often used in jazz.

Baritone Male voice range lower than a tenor and higher than a bass.

Baritone horn Brass instrument similar in shape to the tuba, with a higher range, commonly used in bands.

Baroque A stylistic period from the 1600 to 1750 that can be divided into three phases.

Bass (1) Male voice of low range. (2) See *double bass.*

Bass clarinet Member of the clarinet family, having a low range. Its shape is curved at the end before flaring into a bell.

Bass drum Percussion instrument of indefinite pitch, the largest of the orchestral drums.

Basso continuo Baroque accompaniment made up of a bass part usually played by two instruments: a keyboard plus a low melodic instrument. (See also *figured bass.*)

Basso ostinato See *ground bass.*

Bassoon Double-reed woodwind instrument, made of wood, having a low range.

Baton Thin stick used by many conductors to beat time and indicate pulse and tempo.

Beam Horizontal line connecting the flags of several eighth notes or sixteenth notes in succession, to facilitate reading these notes.

Beat Regular, recurrent pulsation that divides music into equal units of time.

Bebop (bop) Complex jazz style, usually for small groups, developed in the 1940s and meant for attentive listening rather than dancing.

Binary form See *two-part form.*

Bitonality Approach to pitch organization using two keys at one time, often found in twentieth-century music.

Blues Term referring both to a style of performance and to a form; an early source of jazz, characterized by flatted, or "blue," notes in the scale; vocal blues consist of three-line stanzas in the form a a' b.

Bop See *bebop.*

Bow Slightly curved stick strung tightly with horsehair, used to play string instruments.

Brass instrument Instrument, made of brass or silver, whose sound is produced by the vibrations of the player's lips as he or she blows into a cup- or funnel-shaped mouthpiece. The vibrations are amplified and colored in a tube that is flared at the end.

Break Brief unaccompanied solo in jazz.

Bridge (transition) In the exposition of the sonata form, a section that leads from the first theme in the tonic, or home, key to the second theme, which is in a new key.

Broken chord (arpeggio) Sounding of the individual tones of a chord in sequence rather than simultaneously.

Cadence (1) Resting place at the end of a phrase in a melody. (2) Progression giving a sense of conclusion, often from the dominant chord to the tonic chord.

Cadenza Unaccompanied section of virtuoso display for the soloist in a concerto, usually appearing near the end of the first movement and sometimes in the last movement.

Call and response (1) In jazz, a pattern in which one voice or instrument is answered by another voice, instrument, or group of instruments. (2) Performance style in which the phrases of a soloist are repeatedly answered by those of a chorus, often found in African and other nonwestern music.

Camerata In Italian, *fellowship* or *society;* a group of nobles, poets, and composers who began to meet regularly in Florence around 1575 and whose musical discussions prepared the way for the beginning of opera.

Cantata Composition in several movements, usually written for chorus, one or more vocal soloists, and instrumental ensemble. The church cantata for the Lutheran service in Germany during the baroque period often includes chorales.

Castrato Male singer who had been castrated before puberty.

Celesta Percussion instrument of definite pitch, with metal bars that are struck by hammers controlled by a keyboard.

Cello (violoncello) String instrument with a range lower than that of the viola and higher than that of the double bass.

Chamber music Music using a small group of musicians, with one player to a part.

Chance (aleatory) music Music composed by the random selection of pitches, tone colors, and rhythms; developed in the 1950s by John Cage and others.

Chimes Percussion instrument of definite pitch, with suspended metal tubes that are struck with a hammer.

Chorale Hymn tune sung to a German religious text.

Chorale prelude Short composition for organ, based on a hymn tune and often used to remind the congregation of the melody before the hymn is sung.

Chord Combination of three or more tones sounded at once.

Chordophone Instrument—such as a harp or lute—whose sound is generated by a stretched string.

Chorus (1) A group of singers performing together, generally with more than one to a part. (2) In jazz, a statement of the basic harmonic pattern or melody.

Chromatic harmony Use of chords containing tones not found in the prevailing major or minor scale but included in the chromatic scale (which has twelve tones); often found in romantic music.

Chromatic scale Scale including all twelve tones of the octave; each tone is a half step away from the next one.

Church modes Scales containing seven tones with an eighth tone duplicating the first an octave higher, but with patterns of whole and half steps different from major and minor scales; used in medieval, Renaissance, and twentieth-century music and in folk music.

Clarinet Single-reed woodwind instrument with a beak-shaped mouthpiece, cylindrical in shape with a slightly flared bell.

Classical style A stylistic period in music from 1750 to 1820 that emphasized balance and clarity of structure.

Clavichord Baroque keyboard instrument in which sound is produced by means of brass blades striking strings, capable of making gradual dynamic changes, but within a narrow volume range.

Clef Symbol placed at the beginning of the staff to show the exact pitch of notes placed on each line and space.

Climax Highest tone or emotional focal point in a melody or a larger musical composition.

Coda In a sonata-form movement, a concluding section following the recapitulation and rounding off the movement by repeating themes or developing them further.

Computer Tool used to synthesize music, to help composers write scores, to store samples of audio signals, and to control synthesizing mechanisms.

Concert overture Independent composition for orchestra in one movement, usually in sonata form, often found in the romantic period.

Concertmaster Principal first violinist in a symphony orchestra.

Concerto Extended composition for instrumental soloist and orchestra, usually in three movements: (1) fast, (2) slow, (3) fast.

Concerto grosso Composition for several instrumental soloists and small orchestra; common in late baroque music.

Conductor Leader of a performing group of musicians.

Consonance Tone combination that is stable and restful.

Contrabassoon Double-reed woodwind instrument with a register one octave lower than that of the bassoon.

Contrast Striking differences of pitch, dynamics, rhythm, and tempo that provide variety and change of mood.

Cool jazz Jazz style related to bebop, but more relaxed in character and relying more heavily on arrangements; developed around 1950.

Cornet Brass instrument similar in shape to the trumpet, with a mellower tone.

Countermelody Melodic idea that accompanies a main theme.

Counterpoint Technique of combining two or more melodic lines into a meaningful whole.

Countersubject In a fugue, a melodic idea that accompanies the subject fairly constantly.

Countertenor Male who sings in a female pitch range using a special kind of voice production.

Country music (Also known as country and western), a folk-like guitar-based style associated with rural Americans.

Crescendo Gradually louder. (Often abbreviated *cresc.*)

Cymbals Percussion instrument of indefinite pitch, consisting of a pair of metal plates, played by striking the plates against each other.

Da capo From the beginning; an indication usually meaning that the opening section of a piece is to be repeated after the middle section.

Da capo aria Aria in A B A form; after the B section, the term *da capo* is written; this means *from the beginning* and indicates a repetition of the opening A section.

Decrescendo (diminuendo) Gradually softer.

Development Second section of a sonata-form movement, in which themes from the exposition are developed and the music moves through several keys.

Diminuendo See *decrescendo.*

Dissonance Tone combination that is unstable and tense.

Dominant chord Triad built on the fifth note of the scale, which sets up tension that is resolved by the tonic chord.

Dotted note Note with a dot to the right of it. This dot increases the note's undotted duration by half.

Dotted rhythm Long-short rhythmic pattern in which a dotted note is followed by a note that is much shorter.

Double bass (bass) Largest string instrument, having the lowest range of the string family.

Double-reed woodwinds Instruments whose sound is produced by two narrow pieces of cane held between the player's lips; these pieces vibrate when the player blows between them.

Double stop See *stop.*

Downbeat First, or stressed, beat of a measure.

Drone Long, sustained tone or tones accompanying a melody.

Duple meter Pattern of two beats to the measure.

Dynamics Degrees of loudness or softness in music.

Electric guitar Instrument using a built-in pickup to convert the vibration of its strings into electrical impulses for amplification.

Electronic instrument Instrument whose sound is produced, modified, or amplified by electronic means.

Electronic music Music using synthesizers, computers, and other electronic instruments.

English horn Double-reed woodwind instrument, slightly larger than the oboe and with a lower range, straight in shape with an egg-shaped bell.

Ensemble In opera, a piece performed by three or more solo singers.

Episode Transitional section in a fugue between presentations of the subject, which offers either new material or fragments of the subject or countersubject.

Estampie A medieval dance that is one of the earliest surviving forms of instrumental music.

Étude In French, *study;* a piece designed to help a performer master specific technical difficulties.

Euphonium Brass instrument similar in shape to the tuba and the baritone horn, with a higher range than the tuba's, commonly used in bands.

Exoticism Use of melodies, rhythms, or instruments that suggest foreign lands; common in romantic music.

Exposition First section of a sonata-form movement, which sets up a strong conflict between the tonic key and the new key, and between the first theme (or group of themes) and the second theme (or group of themes).

Expressionism Musical style stressing intense, subjective emotion and harsh dissonance, typical of German and Austrian music of the early twentieth century.

Figured bass Bass part of a baroque accompaniment with figures (numbers) above it indicating the chords to be played. (See also *basso continuo.*)

Film music Music accompanying a film.

Flag Wavy line attached to the stem on a note, indicating how long that note is to be held relative to the notes around it.

Flat sign (♭) Symbol that notates a pitch one half step lower than the pitch that would otherwise be indicated—for example, the next lower key on the piano.

Flute Woodwind instrument, usually made of metal, with a high range, whose tone is produced by blowing across the edge of a mouth hole.

Folk music Songs of unknown authorship passed down through oral tradition, usually accompanied by acoustical guitar and harmonica.

Form Organization of musical ideas in time.

Forte (*f*) Loud.

Fortissimo (*ff*) Very loud.

Fourth chord Chord in which the tones are a fourth apart, instead of a third; used in twentieth-century music.

Free jazz Jazz style that departs from traditional jazz in not being based on regular forms or on established chord patterns; developed during the 1960s.

French horn Brass instrument of medium range, whose tube is coiled into a roughly circular shape and fitted with valves; commonly used in symphony orchestras and in bands. (Sometimes called simply a *horn.*)

French overture Common opening piece in baroque suites, oratorios, and operas; usually in two parts: the first slow, with characteristic dotted rhythms, full of dignity and grandeur; the second quick and lighter in mood, often starting like a fugue.

Front line In New Orleans or Dixieland jazz, the group of melodic instruments that improvise on a melody, supported by the rhythm section.

Fugue Polyphonic composition based on one main theme, or subject.

Fusion See *jazz rock.*

Glissando Rapid slide up or down a scale.

Glockenspiel Percussion instrument of definite pitch, made up of flat metal bars set in a frame and played by striking with small metal hammers.

Gong (tam-tam) Percussion instrument of indefinite pitch, made up of a large flat metal plate that is suspended and struck with a mallet.

Grand staff Combination of the treble and bass staves, used in keyboard music to encompass the wide range of pitches produced by both hands.

Grave Very slow, solemn.

Gregorian chant Melodies set to sacred Latin texts, sung without accompaniment; Gregorian chant was the official music of the Roman Catholic Church.

Ground bass (basso ostinato) Variation form in which a musical idea in the bass is repeated over and over while the melodies above it continually change; common in baroque music.

Guitar Plucked string instrument with six strings stretched along a fretted fingerboard.

Half step Smallest interval traditionally used in western music; for example, the interval between *ti* and *do.*

Harmonics Very high-pitched whistle-like tones, produced in bowed string instruments by lightly touching the string at certain points while bowing.

Harmony How chords are constructed and how they follow each other.

Harp Plucked string instrument, consisting of strings stretched within a triangular frame.

Harpsichord Keyboard instrument, widely used from about 1500 to 1775, whose sound is produced by plectra that pluck its wire strings. The harpsichord was revived during the twentieth century.

Heterophonic texture Simultaneous performance of the same basic melody by two or more voices or instruments, but in versions that differ in ornamentation or rhythm; common in nonwestern music.

Hip hop A cultural movement created in the 1970s by African Americans and immigrant Caribbean-Americans in the Bronx, a borough of New York City. It includes rapping (a rhythmic and rhyming vocal style), disc jockeying (using record players and DJ mixers), breakdancing, and graffiti.

Home key See *tonic key.*

Homophonic texture Term describing music in which one main melody is accompanied by chords.

Humanism The dominant intellectual movement of the Renaissance, focusing on human life and its accomplishments.

Idée fixe Single melody used in several movements of a long work to represent a recurring idea.

Idiophone Instrument—such as bells, a gong, a scraper, a rattle, or a xylophone—whose sound is generated by the instrument's own material (no tension is applied).

Imitation Presentation of a melodic idea by one voice or instrument that is immediately followed by its restatement by another voice or instrument, as in a round.

Impressionism Musical style that stresses tone color, atmosphere, and fluidity, typical of Debussy (flourished 1890–1920).

Improvisation Creation of music at the same time as it is performed.

Incidental music Music intended to be performed before and during a play, setting the mood for the drama.

Interval "Distance" in pitch between any two tones.

Jazz Music rooted in improvisation and characterized by syncopated rhythm, a steady beat, and distinctive tone colors and performance techniques. Jazz was developed in the United States predominantly by African American musicians and gained popularity in the early twentieth century.

Jazz rock (fusion) Style that combines the jazz musician's improvisatory approach with rock rhythms and tone colors; developed in the 1960s.

key (tonality) Central note, scale, and chord within a piece, in relationship to which all other tones in the composition are heard.

Key signature Sharp or flat signs immediately following the clef sign at the beginning of a piece of music, indicating the key in which the music is to be played.

Keyboard instrument Instrument—such as the piano, organ, or harpsichord—played by pressing a series of keys with the fingers.

Keynote (tonic) Central tone of a melody or larger piece of music. When a piece is in the key of C major, for example, C is the keynote.

Largo Very slow, broad.

Leap Interval larger than that between two adjacent tones in the scale.

Ledger lines Short, horizontal lines above or below the staff, used to indicate a pitch that falls above or below the range indicated by the staff.

Legato Smooth, connected manner of performing a melody.

Leitmotif Short musical idea associated with a person, object, or thought, characteristic of the operas of Wagner.

Librettist Dramatist who writes the libretto, or text, of an opera.

Libretto Text of an opera.

Lute Plucked string instrument shaped like half a pear; used in Renaissance and baroque music.

Lute song Song accompanied by a lute.

Madrigal Composition for several voices set to a short secular poem, usually about love, combining homophonic and polyphonic textures and often using word painting; common in Renaissance music.

Major key Music based on a major scale.

Major scale Series of seven different tones within an octave, with an eighth tone repeating the first tone an octave higher, consisting of a specific pattern of whole and half steps; the whole step between the second and third tones is characteristic.

Mass Sacred choral composition made up of five sections: Kyrie, Gloria, Credo, Sanctus, and Agnus Dei.

Mass ordinary Roman Catholic Church texts that remain the same from day to day throughout most of the year: Kyrie, Gloria, Credo, Sanctus, and Agnus Dei.

Measure Rhythmic group set off by bar lines, containing a fixed number of beats.

Melody Series of single tones that add up to a recognizable whole.

Membranophone Instrument—basically, a drum—whose sound is generated by a stretched skin or another membrane.

Meter Organization of beats into regular groups.

Metronome Apparatus that produces ticking sounds or flashes of light at any desired constant speed.

Mezzo forte (mf) Moderately loud.

Mezzo piano (mp) Moderately soft.

Mezzo-soprano Female voice of fairly low range, though not so low as alto.

Microtone Interval smaller than a half step.

Middle Ages Period from around 450 CE to around 1450 CE.

Middle C Note C nearest to the center of the piano keyboard, notated as the pitch on the ledger line below the treble clef and above the bass clef.

Minimalism *See* minimalist music.

Minimalist music Music characterized by steady pulse, clear tonality, and insistent repetition of short melodic patterns; its dynamic level, texture, and harmony tend to stay constant for fairly long stretches of time, creating a trancelike or hypnotic effect; developed in the 1960s.

Minor key Music based on a minor scale.

Minor scale Series of seven tones within an octave, with an eighth tone repeating the first tone an octave higher, composed of a specific pattern of whole and half steps; the half step between the second and third tones is characteristic.

Minstrel Medieval wandering performers who provided entertainment in castles, taverns, and town squares.

Minuet and trio (minuet) Compositional form—derived from a dance—in three parts: minuet (A), trio (B), minuet (A). Often used as the third movement of classical symphonies, string quartets, and other works, it is in triple meter (3/4 time) and usually in a moderate tempo.

Mixed media Technique in which music is presented together with visual counterparts such as slide projections, films, or theatrical action.

Moderato Moderate tempo.

Modified strophic form Form in which two or more stanzas of poetry are set to the same music, whereas other stanzas have new music; found in art songs of the romantic period.

Modulation Shift from one key to another within the same piece.

Monophonic texture Single melodic line without accompaniment.

Motet Polyphonic choral work set to a sacred Latin text other than that of the mass; one of the two main forms of sacred Renaissance music.

Motive Fragment of a theme, or short musical idea that is developed within a composition.

Movement Piece that sounds fairly complete and independent but is part of a larger composition.

Musical (musical comedy) Type of American theater created to entertain through fusion of a dramatic script, acting, and spoken dialogue with music, singing, and dancing—and scenery, costumes, and spectacle.

Musical texture Number of layers of sound that are heard at once, what kinds of layers they are, and how they are related to each other.

Mute Device used to veil or muffle the tone of an instrument. For string instruments, the mute is a clamp that fits onto the bridge; for brass instruments, it is a funnel-shaped piece of wood, metal, or plastic that fits into the bell.

Nationalism Inclusion of folksongs, dances, legends, and other national material in a composition to associate it with the composer's homeland; characteristic of romantic music.

Natural sign (♮) Symbol used in notation of pitch to cancel a previous sharp or flat sign.

Neoclassicism Musical style marked by emotional restraint, balance, and clarity, inspired by the forms and stylistic features of eighteenth-century music, found in many works from 1920 to 1950.

New art (*ars nova*) A term used by musical theorists to describe the profound stylistic changes of Italian and French music in the fourteenth century.

New Orleans (Dixieland) jazz Jazz style in which the front line, or melodic instruments, improvise several contrasting melodic lines at once, supported by a rhythm section that clearly marks the beat and provides a background of chords; usually based on a march or church melody, a ragtime piece, a popular song, or twelve-bar blues.

Nocturne In French, *night piece;* a composition, usually slow, lyrical, and intimate in character, often for piano solo.

Notation System of writing down music so that specific pitches and rhythms can be communicated.

Note In notation, a black or white oval to which a stem and flags can be added.

Oboe Double-reed woodwind instrument with a relatively high range, conical in shape with a small flared bell.

Octave Interval between two tones in which the higher tone has twice the frequency of the lower tone.

Opera Drama that is sung to orchestral accompaniment, usually a large-scale composition employing vocal soloists, chorus, orchestra, costumes, and scenery.

Oratorio Large-scale composition for chorus, vocal soloists, and orchestra, usually set to a narrative text, but without acting, scenery, or costumes; often based on biblical stories.

Organ (pipe organ) Keyboard instrument with many sets of pipes controlled from two or more keyboards, including a pedal keyboard played by the organist's feet. The keys control valves from which air is blown across or through openings in the pipes. (The *electric organ* is an electronic instrument that is sometimes designed to imitate the sound of a pipe organ.)

Organ point See *pedal point.*

Organum Medieval polyphony that consists of Gregorian chant and one or more additional melodic lines.

Ostinato Motive or phrase that is repeated persistently at the same pitch, used in music of the twentieth and early twenty-first centuries to stabilize a group of pitches.

Overture (prelude) Short musical composition, purely orchestral, that opens an opera and sets the overall dramatic mood. Orchestral introductions to later acts of an opera are called *preludes.*

Pedal point (organ point) Single tone, usually in the bass, that is held while the other voices produce a series of changing harmonies against it; often found in fugues.

Pentatonic scale Scale made up of five different tones, used in folk music and music of the far east.

Percussion instrument Instrument of definite or indefinite pitch whose sound is produced by striking by hand, or with a stick or hammer, or by shaking or rubbing.

Phrase Part of a melody.

Pianissimo (*pp*) Very soft.

Piano Widely used keyboard instrument of great range and versatility, whose sound is produced by felt-covered hammers striking against steel strings.

Piano trio A type of chamber music with a small group of three instruments, one of which is a piano, with one player to a part.

Piccolo Smallest woodwind instrument, having the highest range; a smaller version of the flute.

Pipe organ See *organ.*

Pitch Relative highness or lowness of a sound.

Pitch range Distance between the highest and lowest tones that a given voice or instrument can produce.

Pizzicato Means of playing a string instrument by which the strings are plucked, usually with a finger of the right hand.

Plectrum Small wedge of plastic, leather, or quill used to pluck the strings of certain instruments, such as the guitar, koto, and harpsichord. (Plural, *plectra.*)

Polonaise Composition in triple meter with a stately character, often for piano solo; originally a Polish court dance.

Polychord Combination of two chords sounded at the same time, used in twentieth-century music.

Polyphonic texture Performance of two or more melodic lines of relatively equal interest at the same time.

Polyrhythm Use of two or more contrasting and independent rhythms at the same time, often found in music after 1900.

Polystylism The use of different styles or techniques in a musical composition.

Polytonality Approach to pitch organization using two or more keys at one time, often found in twentieth-century music.

Popular music Music enjoyed by a large segment of the population and marketed by the music industry.

Postlude Concluding section; the section at the end of an art song that sums up its mood, played by the piano or orchestra, without the voice.

Prelude (1) Short piece usually serving to introduce a fugue or another composition; a short piece for piano. (2) See *overture.*

Prepared piano A piano whose sound is altered by placing objects such as bolts, screws, rubber bands, or pieces of felt between the strings of some of the keys.

Prestissimo As fast a tempo as possible.

Presto Very fast tempo.

Primitivism Evocation of primitive power through insistent rhythms and percussive sounds.

Program Explanatory comments specifying the story, scene, or idea associated with program music.

Program music Instrumental music associated with a story, poem, idea, or scene, often found in the romantic period.

Program symphony Symphony (a composition for orchestra in several movements) related to a story, idea, or scene, in which each movement usually has a descriptive title; often found in romantic music.

Progression Series of chords.

Prompter Person who gives cues and reminds singers of their words or pitches during an opera performance. The prompter is located in a box just over the edge of center stage, which conceals him or her from the audience.

Quadruple meter Pattern of four beats to the measure.

Quadruple stop See *stop.*

Quintuple meter Pattern of five beats to the measure.

Quotation music Works that make extensive use of quotations from earlier music; common since the mid-1960s.

Raga Pattern of notes serving as a melodic framework for the creation of an improvisation, characteristic of Indian classical music.

Ragtime Style of composed piano music, generally in duple meter with a moderate march tempo, in which the pianist's right hand plays a highly syncopated melody while the left hand maintains the beat with an "oom-pah" accompaniment. Ragtime was developed primarily by African American pianists and flourished from the 1890s to about 1915.

Rap music Derived from African American oral poetry, it is made up of rhythmic and rhymed chanting with a percussive background of steady beats and complex rhythms.

Recapitulation Third section of a sonata-form movement, in which the first theme, bridge, second theme, and concluding section are presented more or less as they were in the exposition, with one crucial difference: all the principal material is now in the tonic key.

Recitative Vocal line in an opera, oratorio, or cantata that imitates the rhythms and pitch fluctuations of speech, often serving to lead into an aria.

Recorder Family of woodwind instruments whose sound is produced by blowing into a "whistle" mouthpiece, usually made of wood or plastic.

Reed Very thin piece of cane, used in woodwind instruments to produce sound as it is set into vibration by a stream of air.

Register Part of the total range of an instrument or voice. The tone color of the instrument or voice may vary with the register in which it is played or sung.

Renaissance Term used to describe the fifteenth and sixteenth centuries in Europe, a period of geographic exploration and adventure as well as intellectual curiosity and individualism.

Repetition Reiteration of a motive, phrase, or section, often used to create a sense of unity.

Requiem Mass for the dead.

Resolution Progression from a dissonance to a consonance.

Rest In notation of rhythm, a symbol to indicate the duration of silence in the music.

Rhythm The ordered durations of sounds and silences.

Rhythm and blues (R&B) African American dance music that fuses blues, jazz, and gospel styles. It differed from earlier blues in its more highly emphasized beat and its use of saxophones and electric guitars.

Rhythm section Instruments in a jazz ensemble that maintain the beat, add rhythmic interest, and provide supporting harmonies. The rhythm section is usually made up of piano, plucked double bass, percussion, and sometimes banjo or guitar.

Riff In jazz, a short repeated phrase that may be an accompaniment or a melody.

Ritardando Becoming slower.

Ritornello In Italian, *refrain;* a repeated section of music usually played by the full orchestra, or tutti, in baroque compositions.

Ritornello form Compositional form usually employed in the baroque concerto grosso, in which the tutti plays a ritornello, or refrain, alternating with one or more soloists playing new material.

Rock First called *rock and roll,* a style of popular vocal music that developed in the 1950s, characterized by a hard, driving beat and featuring electric guitar accompaniment and heavily amplified sound.

Romantic period A stylistic movement of the late nineteenth century with an emphasis on the individual expression.

Rondeau One of the main poetic and musical forms in fourteenth- and fifteenth-century France.

Rondo Compositional form featuring a main theme (A) that returns several times in alternation with other themes, such as A B A C A and A B A C A B A. Rondo is often the form of the last movement in classical symphonies, string quartets, and sonatas.

Rubato Slight holding back or pressing forward of tempo to intensify the expression of the music, often used in romantic music.

Saxophone Family of single-reed woodwind instruments.

Scale Series of pitches arranged in order from low to high or high to low.

Scat singing Vocalization of a melodic line with nonsense syllables, used in jazz.

Scherzo Compositional form in three parts (A B A), sometimes used as the third movement in classical and romantic symphonies, string quartets, and other works. A scherzo is usually in triple meter, with a faster tempo than a minuet.

Septuple meter Pattern of seven beats to the measure.

Sequence In a melody, the immediate repetition of a melodic pattern on a higher or lower pitch.

Serenade Instrumental composition, light in mood, usually meant for evening entertainment.

Serialism Method of composing that uses an ordered group of musical elements to organize rhythm, dynamics, and tone color, as well as pitch; developed in the mid-twentieth century.

Series See *tone row.*

Set See *tone row.*

Sextuple meter Pattern of six beats to the measure.

Sharp sign (♯) Symbol that notates a pitch one half step higher than the pitch that would otherwise be indicated—for example, the next higher black key on the piano.

Single-reed woodwinds Instruments whose sound is produced by a single piece of cane, or reed, fastened over a hole in the mouthpiece. The reed vibrates when the player blows into the mouthpiece.

Sitar Most popular chordophone of north India. It is a long-necked lute with nineteen to twenty-three movable frets. Seven strings are plucked, and nine to thirteen strings vibrate sympathetically.

Snare drum (side drum) Percussion instrument of indefinite pitch, in the shape of a cylinder with a stretched skin at either end. A "snare" of gut or metal is stretched below the lower skin and produces a rattling sound when the drum is struck.

Solo concerto A piece for a single soloist and an orchestra.

Sonata In baroque music, an instrumental composition in several movements for one to eight players. In music after the baroque period, an instrumental composition usually in several movements for one or two players.

Sonata form Form of a single movement, consisting of three main sections: the exposition, where the themes are presented; the development, where themes are treated in new ways; and the recapitulation, where the themes return. A concluding section, the coda, often follows the recapitulation.

Sonata-rondo Compositional form that combines the repeating theme of rondo form with a development section similar to that in sonata form, outlined A B A—development—A B A.

Song cycle Group of art songs unified by a story line that runs through their poems, or by musical ideas linking the songs; often found in romantic music.

Soprano Female voice of high range.

Sound Vibrations that are transmitted, usually through air, to the eardrum, which sends impulses to the brain.

Sprechstimme In German, *speech-voice;* a style of vocal performance halfway between speaking and singing, typical of Schoenberg and his followers.

Staccato Short, detached manner of performing a melody.

Staff In notation, a set of five horizontal lines between or on which notes are positioned.

Stem Vertical line on a note indicating how long that note is to be held relative to the notes around it.

Step Interval between two adjacent tones in the scale.

Stop (double, triple, quadruple) Means of playing a string instrument by which the bow is drawn across two, three, or four strings at the same time or almost the same time.

stopping Means of playing a string instrument by which a string is pressed against the fingerboard to vary the length of its vibrating portion and therefore its pitch.

Stretto Compositional procedure used in fugues, in which a subject is imitated before it is completed; one voice tries to catch the other.

String instrument Instrument whose sound is produced by the vibration of strings.

String quartet A type of chamber music, using a small group of four string musicians, with one player to a part.

Strophic form Vocal form in which the same music is repeated for each stanza of a poem.

Style Characteristic way of using melody, rhythm, tone, color, dynamics, harmony, texture, and form in music.

Subdominant chord Triad based on the fourth note—*fa*—of the scale (*fa-la-do*).

Subject Theme of a fugue.

Suite In baroque music, a set of dance-inspired movements all written in the same key but differing in tempo, meter, and character.

Swing Jazz style that was developed in the 1920s and flourished between 1935 and 1945, played mainly by "big bands." *Also,* verb for what jazz performers do when they combine a steady beat and precision with a lilt, a sense of relaxation, and vitality.

Swing band Typically, a large band made up of fourteen or fifteen musicians grouped in three sections: saxophones, brasses, and rhythm. They play swing, a jazz style (*see* above).

Symphonic poem (tone poem) Programmatic composition for orchestra in one movement, which may have a traditional form (such as sonata or rondo) or an original, irregular form.

Symphony Orchestral composition, usually in four movements, typically lasting between 20 and 45 minutes, exploiting the expanded range of tone color and dynamics of the orchestra.

Syncopation Accenting a note at an unexpected time, as between two beats or on a weak beat. Syncopation is a major characteristic of jazz.

Synthesizer System of electronic components that can generate, modify, and control sound; used to compose music and to perform it.

Tabla Pair of single-headed drums in which the right-hand drum is generally tuned to the tonic note and the left-hand drum functions as a bass drum; the most important percussion instrument in north Indian music.

Tala Repeated cycle of beats organizing the rhythm in Indian classical music.

Tambourine Percussion instrument of indefinite pitch, consisting of a skin stretched across a shallow cylinder, with small circular plates set into the cylinder that jingle when the skin is struck or the cylinder is shaken.

Tambura Long-necked lute with four metal strings that are continually plucked in succession; the main drone instrument in Indian music.

Tango Dance of Argentinian origin in quadruple meter for couples in close embrace.

Tape studio Studio with tape recorders and other equipment used to create electronic music by modifying and combining recorded sounds.

Tempo Basic pace of the music.

Tempo indication Words, usually at the beginning of a piece of music and often in Italian, that specify the pace at which the music should be played.

Tenor Male voice of high range.

Ternary form See *three-part form.*

Terraced dynamics Abrupt alternation between loud and soft dynamic levels; characteristic of baroque music.

Thematic transformation Alteration of the character of a theme by means of changes in dynamics, orchestration, or rhythm, when it returns in a later movement or section; often found in romantic music.

Theme Melody that serves as the starting point for an extended piece of music.

Theme and variations Form in which a basic musical idea (the theme) is repeated over and over and is changed each time in melody, rhythm, harmony, dynamics, or tone color. Used either as an independent piece or as one movement of a larger work.

Three-part form (A B A) Form that can be represented as statement (A); contrast (B); return of statement (A).

Through-composed form Vocal form in which there is new music for each stanza of a poem.

Tie In notation of rhythm, an arc between two notes of the same pitch indicating that the second note should not be played but should be added to the duration of the first.

Time signature (meter signature) Two numbers, one above the other, appearing at the beginning of a staff or the start of a piece, indicating the meter of the piece.

Timpani (kettledrums) Percussion instruments of definite pitch, shaped like large kettles with calfskin or plastic stretched across the tops, played with soft padded mallets.

tonality See *key.*

Tone Sound that has a definite pitch, or frequency.

Tone cluster Chord made up of tones only a half step or a whole step apart, used in music after 1900.

Tone color (timbre) Quality of sound that distinguishes one instrument or voice from another.

Tone row (set, series) Particular ordering of the twelve chromatic tones, from which all pitches in a twelve-tone composition are derived.

Tonic See *keynote.*

Tonic chord Triad built on the first, or tonic, note of the scale, serving as the main chord of a piece and usually beginning and ending it.

Tonic key (home key) Central key of a piece of music, usually both beginning and ending the piece, regardless of how many other keys are included.

Treble clef Notation on a staff to indicate relatively high pitch ranges, such as those played by a pianist's right hand.

Tremolo Rapid repetition of a tone, produced in string instruments by quick up-and-down strokes of the bow.

Triad Most basic of chords, consisting of three alternate tones of the scale, such as *do, mi, sol.*

Triangle Percussion instrument of indefinite pitch, consisting of a triangular length of metal suspended from a hook or cord, played by striking with a metal rod.

Trill Musical ornament consisting of the rapid alternation of two tones that are a whole or half step apart.

Trio sonata Baroque composition that has three melodic lines: two high ones, each played by one instrument; and a basso continuo, played by two instruments.

Triple meter Pattern of three beats to the measure.

Triple stop See *stop.*

Triplet In notation of rhythm, three notes of equal duration grouped within a curved line with the numeral 3, lasting only as long as two notes of the same length would normally last.

Trombone Brass instrument of moderately low range, whose tube is an elongated loop with a movable slide, commonly used in symphony orchestras, bands, and jazz ensembles.

Troubadour During the Middle Ages, poet-musician who lived in southern France and wrote poems in the Provençal language.

Trouvère During the Middle Ages, poet-musician who lived in northern France and wrote poems in Old French.

Trumpet Brass instrument with the highest range, commonly used in symphony orchestras, bands, and jazz and rock groups.

Tuba Largest brass instrument, with the lowest range, commonly used in symphony orchestras and bands.

Tutti In Italian, *all;* the full orchestra, or a large group of musicians contrasted with a smaller group; often heard in baroque music.

Twelve-bar blues In vocal blues and jazz, a harmonic framework that is twelve bars in length, usually involving only three basic chords: tonic (I), subdominant (IV), and dominant (V).

Twelve-tone system Method of composing in which all pitches of a composition are derived from a special ordering of the twelve chromatic tones (tone row or set); developed by Schoenberg in the early 1920s.

Two-part form (A B) Form that can be represented as statement (A) and counterstatement (B).

Unison Performance of a single melodic line by more than one instrument or voice at the same pitch or in different octaves.

Upbeat Unaccented pulse preceding the downbeat.

Variation Changing some features of a musical idea while retaining others.

Verse-chorus form A verse followed by a refrain (repeated section, also called a "chorus"). In the verse sections, the different stanzas of text are set to the same music. In the refrain or chorus both text and music are repeated.

Vibrato Small fluctuations of pitch that make the tone warmer, produced in string instruments by rocking the left hand while it presses the string down.

Viola String instrument with a lower range than the violin and a higher range than the cello.

Violin String instrument with the highest range of the string family.

Vivace Lively tempo.

Voice categories of opera Voice ranges that include coloratura soprano, lyric soprano, dramatic soprano, lyric tenor, dramatic tenor, basso buffo, and basso profundo, among others.

Whole step Interval twice as large as the half step; for example, the interval between *do* and *re*.

Whole-tone scale Scale made up of six different tones, each a whole step away from the next, that conveys no definite sense of tonality; often found in the music of Debussy and his followers.

Woodwind instrument Instrument whose sound is produced by vibrations of air in a tube; holes along the length of tube are opened and closed by the fingers, or by pads, to control the pitch.

Word painting Musical representation of specific poetic images—for example, a falling melodic line to accompany the word *descending*—often found in Renaissance and baroque music.

Xylophone Percussion instrument of definite pitch, consisting of flat wooden bars set in a frame and played by striking with hard plastic or wooden hammers.

Digital Music Collection for Music: *An Appreciation Brief*, 10th edition

These audio selections are available in three ways, making accessing the music on a computer or portable device easier than ever:

- Connect Music, where selections stream via computer, tablet, or smartphone in two ways: in a simple audio player or in interactive Listening Outlines.

- Mp3 download card, which instructors can opt to package with the text. Simply use the unique code printed on the card to access and download all of the music to your music device of choice. Note: Selections marked with an asterisk are only available for streaming in Connect, and are not available on the Mp3 download card.